BEYOND THE METROPOLIS

Urban Geography as if Small Cities Mattered

Edited by

Benjamin Ofori-Amoah

University Press of America,® Inc.
Lanham · Boulder · New York · Toronto · Plymouth, UK

Copyright © 2007 by
University Press of America,® Inc.
4501 Forbes Boulevard
Suite 200
Lanham, Maryland 20706
UPA Acquisitions Department (301) 459-3366

Estover Road
Plymouth PL6 7PY
United Kingdom

Library of Congress Control Number: 2006931835
ISBN-13: 978-0-7618-3585-1 (paperback : alk. paper)
ISBN-10: 0-7618-3585-7 (paperback : alk. paper)

Contents

Table of Contents

Preface

Beyond the Metropolis is an attempt to contribute towards the lacuna that exists between large city and small city studies in urban geography, especially in North America. It is designed to bring the study of small cities into mainstream urban geography, and hopefully generate greater interest in small cities among urban geographers. Students and researchers in urban geography and related disciplines in North America, and elsewhere, who want to look beyond the large metropolitan areas as their field of study will find it most useful. It is also intended to be a case study resource for urban practitioners (planners, geographers, sociologists, politicians, and economists) who work in small cities, and whose work is impacted daily by the changing geographies of their cities.

The idea for this book was born out of two sources—my job and my location. In 1991, I assumed a new position as Assistant Professor of Geography at the University of Wisconsin-Stevens Point, with the specific task of revamping the department's urban and economic option. Needless to say, one of the courses I was responsible for was urban geography, and I found myself talking about large cities in my urban geography class in a place no larger than 30,000 people and surrounded by cities that were mostly under 100,000 except for two, Milwaukee and Madison. In addition, my students were mostly drawn from nearby areas and found most of the examples given in the texts and my lectures too far removed from their everyday experiences. The more I traveled around the state the more I became intrigued about what was going on in the many small cities. I began wondering whether the geography of these cities mirrored that of the large cities that dominated so much of the literature I was discussing in my class. With the help of a small grant from the University of Wisconsin-Stevens Point's Professional Development Committee, I finally took the plunge and began studying five of the cities in 1996. Over the next several years, I continued my studies and became increasingly convinced of the need for a book on the geography of small cities. At the 99th Annual Meeting of the Association of American Geographers, held in New Orleans, in 2003, I organized a special session on small cities. Four of the chapters in this book were presented in that session. The rest were obtained by invitation.

The book covers a wide range of topics that can be loosely organized around some of the most common themes that urban geographers have addressed in their study of large cities. Thus, in addition to a general introduction and conclusion, the book is divided into three parts. Part I focuses on the evolution and growth of small cities. Part II deals with the internal structure of small cities, while Part III examines issues related to planning and managing change in small cities. The chapters examine established conventions in urban geography, from the perspectives of small cities, some for purposes of comparison with trends in large cities, and others for purposes of understanding small cities. It is the hope that this book will generate more interest in the study of small cities within urban geography and related disciplines, and that this interest will yield more useful information that will lead to better understanding of small cities and implications of their changing geography.

Benjamin Ofori-Amoah
Stevens Point, Wisconsin, USA
May 1, 2005

Acknowledgements

I am indebted to many people for the publication of this book. The University of Wisconsin-Stevens Point's Professional Development Committee provided the seed grant that enabled me undertake the initial research on small cities in Wisconsin, which eventually kindled my interest in small cities. I am very grateful.

Several local government officials and business leaders in Wisconsin also generously shared their insights and perspectives on their respective small cities with me. My special thanks go to Mr. Jim Van Dyke, Economic Development Specialist of Appleton, Mr. John Pfefferle of Appleton, Mr. Wayne Rollin, the Community Development Director of Fond du Lac, Mr. Bruce Roskom, former city planner of Oshkosh, Mr William Freuh, former City Manager of Oshkosh, Mr. Bob Fick of Oshkosh Chamber of Commerce, Mr. Pat Vale, former planner of Brown County Planning Commission, Mr. Mike Morrissey, Community Development Director of Wausau and Mr. Roger Luce, Executive Director of McDEVCO, Inc, also of Wausau.

I have also benefited greatly from the help of several of my students who in many different ways contributed to my research on small cities. To Erica Hayes, Brad Bastian, Luke Behling, Andy Levy, Mark Lyons, and Travis Clemens, I say thanks. My thanks also go to my long-term friends and academic mentors, Roger Hayter, Professor of Geography at Simon Fraser University, BC, Canada, and Senyo Adjibolosoo, Professor of Economics at Point Loma the Nazarene University in California, for their support in all my endeavors.

To the contributors of this volume who worked willingly and patiently with me on this project, and to University Press of America, I say thanks as well. Without them, this book would never have seen daylight.

Last but not the least, my sincere thanks go to my wife Agnes, and three children David, Jonathan, and Abigail for all the difference they have made and continue to make in my life.

Introduction

1

Small City Studies and Geographic Perspectives

Benjamin Ofori-Amoah
University of Wisconsin-Stevens Point

INTRODUCTION

This chapter provides the rationale for this book. It outlines in very broad terms the status of small city studies within urban studies, in general, and urban geography, in particular, to underscore the relatively little attention that has been given to small cities. It makes a case for studying small cities from geographic perspectives and describes how the chapters in the book attempt to address this rationale. The chapter is in three sections and a conclusion. Section one deals with the relative neglect of small cities in mainstream urban studies and geography. Section two highlights the main themes and approaches to city studies from geographic perspectives. Section three provides a summary of the chapters in the book. Throughout a small city is loosely defined as a city with 100,000 people or less (Ofori-Amoah 1997).

SMALL CITIES, URBAN STUDIES, AND GEOGRAPHY

The urban system is a collection of cities of different sizes and functions, nested into each other in a complex web of functional interrelationships (see e.g. Geddes 1915; Christaller 1933; Hall 1966; Bourne 1975; Sassen 1991; Markusen et al. 1999). However, a cursory survey of urban studies literature on North America reveals that much more attention has been paid to the extreme ends of the system than what lies between them. Thus, mainstream urban studies have overwhelmingly focused on the upper end of the system, which consists of cities of national or global, and in a few instances, regional or provincial importance. Such cities are very large in terms of population, and are economically, socially, and politically domineering. From this group of cities a few select ones have played a more dominant role in driving the evolution and development of theory in urban studies. For most of the last century, Chicago played this dominant role, while in recent years Los Angeles appears to be taking over (Soja 1989; Scott and Soja 1996). This research dominates mainstream urban studies journals.[1]

At the same time, a smaller but considerable amount of work has focused on the lower end of the urban system, which consists of incorporated and unincorporated places with fewer than 20,000 people. This literature has found an outlet mostly in two periodicals, the *Small Town* journal, published by Eastern Washington University, and *The Small City and Regional Community Conference Proceedings* from the University of Wisconsin-Stevens Point, and sometimes in books such as Dane (1997) Schaeffer and Loveridge (2000), and Burayidi (2001).

There may be very good reasons for urban studies to focus on the two ends of the urban system. In one respect large cities are the very embodiment of what most people would consider "urban." In addition, the dynamic influence of these cities on the economic, social, and political life of regions and nations demand continuous attention. On their part, places at the lower end of the system are not only more numerous, but they also stir up some curiosity as to their very existence and what keeps them going. What is amiss, however, is that most cities in North America have less than 100,000 people. According to the US Census Bureau, 40% of all Americans lived in cities with population between 10,000 and 100,000 in 2000; 54.7% lived in cities between 10,000 and 250,000 (United States Bureau of the Census 2004). Yet, within mainstream urban studies, these cities have received very little attention. The result is that we do not know much about them. For example, we do not know whether or not patterns and trends that have been identified in large cities also exist in small cities. Consequently, planners and other urban practitioners in small cities, who have to deal with issues arising from the changing conditions of their respective cities, have to rely on models and policies that may not be suited to their particular situations.

To be sure, this does not mean that no work has been published on small cities outside of the two periodicals cited earlier on. On the contrary, in most disciplines of urban studies there has been some focus on small cities. For example, during the 1970s and early 1980s population growth in non-metropolitan areas generated some interest as evidenced by the work of Bryce (1977, 1979); Swanson, Cohen, and Swanson (1979); US Department of Housing and Urban Development (1979) and Brower et al. (1984). Similarly, the growth of manufacturing employment in nonmetropolitan America in the 1960s and 1970s caused Summers et al. (1976) as well as Lonsdale and Selyer (1979) to examine whether such trends could in fact solve the problems of rural poverty as some believed. Much more recently, Burayidi (2001) and Schaeffer and Loveridge (2000) have, respectively, focused on downtowns of small urban areas and small town economic development. However, these works are relatively few. Besides, most of them are either dated or have focused on specific aspects of small cities such as downtowns (Burayidi 2001) and economic development (Schaeffer and Loveridge 2000). Thus, while these works have informed us about particular aspects of small cities, there is a lot more about small cities that we do not know.

In geography, the relative neglect of small cities is quite evident. For example, a cursory survey of articles published in the *Small Town* journal indicated that geographers have contributed about 34 articles on small cities since 1976. With respect to mainstream geographic journals in the US, the number is even much less. At the same time, some of this research shows that geographic patterns and trends in small cities and the forces that influence them can be distinctively different. For example, Zelinsky (1977) found a distinctive morphology of Pennsylvania towns. In a study of morphology and vitality of business districts in upstate New York villages, Lamb (1985) also found that though small city business districts were influenced by the same forces that have operated in metropolitan areas, the resulting pattern was different. Thus, while multiple shopping trips created a hierarchy of centers in metropolitan areas, in upstate New York they created downtowns and outlying shopping plazas. In an exploratory study of the causes of manufacturing decline in small cities in Illinois, Esparza (1990) also found that technology lags contributed more significantly to decline in small cities and especially those in remote locations than in small cities closer to major urban centers. In contrast, small cities near large urban centers experienced more decline in manufacturing as a result of regional shifts in manufacturing and foreign trade policies. In another Illinois study that focused on location dynamics of physician offices in Bloomington-Normal, Mattingly (1991) identified more differences than similarities between small and large urban areas. In particular, he found that contrary to all the studies on office location, the Central Business District of the two cities saw a decline in office concentration. Johnson (1999) also found that waterfront development in Sheboygan, Wisconsin, seemed to be working better than its large city model due to relatively unique physical characteristics of local water and local history. Thus, just as Markusen et al (1999) have argued for the need to understand "second-tier" cities, there is the need to know more about the nature, characteristics, and dynamics of small cities, and especially those that appear to have fallen through the cracks (cities with 20,000 – 100,000 people), because they are neither too small nor too big to attract attention.

The contributions in this volume aim at addressing this gap in urban studies, from geographic perspectives. The goal is to ascertain whether geographic patterns and trends that have been identified in large cities also exist in small cities to the same degree and for the same reasons. The choice is deliberate for two reasons. First, most of the contributors are geographers by training and they all agree that of all the disciplines of urban studies, urban geography is perhaps the one that has paid the least attention to small cities, and especially to the types of cities being considered in this volume. Second, the contributors also believe that, in spite of this neglect, geographic perspectives have some very important contributions to make towards understanding the dynamics of growth and change in small cities that will complement the work from all the other disciplines that study cities (Clark 1982). So what are these geographic perspectives, and how can they be brought to bear on the study of small cities?

GEOGRAPHIC PERSPECTIVES ON CITY STUDIES

Geography deals with distribution patterns of phenomena, and factors that influence the ever-changing nature of those patterns. Urban geography, the branch of geography that studies cities, is particularly concerned with an understanding of the distribution patterns of places, the distinctive nature of these places as well as the regularities that exist among them in terms of spatial relationships between people and their environment (Knox 1994; Cadwallader 1996). Geographic studies of large cities have, traditionally, followed three broad topical areas.[2] The first of these is the evolution, organization, and dynamics of cities as members of the urban system. In this topical area, the focus is on understanding the evolution and growth of cities. Explanations of the sources of growth and decline of cities are sought in various factors that are physical environmental, economic, sociological, political, and historical in nature (see e.g. Berry and Horton 1970; Murphy 1974; Palm 1981; Clark 1982; Short 1984; Yeates 1990; Herbert and Thomas 1990; Hartshorn 1991; Knox 1994; Knox and McCarthy 2005).

The second topical area that geographic studies of large cities have focused on is the internal structure of the city. The objective here is to understand the urban form with respect to space and time. The main topics considered here include the spatial structure, the social structure, urban land market, housing, neighborhoods, transportation and mobility, and economic activities within the city, and the forces that influence them.

The third area of geographic study of large cities is planning and managing change in the city. The main focus here is to address problems that arise from growth, decline, and stagnation of cities. Common topics here include planning and policy issues as they relate to housing, employment, and transportation, neighborhood revitalization, downtown revitalization, growth management, local economic development, and globalization (see e.g. Palm 1981; Clark 1982; Short 1984; Yeates 1990; Herbert and Thomas 1990; Young 1990; Hartshorn 1991; Swyngedouw 1997; Ellis and Wright 1998; Clarke and Gaile 1998; Knox 1994; Knox and McCarthey 2005).

To address these topical areas, urban geographic studies have used several approaches, which have been drawn from such cognate disciplines as economics, sociology, political science, and urban planning, as well as geography. The four most common approaches have been the neoclassical, behavioral, ecological or sociological, and political economy. With respect to the evolution and growth of cities, for example, the neoclassical and sociological approaches have been dominant (Yeates 1990; Short 1984). The neoclassical approach explains the growth of cities in terms of economic base theory, which says that a city's growth is determined by the amount of goods it can export. The dynamic nature of the export sector, which in this case is referred to as the basic sector, reinforced by other factors such as innovation, agglomeration forces, and geographic inertia, accounts for the differences between growth and stagnation of cities (see e.g. Thompson 1965; Pred 1977; Clark 1982). On its part, the ecological or sociological explanation emphasizes the roles of social institutions and communication. It argues that cities cannot grow unless appropriate sets of institutions are in place, and cities cannot grow geographically unless communication technology allows it (e.g. Childe 1950; Adams 1960; Lampard 1965; Meier 1962).

Explanations of the internal structure of the city have also followed similar theoretical approaches. For example, the neoclassical approach emphasizes the role of economic forces as the most important factor in shaping the city. Thus, the urban landscape emerges from optimizing behavior of rational economic persons operating in a perfectly competitive market in which all have equal access to resources (Alonso 1964). From its perspective, the ecological approach sees the urban form as a product of a repeated process of invasion-succession over the geographic space of one social group by another social group that tends to be different, just as it occurs in the ecological system (Park et al 1925). In contrast, the behavioral approach argues that the rationality of the neoclassical approach is tempered by individual limitations when it comes to decision-making. Explanations of the internal structure of the city should therefore be sought in the decision-making process (see e.g. Brown and Moore 1970; Rossi 1980). Finally, the political economy approach sees the internal structure of the city as resulting from conflict within the social structure of the urban society, a struggle between those who own the means of production and those who do not (Scott 1988; Harvey 1973; 1989; 1996). With respect to the problems, planning, and management of cities, geographic studies of large cities have used the same approaches applied to the study of the evolution of cities and the internal structures of the cities.

In recent years, however, urban geographers have broken away from theories derived largely from other cognate fields and have developed spatial theories that originate from two main sources—critical geography, and technology and space (Aitken, Mitchell, and Staeheli 2004). These theories have particularly focused on understanding social and spatial difference, social control in urban areas, and the transformation of space in urban areas (e.g. Harvey 1989; Soja 1996; Valentine 1989; Hanson and Pratt 1990; Smith 1996; Massey 1994; Mitchell 1992; 1995; Cox 1998). The chapters in this volume attempt to blend these traditions.

CHAPTER SUMMARIES

The contributions in this book are loosely arranged to conform to the three areas that have been the focus of the geographic study of large cities. As a result, the book is divided into three parts and a conclusion. Part I deals with the evolution and growth of small cities. There are five chapters in this section. In Chapter 2, Halseth, Sedgwick, and Ofori-Amoah address the evolution and growth of small cities with respect to Prince George, a regional center in northern British Columbia, Canada. The authors examine how the city of Prince George transformed itself from a frontier outpost into the regional capital of northern British Columbia. They trace the evolutionary phases and the forces that shaped the development of the city through the various phases. The authors highlight the fact that the city's transformation and contemporary urban geography both reflects and challenges aspects of the general trend and patterns of evolution and development of large cities.

In Chapter 3, Adams and VanDrasek focus on another aspect of small city growth that mirrors trends in large cities, namely sprawl. They describe small city sprawl that is taking place in the state of Minnesota. They show that this "urbanization of the countryside" is an expression of a settlement system that is in the process of catching up with the economic and social transformation that has occurred in the State. The authors compare the growth of the greater Twin Cities area, which sprawls over 24 counties in Minnesota and Wisconsin, and the small cities in Minnesota and find that the growth in the small cities seems to be occurring irrespective of population changes. Instead, increasing ease of commuting brought about by an efficient highway network and rising incomes seem to be the main driving forces behind these changes.

In Chapter 4, Brennan and Hoene use the US Census 2000 data to reveal recent demographic changes and growth trends in cities under 100,000 people in America. Comparing 1990 and 2000 data of a sample of cities, Brennan and Hoene highlight the similarities and differences between trends in large and small cities, with special attention to racial and ethnic composition, and the rise and decline of smaller incorporated cities as central and satellite cities within Metropolitan Statistical Areas.

In Chapter 5, González Sánchez and Gutiérrez de MacGregor relate similar trends with respect to small cities in Mexico, where rapid urbanization has currently become one of the major problems of the country. The chapter focuses on the role of small urban areas, cities under 100,000 people, in this urban demographic growth. The chapter analyzes population growth, demographic changes, and the spatial distribution of these cities, from 1970 to 2000, and the forces that have fostered the resulting patterns. The chapter shows that the total number of inhabitants in these cities doubled between 1970 and 2000. However, the percentage that this population represented with respect to the total urban population decreased from 23.9 to 18.8%. The authors hope that their study will motivate other researchers to study small cities in Mexico and thereby draw more attention to how conditions in them might be improved to stem the declining population they are experiencing.

Part II shifts attention to the internal structure of small cities. There are four chapters in this part. In Chapter 6, Fonseca examines the socio-economic and spatial characteristics of micropolitan areas in Ohio. Micropolitan areas are urban areas with population ranging from 10,000 to 49,999. Fonseca examines Ohio's micropolitan areas against the backdrop of the socio-economic and spatial characteristics of large cities and uncovers some supporting and deviating evidence of patterns identified in large cities.

In Chapter 7, Yoder describes how local and external forces are shaping the spatial structure of Ciudad Lerdo, a small city in Northern Mexico. Based on existing literature, Yoder establishes a link between globalization and Mexican political ideology, on the one hand, and Lerdo's evolving urban landscape, on the other. He concludes with recommendations for policy implementation regarding historic preservation and avoidance of an imitation of North American elements of urban design that have created traffic, segregation, and pollution problems elsewhere in northern Mexico.

In Chapter 8, Bell and Gripshover examine the changing structure of small cities as central places using examples from central Iowa. Based on Bell's (1973) work, the authors trace how the changes have occurred over a period of three decades, and the forces behind them. They identify a complex set of factors that include big box retailers, the dominant position of Des Moines as a central place, the impact of highway bypasses, and in some cases, peculiar local factors as the main forces behind these changes.

In Chapter 9, Ofori-Amoah examines the trends, patterns, causes, and effects of location dynamics of economic activities in five small cities in Wisconsin. He describes the changes in business location between downtowns and outskirts of the small cities in the light of existing literature, to verify whether the general trends identified in large cities are the same in small cities. He finds that while some of the trends and patterns in the small cities mirror those of large cities others differ dramatically. He discusses the implications of his findings for understanding the geography of small cities.

Part III of the book deals with planning and managing change in small cities. There are six chapters in this part. In Chapter 10, Ramsey, Erberts, and Everitt look at attempts to counter the decline of traditional commercial Main Street, revive historic areas and improve the quality of life of the people of Brandon, a small city in the Canadian province of Manitoba. The authors find that these efforts are a result of input from key actors and concerned citizens and citizen groups, rather than a "city-driven" plan. Interestingly, these key actors and concerned citizens are of a variety of political stripes and are to be found in opposing camps on many issues that are outside the philosophical boundaries of central area revival.

In Chapter 11, Otto focuses on downtown revitalization and retail re-development as it occurs in small cities. He challenges the simple scheme of "downtown in decline" vs. "succeeding suburban locations" as an obsolete notion. He argues that there still exists a considerable number of inner city retail and services, which represent remnants of the former variety of downtown stores as well as newly created commercial uses. Using empirical case studies from Chillicothe and Mount Vernon, two small cities in Ohio, Otto shows an advanced specialization of downtown with an increasing importance of specialty retail, such as antique shops, gift stores, art galleries, and also reveals a prevailing positive attitude of local merchants to downtown as a commercial location.

In Chapter 12, Smith addresses the factors that contribute to the active or inactive status of Main Street communities in Kentucky. Using data on 37 Main Street communities from 1979 – 1999, Smith shows that the most important predictor of on-going Main Street activity is whether or not the city was within the sphere of influence of a metropolitan area. Specifically, smaller, more rural Main Street communities are better able than their urban counterparts to manifest the "tyranny of space" (i.e., the potential to gain excessive entrepreneurial profits) that Lösch's version of central place theory struggled so hard to eliminate.

In Chapter 13, Irion discusses one of the most difficult issues facing local governments in small cities, namely public transportation. Using two nearby cities in California, Marysville and Yuba City, as case studies, Irion traces the checkered history of public transportation in small cities and highlights the difficulty small cities face in maintaining such a service. He offers some suggestions to meet the future transportation needs of the cities of his study.

In Chapter 14, Cabrales Barajas addresses the problem of housing and urban development in Ciudad Guzman, a small city that is located in one of the most environmentally fragile regions of Mexico. Cabrales Barajas provides an analysis of the contemporary production of housing and urban space through a typology of four housing types: self-built housing, custom built housing, speculative new housing, and social housing, in the wake of rebuilding the city after a major earthquake. He illuminates environmental problems of a small city and how housing analysis in the urban environment portrays social differentiation, and the dilemmas of transforming the urban environment in a small city.

In Chapter 15, Tzfadia provides yet another example of the relationship between problems of urban development of small cities and the public policy framework within which the cities exist. Using examples from Israel, Tzfadia searches for a plausible explanation of the stagnation and backwardness of Israel's development towns. He argues that the factors that have combined to thwart the success and viability of these planned cities are rooted in the socio-economic structures and processes, power relations, and national ideologies of the Israeli government.

Part IV is the concluding section of the book and it has one chapter— Chapter 16. In this chapter, Ofori-Amoah reiterates the perceived need to bring small cities into the mainstream discussion of urban studies. He outlines the main findings of each contribution, pointing out those that confirm what we already know from large cities, as well as those that challenge the existing traditions, understandings, and notions. For the findings that confirm what we already know, Ofori-Amoah argues that there may not be any need to belabor the differences in small and large cities. However, for those findings that differ in trend, pattern, or explanation, or challenge existing notions, he raises several questions and argues the need for special attention in order to develop a better understanding as well as better policies for small cities. In whatever way, Ofori-Amoah hopes that this volume will generate more interest within geography as well as in the other disciplines in which small cities have been relatively neglected or on the research periphery, and by so doing bring small city issues more into the mainstream literature and discussion.

ENDNOTES

1. These include *American Journal of Political Science, American Journal of Sociology, American Planning Association Journal, Annals of Association of American Geographers, Canadian Geographer, Canadian Journal of Urban Research, Environment and Planning A, Urban Studies, Journal of Urban Affairs, Regional Studies, Urban Affairs Review, Urban Affairs Quarterly, Journal of Urban Economics*, and *Urban Geography.*

2. The areas of study and approaches reviewed here are only for purposes of summarizing the most common traditions of urban geography. They by no means represent all the research interests and approaches used by urban geographers, and neither do they represent the most current trends in the discipline. For a more comprehensive review of the most current urban geographic research trends, see S. Aitken, D. Mitchell and L. Staeheli., "Urban Geography." In *Geography in America at the Dawn of the 21st Century, eds.* G. L. Gaile and C. J.Willmott (Oxford: Oxford University Press, 2003): 237-263.

REFRENCES

Adams, R. M. 1960. The origins of cities. *Scientific American* 203: 153 – 68.

Aitken, S., D. Mitchell, and L. Staeheli. 2003. Urban Geography. In *Geography in America at the Dawn of the 21st Century, ed.* G. L. Gaile and C. J. Willmott, 237 – 263. Oxford: Oxford University Press.

Alonso, W. 1964. *Location and Land use: Toward a General Theory of Land Rent.* Cambridge, MA: Harvard University Press.

Berry, B. J. L. and F. E. Horton. 1970. *Geographic Perspectives on Urban Systems with Integrated Readings.* Englewood Cliffs, NJ: Prentice-Hall, Inc.

Bourne, L. 1975. *Regulating Urban System: A comparative Review of National Urban Strategies: Australia, Canada, Great Britain, Sweden*. London: Oxford University Press.

Brower, D. J., American Planning Association, and Center for the Small City 1984. *Managing Development in Small Towns*. Washington, DC: Planners Press.

Brown, L. A. and E. Moore. 1970. The intra-urban migration process: a perspective. *Geografiska Annaler* 52B: 1 – 13.

Bryce, H. J., ed. 1977. *Small Cities in Transition: The Dynamics of Growth and Decline*. Cambridge, MA: Ballinger Publishing Company.

Bryce, H. J. 1979. *Planning Smaller Towns*. Lexington, MA: DC Heath and Company.

Burayidi, M. A., ed. 2001 *Downtowns: Revitalizing the Centers of Small Urban Communities*. New York: Routledge

Cadwallader, M. 1996. *Urban Geography: An Analytical Approach*. Upper Saddle River, NJ: Prentice-Hall, Inc.

Childe, V. G. 1950. The urban revolution. *Town Planning Review*. 21: 3 – 17.

Christaller, W. 1933. *Die Zentralen Orte in Suddeutschland*. Jena: Gustav Fischer. *Central Places in Southern Germany*. Trans. C. W. Baskin. 1966. Englewood Cliffs, NJ: Prentice-Hall.

Clark, D. 1982. *Urban Geography*. Baltimore: Johns Hopkins University Press.

Clarke, S., and G. Gaile. 1998. *The Work of Cities*. Minneapolis: University of Minnesota Press.

Cox, K. 1998. Spaces of dependence, spaces of engagement, and the politics of scale, or: looking for local politics. *Political Geography* 17: 1 – 24.

Dane, S. G. 1997. *Main Street Success Stories*. Washington, D.C.: National Main Street Center, National Trust for Historic Preservation.

Ellis, M., and R. Wright. 1998. The balkanization metaphor in the analysis of US immigration. *Annals of the Association of American Geographers* 83: 686 – 98.

Esparza, A. 1990. Manufacturing decline and technology lags in nonmetropolitan Illinois. *Growth and Change*. 21 (4): 19 – 32.

Geddes, P. 1915. *Cities in Evolution: An Introduction to the Town Planning Movement and to the Study of Civics*. London: Ernest Bean.

Hall, P. 1966. *The World Cities*. New York: McGraw-Hill.

Hanson, S. and G. Pratt. 1990. Geographic perspectives on occupational segregation of women. *National Geographic Research* 6: 376 – 99.

Hartshorn, T. A. 1991. *Interpreting the City: An Urban Geography*. New York: Wiley.

Harvey, D. 1973. *Social Justice and the City*. London: Edward Arnold.

———. 1989. *The Condition of Postmodernity*. Oxford: Blackwell.

———. 1996. *Justice, Nature and the Geography of Difference*. Cambridge, MA: Blackwell.

Herbert, D. T. and C. J. Thomas. 1990. *Cities in Space: City as Place*. Savage, MD: Barnes & Noble.

Johnson, P. C. 1999. Historic preservation and urban waterfront development in Sheboygan, Wisconsin. *Small Town* 29 (5): 4 – 15.

Knox, P. L. 1994. *Urbanization. An Introduction to Urban Geography*. Englewood-Cliffs, NJ: Prentice Hall.

Knox, P. L. and L. McCarthy. 2005. *Urbanization An Introduction to Urban Geography*. Second Edition. Upper Saddle River, NJ: Prentice Hall.

Lamb, R. F. 1985. The morphology and vitality of business districts in Upstate New York villages. *Professional Geographer* 37 (2): 162 – 172.

Lampard, E. E. 1965. Historical aspects of urbanization. In *The Study of Urbanization.*, ed. P. M Hauser and L. F. Schnore, 519 – 554. London: John Wiley.

Lonsdale, R. E. and H. L. Seyler. eds. 1979. *Nonmetropolitan Industrialization*. Washington, DC: V. H. Winston & Sons.

Markusen, A. R., Y-S. Lee, and S. Digionanna, ed. 1999. *Second-Tier Cities: Rapid Growth Beyond the Metropolis*. Minneapolis: University of Minnesota Press.

Massey, D. 1994. *Space, Place, and Gender*. Minneapolis: University of Minnesota Press.

Mattingly, P.F. 1991. The changing location of physician offices in Bloomington-Normal, Illinois: 1870-1988. *Professional Geographer* 43 (4): 465 – · 474.

Mitchell, D. 1992. Iconography and locational conflict from the underside: free speech, people's park, and the politics of homelessness in Berkeley, California. *Political Geography Quarterly* 11: 152 – 69.

————. 1995. The end of public space? People's park, definitions of the public, and democracy. *Annals of Association of American Geographers*. 85: 108 – 33.

Meier, R. L. 1962. *A Communication Theory of Urban Growth*. Cambridge, MA: MIT Press.

Murphy, R. 1974. T*he American City: An Urban Geography*. New York: McGraw-Hill.

Ofori-Amoah, B. 1997. *Geographic Shifts in Economic Activities between Downtowns and Outskirts: The Case of Five Wisconsin Cities*. Stevens Point, WI: Department of Geography and Geology.

Palm, R. 1981. *The Geography of American Cities*. New York: Oxford University Press.

Park, R. E., E. W. Burgess, and R. D. McKenzie. 1925. *The City*. Chicago: Chicago University Press.

Pred, A. 1977. *City Systems in Advanced Economies*. London: Hutchinson.

Rossi, P. H. 1980. *Why Families Move*. 2nd Edition. Beverly Hills: Sage.

Sassen, S. 1991. *The Global City*. Princeton, NJ: Princeton University Press.

Schaeffer, P. V., and S. Loveridge, ed. 2000. *Small Town and Rural Economic Development: A Case Study Approach.* Westport, CT: Praeger Publishers.

Scott, A. J. 1988. *Metropolis: From Division of Labor to Urban Form.* Berkeley: University of California Press.

Scott, A., and E. Soja, ed. 1996. *The City: Los Angeles and Urban Theory and the End of the Twentieth Century.* Berkeley: University of California Press.

Short, J. R. 1984. *An Introduction to Urban Geography.* New York: Routledge.

Smith, D. M. 1996. *The New Urban Frontier: Gentrification and the Revanchist City.* London: Routledge.

Summers, G. F., S. D. Evans, F. Clemente, E. M. Beck, and J. Minkoff. 1976. *Industrial Invasion of Nonmetropolitan America.* New York: Praeger Publishers.

Soja, E. W. 1989. *Postmodern Geographies: The Reassertion of Space in Critical Social Theory.* London: Verso.

Swanson, B. E., R. A. Cohen, and E. F. Swanson. 1979. *Small Towns and Small Towners: A Framework for Survival and Growth.* Beverly Hills, CA: Sage Publications Vol. 79.

Swyngedouw, E. 1997. Neither global nor local: 'globalization' and the politics of scale. In *Spaces of Globalization, ed.* K. Cox, 137 – 66. New York: Guildford Press.

Thompson, W. R. 1965. *A Preface to Urban Economics.* Baltimore: Johns Hopkins Press.

United States Bureau of the Census. 2004. *Statistical Abstract of the United States.* Washington, D.C.: U.S. Dept. of Commerce, Bureau of the Census.

US Department of Housing and Urban Development. 1979. *Developmental Needs of Small Cities: A Study Required by Section 113 of the Housing and Community Development Act of 1977.* Washington, DC: The Department of Housing and Urban Development.

Valentine, G. 1989. The geography of women's fear. *Area* 21: 385 – 90.

Yeates, M. 1990. *The North American City.* 4th Edition. New York: Harper & Row Publishers, Inc.

Young, I. M. 1990. *Justice and Politics of Difference.* Princeton: Princeton University Press.

Zelinsky, W. 1977. The Pennsylvania small town: an overdue geographical account. *Geographical Review* 67 (1): 127 – 147.

Part I

Evolution and Growth of Small Cities

From Frontier Outpost to Northern Capital: The Growth and Functional Transformation of Prince George, BC, Canada

Greg Halseth[1], Kent Sedgwick[1], and Benjamin Ofori-Amoah[2]
[1]*University of Northern British Columbia*
[2]*University of Wisconsin-Stevens Point*

INTRODUCTION

The origins and growth of cities have fascinated researchers in urban studies for a long time. This fascination in part may be due to the complexity and unpredictability of the city growth process itself. Thus, two settlements may start at the same time and yet one will grow to become a large city while the other may not. Efforts to understand these processes and the factors behind them have led to different theoretical frameworks and interpretations. For example, earlier geographers emphasized the site and situation of places as a way of understanding the growth of cities. Economists have emphasized economic reasons, while sociologists have focused on social organization and communication-related factors. Later works by geographers have reflected all these perspectives, sometimes emphasizing more on the economic factors (e.g. Pred 1977). Beyond these theoretical perspectives, a great deal has been learned about city growth in the United States and Canada, and elsewhere, through historical perspectives. Under these perspectives, the growth of cities has been studied through a stages-of-growth approach by which the factors that led to either the growth or decline of cities have been identified and analyzed. Indeed, much of what we know about city growth has resulted from these studies. However, these studies have been characterized by two main features: they have either been conducted at a very high spatial scale such that only the large cities usually get mentioned or they have specifically focused on these large cities in the urban system. The result is that while we know the major phases of evolution of large cities, we do not know much about the growth and transformation of small cities. Have small cities grown through the same stages as we read about in the literature? Have they been influenced by the same factors and to the same degree? Or do they have a different story to tell? If so what lessons can be learned from the similarities and or differences in the evolution and development of small cities?

This chapter makes a modest contribution to this research lacuna in the growth and transformation of small cities. It examines the growth and transformation of Prince George, a small city of 72,000 located in the central interior of the Canadian province of British Columbia. The chapter traces how from a frontier outpost, Prince George grew and transformed itself into the primate city of northern British Columbia, and the factors that influenced both the growth and transformation. The chapter is divided into four sections. In the first section we review the theoretical perspectives and approaches in studying the growth of cities. Each of the next three sections is devoted to the three stages of growth that have characterized Prince George's growth. The last section concludes with some lessons for further considerations.

PERSPECTIVES ON URBAN GROWTH

Theoretical perspectives on the growth of cities identify the forces that allow a small settlement to grow to become a large city. The identification of these forces has been done from various disciplinary perspectives. Thus, initial efforts by geographers focused on the role of the physical environment in the growth and development of cities, leading to what came to be known as site and situation analysis. However, the most prevalent perspectives in the literature have been economic and sociological interpretations (Clark 1982).

Economic interpretations of urban growth are rooted in economic base theory, which argues that the growth of cities lies in the city's ability to produce and sell outside of its borders. The theory divides the economy of a settlement into two – the basic sector and the non-basic sector. The basic sector is the export activity while the non-basic sector is the supporting activity. As basic sector activity develops, agglomeration economies, advantages from the process of circular and cumulative causation and geographic inertia all combine to attract more activities to the basic sector as well as the non-basic sector, thereby leading to the growth of the city. Within the context of economic interpretations, early research focused on an agricultural surplus model, which emphasized the role of an efficient agricultural system that provided the capital and surplus labor to be invested in other basic and non-basic sector activities. Attention later shifted to manufacturing activities as the basic sector activity that provided the engine for growth, and finally to long-distance trade.

Sociological interpretations highlight the gregarious nature of people and the need to facilitate interpersonal relationships, as a basis for city growth. In this regard, cities will not develop unless the level of social organization is sophisticated enough to allow a large number of people to live in a relatively small area (Adams 1960; Lampard 1965; Fischer 1982). One particular factor in this regard is the role of communication. Meier (1962) points out that the type of communication technology that exists to a large extent explains the urban form. Thus, before modern communication technology, cities were small and compact. As communication technology improved, cities began to spread out.

No single interpretation can provide the definitive answer as to what makes cities grow. Historical studies aimed at understanding the growth of cities have combined factors from a host of interpretations. Arguing the strong relationship between economic development and urban system development, Yeates (1998) used the long wave Kondratieff theory to divide the development of the US urban system into five main eras, which include the Frontier Mercantilism Era (1790 – 1840), the Early Industrial Capitalism Era (1840 – 1885), the National Industrial Capitalism Era (1885 – 1935), the Mature Industrial Capitalism Era (1935 – 1975) and the Global Industrial Capitalism Era (1975 – present).

In Canada, Yeates (1998) has identified three eras of urban development, namely the Frontier – Staples Era (before 1935), the Industrial Capitalism Era (1935-1975) and Global Capitalism Era (1975-present). During the frontier-staples era, Canada made the transition from a frontier mercantile economy to a staples economy that produced raw materials for export (Innis 1956). The factors that made this possible include technological innovations, immigrant population, and industrial growth in Europe. The era of industrial capitalism saw a transformation of the Canadian economy. The tremendous growth in manufacturing in Central Canada was supported by branch plant investments, increased efficiency in agriculture, and the growth of a service sector. East coast cities such as St John's, Halifax, and Saint John that had been prominent in the Canadian urban system before were replaced by new ones such as Winnipeg and Vancouver. In addition, a strong urban agglomeration from Windsor to Quebec City, dominated by Montreal and Toronto, and containing about 60% of Canada's population, emerged in Central Canada (Yeates 1975). The era of global capitalism saw increasing importance of international finance and trade as the key factors in controlling urban growth.

In addition to finding explanatory factors behind the growth of cities, considerable attention has also been paid to changes in the morphology of cities that usually come with city growth. The key factors in this have been transportation and communication innovations, economic and population growth, as well as government policies. Thus, the city of the frontier-staples era began as a compact city since the most important mode of transportation was walking. There was no clear separation of work and residence, and no clear differentiation of urban social structure. This morphology began to change as the city transitioned from mercantile trade into manufacturing. Transportation innovations such as the horse-car and the horse-drawn omnibus made possible both the separation of economic activities from residences, and the separation of social classes across the city. The emergence of the metropolis, from about 1885 to 1935, solidified this process with the help of two more transportation innovations—the street car and rapid transit. Two classic models of urban land use were developed to capture these changes. The first was the concentric zone model by Burgess (Norton 1998) and the second was the sector model by Hoyt (1939). The growth of family formation, the rise of car ownership, government transportation, housing, immigration policies, the actions of financial institutions and the building industry all led to further transformation of the metropolis into a suburban city form after World War II (Jackson 1985). Processes of economic and social sorting resulted in highly differentiated city sectors—from the inner city to the surrounding suburbs. At the same time, new centers of economic activities began to develop in addition to the original central business district. This transformation was clear enough to warrant another model of urban land use, namely the multiple-nuclei model by Harris and Ullman (Norton 1998). From the mid 1970s, most of these suburban downtowns began to mirror those of the core cities they were affiliated with. These concentrations of economic activities across large urban areas gave a galactic look to the cities, earning them the label—the galactic city (Yeates 1998). It is against this theoretical background that we examine the growth and transformation of Prince George.

THE GROWTH AND TRANSFORMATION OF PRINCE GEORGE

The growth and transformation of Prince George from a frontier outpost to the largest urban place in northern British Columbia (BC), Canada can be divided into four main periods. These are the Frontier Outpost Period (Before 1901), the Transitional Period (1901 – 1940), the Industrialization Period (1940 – 1980) and the Post Industrial Period (1980 – Present). In the rest of this section, we will examine the main developments that occurred in each of these periods and the factors that were behind them.

The Frontier Outpost Period (Before 1901)

For millennia, the First Nations people today known as the Lheidli T'enneh inhabited the Fraser and Nechako valleys around what is now Prince George (Morice 1905). The focus on the river confluence resulted in their name 'people from where the rivers meet'. The rivers and the numerous trails across the plateau were later followed by white traders and prospectors (Runnalls 1985). The first contact between the Lheidli T'enneh and Europeans was in 1793 when

Alexander Mackenzie's party, in a single canoe, passed along the Fraser River on his voyage to the Pacific Ocean at Bella Coola (Christensen 1989). Following explorations by the North West Company (NWCo)'s Simon Fraser, Fort St. James (some 110 kilometers northwest of the future site of Prince George) became the fur trade capital of 'New Caledonia' (Pond 1933; Fraser 1960). In 1807, Fort George was established at the confluence of the Fraser and the Nechako rivers as a base for Simon Fraser's 1808 canoe voyage down the Fraser River. Following the voyage, the post was apparently abandoned and was only reestablished in 1821 when the Hudson's Bay Company (HBCo) absorbed the NWCo (Newman 1985). By that year, the site was on the Nechako-Fraser canoe route between Fort St. James and the Columbia River and, importantly, was at the western end of a canoe route that utilized the upper Fraser River to the Yellowhead Pass to import buffalo hides from the prairies. For several decades hides were brought to New Caledonia through this 'Leather Pass'. Although never an important post in the 19th century, Fort George nevertheless began its role as a node along the transportation routes that followed the main valleys and river systems crossing the interior plateau. Around 1901, Fort George was a sleepy village of about 150 native residents, a priest for the church and cemetery, a house for the HBCo factory beside the store, and a small farm supporting the factor and his clerks.

The initial selection and reestablishment of what would become Prince George was partly shaped by provincial topography and partly by transportation. The Interior Plateau on which Prince George is located lies between the Rocky Mountains to the east and the Coast Mountains to the west (Figure 2.1). The plateau is drained by a T-shaped river system with the upright portion formed by the main stem of the south-flowing Fraser River and the crossbar by the upper reaches of the Fraser and its major tributary, the Nechako River system. About 9,000 years ago, much of the area was submerged under a glacial lake that filled the Prince George Basin (often referred to as Glacial Lake George). As the ice sheets melted, tremendous amounts of sediment and other debris that had been eroded by the ice was released, and layers of sands, clays and gravels were sorted and laid down on the lake bottom. When the ice dam holding back Glacial Lake George gave way, the Fraser and Nechako rivers, still swollen with glacial melt water, carved deep into those sediments to create the basis within which Fort George would later be built. The result was a mountainous topography that confined transportation corridors to a limited number of river valleys and mountain passes (Wood 2001). This meant that all transportation routes across the plateau, both north-south and east-west, then and later would be channeled through the Prince George area (Robinson 1972; Bradbury 1987; Leonard 1996).

However, in one respect, Fort George's location on natural transportation routes perhaps thwarted its growth until after 1901. In this regard it is important to note that although Fort George was on the main water route through the inte-

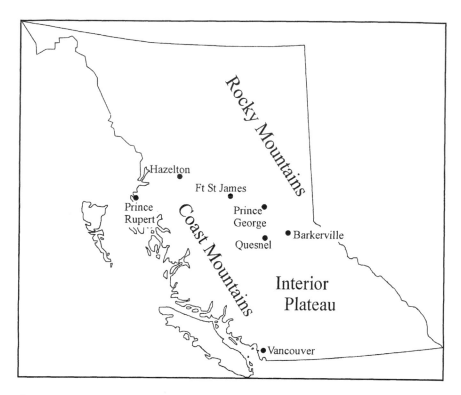

Figure 2.1 British Columbia, Canada
Source: G. Halseth

rior plateau, the Nechako had severe rapids and with major canyons, the Fraser was especially dangerous. The botanist, David Douglas almost drowned and lost many specimens when his canoe capsized in the canyon south of Fort George in 1833. 'Overlanders' trying to reach the Cariboo gold fields from eastern Canada by coming down the Fraser River through the Yellowhead Pass in 1862 suffered a number of fatalities (McNaughton 1986; Wright 1985). The result was that at the end of the 19th century, the only land route to the central interior lay some 55 kilometers to the southwest of Fort George. This was the Telegraph Trail, a route established in the 1860s when Quesnel (120 km south of Prince George) was the main junction on the Cariboo Road from Yale on the lower Fraser River to the gold fields at Barkerville (Downs 1972). The Collins Overland Telegraph project was intended to continue a telegraph line from Quesnel northwest through British Columbia, Yukon, and Alaska, then across Siberia to link with Europe. Work commenced in 1865 but was abandoned in 1867 when a transatlantic cable was successfully laid. Although the line literally came to nothing (it was re-established in 1901 for the Klondike gold rush and operated until about 1930 when radios were brought into use), the 3-meter wide clearing for the line and the packhorse trail supporting it gradually became the main overland route from Quesnel to the Skeena River at Hazelton. A link from the line followed native and fur trade trails to Fort St. James and northeast to Fort McLeod in the Peace River drainage. Thus, from 1865 onward, Fort George was bypassed by the main land route across the central interior (Christensen 1989).

The Transitional Period (1901 – 1940)

This period marked the transition of Prince George from an outpost village to the beginning of a modern city, and the most important factors behind this transition were transportation, land speculation, and the city beautiful philosophy of city planning. The limited overland access of Fort George in the frontier outpost period was changed when a wagon road connected Fort George to the Quesnel-Yukon Telegraph Road (West 1949). The first stagecoach arrived in October 1911 and, using sleighs in winter, Fort George now had an all-season land connection. However, the most important factor was the construction of a second transcontinental railway line during the early 20th century. The Grand Trunk Pacific Railway (GTPR) was chartered in 1903 to build from Winnipeg, a terminus on the Pacific Ocean somewhere near the mouth of the Skeena River (Leonard 1996). Initially, two routes through the Rocky Mountains were considered (neither of which would have led to Fort George), but in 1906 it was announced that a re-evaluation of the Canadian Pacific Railway (CPR) survey through the Yellowhead Pass made that the preferable route. Immediately Fort George was seen as an important node on the proposed line, the major divisional point between Edmonton and the coast. The 'rush to Fort George' began (West 1949).

In advance of GPTR construction, a former North West Mounted Police officer named A.G. Hamilton pre-empted land, opened a store, and began a subdivision survey for a town site about one kilometer south of Fort George. This new area, known as South Fort George, became the paddlewheel steamboat-landing site when boats from Quesnel began service in 1909 to support the railway construction (Hutchison 1982). Soon South Fort George was in competition with another speculative town site called Central Fort George and located west of the Fraser-Nechako confluence and the Lheidli T'enneh Indian Reserve. The speculators developing Central Fort George would eventually acquire more than 800 hectares of land. Like South Fort George, properties were aligned along rectangular streets, which were in turn aligned rigidly to the cardinal directions. When the properties were first marketed in 1909, Central Fort George was very much like a company town with a school, library, hotel, church, community center (including a tennis court), waterworks, and a steamboat—all creations of the land development company (Christensen 1989). Local competition between the town sites was fierce because the GTPR had yet to identify a location for its station.

Eventually, the GTPR decided to locate its railroad yards on the low-lying ground of the Lheidli T'enneh Indian Reserve at the Fraser-Nechako confluence. The GTPR turned to the local Indian Agent to help acquire all of the Lheidli T'enneh Indian Reserve for both the rail yards and the town (Leonard 1996). After much financial and political maneuvering, the Indian Reserve (553 hectares) was purchased (except for the cemetery of 0.91 hectares) for $125,000 in November 1911. In September 1913, the 150 Lheidli T'enneh inhabitants were relocated further up the Fraser River. The village was razed (the cemetery was preserved) and the GTPR had its town site. In keeping with its goal to make the town the most important division point and urban place between Edmonton and the coast, the GTPR commissioned an elaborate plan for a future city. Brett, Hall & Co., landscape architects from Boston, created the plan based on a topographic survey from the summer of 1912 and a brief visit, in September of that year, to the still forested site (Leonard 1996). Following a contemporary American planning concept popular at Harvard University, Brett and Hall created a 'city beautiful' design with a strong geometric aspect (Hall 1988).

City beautiful ideas had grown out of the 1893 Columbian Exposition in Chicago (Levy 2000). Hallmarks of the movement involved symmetry and axial layouts, a formalism over the design of public space, landscaping, promenades and plazas. In Prince George, the Brett, Hall & Co. plan was based around a grid of streets with two main 'axes' at right angles, which were terminated by significant buildings and parks. To relieve the rigidity of the grid, several diagonal streets, and a nested area of crescents following topography and a curving parkway-greenbelt were incorporated. The core of the plan was George Street, a shopping promenade connecting the proposed railroad station to a civic center. Along this street, the properties are aligned east-west to maximize the number of store fronts along the street. For the rest of the downtown, the properties aligned north-south along the streets.

While the earlier town site plans for Central Fort George and South Fort George each emphasized a rectangular grid aligned to cardinal directions, the defining elements of the Brett, Hall, & Co. plan emphasized a focused downtown core, with surrounding residential areas, all connected by greenways and parkways. Curvilinear streets through the Crescents neighborhood even brought diversity to the higher status section of the new town. In many respects, the basic urban structure of the first city plan resembled the concentric zone model first described by Burgess in early Chicago (Ley 1983). There was a focused downtown core immediately adjacent to the rail lines, which was surrounded by small lot residential areas and ringed at the outer edges by larger lot, higher status, neighborhoods whose status was physically imprinted onto the landscape through changes in street layouts. Just as the actual urban landscape of Chicago never perfectly fit with the concentric zone model, the design ideas of the city beautiful movement, which included parkways and greenbelts, acted to modify the Brett, Hall & Co. plan.

The plan was first presented to the public in a local newspaper advertisement in April 1913. The blocks and lots were surveyed and the entire site was cleared in 1913. By 1914, properties were being purchased, and in the summer of that year a number of buildings were constructed creating something of an instant town. The town site was incorporated in March 1915 as the City of Prince George with an area of 442 hectares (Figure 2.2). Immediately following this, the rival town sites of South Fort George and Central Fort George began to decline (Runnalls 1985). In the following winter, buildings were skidded across the snow to Prince George as both developers and speculators concentrated there.

With the coming of the GTPR line, the economy of northern BC began a dramatic transformation (Christensen 1989). All along the new rail line, small sawmills developed to supply the growing needs of both the railroad and the North American market with Prince George becoming a processing center for the rough-cut lumber (Boudreau 1998). It also became an entertainment center with hotels, saloons and theatres to meet the needs of the thousands of workers, mainly young men, employed in the isolated sawmills and bush camps. By 1924, the Cariboo Highway had been extended from Quesnel and the gravel road eventually became part of the provincial road network. The years of WWII were notable for the stationing of approximately 6,000 troops outside the city's western boundary (the largely vacant lands cleared many years earlier for the former Central Fort George town site), and for the completion of the highway westward from Prince George to Prince Rupert.

The growth of Prince George during the Transitional Period is reflected in its population. The first census conducted in the city in 1921 recorded 2,053 people. The population grew to 2,479 by 1931, and then declined through the Depression. By that time, however, Prince George had become a service center supplying a small regional market of agricultural settlers, several sawmills in communities east of the city, as well as the numerous local stores, hotels, restaurants and car dealerships; all the services of an emerging central place (Norton 1998). Over most of this period, the basic characteristics of the city beautiful plan which the GTPR had established remained intact.

The Industrialization Period (1940 – 1980)

From 1940 to 1980, Prince George went through a significant period of growth and change. This change, which was characterized by a growth in the city's industrial base, was made possible by transportation developments, corporate strategies, and government policies.

Following the completion of the highway to Prince Rupert, an upsurge in lumbering took place in Prince George and three more sawmills were added to

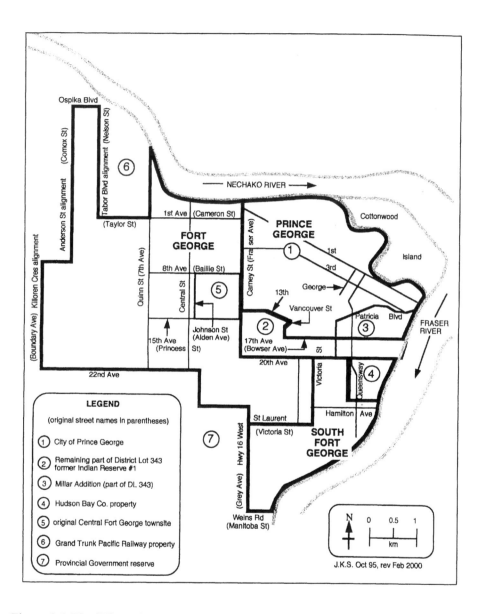

Figure 2.2 The "Three Georges" at the Incorporation of Prince George, 1915
Source: K. Sedgwick

the city's industries. These developments were further enhanced by the completion of a rail line south to Vancouver (Stauffer and Halseth 1998). In 1952, the Pacific Great Eastern Railway (renamed BC Rail in 1972) was extended to Prince George. The W. A. C. Bennett government, which assumed provincial power in 1952, began an extensive northern development program (Williston and Keller 1997). This included completing a highway link north to the Peace River region (Hwy 97 North), a highway eastward to Alberta (Hwy 16), hydroelectric developments on the Peace and Nechako rivers, and a restructuring of the forest tenure system that led to industrial forest activity coming to Prince George through the early 1960s (Marchak 1983; 1989). In the 1970s and 1980s, under different governments, gas and oil pipelines were routed through Prince George and northern extensions were made to the BC Rail line.

Through this period, the application of improved technology led to the consolidation of forest companies and the creation of larger, capital intensive, sawmills (Hak 1989). Such mills were attracted to the Prince George area to make use of its transportation networks and nearby wood supply base. The public policy changes of the 1950s had also attracted three large pulp and paper mills to Prince George by 1965. This investment further concentrated large-scale industrial forestry in the city and created tremendous growth through spin-off industries in transportation, maintenance, and supply (Edgell 1987).

This transition to a major processing center was accompanied by tremendous population growth as young families came seeking work. From a census population of 2,027 in 1941, an estimate based on ration cards put the city's population at 3,800 in 1945 (Runnalls 1985), while a post-war census recorded 4,703 in 1951. After 1951, the city grew primarily as a result of immigration from the Prairies and Europe. From 1951, Prince George's population went from 4,703 to 67,600 in 1981 (Figure 2.3). This rapid growth of Prince George's population also changed its position within the urban hierarchy of northern BC. Thus, in 1961, Prince George, together with Prince Rupert and Dawson Creek, were the three largest places in northern BC. None of these places was larger than 15,000 people and none was distinctly larger than the others. However, by 1981, Prince George's population of almost 70,000 was more than 4 times the size of its nearest rival, Prince Rupert. While places like Prince Rupert, Fort St. John, Dawson Creek, and others continued to serve local economic interests as focal points not only for their respective towns, but also small tributary rural settlement zones (Forward 1987), Prince George had become the 'command and the control' government center and industrial heart of northern BC (Figures 2.4 and 2.5).

Together with population growth came a maturing of the population profile and a sorting of the urban landscape by socio-economic characteristics (Cater and Jones 1989). In the 1960s, this structure looked very typical for a frontier boomtown (Marchak 1983). Attracted to the large number of new industrial jobs

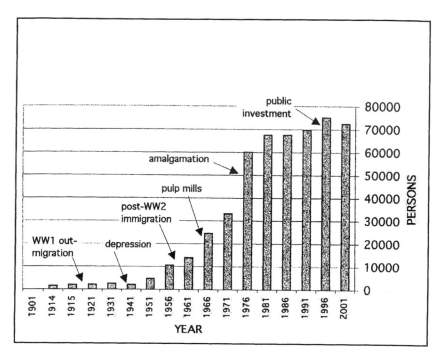

Figure 2.3 Population Growth of Prince George.
Source: K. Sedgwick

being created in the forest industry, that population was comprised largely of young families with young children (Stauffer and Halseth 1998). As is typical across Canada, resource towns often have high wage employment, and many of those coming to Prince George moved into these high wage jobs (Rennie and Halseth 1998). Through the 1960s, 1970s, and 1980s, however, this age structure was changing (Figures 2.6 and 2.7). In the pattern typical of maturing industrial centers, the workforce was aging. Limitations on opportunities for young people also meant an out-migration of youth and proportionately fewer young children as smaller numbers of young families were moving to the city. The share of the population in older age groups was also beginning to grow as many of those who came with young families during the 1960s were now starting to retire and these people desired to stay in the community where they had friends and family.

Prince George's population growth also radically changed its morphology. The tight focus upon the original GTPR city beautiful plan had lent a concentric zone pattern to the city structure; a downtown core surrounded by successive

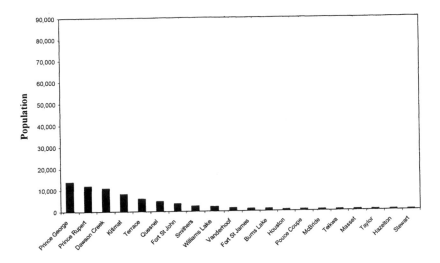

Figure 2.4 Places of North Central British Columbia, 1961.
Source: From Census Canada Data

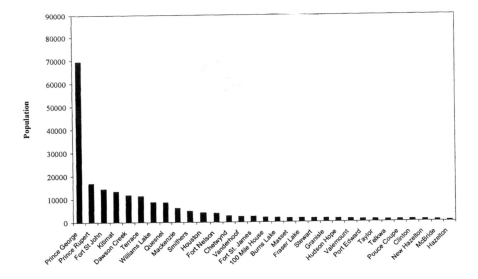

Figure 2.5 Places in North Central British Columbia, 1981.
Source: Census Canada Data

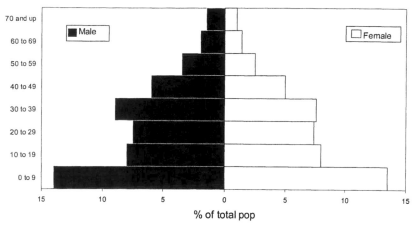

Figure 2.6 Population Pyramid of Prince George, 1961.
Source: Census Canada Data

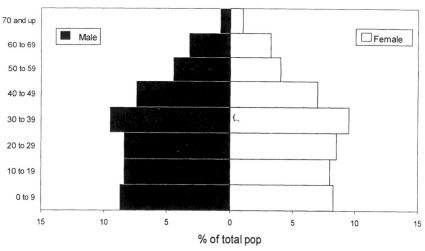

Figure 2.7 Population Pyramid of Prince George, 1981
Source: Census Canada Data

waves of residential and industrial areas. One consequence of this growth was that considerable developments were started just outside of municipal boundaries (Stauffer and Halseth 1998). As in other jurisdictions, uncontrolled suburban and exurban developments strained city services and threatened unsustainable environmental costs (Bryant et al. 1982; Jackson 1985; Hodge 1991). Many of these new spillover developments involved rectangular grid surveys that departed from the design and intent of the original city beautiful plan. This design departure can still be seen on the urban landscape as the original town site is ringed with a number of grid housing areas.

To coordinate planning, development and service provision, the city decided to expand its boundary. The first expansion occurred in 1953, when 577 hectares were added to the west of the city (the former Central Fort George area), more than doubling the city's size. Eight more municipal expansions occurred up to 1974 to bring the city size to more than 6,885 hectares. The last significant expansion occurred in 1975 when the provincial government mandated an amalgamation of the surrounding areas to address the problems of decades of unplanned rural growth. The result created an urban center of 32,400 hectares.

To manage this growth, the city employed an urban planner from Australia who was schooled in the post-war British 'New Town' movement. The former military camp in part of old Central Fort George became a light industrial area and exhibition grounds, and a four-lane arterial road network was designed to provide both 'ring-road' and connection functions. The new suburban housing areas of the 1970s and 1980s emphasized both city beautiful designs and the neighborhood concept (Hodge 1991; Hoare 1994). This is most clearly seen in the College Heights development on the plateau south of the city's core. Curvilinear streets, parks, connecting pathways and greenbelts, and retention of the natural forest landscape all feature prominently in these neighborhoods – features which link back to the city beautiful ideas of the earlier GTPR plan. Application of the neighborhood concept also meant that each of these new suburban areas developed as nodes with a self-contained set of basic services, specifically elementary schools and shopping plazas. Between 1965 and 1975, four shopping malls were constructed outside of the CBD area. These included Spruceland Mall in the area long ago known as Central Fort George, Parkwood Mall in an area southwest of the CBD, and the Hart Centre Mall and College Heights Plaza, both built along the suburban edges north and south (respectively) of the city.

The result of these mall developments was that the percentage of commercial floor space captured by the CBD declined from 78% to 53%. It also set the pattern for suburban commercial hubs around which satellite housing developments would be built. This pattern of suburban shopping development, coupled with a declining share of commercial floor space in the CBD, continued in the following decades. Prince George was now set towards a sprawling urban form punctuated by commercial nodes (Benfield et al. 2001).

Along with private developers, the city engaged in subdivision development and lot sales to control prices. In an innovative program, Crown land was purchased for $1, fully-serviced lots were developed for sale, and the Crown was reimbursed for the raw land value after sale. The contrasts in planning concepts over the years are evident on the street map of Prince George today. In the urban core, the city beautiful downtown and crescents neighborhoods of the GTPR town site are ringed with the grid neighborhoods of Central and South Fort George that developed ad-hoc outside of early municipal control. To the north and southwest are the low density sprawl of suburban areas developed around the neighborhood concept with an attempt to bring back some of the defining city beautiful and garden city planning ideas. These neighborhoods of curved and looped roads, local parks and connecting pedestrian pathways, schools and greenbelt areas, and self-contained shopping plazas created urban nodes along the edge of the original town site through the Hart Highlands, Spruceland, Pine Centre, and College Heights areas. By the 1980s, these nodes together with their shopping plazas and other economic activities away from the core, had laid the foundation for a multi-nuclei form of urban structure, where people functioned within these edge nodes with little or no connection to the original downtown core (see also Garreau 1991).

The Post-Industrial Period, 1980 – Present

Following the very rapid 1960-1980 growth, Prince George was affected by the worldwide economic recession of 1981 – 1982. Economic restructuring in Canada's resource-based industries (Barnes and Hayter 1997; Hayter 2000; 2003) led to consolidation of the forest products firms operating in Prince George in the hands of one company, namely Canadian Forest Products Limited (CANFOR). Thus, in the Prince George area alone, CANFOR came to operate three sawmills, a plywood mill, two pulp and paper mills, a pulp mill, a wood preserving plant, and a reforestation research center. In addition, there was an increasing application of technology, replacement of labor with capital, and the application of flexible work practices in order to reduce costs and remain competitive in the international market (Grass and Hayter 1989; Mackenzie and Norcliffe 1997). The application of these restructuring strategies helped the industry to remain competitive against low cost offshore producers and US softwood lumber tariffs, but the result was an industry that employed fewer people than it once did. The loss of employment in the forest industry was especially notable over the 1990s, when it was reflected in population loss for the city.

These changes in the forest industry were also accompanied by the transformation of the city into retail, educational, and service center for northern BC, which were in turn influenced by the actions of both the provincial and municipal governments as well as the local business community. Thus, to stimulate the local economy, the municipal government initiated a public investment program in the late 1980s. A civic center, sports arena, and aquatic center were built. Local political and business leadership also worked hard to try to position Prince George within the emerging service and information economy. The goal was to maintain a strong economic base and develop others to support additional growth. The city adopted the motto: "BC's Northern Capital" (Halseth and Hal-seth 1998).

The 1990s brought the emergence of a service economy in Prince George, which included the expansion of post-secondary education, the relocation of many federal and provincial government services from smaller communities around northern BC, and private sector investments in the form of big box retail outlets to serve both the Prince George and regional markets. Among the major highlights of this emerging service economy were the opening of the Great Canadian Superstore, Costco Wholesale, Wal-Mart, Home Depot Outlet, and Canadian Tire, the expansion of the College of New Caledonia (CNC), and the opening of the University of Northern British Columbia (UNBC). When UNBC opened in 1994 it had about 900 students and 150 faculty and staff. By 2004, it had over 3,500 undergraduate students, over 600 graduate students, and about 220 faculty and staff. Both of these educational centers have contributed to a local knowledge economy, which now supports a range of high-tech and computer-based information and software companies. By 2004, there were more than 85 high tech firms operating in the city, including more than 60 firms engaged in software design and the development of information technology applications and support. The growth of high tech firms in locations offering lower operating costs and a higher quality of life than large metropolitan agglomerations has been noted elsewhere (Allen and Dillman 1994). Many of these firms have been an outgrowth of the increasing application of computer-based technologies in the forestry sector, the consolidation of government offices from smaller towns and their need for technical services and support, and the research and training role of UNBC and CNC as high tech incubators. All these developments reinforced the position of Prince George as the primate city of northern BC (Figure 2.8).

Together, these changes also helped to reinforce the emerging multi-nuclei form of urban structure described by Harris and Ullman (Knox and Marston 2001). By 2004, the CBD contained only 34% of commercial floor space in Prince George, down from 78% in 1965. This is despite the fact that the volume of the CBD's floor space had increased from 88,000 square meters in 1985 to 96,000 square meters in 2004. Between 2000 and 2003, overall vacancy rates in the CBD ranged between 12% and 23% depending on location and type of commercial space.

By 2001, the age structure of Prince George's population clearly showed the characteristics of a mature industrial town (Figure 2.9). Workplace aging was evident in the shares of the local population in the 30 to 50 year age categories. The outcomes of economic restructuring (especially workplace flexibility and the substitution of capital for labor) had limited new resource industry job growth even though more activity took place in these sectors. One result of the relatively limited employment opportunities being created for young people was also evident through the proportionally smaller share of the local population

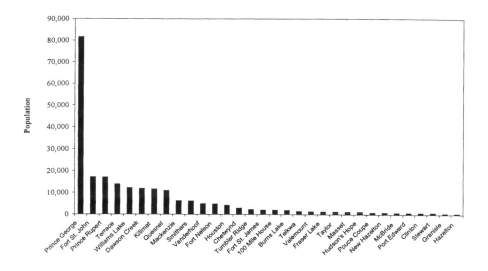

Figure 2.8 Places in North Central British Columbia, 2001.
Source: Census Canada Data

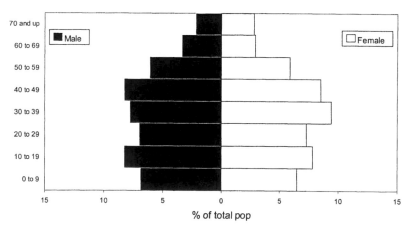

Figure 2.9 Population Pyramid of Prince George, 2001
Source: Census Canada Data

aged 20 to 29 years. Collectively, these changes meant a continued aging of the local population. Like many industrial towns along the resource frontier, the range of services, community facilities, and housing designs were mostly aimed at young families. The city continued to see new immigrant population, with most of these immigrants now having Asian backgrounds compared to the 1920 immigration waves from Scandinavia, Germany, and Britain. This shift in immigration corresponds with many of the general characteristics and changes that have been witnessed in Canadian immigration patterns over the last quarter century (Moore et al. 1990; Elliot and Fleras 1999).

There were also changes in the population distribution. Data from 1996 showed that Prince George's population was concentrated in the suburban neighborhoods along the western edge of the city and in the College Heights area (Figure 2.10). This hollowing out of the downtown core and emphasis on suburban development clearly showed in the structure of the housing market. Thus, average dwelling values increased away from the downtown core. The large rural estate properties commonly found on Cranbrook Hill recorded the highest average dwelling values. The next highest areas of average dwelling values were found in the suburban neighborhoods along the western edge of the city, the College Heights area, and the Hart Highlands area, all neighborhoods built during the 1960s and 1970s economic boom and characterized as single-family neighborhoods, complete with elementary schools and local shopping plazas (Figure 2.11).

Similarly, rental housing had in-filled the lower demand property areas, and were primarily found in the downtown core and the east-west axis that joined the downtown with Cranbrook Hill. This pattern of housing demand movement away from the original urban core, and of a replacement of that demand by rental housing, followed many of the expectations from the housing filtering literature and set up some of the preconditions to disinvestment described in the gentrification literature (Ley 1983; Badcock 2002).

The structure of the local housing market also mirrored the social geography of households and the distribution of recent immigrants. For example, high and middle-income family households were located outside of the downtown core and in the suburban and rural areas of the city, while low-income households were concentrated in the central and downtown portions of the city. The distribution of recent immigrants was focused on two clusters. The first cluster was associated with the low income and rental housing neighborhoods adjacent to the original urban core, while the second cluster involved the suburban neighborhoods along the western edges of the city and into the College Heights area.

In many small communities, the development of a big box retail and service economy has generated fierce debates about the effect of such developments on the local economy, and Prince George has not escaped this. As reenacted in Prince George, it is clear that while some retail establishments face a loss of

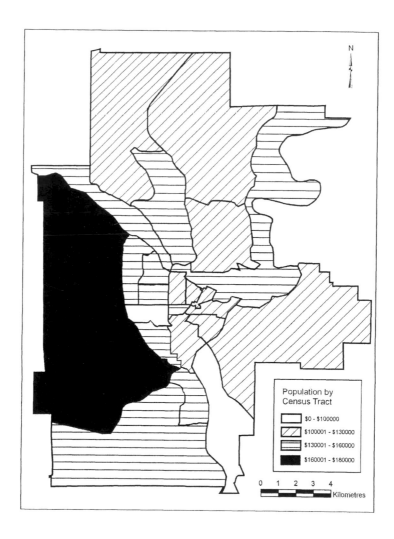

Figure 2.10 Prince George Population Distribution, 1996.
Source: J. Doddridge and S. Stauffer from Census Data

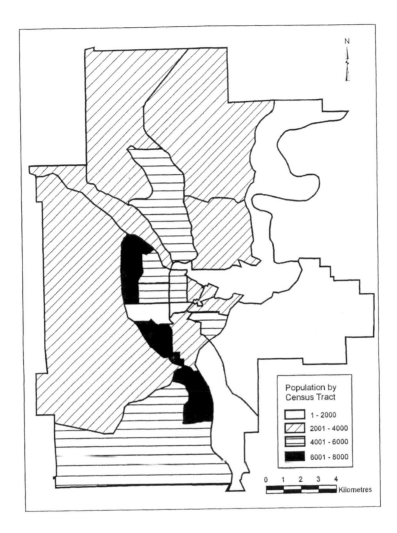

Figure 2.11 Average Values of Dwelling in Prince George, 1996
Source: J. Doddridge and S. Stauffer from Census Data

business and possible closure, other opportunities are being created through the additional traffic these large stores are attracting. There is a notable consequence for retailers in the towns and villages adjacent to Prince George, as shoppers from those places now have more reason to travel and spend money outside of their community (Halseth and Sullivan 2000). There is an increased concern over economic leakage from Prince George as well. In the past, most of the profits made by locally owned businesses had stayed in the community where it was reinvested in other activities and re-circulated through other businesses. Now, profits made by the big box chains are sent out of the community.

A further challenge posed by big box development concerns its geography and the perpetuation of an inefficient urban morphology. The development of big box retail on suburban greenfield sites (the most recent example being the Westgate development adjacent to College Heights and along Highway 16) away from the downtown core has resulted in a very low population and development density in Prince George. This low-density sprawl creates an energy-inefficient city with high servicing and maintenance costs (Hodge 1991). The extension of basic city services such as roads, sewer and water lines, and power has been a heavy burden on the general tax base (even where some of the initial installation costs are borne by developers through fees) and includes the annual costs associated with street cleaning, snow plowing and maintenance on an urban road network that now covers more than 640 kilometers.

However, the approval of big box developments along the suburban frontier is not the only pressure on the downtown core. A municipal golf course close to Costco, and along one of the major highways (Hwy 16) which bisects the city, was recently sold to developers who were seeking to relocate a car dealership from the downtown. The city also recently approved the construction of a large hotel and casino complex at the intersection of Hwy 97 (north-south) and Hwy 16 (east-west) on land which had previously been publicly owned forest and green space. The casino in question had been located downtown, and the traffic it attracted was important for the viability of local hotels, shops, and restaurants.

Thus, like most other small cities in North America, Prince George has been dealing with the problem of revitalizing a downtown that continues to lose business and population to the outskirts, only to be replaced by low income and rental housing. Consequently, like many other places, Prince George has opted to try streetscape and other cosmetic changes to the downtown core rather than changing the fundamentals of housing availability and commercial/retail siting approvals to draw people, investment and economic activity back downtown.

CONCLUSION

Over the past 100 years, Prince George has been transformed from a small village to BC's Northern Capital. The evolutionary phases of this transformation mirror those generally identified in the context of Canada's urban system development. However, instead of three phases, we have identified that Prince George's transformation has occurred in four phases, a frontier outpost period, a transitional period, an industrialization period, and a post-industrial period. One could argue that our first two phases, the frontier outpost period and the transitional period, could be equated to the frontier-mercantile period used to describe Canada's urban system in general. However, in Prince George we found the frontier outpost and the transitional period phases distinct enough to separate them. We also found some slight time lags in the evolutionary phases of Prince George. For example, the industrialization period did not begin until 1940, and the post-industrial industrial period not until 1980. In terms of large cities, both of these periods began 5 years earlier. This could be due to natural tendency that innovation diffusion through an urban system usually starts from large cities.

The factors that have shaped Prince George's transformation are no different from those of large cities, and include the geographic location advantages, development of transportation systems, especially road and rail, land speculation, government policies, and corporate strategies. Like in other cities, this transformation has been accompanied by changes in urban morphology, as well as the social and economic geography of the city. For example, the urban morphology of the city changed from a compact core with surrounding neighborhoods to a dispersed set of suburban neighborhoods and shopping centers loosely connected by an urban road network emphasizing the use of private automobiles over four lane arterial roads. In addition, as economic change has resulted in the closure of some local mills and the expansion of others, the city has seen the expansion of the service economy by way of educational institutions and the creation of a high tech and computer software sector. These are posing new challenges in the areas of location, planning, and redevelopment. These challenges are not unique to Prince George, but to all small cities across North America. More research focusing on the changing geography of small cities will be useful to small cities as they deal with these challenges.

REFRERENCES

Adams, R. M. 1960. The origins of cities. *Scientific American*. 203: 153 – 68.

Allen, J. and D. Dillman. 1994. *Against All Odds: Rural Community in the Information Age*. Boulder, CO: Westview Press.

Badcock, B. 2002. *Making Sense of Cities: A Geographical Survey*. London: Arnold/Oxford University Press.

Barnes, T. and R. Hayter, ed. 1997. *Troubles in the Rainforest: British Columbia's Forest Economy in Transition*. Canadian Western Geographical Series 33. Victoria, BC: Western Geographical Press, University of Victoria Department of Geography.

Benfield, F. K., J. Terris, and N.Vorsanger. 2001. *Solving Sprawl: Models of Smart Growth in Communities across America*. New York: Natural Resources Defense Council.

Boudreau, J. 1998. *Crazy Man's Creek*. Prince George, BC: Caitlin Press.

Bradbury, J. 1987. British Columbia: metropolis and hinterland in microcosm. In *Heartland and Hinterland: A Geography of Canada*, ed. L. McCann., 400 – 401. Scarborough, ON: Prentice-Hall Canada.

Bryant, C., L Russwurm, and A.G. McLellan. 1982. *The City's Countryside: Land and its Management in the Rural-urban Fringe*. London and New York: Longman.

Cater, J. and T. Jones. 1989. *Social Geography: An Introduction to Contemporary Issues*. New York: Edward Arnold.

Christensen, B. 1989. *Prince George: Rivers Railways, and Timber*. Burlington, ON: Windsor Publications.

Clark, D. 1982. *Urban Geography*. London: Croom Helm.

Davis, H. C., and T. A. Hutton. 1989. The two economies of British Columbia. *BC Studies* 82: 3 – 15.

Downs, A. 1972. *Paddlewheels on the Frontier*. Seattle, WA: Gray's Publishing Ltd./Superior Publishing.

Edgell, M. C. R. 1987. Forestry. In *British Columbia: Its Resources and People*, ed. C. N. Forward, 109 – 137. Victoria, BC: University of Victoria.

Elliot, J. L., and A. Fleras. 1999. *Unequal Relations: An Introduction to Race, Ethnic and Aboriginal Dynamics in Canada*. Scarborough, ON: Prentice Hall.

Fischer, C. S. 1982. *To Dwell Among Friends: Personal Networks in Town and City*. Chicago: University of Chicago Press.

Forward, C. N. 1987. Urban system. In *British Columbia: Its Resources and People*, ed. C. N. Forward, 259 – 382. Western Geographical Series. Victoria: BC: University of Victoria.

Fraser, S. 1960. *The Letters and Journals of Simon Fraser, 1806-1808*, ed. W. K. Lamb. Toronto: Macmillan.

Garreau, J. 1991. *Edge City: Life On the New Frontier*. New York: Anchor Books.

Grass, E., and R. Hayter. 1989. Employment change during recession: the experience of forest product manufacturing plants in British Columbia, 1981-1985. *The Canadian Geographer* 33 (3): 240 – 252.

Hak, G. 1989. The socialist and labourist impulse in small-town British Columbia: Port Alberni and Prince George, 1911 – 33. *Canadian Historical Review* LXX, No. 4: 519 – 542.

Hall, P. 1988. *Cities of Tomorrow: An Intellectual History of Urban Planning and Design in the Twentieth Century*. Oxford, UK / Cambridge, USA: Blackwell Press.

Halseth, G., and R. Halseth, ed. 1998. *Prince George: A Social Geography of British Columbia's "Northern Capital"*. Prince George, BC: University of Northern British Columbia Press.

Halseth, G., and L. Sullivan. 2000. *Implications of Changing Commuting Catterns on Resource Town Sustainability: The example of Mackenzie, British Columbia*. Prince George, BC: Northern Land Use Institute, University of Northern British Columbia.

Hayter, R. 2000. *Flexible Crossroads: The Restructuring of British Columbia's Forest Economy*. Vancouver, BC: University of British Columbia Press.

———. 2003. The war in the woods: post-Fordist restructuring, globalization, and the contested remapping of British Columbia's forest economy. *Annals of the Association of American Geographers* 93 (3): 706 – 729.

Hoare, T. G. 1994. Garden City. In *The Dictionary of Human Geography*, ed. R. J. Johnston, D. Gregory, and D. M. Smith, 213-214. Cambridge, MA: Basil Blackwell.

Hodge, G. 1991. *Planning Canadian Communities: An Introduction to the Principles, Practice, and Participants*. Scarborough, ON: Nelson Canada.

Hoyt, H. 1939. *The Structure and Growth of Residential Neighborhoods in American Cities*. Washington, DC: Federal Housing Administration.

Hutchison, B. 1982. *The Fraser*. Toronto, ON: Clarke & Irwin.

Innis, H.A, and M. Q. Innis, ed. 1956. *Essays in Canadian Economic History*. Toronto, ON: University of Toronto Press.

Jackson, K. T. 1985. *Crabgrass Frontier: The Suburbanization of the United States*. New York: Oxford University Press.

Knox, P. L., and S. A. Marston. 2001. *Human Geography: Places and Regions in Global Context*. Englewood Cliffs, New Jersey: Prentice Hall.

Lampard, E. E. 1965. Historical aspects of urbanization. In *The Study of Urbanization*, eds. P. M. Hauser and L. F. Schnore, 519 – 54. London: John Wiley.

Leonard, F. 1996. *A Thousand Blunders: The Grand Trunk Pacific Railway and northern British Columbia*. Vancouver, BC: University of British Columbia Press.

Levy, J. M. 2000. *Contemporary Urban Planning*. Englewood Cliffs, New Jersey: Prentice Hall. Ley, D. 1983. *A Social Geography of the City*. New York: Harper and Row.

Mackenzie, S., and G. Norcliffe. 1997. Guest editors - Restructuring in the Canadian newsprint industry. *The Canadian Geographer* 41 (1): 2 – 6.

Marchak, P. 1983. *Green Gold: The Forest Industry in British Columbia*. Vancouver, BC: University of British Columbia Press.

———. 1989. History of a resource industry. In A *History of British Columbia Selected Readings*, ed. P. E. Roy, 108 – 128. Toronto, ON: Copp Clark Pitman.

McNaughton, M. 1986. *Overland to Cariboo: An Eventful Journey of Canadian Pioneers to the Gold Fields of BC in 1862*. Toronto, ON: William Bricks.

Meier, R. I. 1962. *A Communication Theory of Urban Growth*. Cambridge, Mass.: MIT Press.

Moore, E., B. Ray, and M. Rosenberg. 1990. *The Redistribution of Immigrants in Canada*. Ottawa, ON: Employment and Immigration Canada.

Morice, A. G. 1905. *The History of the Northern Interior of British Columbia: Formerly New Caledonia, 1660 to 1880*. Toronto, ON: William Briggs.

Newman, P. 1985. *Company of Adventurers*. Markham, ON: Penguin Books Canada.

Norton, W. 1998. *Human Geography*. Toronto, ON: Oxford University Press.

Pond, P. 1933. *Five Fur Traders of the Northwest: The Narrative of Peter Pond and the Diaries of John Macdonell, Archibald N. McLeod, Hugh Fairies, and Thomas Connor*. St Paul, MN: University of Minnesota Press.

Pred, A. R. 1977. *City Systems in Advanced Economies*. London: Hutchinson.

Rennie, B., and G. Halseth. 1998. Employment in Prince George. In *Prince George: A Social Geography of BC's' Northern Capital'*. Prince George, BC, ed., G, Halseth and R. Halseth, 45 – 66. University of Northern British Columbia Press.

Robinson, J. L ed. 1972. *British Columbia*. Toronto, ON: University of Toronto Press, Studies in Canadian Geography Series.

Runnalls, Rev. F. E. 1985. *A History of Prince George*. Prince George, BC: Fraser Fort George Museum Society.

Stauffer, B and G. Halseth. 1998. Population change in Prince George. In *Prince George: A social geography of B.C's 'Northern Capital,'* ed. G. Halseth and R. Halseth, 12 – 44. Prince George, BC: University of Northern British Columbia.

West, W. J. 1949. The 'B.X.' and the rush to Fort George. *British Columbia Historical Quarterly* 13 (3 – 4): 129 – 229.

Williston, E., and B. Keller. 1997. *Forests, Power, and Policy: The legacy of Ray Williston*. Prince George, BC: Caitlin Press.

Wood, C. 2001. Introduction.. In *British Columbia, the Pacific Province: Geographical Essays*. ed. C. Wood, 1 – 12. Canadian Western Geographical Series 36. Victoria, BC: Western Geographical Press, University of Victoria.

Wright, R. T. 1985. *Overlanders: The Epic Cross-Canada Treks for Gold, 1858 – 1862*. Williams Lake, BC: Winter Quarters Press.

Yeates, M. 1975. *Main Street: Windsor to Quebec City*. Toronto, ON: Macmillan of Canada.

————. 1998. *The North American City*. Fifth Edition. New York: Longman.

3

Urbanization of the Midwestern Countryside: The Case of Minnesota's Small Cities

John S. Adams and Barbara J. VanDrasek
University of Minnesota-Twin Cities

INTRODUCTION

The term "urbanization" has at least two well-defined meanings in geography. One emphasizes that the proportion of a place's population (e.g., a state, region, or nation) that is officially defined as urban is rising; the second refers to the fact that the size of the population in places defined as urban is increasing. Other definitions use population density, as well as the nature of work that people *do* to earn a living. It happens that by any of these definitions (percentage, size, density, livelihood), the Midwestern countryside is urbanizing at a steady pace. Like the greater Minneapolis-St. Paul commuting field, which sprawls over at least 24 counties in Minnesota and Wisconsin, Minnesota's small cities have been spawning low-density development nearby whether or not local populations are increasing. Towns, villages and hamlets within highway commuting range of the state's regional centers are becoming bedroom suburbs, and incomes brought home from jobs in those centers supply new vitality to Main Street. In unincorporated townships surrounding Minnesota's regional centers, new houses are going up along major and minor highways and country roads that provide access to nearby malls, schools and recreation areas. Meanwhile our professional and conventional lay understanding of our settlement system is still rooted in the urban-rural or metro-non-metro distinctions. Similarly, political geographies of the state such as county-based functions and locally autonomous planning and zoning activity usually remain anchored to 19th century farm economy needs while service provision to dispersed households takes new forms. Consequently, small cities do not really feature much in scholarly considerations of urbanization.

In this chapter, we examine some selected aspects of the contemporary urbanization of the Minnesota countryside in an effort to understand how production and consumption, population and settlement, resource use and transportation are all connected. We are particularly interested in the transportation and planning implications of the demographic and economic trends underway within the commuting fields surrounding a sample of small cities in Minnesota. From a public policy standpoint, we would like to know how the processes that are unfolding can be effectively managed. In what follows, we first outline the major trends in the evolving settlement system in the US and the Midwest to show that the distinction between rural and urban has been obsolete even before World War II. Next we describe the methodology we used to select a sample of 20 small cities and analyze the changes occurring in and around those cities. Then we present the results of our analysis in terms of population and traffic changes within the study areas, and follow it up with the relationship between the patterns of change and transportation development. Finally, we highlight the planning implications of the results for small cities.

THE EVOLVING AMERICAN SETTLEMENT SYSTEM

A central task of urban geographic scholarship focused on the United States is to create ways to define, measure, and portray important features of the American settlement system. This effort involves both theoretical and empirical inquiry. The theoretical part involves defining the concepts and vocabulary that we use in describing what is happening; and the empirical part includes measuring, mapping, describing, and interpreting how people settle and use the land.

The idea that the urban-rural or metro-non-metro distinctions are fast becoming obsolete represents a major departure from professional as well as conventional lay understandings of our settlement system. At the end of the 19th century, Adna Ferrin Webber published his celebrated monograph, *The Growth of Cities in the 19th Century*, which called attention to how industrialization in the Western world during the previous century had transformed traditional resource-based settlement patterns centered on hunting, fishing, farming, forestry, and mining (Weber 1899). At the time he wrote, railroad and streetcar suburbs were already flourishing around many of the world's major cities, and by 1920 with help from Robert Moses and other planning and infrastructure visionaries, automobile-oriented suburbs were spilling out beyond the limits of New York, Los Angeles and other major American cities.

By the time the US Census Bureau adopted terms like urban and rural, and defined them in quantitative terms, the actual forms of settlement were already moving beyond census practice. As big cities spawned suburbs, an effort got underway at the Census Bureau to characterize, measure and assess what was happening—an effort that came to fruition with the formal definition of Standard Metropolitan Areas following the Census of 1950 (Adams and Van-Drasek 1998; Adams, VanDrasek and Phillips 1999). Even so, there was suspicion especially following World War II that the "urban-rural" and "metro-non-metro" distinctions had become increasingly imprecise as ways to distinguish forms of settlement patterns and ways of life from one another. At most they now represented simply variations in settlement densities and land development patterns, rather than profound differences in ways of life like those that had been significant at the end of the 19th century (Dahmann and Fitzsimmons 1995).

Metropolitan Area Definition

Over the next several decades, the Office of Management and Budget (OMB), the federal agency that defines and adopts official criteria for designating metropolitan areas, worked with the Census Bureau to define metropolitan areas, and use census statistics to describe their characteristics. Following the 1990 Census of Population and Housing, the Census Bureau and OMB raised the question whether the idea of defining metropolitan areas would continue to make sense for the year 2000 and beyond in the same way that it had made theoretical and empirical sense during the early part of the 20th century. After all, they observed, most Americans live modern city-centered lives, and in most ways they engage in forms of livelihood and material consumption that are impossible to differentiate on the basis of place of residence. People hold the same kinds of jobs, drive the same kinds of cars, watch the same TV programs, eat the same food, shop at the same malls, have the same aspirations for their kids, and so forth. So "What is functionally significant about place of residence?" they asked.

Transformation of the Midwestern Countryside

Growth trends in small cities in the Midwest were no different from these national trends. Thus, from the early days of North American settlement up through the 1950s, Midwestern cities were understood as centers of manufacturing and wholesale trade, along with transportation, communication, finance and business management activity that linked their respective tributary regions and market areas with other regional economies of the United States and the world. Meanwhile smaller towns, villages and hamlets served as local central places that assembled the products of field, forest and mine for export while distributing retail goods and services to the households and local businesses that were anchored to the land and to extractive industries (Borchert and Adams 1963; Berry 1967).

After 1970 it became increasingly apparent across the American Midwest and within the northeastern Manufacturing Belt that many small cities outside the commuting range of major metropolitan centers were taking on the geographical characteristics of small metropolitan areas. That is, these small cities were becoming regional centers that were developing economies that were increasingly diversified and progressively less dependent on serving the needs of agriculture. They were spawning new housing and business developments at low densities at the edges of their built-up areas, or within easy commuting distance from new jobs in and around those centers. This recognition prompted a question of how Minnesota's regional centers might be sharing in this trend, and as a consequence might be heading toward some of the problems of sprawl, regional planning challenges, and highway congestion that plague the fast-growing Minneapolis-St. Paul region.

We tackled this question by measuring and analyzing low-density suburban-type residential development after 1970 within commuting ranges of a sample of smaller Minnesota's cities—specifically exurban development in towns and townships beyond any built-up suburban edges of those cities. We suspected that low-density development patterns similar to what had been occurring throughout the 24-county Minneapolis-St. Paul MN-WI commute field were being duplicated in the vicinities of small cities around the state, but at reduced ranges and intensities.

METHODOLOGY

Our research plan involved three tasks. First was to specify criteria for selecting up to 20 small cities for investigation and defining the 1990 commuting fields surrounding them. Census data for 1990 county-to-county commuting flows were used in defining the commuting fields because commuting data from the 2000 census would not become available from the Census Bureau until 2003 or later. The next step was to apply those criteria to define and map the 1990 commuting fields. The commuting fields were to be used as study areas. The second task included estimating rates of population change by minor civil division (MCDs—cities, towns, townships) within commuting fields for each decade between 1970 and 2000, then mapping rates of population change for MCDs in each commuting field in order to illustrate the extent to which population was dispersing in the vicinity of the sample regional centers. The third task was to portray local population changes within commuting fields along with changing volumes of trunk highway traffic in the 1980s and 1990s to measure and assess any road congestion that might be developing. Trends in trunk highway traffic to and from the sample regional centers between 1970 and the end of the 1990s provide additional evidence of changes underway in settlement, economic activity and ways of life in the countryside.

Selection of Regional Centers

In a study of trade centers in the Upper Midwest, Casey (1999) provided a list of regional trade and service centers of various ranks or levels as follows:

1. The 7-county Twin Cities Metropolitan Area (defined by state statute and governed for planning purposes by the Metropolitan Council of the Twin Cities) was identified as the state's only "Major Metropolitan Area."

2. Subsidiary centers in Minnesota and along the state's border with neighboring states included:

   - Five identified as "Level 1 centers or *Primary Wholesale/Retail Centers*," a group that includes large places such as Fargo-Moorhead, Duluth-Superior, St. Cloud, Rochester, and La Crosse-LaCrescent;
   - Twenty-two "Level 2 centers or *Secondary Wholesale/Retail Centers*," a group that includes smaller centers such as Bemidji, New Ulm and Hibbing that provide a full range of wholesale and retail functions to local households and businesses and to their tributary market areas;
   - Twenty-two "Level 3 centers or *Complete Shopping Centers*," a group that includes still smaller and less sophisticated central places such as International Falls and Montevideo.

Our study team used this list to select a sample of regional centers in Minnesota to investigate the questions raised. Almost all of these 50 centers are located on one of Minnesota's principal trunk highways, or at the intersection of two or more trunk highways. It is from the set of 49 regional centers in Minnesota (excluding the Twin Cities Metro Area) that we drew a sample of 20 for analysis (Figure 3.1). We wanted the 20 selected to be (1) centers located outside the Twin Cities 24-county commuting field; (2) half from northern Minnesota, and half from southern Minnesota; and (3) a mix of fast-growing (in the 1990s) and slow-growing (or declining) centers.

We divided Minnesota into a northern zone and a southern zone, with the boundary between them running east-west south of Little Falls and north of Alexandria. Each study area consisted of a central county containing the regional center, plus additional counties that sent at least 5% of daily commuters to the central county in 1990. Study areas within each of the zones were grouped according to their population change during the 1990s. Study areas with population growth equal or exceeding 3% for the decade were classified as moderate

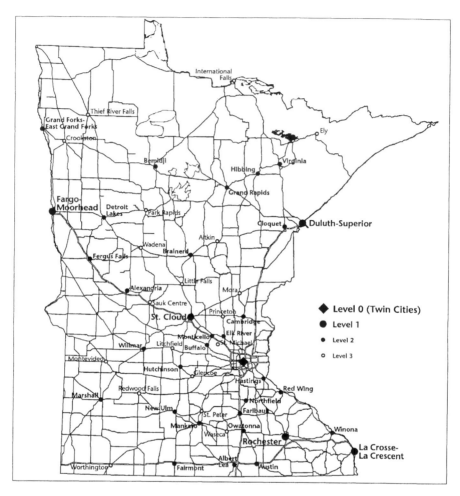

Figure 3.1 Minnesota's Regional Trade Centers

to fast growth. Study areas with population growth below 3% during the 1990s were termed slow-growth or declining. With these distinctions we ended up with four classes of study areas:

- Northern areas of moderate to fast growth;
- Northern areas of slow growth or decline;
- Southern areas of moderate to fast growth; and
- Southern areas of slow growth or decline (Table 3.1).

Table 3.1 Population Change in Study Areas and Regional Key Centers, 1990 – 2000

Study Areas	Population 1990	Population 2000	Population Change (%)	Key City Population 1990	Key City* Population 2000	Population Change %
Northern Areas: Slow Growth or Decline						
Duluth-Superior / Hibbing	322,586	330,189	2.2	85,493	86,918	1.7
Grand Forks - E. Grand Forks	140,717	133,041	-5.5	49,064	49,321	0.5
International Falls	16,149	14,355	-11.1	8,325	6,703	-19.5
Northern Areas: Moderate to fast Growth (3 percent)						
Bemidji	57,690	66,449	15.2	11,245	11,917	6.0
Brainerd	78,661	97,550	24.0	12,353	13,178	6.7
Fargo-Moorhead	213,477	236,945	11.1	73,198	90,599	23.8
Little Falls	52,967	56,138	6.0	7,232	7,719	6.7
Park Rapids	14,939	18,376	23.0	2,863	3,276	14.4
Wadena	36,539	38,139	4.4	4,131	4,244	2.7
Southern Areas: Slow Growth or Decline						
Albert Lea	33,954	32,584	-4.0	18,310	18,356	0.3
Marshall	70,298	68,914	-2.0	12,023	12,735	5.9
Montevideo	33,837	32,235	-4.7	5,499	5,346	-2.8
New Ulm	55,721	56,682	1.7	13,132	13,594	3.5
Worthington	48,436	48,268	-0.3	9,977	11,283	13.1

* Key City identified in italics
Source: US Bureau of the Census

Table 3.1 (Continued)

Study Areas	Population 1990	Population 2000	Population Change (%)	Key City Population 1990	Key City* Population 2000	Population Change %
Southern Areas: Moderate to Fast Growth (3%)						
Alexandria	39,462	44,057	11.6	7,838	8,820	12.5
Mankato / N. Mankato	124,687	130,664	4.8	31,477	32,427	3.0
Rochester	248,142	267,470	7.8	70,745	85,806	21.3
Waseca	18,102	19,526	7.9	8,385	8,493	1.3
Willmar	63,292	66,247	4.7	17,531	18,351	4.7

* Key City identified in italics
Source: US Bureau of the Census

Definition of Commuting Fields

To define study areas surrounding and including the 20 regional centers, and to assess patterns of population change within the study areas during the 1990s, we identified the commuting fields focused on our sample regional centers (Figure 3.2). Each commuting field focuses on one of the regional centers and is composed of one or more counties, which are subdivided into incorporated cities and towns and unincorporated townships. In some cases, (e.g., Fargo-Moorhead) two or more cities comprise the regional center so in each study area we designated a key city, which is understood as the study area's functional center and the largest single job center in the commuting field. Duluth is the key city for the Duluth-Superior and Hibbing study areas where we combined the two overlapping commuting fields into a single study area. Each of the key cities serves as a business, employment and highway transportation node for its tributary area. Portraying population change, trunk highways, and highway traffic in the vicinity of a regional center requires defining and showing each center's functional region, which it serves and that supports it.

However, because of data availability, daily journey-to-work commuting activity turns out to be the only convenient measure of the extent of a center's functional region. Accordingly, we used county-to-county commuting data from the 1990 Census of Population and Housing to define each center's commuting field (Figure 3.3). Centers generally had two or three counties in their functional region (i.e., their commuting field) in addition to the county containing the regional center. In the case of Albert Lea, only Freeborn County qualified. The largest functional region surrounded Grand Forks-East Grand Forks with seven counties, followed by Rochester and Duluth-Superior with six. Some counties lie in more than one commuting field. The commuting fields defined this way were used as the "study areas," one for each of the sample regional centers. The 20 cities were examined in terms of patterns of growth and sprawl, and the relationships among population growth, dispersion of population, and traffic on major highways serving the sample regional centers, using maps and regression analysis.

POPULATION AND SETTLLEMENT CHANGES, AND TRAFFIC IMPACTS

Population Changes

When the regional centers at the heart of these study areas were highlighted on a map of the state and distinguished as to whether they were in the fast-growth or slow-growth category, it was evident that all of the fast-growth study areas lay within a crescent of growth extending from southeast of Rochester,

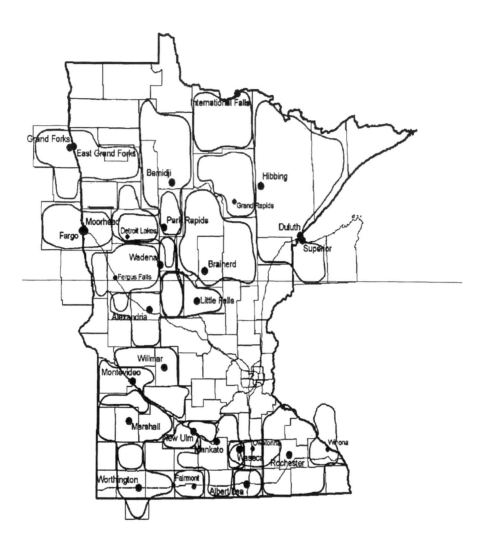

Figure 3.2 Commuting Fields and Study Areas

northwest through Mankato and the greater Twin Cities area, northwest through St. Cloud, and into the lake district north to Park Rapids and Bemidji. The study areas in the "slow-growth or decline" category were in the far southwestern and western parts of Minnesota, and in the far north from the Red River Valley across to northeastern Minnesota's Arrowhead region (Figure 3.3). The slow-growth places are disadvantaged by location—they are remote from major metro centers. Additionally they are disadvantaged by inadequate site resources that they still depend on—an anemic farm economy, weakness in forestry and mining, and limitations in the recreational opportunities they offer compared with resources available throughout the crescent of growth. In contrast, places that experienced moderate to fast growth enjoy advantages of relative location closer to prosperous and growing metropolitan centers, attractive site resources, and an ability to capitalize on scale efficiencies that are impossible to attain in smaller and declining places. Cumulative and circular advantages accompany growth and promote further growth. Once underway, and for a variety of reasons, advantages such as capital investment and net in-migration flow to places that grow faster than their competitors. This process of cumulative and circular causation works in reverse as well because when a place stops growing or slides into decline, the negative economic and demographic effects of stagnation feed off and magnify one another, promoting further decline. Yet regardless of study area location (north or south) or recent growth experience (moderate to fast growth; slow growth or decline), the urbanization of the Minnesota countryside appears to be well on its way. For each of the study areas we also mapped population change within minor civil divisions (MCDs) in the 1970s, 1980s and 1990s to see how changes varied with distance from the regional center. The example of the Bemidji area, a place dotted with lakes, recreational sites, and seasonal and retirement housing illustrates the variation from decade to decade as well as differences between the 1970s and 1980s (Figure 3.4). We made maps for all 20 study areas for each of the three decades (see Adams, Koepp, and VanDrasek 2003).

In addition to maps of population change within MCDs we graphed MCDs according to their respective distances from the regional center and their rates of population change. All MCD observations received equal weight. We anticipated a negative correlation between distance and population increase—that is places closer to the regional center would increase more and the remote places would increase less or decline (Figure 3.5). In the Bemidji example, the outliers in the scatter diagrams dilute the R-square value, but in this case the pattern is pretty clear. We made a graph like this for each decade and for each of the 20 study areas (see Adams, Koepp, and VanDrasek 2003). Finally, we examined changes in highway traffic volumes in the 1980s and 1990s to see how the geography of population change in the vicinity of regional centers showed evidence of sprawl, and was related to the capacity and use of major highways serving the regional centers (Figure 3. 6).

A close look at what happened to populations in incorporated municipalities (i. e., all cities, large and small including key cities) and in unincorporated townships that comprise the commute fields reveals substantial variation among the

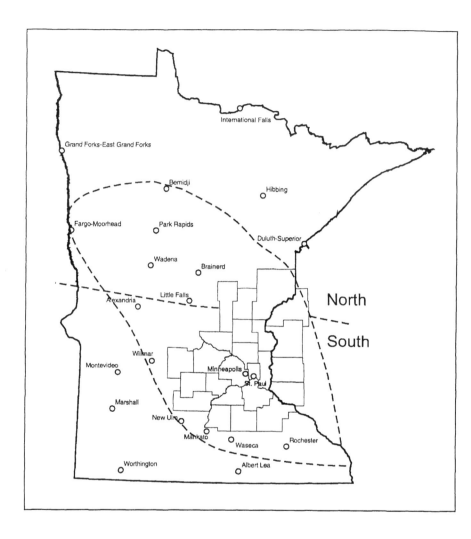

Figure 3.3 Sample Regional Centers and Crescent of Growth

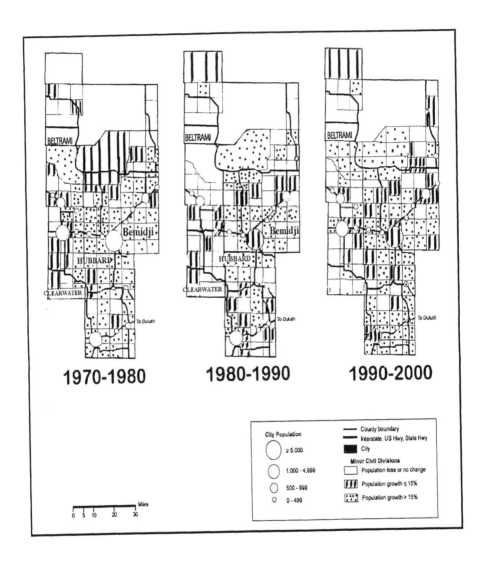

Figure 3.4 Bemidji Area: Population Change in Minor Civil Divisions, 1970 – 2000

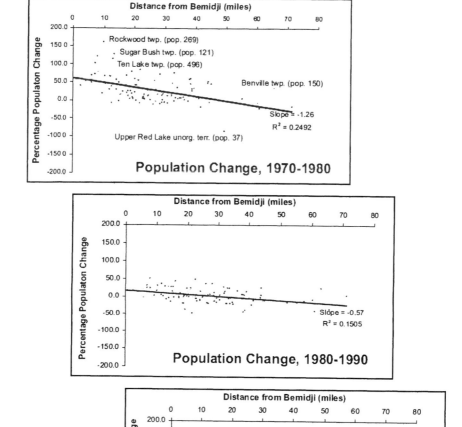

Figure 3.5 Population Change and Distance from Bemidji, 1970 – 2000

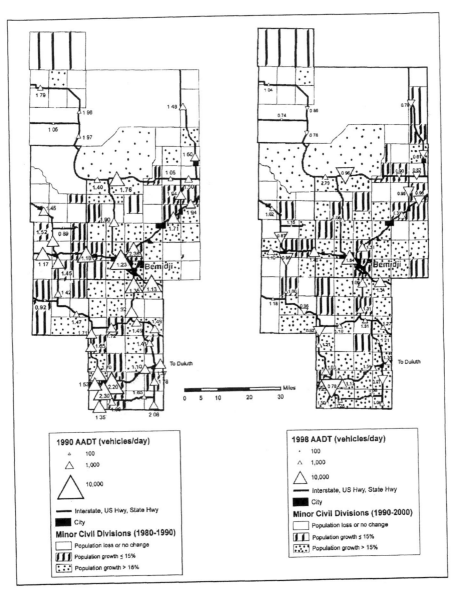

Figure 3.6 Bemidji Area: Highway Traffic Volumes, 1980 – 1998
Maps illustrate changes in annual average daily traffic (AADT) in the 1980s (left) and
the 1990s (to 1998; right). Numbers report ratios of later traffic volumes compared with
earlier.

study areas. We had classified study areas into those that grew fast (more than 3% between 1990 and 2000), and those that grew slower or actually lost population. Yet within the eight slow-growth or declining areas, all but three had population increases in their cities (Table 3.1). Regional and local patterns of population change within study areas can be summarized as follows:

1. In three study areas that lost population in the 1990s, townships in the commute field lost population while cities gained. In two cases, both cities and townships lost, and in one case while the cities lost the townships actually gained, but not enough to offset city losses. (Table 3.2)

2. In nine of the thirteen study areas that gained population in the 1990s, the increases apparently were spilling over into the countryside, while in the four other study areas city gains more than offset townships losses. (Table 3.3)

Table 3.2 Study Areas Losing Population in the 1990s

	Unincorporated Townships in Commute Field that Lost Population	Unincorporated Townships in Commute Field that Gained Population
Incorporated Places that Gained Population	Albert Lea Marshall Worthington	Not Applicable
Incorporated Places that Lost Population	Grand Forks-E. Grand Forks Montevideo	International Falls

Our maps and diagrams define the tributary commuting fields adjacent to the sample regional centers, and portray population changes within MCDs during the 1970s, the 1980s and the 1990s. For each set of population change maps we constructed a corresponding set of scatter diagrams illustrating the relationship between distances of MCDs in the commute sheds from the key city and population change during each decade in each MCD. Population increases during each decade generally were greater in MCDs located closer to the regional centers, and smaller or negative farther away (Table 3.4). Among the 57 cases (i.e., 20 study areas and three decades, with Hibbing combined with Duluth-Superior) 44 had negative slopes indicating population increases dropping off with distance from the key city.

For regional centers and parts of Minnesota experiencing slow growth or decline, places closer to the regional center typically are doing better than places farther away. For regional centers and parts of Minnesota within the crescent of

Table 3.3: Study Areas Gaining Population in the 1990s

	Unincorporated Townships in Commute Field that Lost Population	Unincorporated Townships in Commute Field that Gained Population
Incorporated Places Gained Population	Fargo-Moorhead Mankato-N. Mankato New Ulm Rochester	Alexandria Bemidji Brainerd Duluth-Superior Little Falls Park Rapids Wadena Wascca Willmar
Incorporated Places Lost Population	Not Applicable	None

growth the patterns of growth are more mixed, with growth not necessarily corresponding with distance from regional centers such as where commuting fields overlapped such that increasing distance from one job center meant reduced distance to another one. In other cases of positive regression slopes, some of the fast-growing study areas (e.g., Park Rapids, Little Falls and Wadena) are in the lake and outdoor recreation areas of the state, and those amenities provides a pull that dilutes to some extent the effect of highway distance from key cities and regional centers.

Settlement Changes and Traffic Impacts

In the last 50 years, Minnesota's agricultural areas, mining centers and forest lands underwent a transformation that included consolidation of farms, industrialization of agriculture, contraction of iron and taconite mining, and a convergence of lifestyles for farm families and households living in cities and towns. Many households today continue to live on farmsteads, but they may or may not own the adjacent agricultural land. If they own it, they often rent it to a neighboring farm operation, but often they own or rent only the farmstead and commute daily to jobs in town or at industrial sites scattered across the countryside. Other households have purchased several acres of farmland or forestland, and have built suburban-style houses to create a type of ultra low-density scattered-site exurban development that differs little if at all from conventional automobile-oriented suburbanization. What is deceptive when observing and

Table 3.4 Slopes of Regression Lines Relating Population Change in MCDs and Distance from Regional Centers *

Study Area	1970s	1980s	1990s	Study Area Population Change in 1990s (%)
Albert Lea	+ .08	− .43	+ .49	− 4.0
Alexandria	− 1.58	− .59	− .87	+ 11.6
Bemidji	− 1.26	− .57	− .37	+ 15.2
Brainerd	− .36	− .31	− .26	+ 24.0
Duluth-Superior	− .03	− .10	− .04	+ 2.2
Fargo-Moorhead	− .13	− .22	− .13	+ 11.0
Grand Forks-EGF	− .29	− .13	− .07	− 5.5
International Falls	− .02	− .05	− .20	− 11.1
Little Falls	+ .01	− .83	+ .39	+ 6.0
Mankato-N.M.	− .79	− .76	+ .04	+ 4.8
Marshall	− .05	− .25	− .19	− 2.0
Montevideo	− .44	− .32	− .28	− 4.7
New Ulm	− .40	+ .40	− .67	+ 1.7
Park Rapids	+ .88	+ .60	− .16	+ 23.0
Rochester	− .38	− .71	+ .08	+ 7.8
Wadena	− .00	+.07	+ .74	+ 4.4
Waseca	− 1.80	− 1.16	− 3.60	+ 7.9
Willmar	− .61	− .68	− .17	+ 4.7
Worthington	+ .15	− .25	+ .04	− 0.3

* Estimated by ordinary least squares regression. Distance from place to place is measured between place centroids. Data Source: U.S. Bureau of the Census.

analyzing this phenomenon is the visual impact of cropland and pastureland surrounding what is basically modern, city- or suburban-type housing for residents living daily lives that differ not at all from households living within densely settled urban areas.

With regard to highways and traffic volumes, we are left with the impression that both inside and outside MSAs, a combination of

- larger populations,
- number of households increasing faster than population,
- increasing distances between home and work,
- multiple job holding by household members,
- higher discretionary incomes and more recreational shopping,
- more available leisure,
- increasingly complex household life styles,
- greater numbers of cars and trucks,
- higher rates of participation by women in the paid workforce,

- ever-better highways,
- farm consolidations accompanying longer truck hauls, and
- other factors.

are all contributing to enhanced traffic loads on trunk highways in our study areas. On the other hand, highway capacity serving Minnesota's regional centers is more than sufficient to handle substantial increases in daily traffic loads.

TRANSPORTATION AND DEVELOPMENT OF SMALL CITIES: CAUSE-EFFECT RELATIONSHIPS

The story of the cause-effect relationships between Minnesota's transportation systems and associated agricultural and town development goes back to 19th century railroad construction and even earlier (see for example, Borchert and Yaeger 1968; Richards and Fisher 2001). The first European-American settlers and traders cleared ox-cart and wagon trails, defining overland routes that extended inland from the Mississippi River and from the westernmost point of Lake Superior where Duluth-Superior would develop. Early wagon roads tended to follow still older Indian trails. What eventually became key transportation nodes and town sites in the emerging circulation system were boat landings accessible to uplands such as the bend in the Mississippi at the mouth of Trout Creek at St. Paul, water-power sites, and crossing points on the Minnesota, upper Mississippi and Red Rivers.

The Railroads

Railroad builders pushed west and north across the US and Minnesota between the 1860s and 1900, following (and sometimes leading) the frontiers of farming, lumbering, and mining. At first, local rail lines fanned out from river and lake ports, tending to parallel or supersede the wagon and stage routes previously used to collect resources from tributary areas. By 1880, the national transport system was rapidly becoming an all-rail system with the main rail lines across Minnesota becoming part of the northern transcontinental lines, while branch lines increased in density to drain output, mainly from agricultural areas.

The ways in which natural resource-based economic activity depended on the railroads wielded profound effects on early urban growth patterns. Raw materials moved to towns and cities for processing and markets, while finished manufactured goods and services moved in the other direction. Almost all rail-based economic activity and associated passenger movements eventually converged on the Twin Cities, Duluth or Chicago. Shipments and personal travel perpendicular to these radial lines was difficult, expensive and often impossible.

Urban growth was encouraged at rail nodes and major switching points—of which Minneapolis and St. Paul were the most important in Minnesota and the

Upper Midwest, and along the major rail corridors through agricultural areas such as south-central and southwest Minnesota and the Red River Valley. By 1920 the Minnesota railroad network was virtually complete, and intercity transportation had come to depend almost entirely upon it.

Although automobiles had arrived on the scene during the previous two decades, they were used only for local movement, much of which was purely recreational. After 1920 the railroad network began to thin out slowly, but at the same time passenger train service increased up through World War II while the state highway department was completing the Federal Aid Primary road system (U.S. highways) and the Federal Aid Secondary system (state highways). After the war, rail passenger service slowly dried up and freight service contracted to serve only the main towns and cities, and places fortunately located along the remaining main rail lines.

Highways

In the early 1920s, with financial support and planning assistance from the federal and state government, a coherent and comprehensive highway system began emerging from the mammoth grid of graded section roads that served the farms and mining areas of rural Minnesota. On the eve of World War II, paved roads paralleled the radial rail corridors fanning outward from the Twin Cities and Duluth.

At first the effect of the highways was to reinforce earlier patterns of accessibility. But as the major highway system took shape, selected section roads were upgraded along north-south and east-west lines between and among county seat towns and cities that had been unconnected during the railroad era. In addition, minor radials focused on small cities were paved along routes that had not previously been served by major rail lines because they had not been in the paths from Minneapolis and St. Paul to other major Midwest or Pacific Northwest cities.

Today's network of highways in Minnesota permits, for all practical purposes, freedom of movement from the main population centers of any county to those of any other county. Comparative advantage of location within a "main line" corridor, or the disadvantage of location outside one, has been pretty much eliminated, thereby opening the door to suburbanization of the countryside in the vicinity of each of the state's regional centers.

For large cities and metro areas, the development of the state's freeway system since the 1960s seems to have reestablished or reinforced the historic corridors of accessibility along routes from the Twin Cities to other major centers—northeast to Duluth; east to Chicago and Milwaukee; southeast to Rochester; south to Des Moines and Kansas City; southwest to Mankato, South Dakota, and west; and northwest to Fargo-Moorhead and points west. But as the

Interstate system was supplemented by additional freeways and expressways, interchange between freeways and the remainder of the road system became smooth and unimpeded, posing none of the friction and delays that changing trains posed at an earlier time.

Over the long run, improved highways seem to have reinforced economic advantages and settlement patterns from those of earlier times while increasing the speed and flexibility of the total system. But as differences in accessibility among Minnesota's cities and counties diminished and the capacity and speed of the transportation system improved, other variations among places have emerged to differentiate prospects for economic vitality and population stability or growth in and around small cities.

In parts of the state that traditionally depended for their livelihoods on agriculture and mining, the flagging fortunes of those industries have led directly to population declines.[1] Meanwhile, as the state's metropolitan areas and selected small cities accumulated job and shopping opportunities, retirement and recreational settings capitalized on new economic bases as tourists arrived to purchase goods and services, and retirees settled in with their transplanted wealth, directing their pensions and other income streams into the areas where they choose to live part or all of the year. The combination of spending by tourists and retirees can supplement and eventually replace a local economy formerly based on natural resource extraction. The new economy of the countryside remains tied to natural resources, but in forms and fashions that can be sustained and even enhanced if managed properly.

As small cities such as Rochester, Mankato, Brainerd, Bemidji and Willmar reach a certain size and sophistication they begin competing with the Twin Cities by offering some of the same advantages in the production of goods and services—but without some of the disadvantages that big cities endure. The trunk highways facilitate the activities of the new economy, but are not determinative of which places flourish and which will languish; however, the places that are flourishing have encountered mounting traffic problems in recent years, sometimes during the week and sometimes on weekends.

IMPLICATIONS FOR PLANNING

One of the main planning challenges confronting highway planners and local economic development specialists concerns highways and traffic congestion. Concerns about traffic congestion and reduced mobility on Minnesota's major highways and Interstates in the 1990s prompted the Minnesota Department of Transportation (Mn/DOT) to undertake an Interregional Corridor Study, which was completed in late 1999.[2] The goal of the study was to develop a better understanding of the relationship between small cities and traffic on trunk highways in order to manage proactively the connections among the state's regional centers in a cost-effective manner. The study analyzed all the major highways in the state and identified a system of interregional corridors based on community use and traffic volumes. The 2,930 miles of trunk highways form the corridors that link the regional centers while easing movement between the centers and parts of their commuting fields.

The idea of the corridor study was to provide direction through Mn/DOT's State Transportation Plan, which sets policy for investments on the state's 12,000-mile trunk highway system. That goal was consistent with Mn/DOT's strategic objective "to develop an interregional corridor system that enhances the economic vitality of the state by providing safe, timely, and efficient movement of people and goods to regional trade centers."[3]

Interregional corridors were defined by Mn/DOT as the main transportation channels tying the state together and supporting Minnesota's economic health by linking people with jobs, distributors with manufacturers, shoppers with retail outlets, and tourists and vacationers with recreation opportunities. The state's population has been growing steadily in recent decades, with the Twin Cities and the regional centers as a group growing at above average rates.

The greatest concentration of growth and economic activity occurred in a zone stretching from southeast of Rochester, then west and north through Mankato and the 24-county greater Twin Cities area, to counties in the lake district north and northwest of St. Cloud. Areas of sparse population and general economic weakness include most of the counties in far southwestern and western Minnesota, the Red River Valley, and most of far north and northeastern Minnesota throughout the Arrowhead Region.

Mn/DOT officials noted that growth and sprawl in some places was accompanying traffic congestion on certain trunk highways, with the Twin Cities area experiencing the most serious congestion problems. They went on to argue that growth trends in the state given the present highway transportation system threatened the efficiency of transportation connections among the regional centers statewide and nationwide.

The state's system of major highway routes and the state's pattern of population increase and land development in and around small cities are highly correlated, especially in the zone of growth outlined above. Two kinds of traffic use the state's major trunk highways intensively: local traffic in the vicinity of the growing regional centers and traffic on the interregional corridors. Traffic volumes on the interregional corridor system rose by 50% in the 1990s, and are expected by Mn/DOT to double by 2020. At present, 30% of statewide travel is concentrated on the regional corridors, but these represent only 2% of all highways in the state (Minnesota Department of Transportation, No date).

As selected regional centers grow in size, complexity and spatial extent, a major challenge for transportation officials is improving mobility or preventing loss of mobility on interregional corridors passing through those developing urban areas. One response to increased traffic and accidents in and near busy regional centers is the installation of more traffic signals, which improves safety and minimizes cross-street delays, but reduces the ability of highways to handle through traffic rapidly and efficiently. For example, 16 signals added on US-212 west of Minneapolis between I-494 and Granite Falls over the past 20 years have increased delays and travel times. Eleven signals added on MN-101/US-169 between I-94 and Garrison (north of Minneapolis by Mille Lacs) led to similar results (Minnesota Department of Transportation No date).

Other planning issues accompany the countryside being repopulated by new "suburbanites." As new households move onto 5- 10- or 20-acre lots and into new houses, they push up demand for land and housing, raising average housing prices, land values, and demand for urban-type services, while supporting the gentrification of the main streets of villages. Land uses change as corporate agribusinesses replace small family farms. Conservation movements promote forest expansions and reforestation of marginal farmlands while cropland else-where is replaced by vast expanses of front yard. Industry relocates out of small cities to industrial parks on or beyond the edge of town. Meanwhile recreational uses of the countryside replace other uses, and all-terrain vehicles and snowmo-biles add traffic on logging roads in state and national forests.

Service provision in small cities and nearby commuting fields adjusts as demographic and economic trends support improved housing and health care for some, while poverty and social deprivation afflict others (Ibery 1998). City- and county-sponsored transit systems extend their routes beyond the municipal boundaries of small cities where demand is rising and ability to pay is sufficient. Remote regional hospitals and medical clinics with specialized services and fa-cilities replace smaller generalized facilities that were closer to home. More and better services are now offered, but average distance to services (including emergency services) is increased. School districts consolidate to serve larger areas as the new suburbanites scatter across the countryside. Counties and cities with small or declining population and resources find it increasingly advanta-geous to share "circuit-riding" city clerks, county administrators, county attor-neys, planners, law enforcement and emergency-service personnel.

CONCLUSIONS

Our study of Minnesota settlement changes in and around a sample of the state's regional centers during the past 30 years supports the clear impression that the commuting fields surrounding small cities across the state have become "neighborhoods" in the same way that high density areas within regional centers and metropolitan areas are neighborhoods. To characterize them and to identify their planning requirements is going to require careful empirical work, a move-ment away from the old urban-rural terminology, and a creative effort to describe this new entity that is evolving, and doing it in persuasive and useful ways. To be sure, a drive through the countryside off main highways and past fields of corn, soy beans and alfalfa can lull us into thinking that much has remained unchanged over the decades, but the facts are otherwise. The urbanization of the countryside is well underway with no sign of slowing down.

ENDNOTES

1. Economic and population decline in Minnesota's agricultural regions has occurred steadily, but continued rural decline is neither inevitable, nor does it appear to yield a net benefit for the state. See: Edward G. Schuh, "A Strategy for Developing Rural Minnesota," (Minneapolis: Hubert H. Humphrey Institute of Public Affairs, 2000); Also "Rural Development and the University of Minnesota," Paper presented to the Faribault Rotary Club, Faribault, MN, 22 March 2000; and "Why Rural Human Development Matters," Paper presented in Accra and Cape Coast, Ghana, 4-6 September 2000.

2 For elaboration see: Minnesota Department of Transportation, No date. *Better Connections for Minnesota's Future: Interregional Corridor Study*. St. Paul: Minnesota Department of Transportation, 8pp, which is based in part on: SRF Consulting Group, Inc. 1999. *Statewide Interregional Corridor Study*; submitted to: Minnesota Department of Transportation. At the same time that SRF was completing its study, a parallel investigation was underway with staffing by Minnesota Planning. That effort, *A Generic Environmental Impact Statement (GEIS) on Urban Development*, was a statewide study mandated by the 1999 Minnesota Legislature and ordered by the Minnesota Environmental Quality Board (EQB). The legislation directed the EQB to "... examine the long-term effects of urban development, past, present, and future, upon the economy, environment, and way of life of the residents of the state." The study was ordered because of growing controversy surrounding urban growth and development in Minnesota. See *Final Scoping Document: Generic Environmental Impact Statement on Urban Development in Minnesota*. St. Paul: Minnesota Environmental Quality Board, 21 December 2000.

3. *Better Connections for Minnesota's Future*, p.2. Another major daily traffic generator across Minnesota is the state's collection of colleges and universities—more than 60 public and private campuses, most located in the state's regional centers and most with increasing enrollments. For example, Minnesota State Colleges and Universities (MnSCU) enroll about 150,000 students on 36 campuses. See MnSCU, Performance (a newsletter of Minnesota State Colleges and Universities), Fall 1999, pp. 1ff, and http://www.mnscu.edu

REFERENCES

Adams, J. S., B. J. VanDrasek, and J. Koepp. 2003. *Urbanization of the Minnesota Countryside: Population Change and Low-Density Development Near Minnesota's Regional Centers, 1970-2000*: Transportation and Regional Growth Study. Report No. 10. Minnesota. Department of Transportation, Center for Transportation Studies, University of Minnesota.

Adams, J. S., and B. J. VanDrasek. 1998. Redefining the Metropolitan Region. *CURA Reporter* 28:(3): 13 – 8.

Adams, J. S. and B. J. VanDrasek, with E. Phillips. 1999. The Definition of Metropolitan Statistical Areas. *Urban Geography* 20: 695 – 726.

Berry, B. J. L. 1967. *Geography of Market Centers and Retail Distribution.*

Borchert, J. R., and R. B. Adams. 1963. *Trade Centers and Trade Areas of the Upper Midwest* Minneapolis: Upper Midwest Economic Study.

Borchert, J. R,. and D. P. Yaeger. 1968. *Atlas of Minnesota Resources and Settlement.* Minneapolis, MN: Department of Geography, University of Minnesota. Englewood Cliffs: Prentice Hall.

Casey, W. 1999. *Trade Centers of the Upper Midwest: 1999 Update.* Minneapolis, MN: Center for Urban and Regional Affairs, University of Minnesota.

Dahmann, D. C., and J. D. Fitzsimmons, ed. 1995. *Metropolitan and Nonmetropolitan Areas: New Approaches to Geographical Definition.* Working Paper No. 12. Washington DC: Population Division, U.S. Bureau of the Census.

Ilbery, B. W., ed. 1998. *The Geography of Rural Change.* Harlow, UK: Longmans.

Minnesota Department of Transportation. No date. *Better Connections for Minnesota's Future: Interregional Corridor Study.* St. Paul: Minnesota Department of Transportation.

Richards, R. T., and M. Fisher. 2001. *Highway Improvements and Rural Growth: An Annotated Bibliography.* FHWA/MT-00-001/8117–13. Helena, MT: Montana Department of Transportation. (Available through National Technical Information Service).

Schuh, G. E. 2000a. *A Strategy for Developing Rural Minnesota.* Minneapolis: Hubert H. Humphrey Institute of Public Affairs.

————. 2000b. Rural Development and the University of Minnesota. Paper presented to the Faribault Rotary Club, Faribault, MN, March 22.

————. 2000c. Why Rural Human Development Matters. Paper presented in Accra and Cape Coast, Ghana, September, 4 – 6.

Weber, A. F. 1899. *The Growth of Cities in the Nineteenth Century.* Studies in History, Economics and Public Law. New York: Columbia University.

4

Demographic Changes in America's Small Cities, 1990 – 2000

Christiana K. Brennan and Christopher Hoene[1]
The National League of Cities, USA

INTRODUCTION

In the US, the word "city" generally invokes images of places such as New York, Chicago, Boston, and San Francisco. Yet, the overwhelming majority of cities in America (97%) have less than 50,000 residents (U.S. Census Bureau 1999). These are places such as Lewiston, Maine; Watertown, South Dakota; Jacksonville, Arkansas; and Tualatin, Oregon. Drop the population threshold to 10,000 or less, and the number of incorporated places that falls under this category still includes a large majority of US cities (87%)—from Montpelier, Vermont, and Buffalo, Minnesota, to Whiteville, North Carolina, and Cody, Wyoming (US Census Bureau 1999; Figure 4.1).

While researchers and the media often study large cities to identify trends in American society, small cities have been relatively neglected even though they are more representative of cities nationwide. The focus of this chapter is on small cities and our subject of study is demographic changes. Definitions of what constitutes small cities abound, but in this chapter, we use the National League of Cities' definition of small cities as incorporated places with population of less than 50,000.

We focus on demographic changes in these cities for a number of interrelated reasons. First, understanding the demographic changes under way in these cities is necessary to understanding the changing municipal landscape of America today. Second, most cities with populations of less than 50,000 are

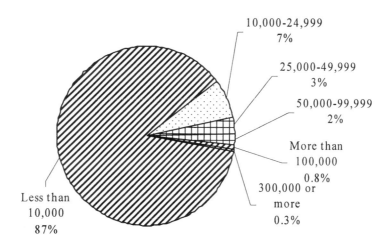

Figure 4.1 US Municipal Governments by Population Size
Source: 1997 US Government Vol. 1 Government Organizations

either suburbs or on the suburban or rural fringe. Understanding how change is occurring in these cities, and comparing those changes across city sizes, can provide valuable perspective on overall population trends in America's metropolitan regions—particularly at a time when research shows that larger metropolitan areas are pushing out and expanding to include smaller communities. Third, small cities have the potential to grow and become what Lang has termed "boomburbs" such as Mesa, Arizona, and Garland, Texas (Lang and Simmons 2001; Lang 2003). "Boomburbs" are rapidly growing suburbs that have maintained their suburban character despite double-digit population growth rates in recent decades. As Lang argues, demographic change in small cities can potentially restructure the dynamics of entire metropolitan areas.

Using census data, this chapter analyzes demographic change in a sample of 100 small cities drawn from across the US. The change is examined with respect to general growth pattern, regional growth pattern, and race and ethnic composition. The rest of the chapter is divided into four sections. The first section outlines the main demographic changes that have occurred in US cities between 1990 and 2000, as reported in recent studies, to provide the context for the similar analysis with regards to small cities. The second section describes the methodology we used to collect and analyze the data for this study. The third section presents the findings of our analysis, and the fourth section discusses the implications of our findings for policy and future research.

DEMOGRAPHIC CHANGES IN THE US, 1990 – 2000

The 2000 decennial census sparked a flurry of studies on demographic change in cities and metropolitan areas in the US. Most of these studies, however, have centered on large and medium-sized cities, offering little perspective on what was happening in the small places that comprise the vast majority of American cities. Among the most comprehensive of these studies are those by the Brookings Institution's Center on Urban and Metropolitan Policy and its staff (The Brookings Institution 2001; Vey and Forman 2002; Berube 2002; Glaesar and Shapiro 2002). Looking at demographic changes in large cities (those with 1990 populations of 175,000 – 7million), the Brookings Institution (2001) and Berube (2002) reported that during the 1990s, large cities as a group grew by 9.1%. At the regional level, they also reported that large cities in the Southwest and West grew rapidly, while those in the Northeast did not grow. In addition, almost half of the largest cities no longer have majority White populations, while increases in Hispanic populations accounted for much of the growth.

Focusing on trends in places defined by the Brookings Institution as medium-sized cities (cities with population of 98,000 – 175,000), Vey and Forman (2002) also reported that medium-sized cities grew faster (12.9%) in population than the largest cities. Although growth was strong among medium-sized cities, there were significant regional disparities, with the fastest-growing cities found largely in the South and West. Like the large cities, the growth of medium-sized cities was driven largely by an influx of new Asian and Hispanic residents.

Glaeser and Shapiro (2001) went a step further to investigate the causes of growth. They attributed the population decline in northeastern cities to that fact that Americans are moving away from Rustbelt manufacturing centers. However, Simmons and Lang (2001) and Lang (2003), while acknowledging that industrial cities have experienced substantial population loss, contend that these cities may be rebounding.

With respect to racial and ethnic trends, Frey (2001) used the census data to show that the 1990s was the first decade during which the Northeast, Midwest, and West experienced a net out-migration of Blacks; 58% of the nation's total Black population gain during the 1990s occurred in the South. In addition, the Census reported that the Hispanic population increased by 57.9% during the 1990s (Guzman 2001). The Hispanic share of the population grew by 2.4% in the Northeast, 2% in the Midwest, 3.7% in the South, and 5.2% in the West.

To date, the only work that has reported on demographic change in small cities during the 1990 – 2000 period is by the staff at the US Census Bureau (Rain, Mackun, and Harper 1999; Perry and Mackun 2001). However, this work looks only at aggregate figures as part of an overall analysis, with no systematic or cross-sectional assessment of the data for small cities. For example, it shows that cities with populations of between 10,000 and 50,000 were the fastest-growing cities in the country during the 1990s. It also shows that of the 892 cities experiencing double-digit growth during the 1990s, 691 (77.5%) had 1998 populations of between 10,000 and 50,000; another 128 had populations of between 50,000 and 100,000. Beyond this, there is nothing about regional growth patterns, differences between metropolitan and non-metropolitan locations, racial/ethnic composition, or other factors. The census study did not include cities under 10,000 in population. Obviously, it will be important to know what is happening in small cities with respect to these changes.

METHODOLOGY

Building on previous work, particularly the Brookings Institution's studies on large and medium-sized cities, we conducted an analysis of demographic changes in small cities for 1990 - 2000, with small cities defined as municipal incorporations with populations under 50,000, as specified in the 1990 decennial census. Data for this analysis were drawn from the 2000 Census Summary File 1 and the 1990 Census Summary Tape File 1.

According to 1997 Census of Governments, the universe of cities under 50,000 in population was 18,803 cities, comprising over 97% of cities in the United States. This research was based on a sample of 100 small cities that was randomly drawn from all cities with populations of less than 50,000 (18,803), using the National League of Cities' database of US cities. To facilitate regional comparisons among the cities, we used the US Census Bureau's regional grouping of states in the country, which is the Northeast, the Midwest, the South, and the West (Table 4.1). Fourteen cities in the sample were located in the Northeast, 29 were in the Midwest, 31 were in the South, and 26 were in the West (Table 4.2).

In order to avoid biasing the analysis towards fast growing cities, we used the 1990 population numbers, instead of the 2000 population numbers, as a basis for the sample selection. Cities in this sample were classified by their population size, region, location, and population growth rate. By population size, the 100 cities, according to the 1990 population census, ranged from 1,594 (Manahawkin, New Jersey) to 49,380 (East Providence, Rhode Island). We categorized them into three main groups—those under 10,000, those between 10,000 and 25,000, and those between 25,000 and 50,000. Thirty-nine cities in the sample had populations of less than 10,000, 36 had between 10,000 and 25,000, and 25 had between 25,000 and 50,000 (Table 4.2). The total population of the sample cities in 1990 was 1.6 million, growing to 1.9 million by 2000.

Table 4.1: US Census Bureau Regional Groupings

Northeast	Midwest	South	West
Connecticut (CT)	Illinois (LI)	Alabama (AL)	Alaska (AK)
Maine (ME)	Indiana (IN)	Arkansas (AR)	Arizona (AZ)
Massachusetts (MA)	Iowa (IA)	Delaware (DE)	California (CA)
New Hampshire (NH)	Kansas (KS)	District of Columbia (DC)	Colorado (CO)
New Jersey (NJ)	Michigan (MI)	Florida (FL)	Hawaii (HI)
New York (NY)	Minnesota MN)	Georgia (GA)	Idaho (ID)
Pennsylvania (PA)	Missouri (MI)	Kentucky (KY)	Montana (MT)
Rhode Island (RI)	Nebraska (NE)	Louisiana (LA)	Nevada (NV)
Vermont (VT)	North Dakota (ND)	Maryland (MD)	New Mexico NM)
	Ohio (OH)	Mississippi (MS)	Oregon (OR)
	South Dakota (SD)	North Carolina (NC)	Utah (UT)
	Wisconsin (WI)	Oklahoma (OK)	Washington (WA)
		South Carolina (SC)	Wyoming (WY)
		Tennessee (TN)	
		Texas (TX)	
		Virginia (VA)	
		West Virginia (WV)	

Source: US Census Bureau

Table 4.2 Small Cities' Sample by Region, Location, and Population Size

Region	Population Size		
	Less than 10,000	10,000 – 25,000	25,000 – 50,000
Northeast	Lewes, DE*	Augusta, ME	Norwich, CT*
	Manahawkin, NJ	Chambersburg, PA	Lewiston, ME
	Monessen, PA*		Millville, NJ
	Montpelier, VT		Easton, PA*
			Wilkes-Barre, PA*
			East Providence, RI*
			North Providence, RI*
			Burlington, VT*

*Metropolitan Location

Table 4.2 (Continued)

Region	Population Size		
Midwest	Less than 10,000	10,000 – 25,000	25,000 – 50,000
	Rock Falls, IL	Coralville, IA*	Greenwood, IN*
	Swansea, IL*	Bradley, IL*	West Lafayette, IN*
	Columbia City, IN*	Park Forest, IL*	Shawnee, KS*
	Abilene, KS	Garden City, KS	Apple Valley, MN*
	Norton Shores, MI*	Ottawa, KS	Blaine, MN*
	Buffalo, MN*	Monroe, MI*	Kirkwood, MO
	Wayzata, MN*	Saline, MI*	
	West Plains, MO	Berkeley, MO*	
	Beulah, ND	West Carrollton, OH*	
	Carlisle, OH*	Watertown, SD	
	Trotwood, OH*		
	Custer, SD		
	North Sioux, SD		
South	Clanton, AL	Jasper, AL	Jacksonville, AR*
	Prescott, AR	Prattville, AL*	North Lauderdale, FL*
	Dade City, FL*	Dublin, GA	Ocala, FL*
	Fairburn, GA*	Baker, LA*	East Point, GA*
	Port Gibson, MS	Bastrop, LA	Bartlesville, OK
	Knightdale, NC*	Cumberland, MD*	Muskogee, OK
	Whiteville, NC	Greenbelt, MD*	Rock Hill, SC*
	Hartsville, SC	Hyattsville, MD*	
	Addison, TX*	Laurel, MD*	
		Starkville, MS	
		Henderson, NC	
		Farragut, TN*	
		Maryville, TN*	
		Coppell, TX*	
		Rockwall, TX*	
West	Kodiak, Ak	Arcata, CA	Beverly Hills, CA*
	Queen Creek, AZ*	La Quinta, CA*	Brea, CA*
	Indian Wells, CA*	Rocklin, CA*	Culver City, CA*
	Estes Park, CO*	Broomfield, CO*	Grand Junction, CO
	Steamboat Springs, CO	Artesia, NM	
	West Wendover, NV	Milwaukie, OR*	

*Metropolitan Location

Table 4.2 (Continued)

Region	Population Size		
West	Less than 10,000	10,000 – 25,000	25,000 – 50,000
	Dallas, OR*	Tualatin, OR*	
	Tillamook, OR	Marysville, WA*	
	Park City, UT	Port Angeles, WA	
	Brewster, WA		
	North Bend, WA*		
	Cody, WY		
	Douglas, WY		

* Metropolitan Location

By location, we categorized the cities as metropolitan or non-metropolitan depending on their location within or outside a metropolitan statistical area (MSA), as defined by the Office of Management and Budget (OMB) in 1990. The Brookings Institution's studies used a different categorization for metropolitan status—central cities and "satellite cities." The central city category comprises the largest cities within metropolitan areas and "satellite cities" include all other cities. However, we did not employ this missing categorization for small cities because so many small cities were located outside of OMB-defined MSAs, that we felt a more important distinction would be whether or not these cities were located within metropolitan areas. In 1990, 62 cities in the sample were metropolitan and 38 were non-metropolitan (Table 4.2). We also categorized the sampled cities according to their population growth rates from 1990-2000, as follows: rapid-growth (>20%), strong-growth (10-20%), moderate-growth (2-10%), no-growth (-2% to 2%), and declining cities (<-2%). Thirty-six cities in the sample were rapid-growth cities, 11 were strong-growth cities, 22 were moderate-growth cities, 15 were no-growth cities, and 16 were declining cities (Table 4.3). This categorization is based on the Brookings methodology and is employed so that growth comparisons can be made across cities of different sizes in terms of population. Following conventional practice for analyzing trends in US population diversity, this study separates the populations of our sample into both racial and ethnic categories.

Finally, since our analysis included race and ethnicity, a word of how we analyzed this will be in order. The US Census Bureau considers race and Hispanic origin to be distinct concepts. All individuals who consider themselves as Spanish, or Hispanic, or Latino are, for the purposes of this survey, considered "Hispanic," regardless of their race. Other race categories discussed in this survey—white, black, Asian/Native Hawaiian/Pacific Islander, and other races—include only those individuals who did not identify themselves as Hispanic. For

Table 4.3 Small Cities' Sample by Region and Population Growth, 1990-2000

Region	Declining Cities (<-2% Growth)	No-Growth Cities (-2 to 2% Growth)	Moderate-Growth Cities (2 to 10% Growth)	Strong Growth Cities (10 to 20% Growth)	Rapid-Growth Cities (>20% Growth)
Northeast	Norwich, CT Augusta, ME Lewiston, ME Monessen, PA Wilkes-Barre, PA East Providence, RI Montpelier, VT	Easton, PA No. Providence, RI Burlington, VT	Millville, NJ Chambersburg, PA		Manahawkin, NJ Lewes, DE
Midwest	Park Forest, IL Monroe, MI Berkeley, MO Belulah, ND West Carrollton, OH	Rock Falls, IL Kirkwood, MO	Abilene, KS Norton Shores, MI Carlisle, OH Wayzata, MN Custer, SD	Bradley, IL West Lafayette, IN Garden City, KS Ottawa, KS Blaine, MN North Sioux, SD Watertown, SD	Swansea, IL Coralville, IA Columbia City, IN Greenwood, IN Shawnee, KS Saline, MI Apple Valley, MN Buffalo, MN West Plains, MO Trotwood, OH
South	Dublin, GA Bastrop, LA Cumberland, MD	Kodiak, AK Clanton, AL Prescott, AR	Jasper, AL Jacksonville, AR Dade City, FL	East Point, GA Starkville, MS Rock Hill, SC	Prattville, AL No. Lauderdale, FL Fairburn, GA

Table 4.3 (Continued)

Region	Declining Cities (<-2% Growth)	No-Growth Cities (-2 to 2% Growth)	Moderate-Growth Cities (2 to 10% Growth)	Strong-Growth Cities (10 to 20% Growth)	Rapid-Growth Cities (>20% Growth)
South	Hartsville, SC	Greenbelt, MD Port Gibson, MS Whiteville, NC Bartlesville, OK Muskogee, OK	Ocala, FL Baker, LA Hyattsville, MD Laurel, MD Henderson, NC		Knightdale, NC Farragut, TN Maryville, TN Addison, TX Coppell, TX Rockwell, TX
West		Culver City, CA Artesia, NM	Arcata, CA Beverly Hills, CA Brea, CA Milwaukie, OR Tillamook, OR Port Angeles, WA Douglas, WY	Cody, WY	Queen Creek, AZ Indian Wells, CA La Quinta, CA Rocklin, CA Broomfield, CO Estes Park, CO Grand Junction, CO Steamboat Springs, CO W. Wendover, NV Dallas, OR Tualatin, OR Park City, UT Brewster, WA Marysville, WA North Bend, WA

the first time, the 2000 Census gave respondents the opportunity to classify themselves as being of more than one race. This new option potentially complicates efforts to compare 2000 census population counts by race or ethnicity to 1990 counts at a city level. In this study, the race categories represent individuals who classified themselves as that race only; individuals who classified themselves as being of more than one race are grouped in a "multiracial" category. Some unknown share of a given city's residents in 1990 could have reclassified themselves as multiracial in 2000; this may introduce a degree of error into the calculation of changes in the population of that city's other race/ethnicity groups. Census analysis of this potential for error suggests that the size of the error is likely insignificant.

With these classifications, we analyzed our sample on the basis of overall growth rates, regional growth patterns, metropolitan or non-metropolitan location, and race and ethnicity. We then compared the findings with those from the studies based on medium and large cities and drew some implications.

DEMOGRAPHIC TRENDS IN SMALL CITIES

Population Growth

Overall, the population of small cities grew substantially during the 1990s, increasing at a rate of 18.5%, compared to 12.9% for medium-sized cities and 9.1% for large cities. Small cities also were more likely than their medium-sized and large counterparts to experience rapid growth; 36% of small cities experienced population growth of more than 20%, compared to 28% of medium-sized cities and 18% of large cities. It is important to note, of course, that increases in population in small cities may appear larger because the total population (the denominator) is smaller. However, small cities outpaced medium-sized and large cities in both the rapid-growth and strong-growth categories, suggesting there are other factors at work. Nearly half of small cities (47%) grew at rapid or strong rates during the 1990s, compared to 51% of medium-sized cities and 41% of large cities (Figure 4.2).

Small cities across population categories grew at a generally fast rate during the 1990s. However, cities under 10,000 in population grew faster than those with populations between 10,000 and 50,000. Cities with populations under 10,000 also were most likely to experience rapid or strong growth (54%), compared to cities with populations between 10,000 and 25,000 (47%) and those with populations between 25,000 and 50,000 (36%).

In addition, the larger small cities (those with populations between 25,000 and 50,000) were far more likely to have declined in population or experienced no growth. Forty-four percent of these cities fell into the no-growth or declining categories, compared to less than 30% of the cities in each of the other two categories.

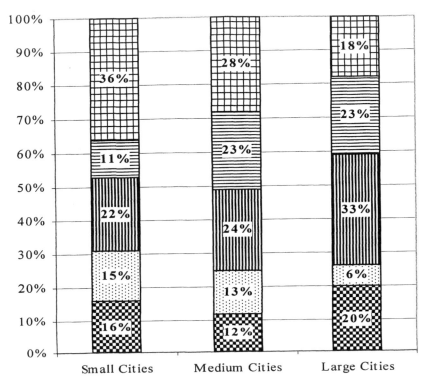

Figure 4.2 Population Growth of US Cities
Source: US Census Bureau Data and Jennifer Vey and Benjamin Forman, (2002)

Regional Growth Patterns

As noted earlier, studies of large and medium-sized cities have found patterns of faster growth in the West and South, confirming notions of long-term population growth and shifts in population from the Frostbelt (Northesat and Midwest) to the Sunbelt (South and West). In contrast, the data on population growth in America's small cities reveals a different trend at work (Figure 4.3).

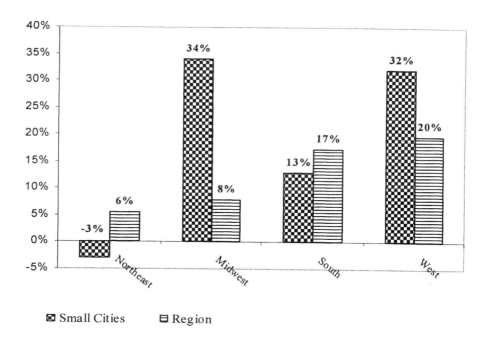

Figure 4.3 Small City Growth versus Regional Growth
Source: Data from US Census Bureau

The small cities that experienced the fastest growth during the 1990s were in the West and the Midwest. Midwestern cities experienced population growth of 34% between 1990 and 2000, compared to 32% in the West, 13% in the South, and population decline of 3% among small cities in the Northeast. Moreover, small cities in both the Midwest and West were growing at a considerably faster pace than their regions as a whole during the 1990s. The 34% growth experienced by small cities in the Midwest was more than four times the region's overall 8% growth rate, while the rate for Western small cities (32%) significantly outpaced the 20% growth rate experienced by the region as a whole (Figure 4.3). In contrast, small city growth in the South (13%) closely approximates the regional growth rate of 17%, and population growth in small cities in the Northeast (-3%) was less than regional growth rate of 6%.

Patterns of faster growth in small cities in the Midwest and West were also evident across cities in different population growth categories. For example, approximately six in ten small cities in the West (62%) and Midwest (58%) experienced rapid or strong population growth in the 1990s, compared to 4 in 10 small cities in the South (40%) and less than one in ten small cities in the Northeast (8%). In perhaps the most dramatic picture of regional differences in small-city growth, one in two small cities in the Northeast (54%) declined in population during the 1990s, compared to 17% in the South, 13% in the Midwest, and no cities declining in the West.

Metropolitan and Non-Metropolitan Small Cities

Small cities in metropolitan areas were more likely to experience rapid population growth than their non-metropolitan counterparts during the 1990s. Eighty-six percent of the small cities that experienced more than 20% population growth from 1990 to 2000 were located in metropolitan areas. At the same time, however, a significant majority of the small cities that declined in population during the 1990s (63%) were metropolitan cities, largely because the declining cities in the Northeast are mostly located in metropolitan areas (Figure 4.4).

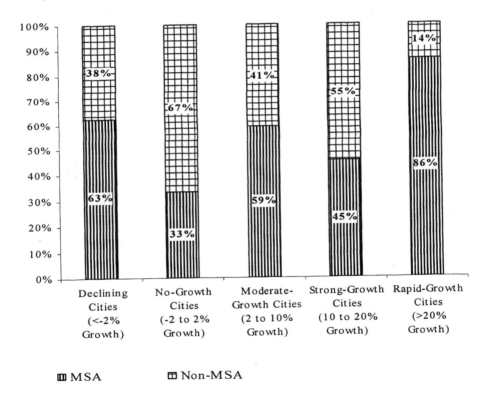

■ MSA   ⊞ Non-MSA

Figure 4.4 Small Cities Population Growth by Metropolitan Location, 1990-2000
Source: Data from the Office of Management and Budget and the U.S. Census Bureau.

Race and Ethnicity

The 1990s were a decade of increased racial and ethnic diversity across cities of all population sizes, although popular images of small-town America as homogeneously White (except in the South) were supported in this analysis. As of 2000, three in four small-city residents (76%) were White, compared to 13% who were Black, 7% who were Hispanic, and 2% who were Asian. The data showed that small cities were considerably less ethnically and racially diverse than their large and medium-sized city counterparts, where 44% and 56% of the 2000 population, respectively, were White (Figure 4.5).

All cities, however, saw the share of the total population that is Black, Hispanic, and Asian increase between 1990 and 2000. Large cities, overall, became non-white majorities, with the White share of the large-city population falling from 52% to 44%. Similarly, the White share of the population in medium-sized cities declined from 67% to 56%. In small cities, the comparable decline was from 83% in 1990 to 75% in 2000. Increases in the Black and Hispanic shares of total small city population accounted for much of this drop, with the Black population growing from 10% to 13% of total small city population, and the Hispanic population growing from 4 to 7% (Figure 4.6).

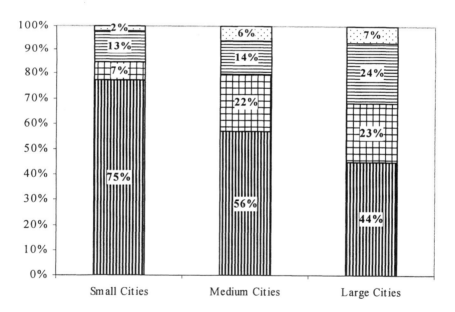

Figure 4.5. Race and Ethnic Composition of Small Cities and Other Cities
Source: 1990 Census STF1 and the 2000 Census SF1 and Jennifer Vey and Benjamin.

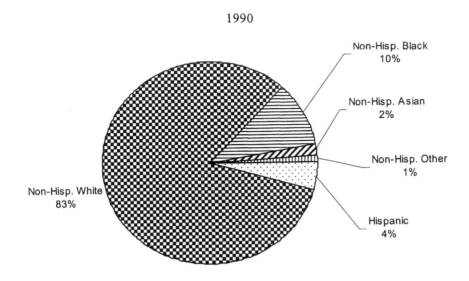

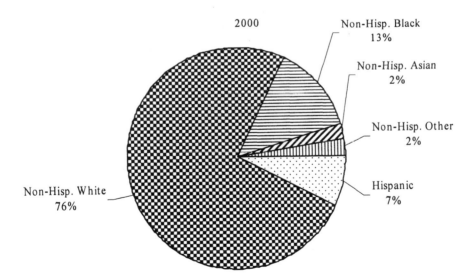

Figure 4.6 Racial and Ethnic Composition of Small Cities, 1990 – 2000
Source: Data from US Census Bureau

For a clearer picture of trends in the racial and ethnic composition of small city populations, it is important to analyze total population growth among different groups, rather than focusing solely on their respective shares of the population. Looking at it this way, we see big population gains across all three of the largest racial and ethnic groups, and especially among Hispanics. In all regions of the country, the Hispanic population in small cities at least doubled between 1990 and 2000, growing by 229% in the South, 191% in the West, 128% in the Northeast, and 102% in the Midwest. The data show that Hispanic population growth is driving overall population growth in all regions. However, the Hispanic population is not the only group experiencing dramatic rates of growth in America's small cities. During the 1990s, the Asian population in small cities doubled in the West (107%) and South (106%) and grew by more than 60% in the Northeast (65%) and Midwest (61%). The Black population in small cities also increased across all regions, particularly in the Midwest (114%) and West (84%).

IMPLICATIONS FOR POLICY AND RESEARCH

This analysis provides an overdue picture of the demographic changes experienced by small cities in the 1990s and of how those changes compare to the experiences of larger and medium-sized cities. Among the key findings are:

- Overall, small cities grew considerably faster than large and medium-sized cities during the 1990s.
- Regional disparities in growth patterns are evident, with small cities in the West and Midwest growing at a fast rate and considerably faster than their regions as a whole. This finding runs counter to conventional assumptions about growth in Frostbelt vs. Sunbelt cities.
- Small cities in metropolitan areas are growing at faster rates than small cities outside of metropolitan areas. At the same time, metropolitan small cities that are declining or not growing are following the trend of their surrounding metropolitan areas.
- Whites are still the most prevalent racial or ethnic group in small cities, although influxes of Hispanic, Black, and Asian residents are gradually changing the face of many small cities and towns in America.

These and other demographic changes affecting America's small cities present challenges and opportunities for municipal leaders and policy makers at all levels. Among the key questions: how to cope with rapidly increasing population growth resulting from the expansion of metropolitan areas and continued increases in the gross population of the United States.

Growing small-city populations pose real challenges to local leaders in areas from infrastructure and service delivery to the fiscal capacity of municipal governments to respond to the needs of increasing numbers of residents. Fiscal capacity also is a challenge confronting those cities that are declining or not growing, which often experience infrastructure problems and increasing poverty at the same time that they see an out-migration of residents and businesses. Increasing racial and ethnic diversity in America's small cities, on the other hand, can create real opportunities for municipal officials as they work to incorporate different cultural perspectives into local policy making and strive to ensure that their cities are inclusive and respectful of the views of all residents. It is important to note that the analysis presented here is merely descriptive, providing summaries of population trends in the 1990s across various categories. We have not attempted to explain precisely why small cities are growing the way they are, or why different categories of cities are experiencing growth in different ways. Further attention to these and other questions can tell us more about how America's cities are changing and why. For example, in their study of the most significant predictors of differences in growth in medium-sized cities, Vey and Forman (2002) point to the effects of immigration, education, age of population, location in the region, and availability of land. What about the impact of such factors as economic growth and access to jobs? It is hard to say precisely what is causing the trends outlined in this analysis. Given that 97% of America's cities are small, more research into the factors affecting these places would be a very valuable exercise.

ENDNOTES

1. The authors would like to thank the Brookings Institution's Center on Urban and Metropolitan Policy for assistance in replicating their methodology.

REFERENCES

Berube, A. 2002. *Census 2000: The Changing Face of Cities.* Washington, DC: Presentation by the Brookings Institution on Urban and Metropolitan Policy to the National League of Cities, Washington, DC, February.

Frey, W. 2001. *Census 2000 Shows Large Black Return to the South, Reinforcing the Region's "White-Black" Demographic Profile* University of Michigan: Population Studies Center at the Institute for Social Research. PSC Research Report No. 01-473.

Glaeser, E., and J. Shapiro. 2001. *City Growth and the 2000 Census: Which Places Grew, and Why.* Washington, DC: The Brookings Institution Center on Urban and Metropolitan Policy.

Guzman, B. 2001. *The Hispanic Population, 2000: Census 2000 Brief.* Washington, DC: US Census Bureau.

Lang, R. 2003. *Edgeless Cities: Exploring the Elusive Metropolis.* Washington, DC: Brookings Institution Press.

Lang, R., and P. Simmons. 2001. *"Boomburbs": The Emergence of Large, Fast-Growing Suburban Cities in the United States*. Census Note 06. Fannie Mae Foundation.

Perry, M., and P. Mackun. 2001. *Population Change and Distribution, 1990-2000: Census 2000 Brief.* Washington, DC: US Census Bureau.

Rain, D. P., Mackun, and G. Harper. 1999. *Phoenix and San Antonio Lead Largest Cities in Growth; Small Cities Grow Fastest, Census Bureau Reports*. Press Release for Population Estimates, Washington, DC: US Census Bureau. (Available at: http//www.census.gov/Press-release/www/1999/cb99-128.html.

Simmons, P., and R. Lang. 2001. The urban turnaround: A decade-by-decade report card on postwar population changes in older industrial cities. Census Note 01. Fannie Mae Foundation.

The Brookings Institution. 2001. *Racial Change in the Nation's Largest Cities: Evidence from the 2000 Census*. Washington, DC: The Brookings Institution Center on Urban and Metropolitan Policy.

US Census Bureau. 1999. *1997 Census of Governments: Volume 1- Government Organization*. Washington, DC.

Vey, J., and B. Forman. 2002. *Demographic Change in Medium-Sized Cities: Evidence from the 2000 Census.* Washington, DC: The Brookings Institution Center on Urban and Metropolitan Policy.

5

Population Growth, Demographic Changes, and Spatial Distribution of Small Cities in Mexico, 1970 – 2000

Jorge González Sánchez
Maria Teresa Gutiérrez de MacGregor
Universidad Nacional Autónoma de México

INTRODUCTION

The main objective of this chapter is to study Mexican cities with less than 100,000 people. Collectively, we will refer to these cities as small cities. In 1970, these cities totaled 234, representing 87.3% of the 268 urban localities in Mexico, and 5.67 million or 23.9% of the total urban population. By 2000, there were 497 small cities, accounting for 87.8% of a total of 566 urban localities and 12.29 million or 18.8% of the total urban population. This growth in the number of small cities has produced a spatial transformation in Mexico, yet these cities have drawn little attention in academic research in Mexico. Instead, most urban research has focused on large cities. This chapter is of the view that differences in city sizes need to be considered for a detailed analysis, since life in a small city is clearly different from that of a large city. This chapter analyzes population growth, demographic changes, and spatial distribution of Mexico's small cities from 1970 to 2000, and the factors that have fostered these changes.

To facilitate detailed analysis, we divided Mexico's small cities into three categories as follows:

- First-tier small cities: from 50,000 to less than 100,000 people
- Second-tier small cities: from 15,000 to less than 50,000 people
- Third-tier small cities: from 10,000 to less than 15,000 people

We analyzed the population and demographic changes using data from Mexico Population and Housing Census. We also produced maps to show the changes in distribution of small cities. The chapter is organized into four sections. In the next section, we examine the population growth of small cities in Mexico. We follow this up with an examination of demographic changes that have occurred in the cities. Next, we examine the spatial distribution of the cities. In the concluding section, we highlight the main findings and their implications for further studies and policy.

POPULATION GROWTH OF MEXICO'S SMALL CITIES

The rapid population growth in Mexico over the past thirty years is undeniable, and can be divided into three different processes: a strong increase in total population, a regression in the rural population's growth rate, and a heavy concentration of population in urban areas. These processes have transformed Mexico from an eminently rural country in 1970 to one where urban population prevails in 2000. From 1970 to 2000, urban population grew at an average rate of 3.4% per year, while the annual growth of rural population was only 0.92% (Table 5.1).

Table 5.1 Total Rural and Urban Population in Mexico, 1970 – 2000

Population Group	1970		2000		Mean annual growth
	Total	%	Total	%	1970 – 2000 (%)
Urban population	23 770 210	49.3	65 310 988	67.0	3.43
Rural population	24 455 028	50.7	32 172 424	33.0	0.92
Total population	48 225 238	100	97 483 412	100	2.37

Note: Urban population = population of villages with 10,000 or more and population of municipalities that conform metropolitan zones.
Source: Based on the IX and XII Population and Housing Censuses, Mexico.

The urban growth process in Mexico stands out because of its intensity and velocity. It has resulted from six major trends (Gutiérrez and Sanchez 2004).

1. Natural growth of the already-settled urban population
2. Immigration of persons previously living in rural areas

3. Increase in the number of urban localities because of the transformation of some rural towns that have acquired urban characteristics and reached the minimum population size to be considered as urban; in this case rural inhabitants become urban without having changed their place of residence. This way of calculating growth is suitable to measure urban growth in small cities.
4. Increase in the degree of urbanization.
5. Increase in the geographic concentration of urban population, implying a concentration of population in large-sized agglomerations—localities with 100,000 or above. In 1970, 76.1% of the urban population lived in such large cities by 2000 it was 81.2% (Table 5.2).
6. A significant decline in mortality rate.

Table 5.2 Population of Mexico's Small Cities, 1970 and 2000

City Size	1970			2000			Mean annual growth
	Population	%	No. of cities	Population	%	No. of cities	1970 – 2000 (%)
Third-tier Small Cities	1,153,570	4.9	95	2,381,359	3.7	194	2.45
Second-tier Small Cities	2,827,533	12.0	115	6,424,133	9.8	255	2.79
First-tier Small Cities	1,674,411	7.0	24	3,489,758	5.3	48	2.41
Below 100,000	5, 673,514	23.9	234	12,295,250	18.8	497	2.61
Above 100,000	18,096,696	76.1	34	53,015,738	81.2	69	3.65
Total Urban Population	23,770,210	100	268	65,310,988	100	566	3.43

Source: IX and XII Population and Housing Censuses. Mexico.

From Figure 5.1, it is evident that large cities dominated the urban population growth rate in Mexico from 1970 to 2000, during which the mean annual growth of cities with more than 100,000 people was 3.6%. However, as already pointed out differences in the size of cities need to be considered for a detailed analysis, since the significance of living in a city with a population size above or below

100,000 inhabitants is clearly different. We will therefore take a closer look at the small cities.

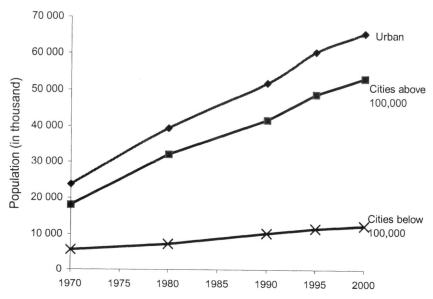

Figure 5.1 Population of Cities Above and Below 100,000, 1970 – 2000
Source: Calculations based on information from IX to XII Population and Housing Censuses, Mexico.

We have already pointed out that from 1970 to 2000 the number of small cities in Mexico went from 234 to 497. Over the same period, their total population grew from 5.67 million or 23.9% of the total urban population to 12.3 million or 18.8%. This translated into an annual growth rate of 2.6% for small cities, which was below the mean annual growth rate of 3.4% for the total urban population, but above the national growth rate of 2.4%. The analysis of these changes within each of the three groups of small cities reveals that both the population size and the number of cities doubled from 1970 to 2000, for all three groups of small cities. However, the second-tier small cities stood out in 2000, accounting for over 51% of all small city localities (Table 5.2) and over 52% of the population living in small cities (Figure 5.2). There were also some variations in terms of growth rate. Second-tier small cities had the highest growth, with a rate of 2.7% well above the overall growth rate for small cities, while first-tier and third-tier small cities had growth rates below the small city average (Figure 5. 3).

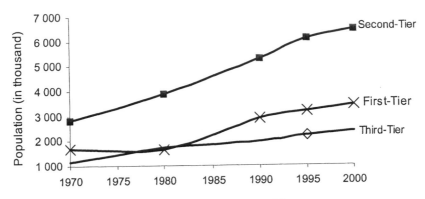

Figure 5.2 Population of Small Cities, 1970 – 2000
Source: Calculations based on information from IX to XII Population and Housing
Censuses, Mexico

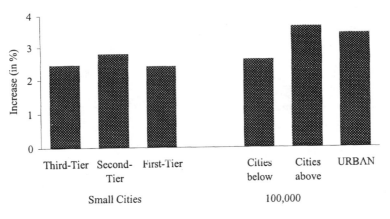

Figure 5.3 Mean Annual Growth of Population by City Size, 1970 – 2000
Source: Table 5.2

In general, the rise in the number of small cities in Mexico derives from the transformation of rural to urban localities. Three hundred and eighteen localities that were rural in 1970 had become urban by 2000, having reached the urban population threshold size of 10,000, over the course of 30 years. By 2000, these 318 localities, with 12.2 million people, represented 64% of all small cities. The population of localities that became urban reached 5.3 million by 2000, resulting in more than 43.3% of urban population living in third-tier small cities. Rural localities that steadily became urban each decade during the period of study were 107 in 1980, 109 in 1990, and 102 in 2000 (Table 5.3). There were 179 urban localities in 1970 that had population sizes below 100,000 in 2000, representing 35% of all small cities in 2000. This accounted for 6.9 million people this same year, or 56.7% of the urban population living in small cities.

Table 5.3 Dynamics of Cities below 100,000 People, 1970 – 2000

City Status	Number of Cities				
	1970	1980	1990	2000	%
New		123	116	102	20.5
Remaining since 1970	234	197	184	179	36.0
Remaining since 1980			113	107	21.6
Remaining since 1990				109	21.9
Incorporated into metropoli-tan zones		19	16	8	
Transformed into Big Cities		18	7	10	
Cities below 100,000	234	320	413	497	100

Source: Calculation based on information from IX and XII Population and Housing Censuses, Mexico

Another important fact is that 35 urban localities with populations less than 100,000 in 1970 displayed a significant dynamism, and as a result they became large cities having surpassed the minimum population size of 100,000. In 34 of them the population reached between 100,000 and 500,000, and only Coatzacoalcos, an oil-producing city located in the Gulf Coast, surpassed 600,000. Out of the 34, 14 are state capitals so they perform significant administrative activities. In addition, they benefit from their location at the intersections of important highways, which have undoubtedly been the key for their demographic and economic growth.

While most of this growth could be attributed to natural increase, local migration from rural to urban areas represents one of the most important demographic and social issues in the Mexican socio-economic process. These migrations have become accentuated during the past decades for different reasons. Among these are impoverishment of the rural sectors due to the lack of investment in farming, the improvement and increase in transportation and communication networks, as well as other communication means such as radio and television, which foster the idealization of the city, increasing the attractiveness of big cities, particularly those located along the country's northern border because of the development of contract manufacturing, and the desire to be able to cross the border and work in the United States of America.

When studying urban immigration, the size of the city must be taken into account, since, theoretically, a bigger city represents better—-real or fictitious—job opportunities, along with a higher order goods and services. In the case of Mexico, this association is confirmed when these two factors are related, that is, bigger cities are the most attractive ones for local immigrants. In 2000, 10.8 million immigrated to 69 cities with more than 100,000 inhabitants. This represented 86.8% of the total urban immigration (Table 5.4). Immigration to small

Table 5.4 Cumulative Urban Immigration in 2000

City Size	Immigrants	%	Number of Cities
Third-tier Small Cities	264,313	2.1	194
Second-tier Small Cities	856,547	6.9	254
First-tier Small Cities	524,474	4.2	49
Cities below 100,000	1,645,334	13.2	497
Cities above 100,000	10,820,508	86.8	69
Urban Immigration	12,465,842	100.0	566

Sources: Calculations based on information from the XII Population and Housing Census, 2000, Mexico.

cities showed a different picture from the one mentioned above. First, the 497 urban localities within this category accounted for only 1.6 million immigrants, which was 13.2% of the total urban immigration. Second, among small cities, it was not the 49 first-tier small cities that received the largest number of immigrants. Instead, it was the 254 second-tier small cities that did. However, this can be explained in part by the large number of these cities. Most small cities recorded an insignificant volume of immigrants. Of the 497 localities, 409 recorded less than 5,000 immigrants, and only 15 recorded more that 15,000 immigrants (Table 5.5).

Table 5.5 Distribution of Immigrants in Small Cities in 2000

Volume of Immigrants (in thousand)	Immigrants	%	Number of Cities	%
Very low (less than 5)	736,076	44.7	409	82.3
Low (5 to less than 15)	553,936	33.7	73	14.7
Moderate (15 to less than 50)	355,322	21.6	15	3.0
Immigration to cities below 100,000 people	1,645,334	100.0	497	100

Source: Calculations based on information from the XII Population and Housing Census, 2000, Mexico

At the same time there were several small cities in which immigration was key to explaining their growth. For example, in 9 small cities immigration accounted for more than 50% of their population growth. For another 27, immigration contributed between 30 to 50% of their growth (Table 5.6). The importance of immigration in many of these localities derives from their proximity to big urban centers, mostly cities located in the northern border and the country's center (Figure 5.4). Thus, small cities close to Tijuana, Mexicali, Ensenda, Ciudad Juarez, Nuevo Laredo, and Reynosa, along the northern border, and small cities close to Mexico City, in the center, recorded higher immigration component in their population growth than other small cities. In addition, to their proximity to big cities, these small cities also benefit from a decentralization process that has increased job opportunities in both industry and services in them.

Table 5.6 Immigration Rates in Small Cities in 2000

Immigration Rates (in percentage)	Immigrants	%	No. of Cities	%
Low (less than 15)	732,841	44.5	373	75.1
Moderate (from 15 to less than 30)	468,361	28.5	88	17.7
High (from 30 to less than 50)	308,591	18.8	27	5.4
Very high (more than 50)	135,541	8.2	9	1.8
Immigration to cities below 100,000	1,645,334	100	497	100

Source: Calculations based on information from the XII Population and Housing Census, 2000, Mexico

Apart from these, small cities close to the Mexican Caribbean, especially the areas close to Cancun, the southern end of the Baja California peninsula and the whole Pacific coast also saw a fair amount of immigration due to the tourist industry as well as such indirectly linked activities like construction.

The urban population boom in Mexico is relatively recent, beginning in the 1940s (Unikel 1978). Urban growth is intimately linked to the country's economic evolution, which in turn has favored industrial growth at the expense of rural development. It can be stated that the urban system in Mexico has not undergone a homogenous evolution, but instead has suffered noticeable changes through time.

DEMOGRAPHIC CHANGES IN MEXICO'S SMALL CITIES

In this section, we examine changes in the age, gender, economic, and educational characteristics of the population of Mexico's small cities.

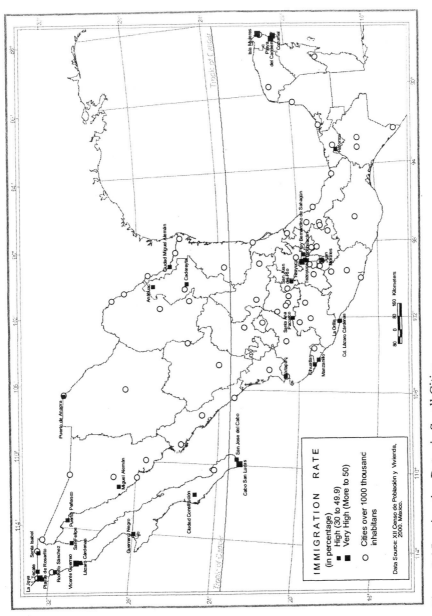

Figure 5.4 Immigration Rates in Small Cities

Age Characteristics

Analysis of the age structure of the total urban population as well as the population in small cities revealed that the age structure in 1970 was identical to that of 2000: a higher percentage of adults and lower percentages of children and the elderly. However, when the age structure of the total urban population was compared to that of small cities some small differences between 1970 and 2000 were identified. The percentage of both children and the elderly was higher in small cities with a slightly lower percentage of adults, compared to the total urban population (Figure 5.5). A detailed analysis of age distribution among the three categories of small cities confirmed that in both 1970 and 2000 the number of children and the elderly was inversely proportional to city size. Thus, the bigger the city, the lower the proportion of children and the elderly; conversely, the proportion of adults increased directly with city size, that is, the bigger the city, the higher the proportion of adults.

Gender Characteristics

In 1970, there were 99.6 men per 100 women in Mexico; by 2000 that ratio had decreased to 95.4. In small cities, the gender ratio fell from 95.6 in 1970 to 93.7 in 2000 (Figure 5.6). Like age structure, the gender structure varied within all the three categories of small cities for both 1970 and 2000. Each of the three categories saw a decline with largest decline occurring in the second-tier category. In 1970, the gender ratio for this group was 96.3%. In 2000, it was 93.8% (Figure 5.8). Emigration of mostly male Mexicans towards the US is one of the major factors balancing or disrupting the proportion between sexes, and explains the main differences at the local level in Mexico. Another possible factor in the decline in male ratio is the longer life expectancy in women compared to men. For example, in 1970, life expectancy at birth was 61.6 years for the nation as a whole, 63.5 years for women, 59.7 years for men. In 2000, life expectancy was 75.3 years for the nation, 77.9 years for women, and 73.4 years for men (CONAPO 2001).

Economically Active Population

In Mexico, the minimum age for the economically active population (EAP) is 12 years old. Due to lack of detailed statistical data at the local level, we will focus on the EAP in the three economic sectors: primary, secondary, and tertiary. A useful measure in this regard is the gross activity rate, which is the EAP divided by the total population, and multiplied by 100. Analysis of the gross activity rate indicated that it is related to city size. Thus, the highest rate, 37.1%, was associated with the first-tier small cities; the second highest rate, 35.3%,

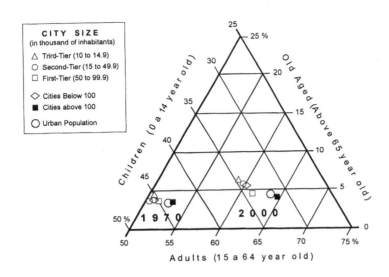

Figure 5.5 Age Structure of the Urban Population in Mexico, 1970 and 2000
Source: Calculations based on information from IX and XII Population and Housing Censuses, Mexico.

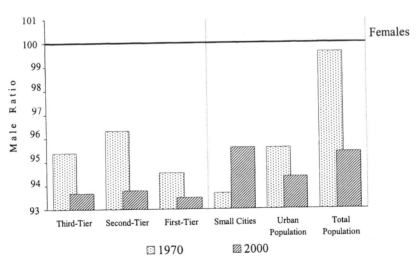

Figure 5.6 Male Ratio in Mexico's Small Cities, 1970 and 2000
Source: Calculations based on information from IX and XII Population and Housing Censuses, Mexico.

was associated with second-tier small cities, and the lowest rate, 33.7%, with third-tier small cities (Figure 5.9).

The economically active population working in the tertiary sector exceeds population working in the secondary sector, the former representing more than 50% of total EAP. A direct relationship was also evident, that is, the bigger the city, the higher the percentage of EAP working in tertiary activities. However, for all three categories of small cities, the percentage of EAP in the tertiary sector was below the average for the total urban population, which was 62.9% (Figure 5.9). The proportion of EAP working in secondary activities was much lower, and did not vary in any significant way among the three categories of small cities, oscillating between 29.1 and 30.7%. It was also evident that the percentage of EAP working in the primary sector varied inversely with city size for the three groups of small cities—the smaller cities had a higher percentage of EAP working in the primary sector.

Education

According to the 2000 population census, education levels in small cities in Mexico varied in three different respects: illiteracy, high school, and college education. These variations were more accentuated in first-tier small cities and became less important in third-tier small cities. Third-tier small cities posted the lowest percentages in the three education categories studied, compared to the average for the total urban population. With respect to literacy, the average for the total urban population was 94.8%, while for the third-tier cities it was 88.9%. In high-school education, it was 62.1%, compared to 44.6% for third-tier small cities, while for population with college education it was 16% for the total urban population compared to only 7.7% for third-tier small cities (Figure 5.8).

SPATIAL DISTRIBUTION OF MEXICO'S SMALL CITIES

The spatial distribution pattern of the population living in small cities from 1970 to 2000 is an interesting phenomenon. In order to analyze this pattern one needs to consider that oftentimes population growth, in terms of absolute numbers, is not necessarily related to growth in relative terms, and vice versa. The maximum concentration of urban population is still occurring in the Mexico City Metropolitan Zone, but it has undergone a noticeable change. In 1970, it accounted for 36.2% of the total urban population. By 2000, it had dropped to 27.1%. However, it is worth remembering that this area doubled its population size in absolute numbers, from 8.6 to 17.6 million inhabitants from 1970 to 2000.

The geographic distribution of small cities in Mexico is highly uneven. A comparative analysis of Figures 5.9 and 5.10 corresponding to the distribution of

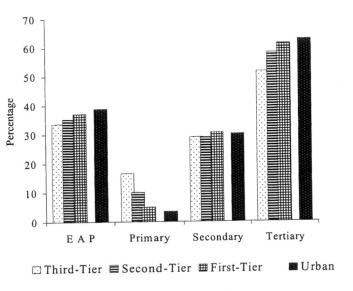

Figure 5.7 Economically Active Population in Small Cities in 2000 by Sector.
Source: Based on data from IX and XII Population and Housing Censuses, Mexico.

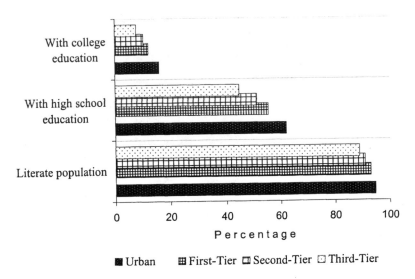

Figure 5.8 Education Indicators in Small Cities in 2000
Source: Based on data IX and XII Population and Housing Censuses, Mexico.

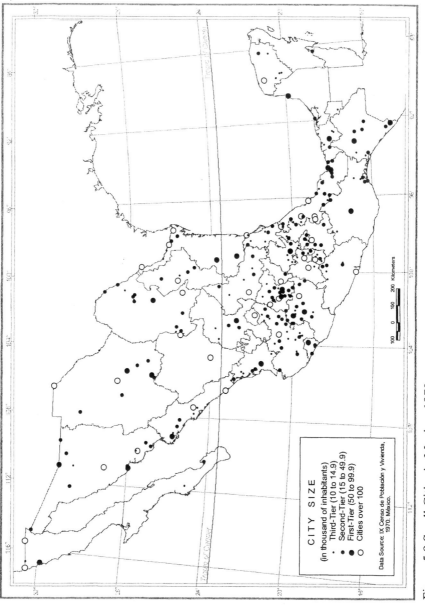

Figure 5.9 Small Cities in Mexico, 1970

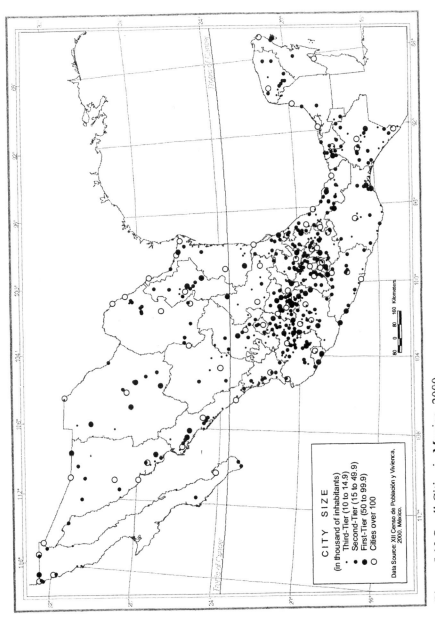

Figure 5.10 Small Cities in Mexico, 2000

small cities in 1970 and 2000, indicate how people have used space in two different times. Both maps reveal profound contrasts, with areas supporting huge concentrations of urban population, areas devoid of urban population, and areas including cities separated by vast empty zones. Relief, climate, and above all, the availability of economic resources, are all the factors that explain the discontinuity and uneven distribution of small cities in Mexico.

The distribution pattern has not significantly changed over the course of 30 years, although the population and the number of cities have doubled, as already mentioned. In general, this pattern is consistent with a heavy concentration of urban population in the country's center between latitudes 17° and 23° north and south to the Tropic of Cancer. Other areas with concentration of small cities are:
1. The area that runs from the Gulf of Mexico coastal plain to the Yucatan peninsula
2. The northeast portion of the Pacific coastal plain, from latitude 19° to 28° North, where the cities are located in a linear pattern.
3. A strip of cities located on the plain's southern end, from the Tehuantepec Isthmus to the border with Guatemala.
4   North to the Tropic of Cancer, in the highlands along two major highways connecting the country's center and northern portion.
5   Along the northern border.

Along the Pacific coastal plain differences between 1970 and 2000 were detected in the three southeastern states of Michoacán, Guerrero, and Oaxaca. There were no urban localities in these states in 1970, but by 2000 a string of urban locations had appeared. Urban localities also increased in the Baja California peninsula, particularly to the south.

The relief of Mexico is mountainous and this restrains the construction of road and communication systems. The climate is also very varied, ranging from warm and humid zones to the south; temperate humid areas to the center; and mountains and deserts to the north. Figure 5.11 illustrates that in both 1970 and 2000, most small city population lived in cities located above 1000 meters. In 1970, small cities located at elevations above 1000 meters accounted for 2.72 million people. In 2000, there were 6.65 millions, a 2.5-fold increase. Coastal plains (with elevations of less than 200 meters) were the second most preferred places to live during the same period. In 1970, these places accounted for 1.94 million. In 2000, the population doubled to 3.97 million. The least preferred places were those between 200 and 1000 meters above sea level, corresponding to mountain slopes. In 1970, a mere 1 million people lived in these places. By 2000, this had increased only slightly to 1.66 million.

From the analysis of the population distribution of small cities, it is evident that second-tier small cities accounted for the largest populations at altitudes below 200 meters, between 200 and 1000 meters, and above 1000 meters, both in 1970 and 2000. During this period, the population of second-tier small cities

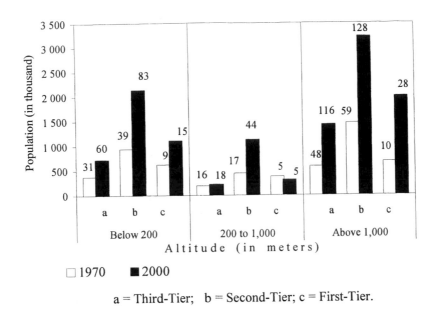

a = Third-Tier;   b = Second-Tier; c = First-Tier.

Figure 5.11 Population of Small Cities by Altitudinal Zones, 1970 and 2000.
(The number of localities on the top of columns)
Source: Calculations based on information from IX and XII Population and Housing
Censuses, Mexico.

in the coastal plains grew from 0.9 to 2.1 million; those on mountain slopes
grew from 0.4 to 1.1 million; those above 1,000 meters grew from 1.4 to 3.2
million (Figure 5.11).

It must be remarked that altitude cannot be separated from latitude (Clarke
1991). In countries located in low latitudes, like Mexico, which is bisected by
the Tropic of Cancer, two zones are formed: a subtropical zone to the north of
the Tropic and an inter-tropical zone to the south. In 1970, the warm-humid climatic zone had the largest portion of small city population, with 1.87 million
people; by 2000 the temperate humid climate had claimed the largest portion of
small city population, with 3.97 million people. In absolute terms there was an
increase in the four climatic zones, especially in the warm humid and temperate
humid zones, where population underwent an almost three-fold increase. However, with the exception of temperate humid climate, the percentage of population living in small cities declined between 1970 and 2000 in the other climatic
zones, namely warm humid, dry, and very dry.

In terms of categories of small cities, the second-tier small cities recorded
the largest population in the four climatic zones in 1970. A slight change

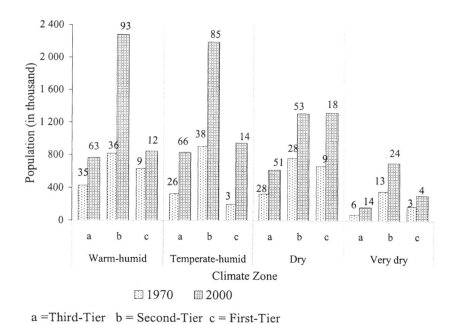

a =Third-Tier   b = Second-Tier   c = First-Tier

Figure 5.12 Population Living in Small Cities by Climatic Zones, 1970 and 2000
(The number of localities on the top of columns).
Source: Calculations based on information from IX and XII Population and Housing
Censuses, Mexico and García, (1987 and 1988).

was observed in 2000, with this group of small cities still accounting for the
largest population in three climatic zones of warm humid, temperate humid, and
very dry. It is only in the dry zone that the first-tier small cities attained larger
population sizes compared to the second-tier small cities (Figure 5.12).

CONCLUSION

The objective of this chapter was to study small cities in Mexico, a segment
of the country's urban system that has been relatively neglected by mainstream
urban research. Specifically, we decided to analyze the changes that have occurred in the size, growth, composition, and distribution of population in these
cities. Our analysis has found that in 1970, there were 234 small cities in Mexico, accounting for 24% of the total urban population in Mexico. In 2000, there
were 497 small cities, but accounted for only 19% of the total urban population.
Thus, in absolute terms, the population of small cities had increased over the 30

year period, but in relative terms it had actually declined. Part of the growth in number of small cities was due to a considerable number of rural communities that were able to record the minimum urban population threshold. At the same time, the decline of population was due to emigration from small cities to large cities. In spite of this, we found that 1.6 million people or, 13.2% of the whole population of small cities are immigrants. This makes us believe that migrants usually use small cities as first steps towards eventual migration to large cities.

In terms of composition, we found that the proportion of adults to the total population is smaller in small cities compared to large cities, while the proportion of children and the elderly is larger in small cities. Therefore, in small cities there is a considerable economic dependence on the adults group. Our investigations into the gender structure of small cities showed that the masculinity coefficient decreased in small cities. The education indicators of small cities showed to be considerable smaller than those of large cities and the urban population as a whole, thus revealing the huge differences that can be found in Mexico with respect to education infrastructure.

We also established a relation between the spatial distribution of the small cities, and climate and altitude. We found that 50% of the cities are located in the temperate zone, and at altitude above 1000 meters. This can be explained from the fact that Mexico is located in the subtropical and inter-tropical zones, where altitude helps to improve the climatic conditions, thus promoting human settlement.

Given the finding that Mexico's small cities are declining in population, we hope that this work will help improve the condition of small cities and move them away from the chaotic and disordered development that has become characteristics of them. Moreover, we hope that this work will motivate other researchers to study small cities in Mexico. We believe that such studies might be useful for future planners since they will provide them with valuable guidelines to apply realistic policies, and in accordance to the actual situation of Mexico.

REFERENCES

Aguilar, A.G. 1995. Introducción. en Desarrollo regional y urbano, tendencias y alternativas, ed. J. Pablos, 14 – 22 T.I, Instituto de Geografía, UNAM, Centro Universitario de Ciencias Sociales y Humanidades, Universidad de Guadalajara y, S.A., México.

Clarke, J. I. 1991. Geografía de la población. Trad: Gutiérrez de MacGregor, M.T. and Holt Buttner E., Instituto de Geografía, UNAM, México.

CONAPO 2001. Población de México en el nuevo siglo, Consejo Nacional de Población, México.

Dirección General de Estadística. 1971. *IX Censo general de población. 1970,* *Volúmenes estatales,* Secretaría de Industria y Comercio, México.

García, E. 1987. *Modificaciones al sistema de clasificación de Köppen,* 4th ed. Instituto de Geografía, UNAM. México.

García, E. 1988. *Los Climas de México y catas de clima, esc:1:2500000.* Proyecto y Ejecución Editorial, S.A. de C.V., México.

Gutiérrez de MacGregor, M. T and J. González Sánchez 2004. *Dinámica y distribución espacial de la población urbana en México, 1970-2000.* Instituto de Geografía, UNAM, México.

INEGI. 1991. *XI Censo general de población y vivienda.* 1990, Volúmenes es tatales, Instituto Nacional de Estadística, Geografía e Informática, México.

INEGI. 2001. *XII Censo general de población y vivienda 2000,* Volúmenes estatales, Instituto Nacional de Estadística, Geografía e Informática, México.

Noin, D. 1988. *Géographie de la population,* 2nd ed. Masson, París.

SPP. 1983. *X Censo general de población y vivienda,* 1980, Volúmenes estatales, Secretaria de Programación y Presupuesto, México.

Unikel, L. 1978. *El desarrollo urbano de México,* El Colegio de México, México.

Part II

Internal Structure of Small Cities

6

Micropolitan Ohio: A Study of the Internal Structure of Small Cities

James W. Fonseca
Ohio University – Zanesville

INTRODUCTION

The study of the internal structure of the city is one of the major topics in urban geography and related fields. Essentially, such study seeks to understand both the social structure and spatial structure of cities. Like most areas of urban geography, much of what we know about the social and spatial structures of cities has come from research based on large cities. In 2003 the Census Bureau provided data for a new class of cities called micropolitan areas (US Census 2004). These areas were defined as consisting of a central city of at least 10,000 population and adjoining population clusters totaling up to 50,000 people. In practice they are usually counties or pairs of counties. The recognition of these areas as a new category of urban areas, not only by researchers, but by retailers and American business in general, as noted by Michael McCarthy in an article in the Wall Street Journal, 3 June 2001, raises obvious questions. What are the internal characteristics of this new category of cities? How are they similar or different from traditional metropolitan areas? What are the implications of such similarities and differences, if any? This chapter attempts to answer this question. Specifically, it examines the internal structure of micropolitan areas in Ohio. Ohio is a fertile area for such a study for two reasons. First, it has more micropolitan areas than any other state except Texas. Second, it also has eleven metropolitan areas, three of which are major urban clusters of more than a million people (Cleveland, Cincinnati and Columbus), thus providing a basis for comparison.

The chapter is divided into four sections. Section one reviews some stylized facts about the internal structure of urban areas in general. Section two examines the socioeconomic characteristics of Ohio's micropolitan areas. Section three focuses on the spatial structure of the core cities of these areas. Section four provides a conclusion summarizing the differences and similarities between metropolitan and micropolitan areas and their implications for small city studies. Throughout the chapter the term micropolitan city will be used to refer to the core city of the micropolitan area.

THE INTERNAL STRUCTURE OF URBAN AREAS

Since earliest times, cities have reflected social class in their spatial structure with segregated districts for groups such as the ruler, his family and followers, artisans, soldiers, a small elite class, and larger districts with higher densities for the working commoners (Sjoberg 1960). As cities grew in size with increased trade, transportation improvements, industrialization, and migration, districts expanded in size as well, and the amount of differentiation in these specialized districts increased. In particular, each era of transportation improvements such as canal, railroad, or automobile saw the development of specialized districts around that transport sector.

A variety of centripetal and centrifugal forces interact in complex ways to give us the modern American automobile city, which, even though more decentralized and multi-nodal than cities in the past, still operates according to a few key principles. These principles include the rise of the differentiated central business district, outlying business centers, the sorting of business and residential functions by bid-rent, and the continued segregation of social groups by social, ethnic and economic factors.

Thus, in the modern city, and, as we will see, in Ohio's micropolitan areas, users of land are spatially segregated by their ability to pay for location. This leads to competition and conflicts over land in which the largest users with the best ability to pay, such as factories, corporate headquarters and the highest income residents, locate in the most desirable sites, whether that be the heart of the CBD or prime locations along railroads or key highway intersections. Factory workers take residential sites near factories that are aesthetically less desirable but proximate to work. Professional, white-collar households and retail services are attracted to suburban locations. The heavy industrial sector develops its own differentiated district of industrial supply firms, warehouses, and truck terminals, while the auto-oriented suburban locations develop districts of shopping malls and consumer services.

Within the differentiated CBD space is also sorted vertically, with ground-level activity focused on retailing, entertainment, restaurants, and other services.

In the very large cities, differentiated retail districts develop with clusters of specialty stores such as jewelry and antiques. Services cluster also, and one may find a banking district, law offices and legal services, and a cluster of administrative functions near the courthouse or city hall including government services, library and post office. The main hospital may be the kernel of a cluster of medical services. The central cluster of office buildings gives large cities prominent high-rise CBDs and an office service district may develop to serve clientele in these buildings. In small cities, these functions still cluster, but differentiated districts are less noticeable.

The CBD, and indeed the whole city, is not static but dynamic. The CBD can shift and change over time as new functions are acquired or lost. The core tends to move toward newer and higher-status functions and services, creating a sector called a zone of advance or zone of assimilation as it expands. The area it leaves behind is called the zone of retreat or the zone of discard. In general, the whole area around the CBD can be thought of as a zone of transition.

The driver of land use, or the sorting process among uses, is called bid-rent, the rental or sale value that different users compete to pay for prime locations. Economic geographers and economists such as Alonso (1964) have researched this phenomenon. While, simplistically, there is a peak land value at the intersection of the downtown and the core of the CBD, in reality, land values are complex and more like a "circus tent" model with multiple peaks, of which the downtown CBD may be the highest, but only one such peak. Corridors along key transportation routes, such as railroads and highways, also command higher rent than intervening areas.

Numerous complexities intervene, such as the trade-offs among cost, the convenience of central location, congestion of central location, and commuting time. While, in theory, higher income bidders can best afford the central locations (and every large city has exclusive residential areas near downtown), in practice higher income bidders may shun downtowns due to congestion and industrial use. Some downtown sectors may become so undesirable that lower income housing areas, or even abandoned and vacant structures, abound quite close to the CBD. Zoning, taxes, racial prejudice, and the cultural clustering of ethnic groups are some of the many factors that complicate theoretical models of urban structure in practice.

A variety of models have evolved to explain modern western city structure, such as that of Burgess (1925). Burgess, a sociologist of the Chicago school, pioneered a concentric zone or ecological type of model. The rings or zones around the CBD were first a zone of "independent workingmen's" homes and homes of second-generation immigrants who had moved into the inner city, often in distinct ethnic communities. Second was a zone of "better residences," basically middle-class residential districts made up of single-family homes and ample yards. The farthest zone out was the "commuters' zone," including small towns and villages, that were mainly residential, with some retail but little industry or employment, reflecting the pre-interstate highway era when the auto was first developed. The ecological models recognized the CBD and a zone of transition where buildings deteriorated over time and where different groups competed in waves of invasion and succession.

Hoyt (1939) proposed the sector model that conceptualized the city in terms of radial sectors of rent and socioeconomic status along transportation routes extending out from the CBD. Middle rent sectors adjoin the high rent sector, but the lowest rent sector is usually found on the opposite side of the city from the highest rent sector. The high rent sector follows amenities such as higher elevation land and rivers, if they are scenic and not already occupied by industry. Low rent sectors, conversely, adjoin industrial areas and rivers already occupied by factories. All sectors grow out from the center by accretion along the outer edge of sectors so that the newest structures are along the periphery of the urban area. As structures age, lower rent functions move in, especially in residential areas.

Modern adaptations of these theories have called attention to multiple urban centers as in the multiple nuclei model of Harris and Ullman (1945) who argued that that land use patterns grow from multiple points rather than a single central point. Some of these points, such as those related to physical geography, existed before the urban area began to grow, while others developed as the city expanded. Nuclei might include important transport links such as railway stations, docks and the airport, as well as the original downtown. More recently, suburban "downtowns" along beltways or "edge cities," as popularized by Garreau (1991), can be seen as an extension of the multiple nuclei model.

The social structure of the city has grown hand in hand with its industrial and physical structure. From the very beginning of modern analysis, Sjoberg called attention to differentiation of the city by class status and Mumford (1961) noted ethnic and class districts. Hoyt's sectors were "class driven" in the sense that the highest income class had the "first choice," so to speak, of prime sites; the middle class followed and the lower class took what was left. Burgess's zones were heavily interrelated with class as seen by his nomenclature such as "workingmen's homes." The multiple nuclei model, in part, was created to account for ethnic districts. Even in the evolving suburbs, traditionally thought of as white collar and middle and upper middle class, there is a growing awareness of the urbanization of the inner suburbs, including the movement of low income African Americans and recent immigrants. Indeed, researchers increasingly recognize that suburban downtowns function as "true downtowns" including serving as arrival points for very recent immigrants, thus greatly diversifying the suburbs of the very largest metropolitan areas.

A synthesis of sorts has been achieved by researchers such as Shevkey and Williams (1949) who did a factor analysis of many American cities and found validity, to some extent, in the social components of all of these models. Indeed, one would expect this to be the case as geographers and other observers recognize that most cities have aspects of concentric zones and transport sectors and multiple nuclei. In their model, sometimes referred to as urban factorial ecology, Shevkey and Williams (1949) found social class to correspond best with sectors, family status (age, marital status, presence of children) to correspond with zones, and ethnic and racial districts to be best described by multiple nuclei. In the remaining sections of this chapter, I will examine the internal structures of micropolitan areas in the state of Ohio. I will do so with respect to their socio-economic as well as spatial structures.

According to the US Census Bureau, there were 29 micropolitan areas in Ohio in 2000 (Figure 6.1). Each micropolitan area has a micropolitan city, which is the core city from which the area derives its name. Like metropolitan areas, the suburbs of these cities frequently extend into the surrounding county. Generally, the micropolitan city has at least 10,000 people. There are a few exceptions, such as Gallipolis, which had only 4,180 people because it was part of the larger bi-state, two-county micropolitan area, Point Pleasant, with neighboring Mason County, West Virginia. (In this chapter only Gallipolis City and Gallia County in Ohio are considered in the statistics that are presented.). Wapakoneta in Auglaize County was also an exception with only 9,474 residents, and thus it seems only fair to also consider St. Marys (population 8,342) in the same county as a second core city. The average micropolitan core city in Ohio has about 16,250 residents. Cities ranged in size from the three just mentioned with less than 10,000 people, to Findlay with about 38,000 and Marion with about 35,000. Besides these two largest core micropolitan cities, only Zanesville and Wooster had at least 25,000 people.

THE SOCIO-ECONOMIC CHARACTERISTICS OF OHIO'S MICROPOLITAN AREAS

In this section, I focus specifically on population size and growth, ethnicity, educational attainment, income, employment, and housing characteristics of these areas. I will attempt to compare the micropolitan core city in relation to its micropolitan area as well as metropolitan core to metropolitan area.

Population Size and Growth

The 29 micropolitan areas in Ohio ranged from about 28,000 people (Van Wert, Washington and Gallipolis) to 112,000 in East Liverpool-Salem (Columbiana County), Wooster and Ashtabula, with an average of about 60,000 residents. Together they accounted for a total of 1,708,392 or 15% of Ohio's total population (Table 6.1). Exactly one-third of total population of micropolitan areas lived in the 35 micropolitan core cities. Only two core cities had more than 50% of their micropolitan area populations: Findlay with 55% of Hancock County's population and Marion with 50% of Marion County's population. In

Figure 6.1 Ohio's Micropolitan Areas

Crawford County, the dual core cities of Bucyrus and Galion accounted for 52% of the county population. The same was true for Seneca County, where Tiffin and Fostoria, combined, had 55% of the county population. A few core cities had only about 10% of their micropolitan area populations, but these cities, like Salem and East Liverpool in Columbiana, tended to be cases where dual core cities are located in populous counties. The smallest proportion of micropolitan area population in a single core city was Wooster where its 24,800 people made up only 22% of Wayne County's population. However, in this case, this small

Table 6.1 Population of Ohio's Micropolitan Areas

Micropolitan Area (MA) *		Micropolitan Area Core City*		
Name	Population	Name	Population	% of MA Population
Ashland	52,523	Ashland	21,249	40.5
Ashtabula	102,728	Ashtabula	20,962	20.4
Ashtabula		Conneaut	12,485	12.2
Athens	62,223	Athens	21,342	34.3
Bellefontaine	54,500	Bellefontaine	13,069	28.4
Bucyrus	46,966	Bucyrus	13,224	28.2
Bucyrus		Galion	11,341	24.1
Cambridge	40,792	Cambridge	11,520	28.2
Celina	40,924	Celina	10,303	25.2
Chillicothe	73,345	Chillicothe	21,796	29.7
Coshocton	36,655	Coshocton	11,682	31.9
Defiance	39,500	Defiance	16,465	41.7
Findlay	71,295	Findlay	38,967	54.7
Fremont	61,792	Fremont	17,375	28.1
Gallipolis	31,069	Gallipolis	4,180	13.5
Greenville	53,309	Greenville	13,294	24.9
Marion	66,217	Marion	35,318	53.3
Mount Vernon	46,005	Mount Vernon	14,375	26.4
New Philadelphia	90,914	New Phila.	17,056	18.8
New Philadelphia		Dover	12,210	13.4
Norwalk	59,487	Norwalk	16,238	27.3
Portsmouth	79,195	Portsmouth	20,909	26.4
Salem-East Liverpool	112,075	East Liverpool	13,089	11.7
Salem-East Liverpool		Salem	12,197	10.9
Sidney	47,910	Sidney	20,211	42.2
Tiffin	58,683	Tiffin	18,135	30.9
Tiffin		Fostoria	13,931	23.7
Urbana	38,890	Urbana	11,613	29.9
Van Wert	29,659	Van Wert	10,690	36.0
Wapakoneta-St Marys	46,611	Wapakoneta	9,474	20.3
Wapakoneta-St Marys		St Marys	8,342	17.9
Washington	28,433	Washington	13,524	47.6
Wilmington	40,543	Wilmington	11,921	29.4
Wooster	111,564	Wooster	24,811	22.2
Zanesville	84,585	Zanesville	25,586	30.2
Total	1,708,392	Total	568,884	33.3

*Micropolitan areas are named after their core cities hence duplication of place names

proportion reflected the large micropolitan area population: Wayne County had the second largest population (111,500) of all micropolitan area populations in Ohio.

Relative growth varied greatly among the 29 micropolitan areas. As a whole, micropolitan areas grew by 4.4% between 1990 and 2000, slightly less than Ohio's metropolitan areas, which grew at 4.6%, and also slightly less than Ohio's rate of 4.7% (Table 6.2). Twenty-four micropolitan areas gained population and five lost slightly. Generally, those adjacent to major metropolitan areas grew most rapidly. Plane (2003) and Khan, et. al. (2001) have discussed the economic impact of proximity to metropolitan areas upon small cities and counties. Mt. Vernon, adjacent to Columbus, and Wilmington, adjacent to both Cincinnati and Dayton, experienced more than 14% population growth. Ashland and Wooster, both adjacent to Cleveland, grew by more than 10%. Wooster was also the largest absolute gainer, adding more than 10,000 people in the decade. While the majority of micropolitan areas grew, six declined. Van Wert, declined the most, 2.6%, while Fremont, Portsmouth, Tiffin, and Bucyrus all declined in population by smaller proportions (Table 6.2).

Population growth in the core cities was decidedly mixed between 1990 and 2000 (Table 6.2). Sixteen of the 35 cities gained population while 19 lost population. Total population in the 35 core cities grew by only 1.3% over the decade, compared to Ohio's overall slight growth rate of 4.7%, and the overall micropolitan growth rate of 4.4%. The biggest gainers were Wooster, 11.8% and Norwalk 10.2%. Substantial population losses occurred in Gallipolis, down 13.5%, and in Portsmouth, down 7.8%. Cities away from metropolitan areas, especially those in southern Ohio and Appalachia, tended to decline. Of course, this decline in population in the urban core was also true of Ohio's major metropolitan areas in recent decades, with the exception of Columbus.

Relative population growth or loss between city and the rest of its county was complex. Every possible combination was found in Ohio between 1990 and 2000. The typical scenario (16 of the 35 micropolitan core cities) was that both core city and county gained population, usually with the county gaining more than the core city. These micropolitan areas were more likely to be in northwest and north central Ohio. Bellefontaine was an example where the micropolitan area (Logan County) grew by 8.7% over the last decade and the core city of Bellefontaine grew by 7.6%. Next most common were 11 cases where the micropolitan area gained population, despite losses in the core city, partly due to "suburbanization" of residents. Most of these areas were in Appalachia. The city of Zanesville, for example, lost 4.5% of its population in the decade, yet the Zanesville micropolitan area (all of Muskingum County) showed a net gain of 3.1%. In five micropolitan areas that declined in population, seven core cities likewise lost residents. Interestingly all these micropolitan areas, except Portsmouth, were in northwest and north central Ohio where metropolitan areas with population gains were otherwise concentrated.

Table 6.2 Population Growth in Ohio's Micropolitan Areas

Micropolitan Area (MA)*		Micropolitan Area Core City*	
Name	Population Growth (%) 1990-2000	Name	Population Growth (%) 1990-2000
Ashland	10.6	Ashland	5.8
Ashtabula	2.9	Ashtabula	-3.1
Ashtabula		Conneaut	-5.7
Athens	4.5	Athens	0.4
Bellefontaine	8.7	Bellefontaine	7.6
Bucyrus	-1.9	Bucyrus	-2.0
Bucyrus	-0.6	Galion	-4.4
Cambridge	8.8	Cambridge	-1.9
Celina	3.8	Celina	6.8
Chillicothe	5.8	Chillicothe	-0.6
Coshocton	3.5	Coshocton	-4.2
Defiance	3.5	Defiance	-1.8
Findlay	8.8	Findlay	9.1
Fremont	-0.3	Fremont	-1.5
Gallipolis	4.5	Gallipolis	-13.5
Greenville	0.4	Greenville	3.4
Marion	3.0	Marion	3.6
Mount Vernon	14.8	Mount Vernon	-1.2
New Philadelphia	8.1	New Philadelphia	8.7
New Philadelphia		Dover	7.8
Norwalk	5.8	Norwalk	10.2
Portsmouth	-1.4	Portsmouth	-7.8
Salem-East Liverpool	3.5	East Liverpool	-4.1
Salem-East Liverpool		Salem	-0.3
Sidney	6.7	Sidney	8.0
Tiffin	-1.8	Tiffin	-2.5
Tiffin		Fostoria	-7.0
Urbana	8.0	Urbana	2.3
Van Wert	-2.6	Van Wert	-1.8
Wapakoneta-St Marys	4.5	Wapakoneta	2.8
Wapakoneta-St Marys		St. Marys	-1.2
Washington	0.4	Washington	4.2
Wilmington	14.5	Wilmington	6.4
Wooster	10.0	Wooster	11.8
Zanesville	3.1	Zanesville	-4.5
Average	4.4	Average	1.3

*Micropolitan areas are named after their core cities hence duplication of place names

Ethnicity

The proportion of minority population in Ohio's micropolitan areas was 4.4%, compared to metropolitan areas (17.7%) and Ohio (16.0%). Most of this population was African American with a small number of Asian, Native Americans, and Hispanics. Micropolitan areas with the smallest proportions of minority population tended to be in the western half of the state, such as Celina, Wapakoneta-St. Marys, and Greenville all of which had (2% or less). Micropolitan areas with more substantial non-white populations were scattered across Ohio. Chillicothe was highest with 8.3% and Marion, Fremont, Defiance, Athens and Zanesville all had more than 6% (Table 6.3).

Hispanics were the largest ethnic minority group in Ohio's micropolitan areas. In Ohio as a whole, only 1.9% of the state's population was Hispanic, and this population was relatively homogeneously distributed between metropolitan areas (2.0%) and micropolitan areas (1.5%). Five micropolitan areas in northern Ohio had the largest proportion of Hispanic population including Defiance and Fremont (more than 7%) and Norwalk, Tiffin and Findlay (all between 3% and 3.6%). This could be a spill-over from adjacent metropolitan areas as these five micropolitan areas are close to Ohio's largest clusters of Hispanic population in Toledo and Cleveland. Many Hispanics arrived in this area as migrant laborers and some stayed to work in the meat and agricultural processing firms. Micropolitan areas with the smallest proportion of Hispanics (0.6% or less) are in Appalachian Ohio, specifically, Zanesville, Chillicothe, Coshocton, Portsmouth, Gallipolis and Cambridge.

Micropolitan core cities had 7.5% non-white population, and thus were substantially more diverse than many other areas of Ohio (Table 6.3). Three core cities with higher than average concentrations of non-white population were Fremont (17.8%), Ashtabula (15.3%) and Zanesville (14.5%). Hispanic population was even more concentrated in micropolitan core cities; indeed the concentration here was higher than any other grouping in Ohio, including metropolitan core cities. While Ohio as a whole had only 1.9% Hispanic population, Hispanics made up 2.4% of micropolitan core city population (and 1.5% of micropolitan area population). Defiance (12.8%) and Fremont (12.3%) were two core cities with substantial Hispanic population, again, perhaps related to initial attraction of Hispanics to western Ohio as farm and agricultural processing workers.

Educational Attainment

Two measures were selected to examine educational attainment of the population over age 25: the percentage of the population without a high school degree, and the percentage of the population with a bachelor's degree or higher (that is, a graduate or professional degree). About 18.9% of the population over

Table 6.3 Non-White Population in Micropolitan Ohio

Micropolitan Area (MA)*		Micropolitan Area Core City*	
Name	Non-White Population (%)	Name	Non-White Population (%)
Ashland	2.5	Ashland	3.7
Ashtabula	5.9	Ashtabula	15.3
Ashtabula		Conneaut	3.7
Athens	6.5	Athens	10.8
Bellefontaine	3.9	Bellefontaine	9.2
Bucyrus	2.0	Bucyrus	2.6
Bucyrus		Galion	1.7
Cambridge	3.7	Cambridge	7.2
Celina	1.6	Celina	3.0
Chillicothe	8.3	Chillicothe	10.8
Coshocton	2.6	Coshocton	4.0
Defiance	7.4	Defiance	12.9
Findlay	4.9	Findlay	6.3
Fremont	7.8	Fremont	17.8
Gallipolis	4.7	Gallipolis	9.4
Greenville	1.9	Greenville	2.7
Marion	7.9	Marion	9.6
Mount Vernon	2.3	Mount Vernon	3.3
New Philadelphia	2.1	New Philadelphia	3.1
New Philadelphia		Dover	2.9
Norwalk	4.0	Norwalk	5.5
Portsmouth	5.1	Portsmouth	8.5
Salem-East Liverpool	3.6	East Liverpool	7.2
Salem-East Liverpool		Salem	1.6
Sidney	4.0	Sidney	7.4
Tiffin	5.0	Tiffin	3.7
Tiffin		Fostoria	12.7
Urbana	4.3	Urbana	9.0
Van Wert	2.6	Van Wert	3.9
Wapakoneta-St Marys	1.9	Wapakoneta	2.0
Wapakoneta-St Marys		St. Marys	2.5
Washington	4.4	Washington	5.5
Wilmington	4.0	Wilmington	9.3
Wooster	3.5	Wooster	7.4
Zanesville	6.1	Zanesville	14.5
Average	4.4	Average	7.5

*Micropolitan areas are named after their core cities hence duplication of place names

age 25 in micropolitan areas did not graduate from high school, compared to 16.3% in metropolitan areas and 17% in Ohio (Table 6.4). There was a fairly distinct regional pattern at least among clusters of micropolitan areas with the highest and lowest rates. All six of the micropolitan areas with the highest proportion of adults who did not complete high school were in Appalachia. Gallipolis (26.3%) and Portsmouth (25.9%) had the highest rates. All six micropolitan areas with the lowest rates were in northern and western Ohio. The very lowest rates (in Findlay, 11.6%, and Van Wert 13.4%) are about half those in the Appalachian counties cited.

Micropolitan areas were also much more different than metropolitan areas in terms of the number of people over age 25 that had a baccalaureate degree or higher. In all of Ohio 21.1% of the adult population had at least a college degree (or a graduate or professional degree as well). The figure in metropolitan areas (23.2%) was much higher than in micropolitan areas (13%). A few micropolitan areas that were homes to colleges had higher rates of population that had college degrees. These included Athens (25.7%), a rate higher than the metropolitan rate, Findlay (21.7%), Wooster (17.2%), Mt. Vernon (16.7%) and Ashland (15.9%).

In Appalachian Ohio, core cities had lesser educational attainment rates than their surrounding counties. Thus, Gallipolis, East Liverpool and Portsmouth had 25%-30% of their residents without a high school diploma. Core cities with the lowest dropout rates tended to be in northwestern and north central Ohio such as Findlay (11.6%) and Van Wert (13.4%). Baccalaureate degree holders were also lowest in East Liverpool (7.3%) and Fostoria and Galion (8.5%).

Table 6.4 Educational Attainment in Micropolitan Ohio

Micropolitan Area (MA)*		Micropolitan Area Core City*	
Name	% Without HS Diploma	Name	% Without HS Diploma
Ashland	16.7	Ashland	16.7
Ashtabula	20.1	Ashtabula	22.0
Ashtabula		Conneaut	19.0
Athens	17.1	Athens	17.1
Bellefontaine	16.4	Bellefontaine	15.3
Bucyrus	19.8	Bucyrus	24.2
Bucyrus		Galion	22.5
Cambridge	21.6	Cambridge	21.6
Celina	16.0	Celina	15.6
Chillicothe	23.9	Chillicothe	23.9
Coshocton	21.3	Coshocton	21.3
Defiance	15.3	Defiance	15.3

*Micropolitan areas are named after their core cities hence duplication of place names.

Table 6.4 continued

Micropolitan Area (MA)*		Micropolitan Area Core City*	
Name	% Without HS Diploma	Name	% Without HS Diploma
Findlay	11.6	Findlay	11.6
Fremont	17.9	Fremont	17.9
Gallipolis	26.3	Gallipolis	29.4
Greenville	17.2	Greenville	17.2
Marion	19.7	Marion	19.7
Mount Vernon	18.2	Mount Vernon	18.2
New Philadelphia	19.7	New Philadelphia	19.7
New Philadelphia		Dover	15.8
Norwalk	19.0	Norwalk	19.0
Portsmouth	25.9	Portsmouth	25.9
Salem-East Liverpool	19.4	East Liverpool	26.6
Salem-East Liverpool		Salem	17.8
Sidney	18.5	Sidney	18.5
Tiffin	16.9	Tiffin	16.9
Tiffin		Fostoria	22.5
Urbana	17.7	Urbana	17.7
Van Wert	13.4	Van Wert	13.4
Wapakoneta-St Marys	14.3	Wapakoneta	17.6
Wapakoneta-St Marys		St. Marys	17.9
Washington	21.3	Washington	21.3
Wilmington	16.9	Wilmington	15.0
Wooster	20.0	Wooster	20.0
Zanesville	19.4	Zanesville	19.4
Average	18.9	Average	19.2

*Micropolitan areas are named after their core cities hence duplication of place names.

Income

Median income per capita in micropolitan areas according to the 2000 Census was $17,740, which was 81% that of the state's metropolitan areas ($21,882) and 84% of Ohio's median income per capita ($21,003). None of the 29 micropolitan areas exceeded the state median (Table 6.5). Findlay had the highest with a median of almost $21,000. Athens had the lowest ($14,170), reflecting both its Ohio University student population and its location in Appalachian Ohio. Nine of the ten micropolitan areas with the highest median per capita

Table 6.5 Per Capita Income (PCI) and Family in Poverty (FIP) in Micropolitan Ohio

Micropolitan Area (MA)*			Micropolitan Area Core City*		
Name	PCI $	FIP (%)	Name	PCI $	FIP (%)
Ashland	17,308	7.1	Ashland	16,760	7.1
Ashtabula	16,814	9.2	Ashtabula	14,034	17.8
Ashtabula			Conneaut	14,703	10.7
Athens	14,171	14.0	Athens	11,061	14.0
Bellefontaine	18,984	7.1	Bellefontaine	17.781	12.9
Bucyrus	17,466	7.8	Bucyrus	17,027	8.9
Bucyrus			Galion	16,113	11.9
Cambridge	15,542	12.9	Cambridge	14,452	12.9
Celina	18,531	4.6	Celina	18,200	8.1
Chillicothe	17,569	9.1	Chillicothe	19,101	9.1
Coshocton	16,364	7.0	Coshocton	17,436	7.0
Defiance	19,667	4.5	Defiance	19,790	4.5
Findlay	20,991	5.2	Findlay	21,238	5.2
Fremont	19,239	5.7	Fremont	16,014	5.7
Gallipolis	15,183	13.5	Gallipolis	16,728	13.6
Greenville	18,670	6.0	Greenville	18,830	6.0
Marion	18,255	7.4	Marion	16,247	7.4
Mount Vernon	17,695	7.4	Mount Vernon	16,471	7.4
New Philadelphia	17,276	7.2	New Phila.	18,745	7.2
New Philadelphia			Dover	18,928	7.5
Norwalk	18,133	6.5	Norwalk	18,519	6.5
Portsmouth	15,408	15.2	Portsmouth	15,078	15.2
Salem-East Liverpool	16,655	9.0	East Liverpool	12,656	21.5
Salem-East Liverpool			Salem	16,579	9.8
Sidney	20,255	5.3	Sidney	19,075	5.3
Tiffin	17,027	6.1	Tiffin	16,580	6.1
Tiffin			Fostoria	15,568	9.0
Urbana	19,542	5.1	Urbana	17,831	7.2
Van Wert	18,293	4.2	Van Wert	17,413	4.2
Wapakoneta-St Marys	19,593	4.9	Wapakoneta	18,976	8.4
Wapakoneta-St Marys			St. Marys	17,682	5.7
Washington	18,063	7.7	Washington	18,618	7.7
Wilmington	18,462	6.4	Wilmington	17,346	8.9
Wooster	18,330	5.4	Wooster	21,505	5.4
Zanesville	17,533	9.9	Zanesville	15,192	9.9
Median/Average	17,740	7.8	Median/Avge	17,208	7.6

*Micropolitan areas are named after their core cities hence duplication of place names

incomes were located in the northwestern quadrant of the state. The six with the lowest per capita incomes were located in Appalachian Ohio.

In Ohio as a whole, 7.8% of families were below officially defined standards of poverty. Micropolitan areas had an identical rate, and almost the same as the 7.7% found in metropolitan areas. Among micropolitan areas, Van Wert had the lowest percentage of families in poverty, 4.2%, and Portsmouth had the highest rate, 15.2%. As before, the micropolitan areas with the lowest percentage of families in poverty (that is, the least poverty) were all located in northwest or western Ohio, while all but one of the eight micropolitan areas with the highest rates of family poverty were in Appalachian Ohio.

Families with children under five years of age were more likely to be in poverty than families in general in all groups of Ohio counties. In all of Ohio 17.7% of these families were in poverty (compared to 7.8% of all families). Micropolitan areas averaged 17.9% of families with children under five in poverty, higher than the state and also higher than metropolitan areas (17.5%). A half dozen micropolitan areas in the Northwestern part of the state again had the lowest rates (6% in Van Wert, for example) while micropolitan areas in Appalachia had the highest rates. All six of the micropolitan areas with 20% or more of families with children under five in poverty were in Appalachian Ohio: Salem-East Liverpool, Zanesville, Athens, Cambridge, Portsmouth, and Gallipolis. The last three had startling percentages of families with children under five in poverty: 27%, 28% and 29%, respectively.

One last interesting measure of income is total transfer payment (TTP) as a percentage of total personal income (TPI). This is a measure of what proportion of income is "unearned" income from payments from such sources as welfare, black lung payments, and social security income. Total transfer payments averaged 17.1% of total personal income in micropolitan areas, compared to 13.7% in metropolitan areas and 14.3% for the state of Ohio. The northwest Ohio/Appalachia split was again evident in the TTP/TPI ratio. Five of the six micropolitan areas with the lowest TTP/TPI ratios were in northern and western Ohio, while four of the five counties with the highest ratios were all in Appalachian Ohio.

Per capita income was generally lower in the core cities than in the micropolitan areas as a whole. Thus, micropolitan areas are miniature parallels to Ohio's metropolitan areas, where the suburbs have a higher per capita income than the core cities. In 2000 micropolitan core cities had an average per capita income of $17,030 while the collective micropolitan areas averaged $17,740. The nine core cities that were wealthier than their respective micropolitan areas by at least $500 per capita were Chillicothe, Coshocton, Dover, Findlay, Gallipolis, New Philadelphia, Norwalk, Washington and Wooster. The core city that was most like an island of wealth was Wooster, $3175 wealthier per capita than its surrounding micropolitan area (Wayne County). On the other hand, one micropolitan core city stood out as an island of poverty: East Liverpool, which was $3999 poorer than its surrounding micropolitan area, Columbiana County.

The measure of families in poverty within micropolitan core cities paralleled other geographic patterns of well being we have seen (Table 6.5). The poverty figures were highest in core cities in Appalachia, such as East Liverpool (21.5%), Portsmouth, Athens and Gallipolis (around 14%) and in Ashtabula (17.8%). Family poverty rates were lowest in western and north central Ohio, such as Van Wert, Defiance, Findlay and Sidney, where rates were only 4% to 5%.

Employment

Manufacturing remains a mainstay of Ohio's micropolitan areas. In 2000, 16.4% of workers in Ohio were employed in manufacturing. In Micropolitan Ohio, 22.1% of workers earned wages in manufacturing, compared to only 15% in Metropolitan Ohio. Branch plant factories are particularly attracted to micropolitan areas, a phenomenon noted by Leinbach and Cromley (1982). The micropolitan area with the highest percentage of manufacturing employees was Sidney, with a phenomenal 43.8% of workers in manufacturing, followed by Wapakoneta, Fremont, Van Wert, Bucyrus and Norwalk, all with more than 28% of their workers in manufacturing (Table 6.6). Generally, Micropolitan areas in northwest Ohio and the northern half of the state had the highest percentages employed in manufacturing, while Appalachian micropolitan areas had the lowest percentages. Micropolitan workers were found to be commuters, with an average commuting time of 22 minutes compared to 23 minutes for metropolitan areas as well as the state. Commuting time ranged from a low of 17 and 18 minutes in northern and western Ohio, respectively, to a high of 28 minutes in Appalachia.

With only a few exceptions, all micropolitan cities are county seats. Consequently, employment in government, social services, school administration, law offices, jails, and bail bond offices, is quite substantial. These cities also function as regional medical, banking, and retail, as well as tourist centers, all of which translate into a fairly diversified economic base for the cities with additional employment in small museums, hotels, and restaurants. The biggest surprise yet was the extent to which the micropolitan core cities are specialized in manufacturing. Thus, micropolitan core cities were even more specialized than their surrounding counties. On average 27.6% of core city workers were employed in manufacturing. Fourteen of the 35 micropolitan core cities had over 30% specialization, with Sidney the highest at 43.8%. In fact, only three of the 35 micropolitan core cities had less than the state average of employment in manufacturing. These were Athens (2.2%), Gallipolis (7.7%), and Portsmouth (12.0%).

Table 6.6 Manufacturing Employment in Micropolitan Ohio

Micropolitan Area (MA)*		Micropolitan Core Area City*	
Name	Manufacturing Employment (%)	Name	Manufacturing Employment (%)
Ashland	24.4	Ashland	26.9
Ashtabula	22.5	Ashtabula	28.7
Ashtabula		Conneaut	35.4
Athens	4.7	Athens	2.2
Bellefontaine	25.0	Bellefontaine	28.2
Bucyrus		Bucyrus	35.9
Bucyrus	28.9	Galion	31.1
Cambridge	14.3	Cambridge	21.5
Celina	17.9	Celina	30.4
Chillicothe	14.4	Chillicothe	19.3
Coshocton	22.0	Coshocton	35.7
Defiance	27.6	Defiance	36.5
Findlay	25.8	Findlay	26.4
Fremont	30.9	Fremont	35.6
Gallipolis	7.1	Gallipolis	7.7
Greenville	19.0	Greenville	25.5
Marion	20.1	Marion	27.9
Mount Vernon	18.8	Mount Vernon	23.8
New Philadelphia	20.3	New Philadelphia	28.1
New Philadelphia		Dover	22.9
Norwalk	31.7	Norwalk	30.5
Portsmouth		Portsmouth	12.0
Salem-East Liverpool	19.8	East Liverpool	25.2
Salem-East Liverpool		Salem	31.0
Sidney	43.8	Sidney	43.8
Tiffin	22.4	Tiffin	30.1
Tiffin		Fostoria	39.1
Urbana	22.1	Urbana	33.3
Van Wert	28.9	Van Wert	36.2
Wapakoneta-St Marys	30.9	Wapakoneta	28.2
Wapakoneta-St Marys		St. Marys	38.8
Washington	19.3	Washington	23.7
Wilmington	15.8	Wilmington	17.1
Wooster	26.8	Wooster	22.9
Zanesville	20.6	Zanesville	24.3
Average	22.1	Average	27.6

*Micropolitan areas are named after their core cities hence duplication of place names

Micropolitan cities averaged 21% employment in education, health, and social services. These activities tended to be highest in those cities with the lowest percentage of workers in manufacturing, including Athens (52%), Gallipolis (38%) and Portsmouth (27%) and lowest in some of the west central cities most highly specialized in manufacturing, such as Sidney. In Sidney, the percentage of workers in education, health, and social services was only 14%. Since all micropolitan cities are retail centers, retail employment varied much less than employment in manufacturing, ranging from a high of 16% in Gallipolis to a low of 10% in Tiffin.

Unemployment for 2000 averaged 4% in Ohio. Metropolitan residents, with a 3.8% rate, fared better than micropolitan areas (4.7%). Four of the five micropolitan areas with the highest rates of unemployment were in Appalachia with Portsmouth being the highest (8.7%) followed by Cambridge (8.2%). Lower rates were generally found in Northwestern Ohio, particularly Findlay (2.8%) and Wapakoneta (3.2%), although the Northwest/Appalachian split was not as prominent as in most other socio-economic indicators.

Housing

A number of indices related to housing cast light on the differences between micropolitan and metropolitan areas. The median value of the typical owner-occupied housing unit in the micropolitan areas of Ohio in 2000 was about $86,900. This figure was about 84% of the state-wide median of $103,700, and lower still than the metropolitan median value of almost $109,800. Micropolitan areas with median home values exceeding the state average tended to be in northern Ohio (Wooster, Findlay, Ashland, and Norwalk) or in western Ohio (Sidney, Wilmington, Urbana, Celina). Those with the lowest values tended to be in Appalachia, including the two very lowest, Portsmouth and Cambridge, where median values were less than $66,000.

The median gain in housing value in micropolitan areas between 1990 and 2000 averaged 35.2% compared to Ohio's 29.8%. This was also higher than the gain for metropolitan areas (28.8%), because lesser increases in value in metropolitan urban core areas canceled gains in fringe counties. Individual micropolitan areas were quite disparate when this figure was examined. Eight micropolitan areas were among the top quartile of Ohio counties experiencing the greatest gains in housing values over the decade. These were Washington (highest with a 55.8% increase), East Liverpool-Salem, Mt. Vernon, Ashtabula, Wilmington, Marion, Bucyrus, and Ashland. The last seven all had gains of at least 43%. On the other hand, seven micropolitan areas were among the lowest quartile of all Ohio counties: Celina (lowest at 20.8%), Wapakoneta, Fremont, Findlay, Gallipolis, Sidney and Defiance. Each of the last six had gains of less than 28%. The largest gainers in housing value tended to be close to large metropolitan areas. The smallest gainers tended to be in northwestern Ohio (all except Gallipolis).

Micropolitan areas tended to have some of Ohio's oldest housing stock. The proportion of residential structures that was built before 1939 averaged 29.8% in micropolitan areas, much older than metropolitan areas (20.9%) and all of Ohio (22.5%). There was great variation among the micropolitan areas, but without apparent geographic pattern. Gallipolis has the smallest proportion of pre-1939 housing (17.6%) and Tiffin had the largest, 41.3%.

Median values of owner-occupied housing in micropolitan core cities of $87,700 were about 85% of the State of Ohio median, about 80% of the median for metropolitan areas, and about $1000 higher than their micropolitan areas as a whole. The distribution of values showed a similar geographic pattern in core cities to that of micropolitan areas in general. Western central and north central micropolitan areas had the highest median values of homes and Appalachian areas had the lowest, with a few exceptions. Wooster had the highest median housing value, $108,000, more than twice the median value in East Liverpool, the lowest, at $41,700.

THE SPATIAL STRUCTURE OF OHIO'S MICROPOLITAN AREAS

As already pointed out, all micropolitan areas have a core city and its surrounding areas, which usually include the county in which the core city is located. In this section, I will focus mainly on the micropolitan core city. Like all cities, Ohio's micropolitan cities reflect differential spatial structures that have been largely shaped by the transportation technology of the day. Thus, all Ohio micropolitan cities grew up along water including rivers and lakefront. These cities boomed when the rivers were improved to create canals. Sixteen of Ohio's 29 micropolitan areas were connected to the two great canal systems that were developed in Ohio. Both systems connected the Ohio River with Lake Erie. One, the Miami and Erie, ran along the western half of the state and the other, the Ohio and Erie, connected cities primarily along the eastern half and in central Ohio. Activities clustered around the canals as the cities boomed. However, the canal era was short-lived and it was largely over before the Civil War.

Railroads replaced canals and connected every Ohio micropolitan area, giving them an industrial location advantage that lasted into the early 20th Century. Gradually, micropolitan cities with railroads lost their economic edge because the next shift, to truck transportation, gave the next industrial location advantage to the suburbs which had better road access—literally more room and quicker access for trucks to maneuver into loading docks and to park. Most micropolitan cities still have some railroad service, but the river-canal-railroad corridors within these small cities today are almost equally important for the opportunities they present for beautification and tourism through the creation of river walks, such as that in Findlay, or bicycle paths along abandoned railway rights of way, as in Zanesville.

In the automobile era railroad tracks may even be more of an aggravation than a benefit. Indeed, Marion has incurred considerable expense building overpasses for the railroad tracks that bisect the central business district. One result of this change in transportation mode is that the spatial structure of the micropolitan city is now characterized by linear sectors along roads, along with rings of density of use, usually denser toward the center, just as would be expected from the Hoyt and Burgess models. These rings and sectors give the micropolitan city a different appearance depending upon by what road one approaches the city. This is true of the city, in general, and the central business district, in particular.

The Central Business District (Downtown)

The central business districts of Micropolitan Ohio combine a fascinating mixture, or even polarity, of uses and conditions: offices and retail, old and new, urban and suburban, modern and traditional, well maintained and decrepit. While most of these CBDs are too small to have any large distinct zones, it is possible, especially in the relatively larger cities, to distinguish two zones—the "zone of advance" and the "zone of retreat".

The zone of advance is the part of the CBD closest to the main road or street that has become suburbanized at the outer limits of the city. Activities in this section are a little more vibrant and the look of buildings a little perkier, a reflection of higher rents. This side of downtown will have a more vibrant look with banks, restaurants, gift shops, a gourmet coffee shop (but probably not a national chain like Starbucks), and social services, especially if they are in old buildings. Perhaps this sector has a "boutique look," such as Urbana does. Often however, downtown retail establishments are scarce and those found tend to be such low traffic operations that one wonders how they can pay the rent: video rental stores, the ubiquitous schools of hair dressing, cosmetology, tanning and nail salons, and hobby shops open only on weekends. Within this zone are also the churches whose impressive old brick and stone architecture makes one wonder how a city of this size can support such a large number of churches. In cities with declining populations, church membership has also dropped, and some of these churches, built in days gone by, are being kept afloat only by endowments from wealthy parishioners.

In contrast, the "zone of retreat" consists of the old industrial corridor, which usually follows the road along the main river and leads outward from the CBD. In this zone lie the county jail and the former canal and current railroad bed where manufacturing activities were located during the heyday of manufacturing. Activities in this zone reflect the low rents in this part of the city and the agricultural central place functions of the city. Thus, closer to the CBD in this sector, are pawnshops, used video stores, used furniture stores, and second-hand shops struggling to be seen as antique stores. Here one also finds a collection of grain elevators and cattle auction houses, as well as farm machinery suppliers and repair firms. These statements are truer of the central, west central and north central Ohio micropolitan areas than of the eastern and Appalachian micropolitan areas because the central and western portions of the state are more agricultural. This sector also blends into the factory district and adjacent workers homes and may comprise a miniature "inner city" with all its characteristics of older, deteriorated structures and abandoned and boarded-up buildings. Although based on cities of less than 10,000 population a recent work by Davies (1998) discussed these problems of urban decline in Ohio. The minority population of the city will be over-represented in this district of older homes and abandoned homes adjacent to the old factories.

At the center of the CBD, somewhat in between the two zones, are the courthouse, the city hall, the old hotel, a restored theater, and the library. Some cities, like Zanesville, may have a small convention center or a municipal auditorium. Almost all of Ohio's micropolitan cities are county seats, so the county courthouse dominates downtown with its classical columns or its Second Empire wedding-cake look. A plaza or circle, as in Mount Vernon, gives open space from which to view the building. Monuments to important native sons and to wars give the courthouse plaza a European look. Urbana, for example, has a monument to those lost at Gettysburg. In most cities, a corner of the plaza or the edge of the circle has been taken over for parking spaces. Nearby to the courthouse, and much less architecturally impressive, will be an old brick or granite City Hall. Associated with the county courthouse will also be lawyers' offices, a police station, a bail bonds office and the like; all representing a significant cluster of employment in the downtown area. Some of the City Hall functions may have expanded into a nearby annex or even moved to a more modern office building nearby. This new city hall is brick if built in the 1960's or 1970's, but glass and steel if of more recent vintage. If the old City Hall has lost its function, the building has been converted into an art gallery, local history museum or community youth center. An interesting and very visible historic remnant may be metal electric towers carrying wires through downtown alleys as can be seen in Zanesville and Marion.

All micropolitan cities in Ohio have been just as subject to suburbanizing influences as have large cities. This competition between suburban and downtown locations sometimes results in a "bipolar" or "schizoid" aspect to land use in these micropolitan areas. It is not just suburban institutions "versus" downtown institutions in general but each specific institution, public or private, struggles with this locational choice and sometimes decides to split its operations. Thus, county offices maintain their presence in the downtown courthouse, but if the adjacent annex built in the 1950's is not sufficient, county authorities will suburbanize social services, such as school district administration, perhaps in a "one stop" center, thus maintaining two locations. Factories may do this too; just as the Bloomer Chocolate Company in Zanesville maintains an older brick factory location downtown and a recently built suburban metal shell building. The traditional downtown restaurant may clone itself along the interstate, as did Adornettos in Zanesville or the Forum in Cambridge.

This competition between the CBD and the outskirts, coupled with declining population in micropolitan cities, has impacted the CBD in several ways. One obvious result is abandoned structures, due to businesses leaving the area or migrating to the outskirts. Thus, many CBD buildings in Ohio's micropolitan areas are for lease or even derelict. In the few CBDs that have high-rise buildings, only the first and sometimes the second floors of most of those buildings are occupied. Large, occupied, multi-story complexes like Ashland Oil in downtown Ashland are exceptions. The size and seating capacity of the old downtown churches dwarf their congregations. Former school buildings lie empty or put to other uses. It is very rare to find an old downtown department store like Freedliner's in Wooster, or the chain department store, such as Peebles in Coshocton. Almost always, the old downtown department stores have been converted to other uses and the upper stories abandoned. All these give the overall appearance of a city wearing an oversized coat: the buildings are usually too big and too numerous for the current population to be served.

The second effect of the competition between the CBD and the outskirts is that to some extent, it has "forced" the CBD to "suburbanize" by adding suburban style buildings and uses. For example, there will be an old granite or sandstone bank decorated with carved eagles and wrought iron grates and on the adjoining block might be a suburban-style bank with a drive-in window and ample parking. There may be an old-fashioned drugstore or a suburban-style chain drugstore, or both, in which case the former business may be in financial peril. In addition, there has been a "flattening" of CBD density by the razing of structures for parking lots. All these have resulted in a landscape that this author has elsewhere described as "semi-urban" (Fonseca 1977).

The Historic District

In most of Ohio's micropolitan cities near downtown is a sector of old established mainline homes. Many of these older homes closest to the CBD may no longer be residences, but have instead acquired new uses such as funeral homes, real estate and dentist offices. One or two old homes with particularly significant architectural restoration will be a bed and breakfast or a restaurant, such as the Fort Ball Bed and Breakfast in Tiffin or Sidney's Great Stone Castle Restaurant. The distinctive architecture of these parts of the micropolitan city is a treasure. Some buildings are so significant as to be noted in architectural guidebooks, such as the People's Savings and Loan building in Sidney designed by Louis Sullivan. Building facades, usually from the late 19th and early 20th century, are impressive, if restored and almost always evident if the observer looks above the renovated retail shops on the first floor. Blank factory walls may exhibit sport murals, as in Bucyrus and East Liverpool, or the one outlining Sidney's industrial history. Portsmouth's floodwall is perhaps the best known of these mural efforts. Palimpsests, barely remaining commercial signs of by-gone eras, are also usually evident. Almost all the Ohio cities have alleys close to downtown. Many alleys may have deteriorated pavement. The alleys and side streets may even be brick or cobble, remnants of an earlier era. If not maintained, as in a historic district, these streets may be in terrible repair. In any case, the micropolitan city will always have a strip of fine, well-maintained older homes that still shows the former grandeur of the city, such as South Main Street in Findlay or the McIntyre historic district of Zanesville. Sometimes these neighborhoods will have a median strip of towering old trees.

The College District

Every micropolitan city in Ohio has an institution of higher education. If this is a public institution, it will be on the outskirts of the core city where the county donated vacant land for the building of a branch campus or community college in the 1960s and 1970s. These suburban-looking structures have ample parking for their commuting population and often occupy the former "poor farm" land across from the county home. Private institutions, on the other hand, are most likely to be found in the ritzy older home area of the city. This is true of colleges such as Findlay, Urbana, Wooster, and Heidelberg (in Tiffin). Some of the nearby older homes may have been acquired by the campus through donation or purchase, and are now used as the president's house, a museum or an administration building. Faculty members have gentrified a few adjacent homes and help keep the older neighborhood of giant homes with giant utility bills looking upscale. Private residential colleges will also develop a small nearby neighborhood of older homes subdivided for rental, retail shops and services not usually found around the commuter-dominated branch campuses.

The Medical District

Most micropolitan cities are also health care centers for the regions they serve. Thus, most have a medium-size hospital and associated health care facilities, pharmacies and doctors' offices. Since health care has been one of the fastest-growing sectors in our modern economy, the hospitals have modernized and expanded and thus many have moved from former downtown locations. So while the medical complex is most likely still located within the city limits, it has probably moved away from downtown to a site where more parking and space for building expansion is available. Like the social services sector of the economy, the space needs of medical services have been increasing and the medical sector expands by acquiring new land, annexing adjoining buildings, and demolishing older adjacent structures for the construction of new buildings and parking lots.

Commercial Strips and Outskirt Clusters

The micropolitan city is centered about a variety of roads, some of which are two-lane, and some four-lane, including Interstate highways. (Twelve of the 29 micropolitan cities have Interstates within their boundaries). Along these roads are commercial strips of the micropolitan city. Older two-lane roads leading out of the city core show less "suburbanization" with the urbanized areas ending fairly abruptly at or close to the city boundary. Along wider roads, urban uses such as gas stations, convenience shops, restaurants, mobile home sales, auto service shops, and new and used car lots, will line the roads between the CBD and the city boundary. The city limit itself will be marked with signs announcing the presence of the local Rotary, Kiwanis and other service clubs. There will almost always be a sign announcing the "home of" something, in some cases United States presidents, but more often a sports hero, inventor, or, as in Bucyrus, a war hero. Athletic achievements of the local high school will be announced such as the boys' high school basketball team won the state Division II finals in 1989. Somewhere within sight from this point, will be a water tower on a hill announcing the city's name. On the wider, more heavily traveled roads, the strip of houses and commercial activities may continue for a mile or more beyond the city boundary.

Along four-lane roads, typical suburban uses will include a mixture of single-family homes, retail shops, fast food restaurants, supermarkets and gas stations. There will be a recently built cluster of apartments, townhouses or condominiums. Here at the outskirts of the city, especially if the four-lane road intersects an Interstate highway, will be a commercial cluster including a Wal-Mart or certainly a K-Mart, and perhaps both. In larger micropolitan cities, this cluster will also include a wider range of modern suburban stores such as an Olive Garden restaurant, Staples office supply store, a mall, and chain motels. Even if there is not an Interstate, some modified version of this suburban tangle will still appear outside the micropolitan core area, and usually along the major four-lane road that leads to the next largest, and closest city, so that these establishments can serve two markets. If an Interstate crosses the micropolitan city, the largest clusters of suburban development will most likely be along the main highway that connects to the Interstate.

Newer Industrial District

Suburban-style industrial parks are the economic lifeblood of many of Ohio's micropolitan cities. Some cities, like Zanesville, have multiple industrial parks. Ideally, the industrial park will be near an Interstate or limited access highway, and ideally at a major highway exit. In the case of modern warehouse distribution centers, for example, they will avoid locating more than three miles from major highways. The scale of activities in these industrial parks can be impressive. Wooster has a wide variety of manufacturing including Akron Brass, Frito Lay, Rayco, Rubbermaid and Gerstenglager (a division of Worthington). Mount Vernon has a Rolls Royce engine plant. Greenville has huge factories of Honeywell, Corning, BASF and Whirlpool. Occasionally there is a substantial high tech company presence, such as Wooster's ProQuest Business Solutions. These factories mainly represent the traditional, but very wide, array of Ohio industries, including food processing, metals manufacturing, appliance assembly, plastics, auto parts manufacture and assembly, and due to Ohio's relatively central location to US population, warehousing and distribution.

Recreational District/Land Use

Ohio's micropolitan cities are small enough and of low enough density to be relatively "green" by American urban standards. Almost every city under discussion has a downtown park and open areas right near the courthouse. However, micropolitan city parks may even be "too" plentiful for cities to maintain, with the result that some are neglected and eventually abandoned, due to budget constraints. The ultimate result is that these parks become hangouts for drug dealers and unsavory characters. The county fairground, located in the county seat, is another function that is near the core city, but not downtown. Fairgrounds will probably be located at the edge of the city because they require a great deal of space.

Residential Areas

With the exception of high-rise luxury apartments, Ohio's micropolitan cities have essentially every standard type of housing available in modern American cities. As with other aspects of the cities discussed, housing is differentiated into neighborhoods by type of structure and socio-economic class of occupant. Near the CBD and adjacent to the old factory district will be some older brick apartment buildings transitioning into an inner city neighborhood of duplexes and single-family homes in need of repair. Another side of the CBD will grade into the sector of older, substantial, well-kept homes. Surrounding both will be a variety of neighborhoods of single-family homes, with larger homes, larger lots, and more recent construction toward the outskirts of the city. More modest, older single-family homes in good repair, occupied by the lower middle class, will be closer to the CBD and grade into the more deteriorated homes adjacent to the old factory district. Outside the traditional urban core, along the suburban highways, will be garden-style apartment buildings or condominiums of three or four stories and townhouses. If newer apartment buildings are found near downtown, they are very likely specialized apartments for the elderly or for lower income residents. Older apartment buildings may be underutilized unless they have been renovated for these specialized uses.

Since Ohio's micropolitan cities are freestanding and not part of existing metropolitan areas, the approach to the city is usually through rural regions. Several miles from the city center a mixture old farmhouses, older single-family residences, and newer single-family residences prevail. Many of the last are mobile or manufactured homes. Low intensity use is a mark of distance from the city and almost all these homes are on a half-acre or acre. Many are "farmettes" of five or ten acres but without significant agricultural activity. Barns abound but most are abandoned or deteriorated.

CONCLUSION

In this chapter, we have examined the social and spatial structures of Ohio's 29 micropolitan areas. In this concluding section, it will be instructive to summarize the extent to which the social and spatial structures of micropolitan areas mirror metropolitan areas and the stylized facts of internal structures of urban areas, and implications for small city studies.

In terms of social structure, the 29 micropolitan areas accounted for 1,708,000 people or 15% of Ohio's population, while the 15 metropolitan areas had a total population of 9,141,000, which was 81% of Ohio's population in 2000. While the proportion of non-white population was much greater in metropolitan areas (almost 17.7% compared to 4.4%) the percentage of Hispanic population was about the same. Population growth rates in both areas were equal. Metropolitan Ohio was wealthier than its micropolitan counterpart, by almost every measure. Per capita income was 24% greater in metropolitan areas; unemployment was less; family poverty and poverty of families with children under five years of age was less. Residents of Micropolitan Ohio had a much higher dependence on transfer payments for income. While the percentage without a high school degree was about the same, Metropolitan Ohio had a substantially greater proportion of college graduates: 23.2% compared to 13.0%.

Metropolitan Ohio's single-family housing was of greater value (19% more) and of more recent vintage, reflecting recent construction to accommodate migration to the suburbs. However, housing values were growing more rapidly in Micropolitan Ohio. Unemployment was about 1% higher in Micropolitan Ohio than in Metropolitan Ohio, in large part reflecting the much greater dependence on manufacturing employment and the continuing decline in that employment.

More than 22% of micropolitan workers were employed in manufacturing compared to 15% of metropolitan workers. Travel time to work in both areas was about the same.

Micropolitan areas are also miniature metropolitan areas, when comparing micropolitan core cities with their fringes, but there were many important differences as well. Thus, micropolitan fringe areas were growing much faster than their cores, just as in metropolitan areas. Per capita income was higher in the fringe than in core in both micropolitan areas and metropolitan areas. Minority population was more concentrated in cores than fringes, in both Metropolitan and Micropolitan Ohio.

However, there were differences between Metropolitan Ohio and Micropolitan Ohio. Even though per capita income fit the expectation of "wealthier fringe/poorer core," family poverty did not fit that mold, at least in micropolitan areas. Metropolitan fringes had much less poverty than urban cores, but in micropolitan areas, fringes had higher poverty rate compared to their core cities. In Metropolitan Ohio, education attainment was lower in the metropolitan core cities than it was in the suburbs. In Micropolitan Ohio, there was only a slight difference between the core and the fringe. In Micropolitan Ohio, 28% of core city workers were employed in manufacturing, compared to only 8% of micropolitan fringe workers. In Metropolitan Ohio, the distribution was reversed: almost 18% of suburban fringe workers were in manufacturing compared to 14% of metropolitan urban core residents. In Metropolitan Ohio, 80% of the population resided in urban core counties; in Micropolitan Ohio, only 33% of the population lived in the micropolitan core cities.

The spatial structure of Ohio's micropolitan areas largely mirrors those of the large urban centers in metropolitan Ohio. As we know from urban geographic theory, these small cities, like their large counterparts, have evolved a CBD, rings of decreasing residential density around that CBD, sectors along radial transportation routes, and multiple nuclei around specialized locations. Specialized districts are smaller and sometimes harder to discern, but among the micropolitan areas there is no question that a trained observer, or even the layperson, can find the CBD or downtown, older factory districts with adjoining multifamily and run-down housing, a historic district or strip of well-kept and large older homes, and in general, distinct neighborhoods or sections of the city easily categorized by social class. Larger micropolitan areas will exhibit a college district, medical district and perhaps a cluster of parks and fairground in a recreational district.

As in Ohio's metropolitan areas, the micropolitan cities have experienced extensive suburban growth along their outskirts, particularly along Interstates and other major highways. These suburban locations provide opportunities for new residences and new styles of residences, sites for national chain retailers and for industries in industrial parks, but at the cost of competition with established businesses in the older core city. As in metropolitan areas, the result in many cases is population loss in the central city and the conversion of older structures to new uses, but more often the vacancy and abandonment of those older structures. Many of Ohio's core metropolitan areas and many micropolitan areas are thus alike in loss of population and tax base and subsequent deterioration of infrastructure in parts of the cities' cores.

Overall, given the small territorial extent and the high density of micropolitan core cities, it will be useful for future research to develop a more accurate comparison between micropolitan core cities and the *urbanized area* population of metropolitan regions. Future research can also analyze the extent to which Ohio's micropolitan areas are typical or atypical of other such cities in the United States, particularly given what we have learned about the extreme specialization in manufacturing of some of Ohio's micropolitan areas and the regional differences among Ohio's small cities based on their location within subregions of the state, such as Appalachian Ohio.

REFERENCES

Alonso, W. 1964. *Location and Land Use: Towards a General Theory of Land Rent.* Cambridge: Harvard University Press.

Burgess, E.W. 1925. The Growth of the City. In *The City*, ed. R.E. Park, E.W. Burgess, and R. D. McKenzie. Chicago: University of Chicago Press.

Davies, R.O. 1998. *Main Street Blues: The Decline of Small-Town America.* Columbus: Ohio State University Press.

Fonseca, J. W. 1977. The Semiurban Landscape. *Landscape* 21: 23 – 25. (Also at   http://www.zanesville.ohiou.edu/geography/semi-urban/index.htm).

Garreau, J. 1991. *Edge Cities: Life on the Frontier.* New York: Anchor Books.

Harris, C. D., and E. L. Ullman. 1945. The Nature of Cities. *Annals of the American Academy of Political and Social Sciences* 242: 7 – 17.

Hoyt, H. 1939. *The Structure and Growth of Residential Neighborhoods in American Cities.* Washington, DC: Federal Housing Administration.

Khan, R., P. F. Orazem, and D. M. Otto. 2001. Deriving empirical definitions of spatial labour markets: the roles of competing versus complimentary growth. *Journal of Regional Science* 41: 735 – 56.

Leinbach, T. R., and R. G. Cromley. 1982. Appalachian Kentucky: the role of manufacturing in micropolitan development. *Growth and Change* 13: 11 – 20.

Mumford, L. 1961. *The City in History: Its Origins, Its Transformation, and Its Prospects.* New York: Harcourt, Brace & World.

Plane, D. A. 2003. Perplexity, complexity, metroplexity, microplexity: perspectives for future research on regional growth and change. *Review of Regional Studies* 33: 104-20.

Shevkey, E., and M. Williams. 1949. *The Social Areas of Los Angeles.* Berkeley: University of California Press.

Sjoberg, G. 1960. *The Preindustrial City: Past and Present.* New York: Free Press.
U.S Census Bureau. About Metropolitan and Micropolitan Statistical Areas http://www.census.gov/population/www/estimates/aboutmetro.html.

7

Globalization, Neoliberal Policies, and the Changing Landscapes of Small Cities: The Case of Ciudad Lerdo, Durango, Mexico

Michael S. Yoder
Texas A&M International University

INTRODUCTION

The changing urban landscape has long been a traditional theme of urban geography and related disciplines. In particular, geographers have sought to understand the forces underlying urban form and have addressed the question from a myriad of ideological and theoretical perspectives. Traditional approaches to the study of urban form generally place transportation technologies at the center of explanation of spatial expansion of cities (for example, see Adams 1970; Thomson 1977; Herbert and Thomas 1997). Such explanations of evolving urban form typically document various transportation eras: pedestrian and animal-drawn carts, horse-drawn streetcars, electric streetcars, and various stages of auto mobility .

In contrast, political economy approaches seek explanations in deep-rooted political, social, and economic forces. Thus, within this tradition, some explanations have emphasized the linkage between monetary flows and the dramatic changes in urban landscapes taking hold in large metropolitan areas, particularly in North America (Harvey 1978 and 1985; Feagan 1987). Others have looked at competing political ideologies and their different impacts upon the evolution of the urban landscape (e.g. Ley 1987). A third approach within political economy that includes "locality studies, and "the Los Angeles School" of urbanism has emphasized globalization, local reactions to it, and the fundamental importance of this duality to the postmodern social construction of places, particularly cities and their hinterlands (See for example Scott and Storper 1986; Warf 1988; Leitner 1990; Amin 1995; Martin 1994; Dear and Flusty 1998; Markusen et al 1999; Nijman 2000; Grant and Nijman 2002; and Rea Becerra 2002).

These studies have been invaluable in highlighting the complex web of forces that condition urban form. However, they generally appear to be lacking in two aspects. First, much of the literature, with the exception of some locality studies, has emphasized global forces over local actors, and second, all of them have focused on large cities with very little inclusion of small or mid-sized cities, especially those in developing countries. With respect to the first, Beauregard (1995), and Markusen et al (1999) argue that planning, political and economic decision-making, labor action, and other reactions to globalization occur, in fact, at the local level. Thus, it is important to understand the global-local connection as not only a world-wide structural phenomenon, but equally as an array of local conditions and actions on the part of investors, political figures, organized labor, chambers of commerce, and other economic promotion agencies. With respect to the second, it is important to emphasize that in Latin America, at least, since the decline of import substitution industrialization (ISI) economies, foreign (multinational) and domestic capital has sought out a multiplicity of places outside the primate cities for reproduction. Such capital has thus targeted mid-sized and smaller cities where labor organization is weak, the cost of doing business is lower, and national and local governments, desperate to attract new job opportunities where traditional economic activities are waning, are willing to offer generous fiscal incentives (Campolina Diniz and Santos 1999; Campolina Diniz and Razavi 1999; Rowland 1999). The result is that in Mexico, for example, during the 1980s, small cities between 50,000 and 100,000 population grew 5% annually, a faster rate than any other category of settlements, followed by mid-sized cities with 250,000 to 500,000 people (4.3%) (Tomas 2000). Yet the impact of these globalizing forces and their associated neoliberal policies on small cities has not been adequately examined.

This chapter examines the impact of globalization and neoliberal policies on Ciudad Lerdo, a small city in the State of Durango, which is in North Central Mexico's rapidly industrializing district of "La Laguna" (Figure 7.1). The region, traditionally strong in agricultural and livestock activities, has fallen on hard times, owing to increasing competition with the US, growing disparities in the region between large-scale and small-scale producers, and a heavy reliance on irrigation. Low-wage manufacturing has replaced farming as the economic sector viewed by many as having the potential to employ thousands of people in the region, and therefore, the sector receiving the lion's share of investment and attention by local officials and transnational investors alike. The chapter focuses

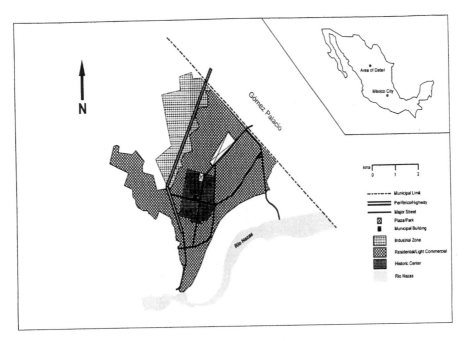

Figure 7.1 Map of Ciudad Lerdo, Durango, Mexico

on Ciudad Lerdo as a case study of the character of urban spatial expansion in the region, in light of globalization and pertinent neoliberal policies identifiable as having a strong impact on urban form. Specifically, it examines the dramatic decline of agriculture, the rise of manufacturing both for export and for domestic markets, and the resulting effects on the region.

I conducted interviews of municipal government officials, including urban planners, rural development personnel, directors of economic promotion, federal agricultural officials located in the area, and local representatives of the national trade association that promotes the textile and apparel sector, the key economic sector of the region. Economic and demographic data related to the region were also incorporated into the analysis.

The remainder of the chapter is organized into five sections. In the first section, I provide a brief overview of the relationships among globalization forces, neoliberal policies, and urban form. The second section provides a brief historical geographic background of the study region. The third section outlines the key neoliberal policies of political decentralization and privatization within the broad context of globalization forces. The fourth section describes the land uses that slowly are replacing agriculture on the former *ejidos*-turned-private small farms as a result of the policies. The final section addresses similarities and differences between large and small cities with respect to the forces of globalization and urban form.

GLOBALIZATION, NEOLIBERAL POLICIES, AND URBAN FORM

By the 1980s human geographers were among the social scientists at the forefront of the study of globalization and its impact upon places and people. This research has focused on the different effects from place to place of the globalization of the world economy, consumer culture, and an increasingly standardized neoliberal style of governance. The latter is synonymous with economic deregulation that permits greater flexibility and maneuverability on the part of industrial and financial capital, the proliferation of free market policies and other facets of trade liberalization, and the greater emphasis by governments on attracting capital flows at the expense of social spending. It includes privatization of state-run industries and utilities, the opening of domestic markets to foreign goods under the banner of "free trade," the emphasis on promoting agricultural and industrial production for export, and the de-emphasis of protectionism and social spending. In short, neoliberalism involves new policy initiatives that facilitate new global capital flows. The built environment, in general, and urban form in particular, change in response to the policies and corresponding fluidity of capital flows.

Geographers have increasingly noted that despite apparently common neoliberal policy making in response to globalization, places react to and are constructed by global forces in fundamentally different ways (Rea Becerra 2002). In particular, the political economy approach within urban geography emphasizes the connections between urban form shifts in governmental policies, and flows of capital. Harvey (1978, 1985) views the ever-changing built environment and corresponding changes in urban form as essential conduits of capital accumulation. He defines the "second circuit of capital" as the reinvestment of industrial and financial capital in real estate development. A notable application of this concept is the case of Houston's edge city development (Feagin 1987).

An interesting and enlightening variant of the political economy approach to the study of urban form is Ley's (1987) study of Vancouver. He contrasts the style of development of the built environment of that city under Liberal Party municipal leadership, which emphasized historic preservation, with that which occurred under Conservative Party leadership, which emphasized private-public partnerships and fiscal incentives for multinationals to construct new shopping, entertainment, and office space.

A more overt focus on globalization underscores the work of Dear and Flusty (1998) as they examine the interconnection of global and local flows of capital and cultural traits in the creation and recreation of Los Angeles. In particular, they emphasize the blending of different and incongruous land use styles that emanate from global flows of capital and cultural information. They claim that Los Angeles is uniquely postmodern in this regard, and call on others to research such issues as they relate to other cities. Nijman (2000), in a somewhat similar vein, argues that global capital has reshaped Miami into a uniquely futuristic city, whose internal structure is shaped by its linkages to distant locales, particularly in Latin America. Grant and Nijman (2002) examine the emergence of global financial zones and the remaking of traditional business and residential sectors of Mumbai (Bombay) and Accra as neoliberal policies are broadly adopted and carried out there as a response to increasingly globalized flows of money.

Goldsmith (1997) provides an ironic twist to the discussion linking neoliberalism, globalization, and urban form by arguing that American urban form ultimately impacts the nature of globalization. He argues that segregation resulting from suburban sprawl in the US subverts the democratic process, and the resulting ideology is exported to Europe in the form of neoliberal policies, whereupon urban form is altered.

Markusen (1999a) focuses more explicitly on industrial policy, industrial organization (linkage) within a region, and how a region is linked to the larger global economy. She defines four basic types of industrial districts. The "Marshallian District," named for the economist, Alfred Marshall, who advocated multiple small-scale firms with tight inter-firm linkages, is commonly associated with the "post-Fordist" style of economic and geographic organization. The Marshallian District has a highly trained and specialized work force and strong loyalty on the part of both labor and investors to the region, such that trade secrets are shared for the benefit of the region. The most widely cited example is the "Third Italy," a district whose success is largely due to Communist Party influence and the creation of a "social safety net" strategy that helps firms and employees to weather periodic economic downturns (Markusen 1999a).

The "Hub and Spoke" industrial district is one dominated by a large firm or complex of firms that serve as the foundation for the district's economy. Multiple subordinate small firms serve as suppliers of inputs or providers of producer services. Japanese automobile companies tend to be located in such localities.

The "State-Anchored Districts" include a government facility of some kind, such as a military complex or university camp that dominates the local economy. Connections between firms can be similar to the hub-and-spoke district if intra-district linkages are strong, or more like the satellite platform district if internal linkages are weak (Markusen 1999a).

The "Satellite Platform District" is a grouping of branch plants of domestic or foreign multinational corporations, usually multi-plant firms, whose key decision-making and investment capital emanate from elsewhere. Such districts in developing countries tend to take on rudimentary manufacturing of textiles, apparel, electronic parts, and the like. Because local suppliers of inputs are virtually non-existent, intra-district connections are much weaker than those between branch plants and other entities of the firms of which they are a part. The strongest linkages involve labor, which usually is non-union and organizationally weak (Markusen 1999a; Yoder 2000). Such regions tend to lack industry-wide trade associations, given the strong competition between firms in the global arena and/or the diversity of activities that the single-activity firms that locate there undertake (Markusen 1999a). The case study, Ciudad Lerdo, and the adjoining mid-sized cities of Torreón and Gómez Palacio exemplify the satellite platform district. This reflects the limits to industrial maturation of neoliberal policy making in a developing country attempting to come to grips with the imperatives of globalization.

Subsequent sections examine the inter-relatedness of neoliberal policies of political decentralization and abandonment of the traditional agricultural social safety net as Mexico pursues fiscal policies friendly to multinational capital, on the one hand, and a decentralized urban form in Ciudad Lerdo, on the other. Thus, a political economy approach that focuses on neoliberalism as an ideological response to globalization, globalization as a set of social and economic forces, and an urban form that reflects both is relevant. The prevailing ideology of Mexico and its numerous localities adapting to globalization is an aggressive pursuit of policies designed to promote export-oriented manufacturing. This ultimately leads to conversion of farmland surrounding cities into real estate that is prime for manufacturing plants, social externalities among small-scale farmers that include the loss of self-sufficiency, and rapid rural-to-urban migration, including to small cities such as Ciudad Lerdo.

THE STUDY AREA

Ciudad Lerdo, Durango, with a population of 80,600, is one of three cities of a conurbation that straddles the Durango-Coahuila state line, and includes Torreón, Coahuila, and Gómez Palacio, Durango. The three-city conurbation, the core of the agricultural region known as La Comarca Lagunera, or simply "La Laguna," has a population of 928,000, while La Laguna in its entirety has a population of 1.25 million (El Siglo de Torreón 2002). The steady population growth in the district throughout the 20th century was first a result of the region's success at cotton production, followed by its emergence by the end of the century as Latin America's primary center of denim manufacturing (Gereffi 1997).

La Laguna, a vast arid plain, is the interior drainage basin of the Nazas and Aguanaval Rivers, both of which deposited valuable alluvium to create the region's productive soils. Both rivers provided irrigation to support a prosperous cotton and grain economy throughout the latter 19th and most of the 20th centuries that stimulated rapid migration to the region (Arreola 1994; Garloch 1944,

Porfirio Hernández 1975; Estado de Durango 1999). Prior to that, the indigenous *Tamazultecas* used the region's lagoon waters, remnants of an ancient sea, *el Mar Mexicana*, and streams entering them for irrigation and took advantage of the local ecosystem's hunting resources (Porfirio Hernández 1975; Santos Valdés 1973). Early Spaniard activities in the area, dating back to 1598, included some limited mining and the establishment in the 1630s of vineyards that produced wines that were sold as far away as Chihuahua and Mexico City by 1700. The *haciendas* of the region flourished from the wine trade and from the production of wheat, maize, beans, and beef for regional and local markets–until the 19th century, when cotton transformed the region (Corona Paéz 2002). This transformation was in part made possible by fine alluvial soils from sediments deposited by the Nazas and Aguanaval Rivers over millions of years. Both rivers are dry today until torrential rains create temporary high-velocity flows, which in turn have created the steep sides of the arroyos or small canyons emptying into the basin (Santos Valdés 1973).

Forty kilometers upstream on the Nazas River from Ciudad Lerdo, the westernmost city of the conurbation, is a canyon, *el Cañon de Fernández*, which the Revolutionary Government of Lázaro Cárdenas began to dam during the late 1930s to provide irrigation water for cotton production in the region. The State completed the dam and reservoir, "*la Presa Lázaro Cárdenas*," in 1946. In 1969-70, the federal government constructed a second dam and reservoir, "*la Presa Francisco Zarco*," located downstream from the canyon to capture rain waters from three arroyos that drain into the Nazas between the Lázaro Cárdenas dam and Ciudad Lerdo, as an additional source of irrigation water. Prior to these large-scale projects, farmers throughout the latter 19th century constructed a series of canals and small dams to capture and divert floodwaters from periodic torrential rains, for the purpose of cotton production. Some canals exceeded a kilometer in length. *Acequías*, or communal irrigation ditches, traversed the entire Laguna Region. While production of basic grains to sustain cattle ranching comprised the majority of cropping activities early in the 19th century, after 1850, cotton rapidly became the dominant activity utilizing these hydraulic resources and alluvial soils. Written accounts of the agricultural landscape of the latter 19th century describe the region as crisscrossed by a dense irrigation network, comprising, in effect, a "lagoon of canals and *acequías*" that irrigated thousands of acres of cotton parcels (Santos Valdés 1973: 22 – 23). The implication is that this hydraulic human landscape forms a secondary basis for the region's nomenclature, "La Laguna."

The region's acute water problems originated from fruit and vegetable horticulture in the first decades of the 20th century. The struggle over irrigation water among farmers culminated in the creation of hundreds of wells that tapped the region's groundwater, first by mule-powered pumps, and in the 1920s, by tractor-driven pumps. In many cases the water originated 20 to 50 meters below the ground. This irresponsible use of water continued throughout the century, such that by the early 1970s, water had to be drawn from as deep as 200 meters, mostly with electric pumps (Santos Valdés 1973).

Today, despite scarce water resources, La Laguna is Mexico's primary center of dairying, which requires the production of irrigated alfalfa in the vicinity and the direct use of most of the region's wells (Expansión 2001; Esparza 2002b). Thus, the conurbation is an important hub of agro-industrial activity. In addition, it is also a rapidly urbanizing "satellite industrial platform" where, despite recent closures and layoffs, assembly in *maquiladoras* employ more labor today than agriculture and agro-industry combined.

However, as it will be shown later, La Laguna deviates from this latter feature considerably, Because of the dominance of the textile/apparel complex and agroindustry. In fact, as illustrated below, La Laguna demonstrates the hybridization of district types that Markusen suggests can occur, as the region takes on some aspects, albeit to a very limited extent, of the Marshallian District. This has implications not only for the region as a whole, but also for the unfolding contemporary urban geography of the case study, Ciudad Lerdo.

NEOLIBERALISM AND THE CHANGING GEOGRAPHY OF CIUDAD LERDO

For nearly two decades, neoliberal policies enacted at the national, state, and local levels in Mexico collectively have reinforced the transformation of the region from one of production and marketing of crops to one that produces consumer goods for domestic and export markets. The competition between different localities to attract investment in this neo-liberal setting can be fierce, and generally requires, under the aegis of political decentralization, the offering by local governments of tax abatements and subsidies. By the late 1980s and early 1990s, the Mexican government had already put in place NAFTA-friendly policies with regard to imports of grains for human and livestock consumption that ultimately have reinforced poverty among *campesinos* and instigated rural-to-urban migration. However, apart from to the signing of NAFTA by Mexican President Carlos Salinas de Gortari in 1992, two other linchpins of Mexican neoliberalism with relevance to Ciudad Lerdo's contemporary urban geography were the alteration of the Constitution in 1983 by President Miguel de la Madrid to decentralize policy making to the local level, and the changing of the constitution by Salinas in 1992 to allow privatization of *ejidos*.

Decentralization and Local Government Planning in Lerdo

By the early 1980s, it had become clear to the federal government that six decades of centralized economic planning and management of revenues had contributed to the fiscal crisis the country faced, and the growing inequities between Mexico City and outlying regions. President de la Madrid changed Article 115 of the Constitution, which outlines the relationships between the federal, state, and municipal governments, in an attempt to both empower states and localities, to relieve the federal government of the burdens of providing services and promoting development country-wide, and pass on accountability for success or failure to states and municipalities. The changes to Article 115 had three primary goals: to decentralize federal agencies spatially throughout the country, to boost the power of states and municipalities (or strengthen federalism), and to instigate economic development in regions other than Mexico City, a primate city in every sense of the word. Monies would continue to flow from Mexico City to the individual municipalities, but the process would involve greater input from the localities themselves, and the municipalities could enjoy locally generated revenues previously unavailable to them (Edmonds Elías 1997; Rodríguez 1997).

Under the changes to Article 115, each municipality oversees the creation of its own "*Plan Director*," or master land use and economic development plan. No longer regulated at the federal level, the creation and changing of the Plan Director can easily be effected to meet the wishes of a potential investor. Thus, a committee comprising the municipal president, department heads appointed by the municipal president, and members of the business community could approve changes quickly, paving the way for land use decisions that suit the interests of capital. As we will see Ciudad Lerdo's emerging west side industrial landscape reflects the numerous changes made to the municipal Plan Director in this manner. Such changes, however, could not have been made without changes in the status of the adjoining farmland.

Ejido Privatization and Ciudad Lerdo's Changing Urban-Rural Fringe

Ejidos are a major outcome of the Mexican Revolution. The revolutionary governments of the 1910s began the process of appropriating portions of huge land holdings of the wealthy rural elite and redistributing them to landless *campesinos* who had worked the lands for the elites. The process was accelerated by President Lázaro Cárdenas in the latter 1930s (Krauze 1995). Though often criticized for their lack of productivity (see for example Brannon and Baklanoff 1987), many social scientists and historians argue that *ejidos* nonetheless served for several decades not only as a safety valve to stifle rural unrest throughout Mexico, but also as a successful mechanism for creating rural social and political stability by offering the poorest of rural Mexicans a form of land ownership (Hart 1986; Joseph and Wells 1982). Still others argue that their lack of productivity was not so much inevitability under agrarian reform, but rather, it resulted from the lack of attention by various administrations, including a lack of provision of credit for inputs and lack of technical assistance and training (Hart 1986; Joseph 1982; Yoder 1993). Neoliberal critics of *ejidos,* such as President Salinas, viewed their privatization as a necessity in the battle to attract investment, either in manufacturing or in agribusiness (El Financiero 1998). Critics of privatization, however, lament that the titled smallholder is more likely to default on loans during times of poor crop prices and rising production costs, and is, therefore, vulnerable to loss of land (Business Mexico 1997; Public Citizen 2001).

Neoliberal food crop policies by the state have hastened the economic collapse of the Mexican *ejido.* The federal government supported *campesinos,* albeit to a minimal level, until the latter 1980s through price floors on food crops guaranteeing favorable prices, and quotas on imports of the most important crops of the *ejidos,* especially corn. Thus, six years before the implementation of NAFTA, which gradually phased in requirements to eliminate price floors and quotas on imports, the state began to enact neoliberal policies designed to boost available corn supplies and to fulfill Mexico's commitments to GATT. The result was the erosion of the credit that created at least some viability to *ejidos* in the past, and is necessary to make *ejidos* competitive today (Moreno 2002; Reforma 2002, Litchfield 2000; Public Citizen 2001). *Campesinos* now have to face the awesome task of competing with large-scale US agribusiness, which is able to produce more efficiently and can afford occasional dumping of corn during years of oversupply and poor prices.

One large *ejido,* "El Ejido Lerdo," created in 1922, completely surrounded Ciudad Lerdo. The town officially became the seat of the *municipio* (roughly speaking, the equivalent of a county) of Lerdo in 1867. Upon establishment of the *ejido* 55 years later, a limited amount of land was designated for the town, whose population at the time was approximately 8,000, in such a way as to hem the town in. As noted, in the late 1930s, President Lázaro Cárdenas oversaw construction of the dam and reservoir along the Rio Nazas in the southern portion of the *municipio* that provided irrigation for the vast cotton *ejidos* throughout La Laguna. The irrigation canals that crisscross the entire region provided irrigation for all the region's *ejidos,* including *Ejido Lerdo,* whose parcels flourished from cotton and corn production for nearly four decades (Esparza 2002a; Villegas 2003). However, as the city's population grew from 13,500 in 1950 to 80,600 in 2000 (see Table 7.1) an enlargement of the urban zone became necessary to accommodate not only new residential areas but manufacturing plants as well. This could not be achieved without a transformation of *ejido* parcels closest to the city into urban space. Thus, the government began appropriating *ejido* lands adjacent to the city's north side (Table 7.2). Together, CORETT (La Comisión Reguladora de la Tenencia de la Tierra, or the Regulatory Commission of Land Tenancy), the federal agency overseeing the allocation of *ejido* lands, and the Secretary of Public Education (SEP) appropriated in that decade, enough

Table 7.1 Population of Cuidad Lerdo, Durango, 1950 – 2000

Year	Population
1950	13,500
1960	17,700
1970	29,700
1980	39,500
1990	63,200
2000	80,600

Note: Figures are rounded off to the nearest 100
Source: INEGI, Ciudad Lerdo, 1993, 2001

ejido parcels to roughly double the size of the original city limits of 1922. This spatial expansion north and northeast of town accommodated the construction of residential neighborhoods and schools, and the broadening of Boulevard Alemán, the primary artery connecting Ciudad Lerdo with Gómez Palacio (Cervantes 2003). Similar *ejido* appropriations for the purpose of residential expansion and related services occurred in 1989 and again in 1993 (Ramos 2003).

Table 7.2 Ejido Lerdo: Selected Statistics, 1992 – 2002

Description	Area (in Hectares)
Original Size of Ejido Lerdo, 1992	3,731
Area Appropriated by CORRET* and SEP,** 1970 – 1991	953
Area Certified Upon Ejido Privatization in 1996	2,778
Area Currently Parceled	
Farmland	1,013
Land in Common Use	388
Land in Ejidal Settlements	480
Ejido Land Sold since 1996	897

* CORETT=La Comisión Reguladora de la Tenencia de la Tierra
** SEP=Secretaria de Educación Pública
Source: Municipio de Lerdo, Departamento de Catastro Municipal, Unpublished Data

The resulting landscape includes formal housing architecturally typical of inner city neighborhoods found throughout cities of Northern Mexico, but, consistent with Ciudad Lerdo's historic urban zone, narrower streetscapes. The one- and two-story homes were constructed close to sidewalks in a higher density fashion than is encountered in urban and suburban neighborhoods typical in the North. A few of the homes have been converted in whole or in part into retail stores that serve the immediate neighborhood. Flanking Boulevard Alemán, between downtown Lerdo and the city limits of Gómez Palacio, are several locally owned, family-run retail establishments, located either in converted homes or in five small strip malls. A gasoline station, three automobile repair shops, a used car dealer, a franchise convenience store, an airplane museum, an abandoned *maquiladora,* a night club, and several tree/plant nurseries, schools, and parks complete the ensemble of new land uses along the boulevard that until recent years was farmland. The commercial boulevard and the neighborhoods that flank it create a continuous urban linkage between the traditional town center and the fully urbanized southwestern edge of Gómez Palacio. Only an arch over the boulevard marking the limits between the two cities provides any indication of where one city stops and the other starts.

West and northwest of Ciudad Lerdo lies a mix of existing (though mostly abandoned) *ejido* parcels crossed by a dried-up concrete irrigation canal, neighborhoods of informal housing, and a growing number of *maquiladoras* along the *periférico,* or perimeter highway that bypasses Ciudad Lerdo and continues northward and eventually eastward to surround Gómez Palacio and Torreón. The west and northwest suburban fringe is the site of the most recent sprawling development, which has occurred since the privatization of *ejidos* and certification of land parcels by Salinas in 1996. Of Ejido Lerdo's original 3,731 hectares, 953 were appropriated by CORETT and SEP prior to 1996, and 2,778 were certified and titled in 1996 to 270 remaining *ejidatarios*, or members of the *ejido*, by the federal government. Of these 2,778 certified hectares, an estimated 897 have been sold by ex-ejidatarios for construction of *maquiladoras*, housing, and infrastructure (Municipio de Lerdo 2003). The majority of this land is immediately adjacent to the *periférico* (Table 7.2).

To the west of Ejido Lerdo and the urbanized zone of the *municipio* are some 34 rural communities with a population of nearly 30,000 combined, many of which are *ejidos*. The failure of the *ejidatario* to persist in the neoliberal era is addressed in part by attempts to attract small manufacturing plants to the *ejidos* of rural Lerdo. Seven *ejidos* have attracted such plants over the past decade. Three are marble processing plants for use in furniture making. Four provide cutting and stitching activities for the denim apparel industry, and serve as ancillary branch plants for either US-or Mexican-owned blue jeans manufacturing plants located in Torreón or Gómez Palacio. The appearance of rural plants near the city of Lerdo is part of a trend to alleviate rural unemployment and rural-to-urban migration by relocating low wage manufacturing jobs in rural settlements themselves. This is quite common throughout La Laguna, as well as other rural areas of Mexico that are suffering poverty and the breakdown of traditional rural lifestyles and social networks (Van Dooren and Verkoren 2002; Esparza 2002b).

Globalization, Local Realities, and the Changing Suburban Landscape

The neoliberal landscape of Ciudad Lerdo is the incarnation of the economic and social dilemmas the locality faces. NAFTA and other facets of globalization force Lerdo to attract manufacturing plants to the former *ejido* lands of the city's western and northwestern fringe. In tandem with the decentralization, the State of Durango legally allows its cities to offer incentives to potential investors, including:

- Exemption for five years from real estate taxes and waste disposal fees
- Subsidies for infrastructure, such as water, drainage, and electricity (in the case of large plants, such infrastructure is provided by the local state. Lerdo has no such large plants)
- Exemption from payroll taxes for four years
- Subsidized training of the work force
- Assistance from the state in preparation of legal documents, paperwork, and procurement of an industrial site, building permits or licenses, and land use permits.

These incentives indicate the flexibility of local governance in appeasing would-be investors, owing to decentralization. However, since these incentives are universal throughout the state of Durango (Twin Plant News 2001), and are almost identical to those offered by other northern states (Rentería 2002), Ciudad Lerdo is at somewhat a disadvantage when compared to the adjoining cities of Gómez Palacio and Torreón. These two cities have well-developed industrial parks, more elaborate road and highway networks, direct rail access, and higher capacity electricity, water and drainage lines (Cervantes 2003). As a result, Torreón and Gómez Palacio have been able to diversify their respective manufacturing bases throughout additional fiscal incentives to include automobile parts, rudimentary electronic components such as wire harnesses, and the bottling of beer. Ciudad Lerdo lacks the rail, highway, and utilities infrastructure to take on these larger activities (Cervantes 2003).

Furthermore, as the state of Durango's third largest city, Ciudad Lerdo does not receive as much state funds as the state's capital city of Durango and its second largest city, Gómez Palacio (Galindo 2002). This is evident in the fact that the Office of Economic Promotion, a converted house four blocks from the central plaza, has no sign marking it. Under the decentralization, municipalities like Lerdo have three primary revenue sources:

1. Locally-generated property taxes.
2. Revenue-sharing or regular transfers of funds from the federal government to the states and from the states to the municipalities.
3. One-time fund transfers from the federal governments to the states for distribution to municipalities for special projects, including infrastructure improvement or social programs (Mendez 1998; Edmonds Elías 1997).

Since the state governments control the distribution of the funds, the mid-sized cities of the state, Durango and Gómez Palacio, receive most federal monies for infrastructure improvement and construction that is necessary to attract *maquiladoras* and other industries. For example, in 2002, Ciudad Lerdo received as a one-time federal funds transfer only 2.2 million Pesos (approximately $200,000 US) of federal funds, barely enough to finance the paving of seventeen blocks of streets (Siglo de Durango 2002). Meanwhile, the adjoining larger city of Gómez Palacio was able to improve two stretches of highway that connect four modest-sized industrial parks to rail yards and national highways that pass through the city. According to the *Directorial Maquiladora 2002* (2002 *Maquiladora* Directory) and the municipality's own directory of manufacturing plants (Municipio de Lerdo 2002), 48 plants with *maquiladora* status, primarily apparel-related, were located in the city of Gómez Palacio, while 12 were in the city of Ciudad Lerdo. Two such *maquiladoras* were located in the rural outskirts of the *municipio*. Of course, not all plants related to textiles and apparel are *maquiladoras*, as many are small operations that carry out ancillary activities to the *maquiladora* assembly plants, such as cutting and washing. The Municipio of Lerdo has nine of the latter, including the two plants located on rural *ejidos*. Moreover, eight small plants in the *municipio*, employing typically 50 or fewer employees each, process marble for furniture. Three of these are located on rural *ejidos* (Araya 2003) (Table 7.3).

Table 7.3: Manufacturing Plants in the Municipio of Lerdo, By Type, Number, Location Summer 2002

Type of Manufacturing Plant	Number of Activities	
	Urban Zone of Lerdo	Rural Ejidos
Maquiladoras, denim	12*	2
Non-*maquiladora* denim	7	2
Marble Processing and/or Furniture	5	3
Total Number of Plants	24	7

Sources: Municipio de Lerdo 2002; Mexico's Maquila Online Directory 2002; Araya 2003.
* One plant closed late in 2002, leaving 11 denim *maquiladoras* in the urban zone.

La Laguna had enjoyed some advantages in textile and apparel production until the end of the 1990s. However, the apparel production did not result in any significant creation of a supply chain involving the forward and backward economic linkages that define the Marshallian District. By the late 1990s, it was expected, and even falsely reported, that a supply chain was developing in the region that would link cotton production, the manufacturing of thread and denim, the cutting of cloth, the assembly of blue jeans, the washing of the jeans, and "finishing operations" (Gereffi and Martinez 2000; Gereffi and Bair 1998). In fact, Gereffi and Martinez (2000) went so far as to claim that in La Laguna, including Ciudad Lerdo,

> the boom of full package production has encouraged the establishment and expansion not only of sewing plants but also textile mills, cutting facilities, laundries, finishing operations and some design and pre-production capabilities.

This, according to La Laguna's regional director of the national chamber for textile and apparel manufacturing, is wishful thinking (Marcos 2002). In general, exported apparel involves the assembly of components that arrive from the US or from elsewhere in Mexico, and some limited finishing processes such as washing, attachment of labels, and the like (Spener and Capps 2001; Litchfield 2000). Laundries are the primary forward linkage of apparel manufacturing, and Lerdo has four of these that link to blue jean plants in La Laguna. The other operations, though they exist, represent less than one-fifth of the apparel manufacturing activity of La Laguna as a whole as well as Ciudad Lerdo, in particular, which suggests that inter-firm linkages remain poor throughout the region (Marcos 2002; Galindo 2002).

The advantages that northern Mexico originally possessed in textile and apparel production are vanishing, because the country's productive capacity in making cloth is largely obsolete (Conocer 2000). Under the terms of the World Trade Organization, member countries are no longer subject to quotas or tariffs (Spener and Capps 2001). This means that places like Ciudad Lerdo now have to compete with lower wage producers such as China and Central America. Still, while local officials strongly desire the transformation of La Laguna into a Marshallian apparel manufacturing district that could generate new manufacturing activities in Ciudad Lerdo and the region's other cities, they acknowledge that global competition and the downward pressures on production costs will make such a development difficult if not unlikely (Marcos 2002, Rentería 2002).

In all of 2002, Ciudad Lerdo gained no new *maquiladoras*, and in fact lost one to closure (Galindo 2002). The softened demand in the US for consumer goods owing to the struggling economy since 2001, coupled with the movement of apparel plants to lower wage countries such as China, Guatemala and Honduras, spelled trouble for La Laguna's employment profile, and Ciudad Lerdo was no exception. That same year, agricultural employment throughout La Laguna continued its downward trend, declining by 12.9% (Siglo de Torreón 2002).

Nonetheless, officials of the Department of Economic Promotion and the Department of Urban Development of the Municipality of Lerdo aspire to lure more manufacturing plants to the city's west side, where most of the city's eighteen remaining denim plants, including *maquiladoras* and small finishing operations, are scattered along the *periférico*. Their warehouse-like architecture and land-extensive layout, indicative of the drive to reap profits in the short term by investors, has changed the aesthetic character of the city, and is architecturally misaligned with its traditional narrow tree-lined streetscapes.

The assigning of so much land to manufacturing, in a sprawling manner, illustrates the high degree of flexibility of the planning process, and in particular the alteration of the *Plan Director Municipal*, a key factor in the creation of the landscape of globalization at the urban-rural fringe of Ciudad Lerdo. In accordance with Mexico's municipal decentralization, Ciudad Lerdo's urban planning, regulated by its *Plan Director Municipal*, is created at the local level under the Development Code of the State of Durango. Businessmen representing various interests meet with local government officials every two to four years to propose changes to the master plan, subject to approval by state-level officials in Durango. However, as I pointed out earlier, the approved plan can be altered at any time by municipal government to suit the desires of a domestic or international investor. A case in point is the use of municipal funds to promote a modest-sized industrial park owned by the current Municipal President, who oversees the budget for such promotions.

The rapid rural-to-urban migration spawned by the establishment of *maquiladoras* in La Laguna over the past two decades has created a housing shortage in Ciudad Lerdo, which in turn has changed the housing landscape. Makeshift informal housing is rapidly encroaching on the ex-*ejido* lands on the city's western side. Building materials include pallets, non-uniform planks of wood and concrete blocks for exterior walls, and corrugated aluminum or recycled plywood roofs. The roads on this side of town remain largely unpaved. This type of housing is typical throughout Northern Mexican suburban zones (Ward 1999). Private contractors construct formal housing, largely of concrete block or cement, on former *ejido* land at the city's southern edge. Much of it is financed by INFONAVIT, the federal public housing agency that subsidizes mortgages for salaried Mexicans and oversees social housing (Cervantes 2002; Yoder 2001). This housing is more like an extension of older residential areas, whereas the informal housing, like the manufacturing plants, are scattered in a non-contiguous fashion throughout the sprawling suburban zone.

Apart from this, decentralization has also changed the character of how social housing is constructed in Mexico over the past decade. Rather than construction of modern-style row housing projects by the state and direct sales of housing units by the state, INFONAVIT, the primary agency that oversees social housing, is primarily involved in providing mortgage subsidies, brokered through private real estate companies (Yoder 2001). INFONAVIT-financed projects in Lerdo, as elsewhere in small and mid-sized cities of northern Mexico, tend to be smaller in size and built by private developers one block at a time within or adjacent to existing neighborhoods. They are unlike the government-built mega-projects of the 1970s and 1980s that dominate suburban residential landscapes of Torreón, Saltillo, Monclova, Nuevo Laredo, and other mid-sized industrial cities of northern Mexico. Such housing does not keep up with demand, and informal housing is the only alternative for many families (Esparza 2002b).

CONCLUSION

This case study illustrates that the interrelatedness of urban form and global forces, produced through the compatible ideologies of neoliberalism and free trade, is quite different in the case of a small Mexican city and those of large cities of North America, Europe, or elsewhere. Ciudad Lerdo clearly holds a marginal place in the global semi-periphery. It lacks the financial institutions housed in such cities as New York, Los Angeles, Miami, London, or Mexico City, and the political clout of these large cities. Yet, like large cities across the globe, and mid-sized cities for that matter, investment decisions made from abroad ultimately impact land use in a small city such as Ciudad Lerdo, and produce somewhat similar decentralizing effects.

The neoliberal landscape of Ciudad Lerdo is the result of a conjuncture of national policy making that is generally turning small-scale Mexican farmers into urbanites scrambling for manufacturing jobs in cities, a new culture of local governance given the political decentralization, and unique conditions of local geography and economic history in a traditional stronghold region of cotton and corn production. The events that affect Ciudad Lerdo's contemporary urban geography are, thus, both urban and rural in nature. The PRI and PAN ideologies of promoting manufacturing for export forces agricultural policy favorable to small-scale farmers to take a back seat. As a result, nearly all of *Ejido* Lerdo is incapable of achieving the levels of productivity necessary to compete with agribusiness in the global marketplace. The results are the sale of *ejido* lands, which until 1989 served to hem in the original city, and the steady exodus of *ejidatarios* to cities of La Laguna and beyond. Furthermore, the promised expansion of the apparel industry to include a more complete production chain, and a favorable climate for additional manufacturing activities that this implies, has yet to materialize in the region. Nor has a stabilization of manufacturing, as apparel and textile-related employment has stagnated in the wake of employee layoffs in Ciudad Lerdo and the continuing threat of cheaper wages elsewhere in Latin America and in East Asia. Ciudad Lerdo's spatial growth is nonetheless unfettered, without any appreciable prospects for economic expansion. The unhealthy suburban form taking hold of Northern Mexico that is so wasteful of space and other resources, and clashes with traditional architecture, is becoming the defining element of the city's urban design, thus far without producing any appreciable benefits or upward social mobility.

The same sorts of sprawling landscape features are appearing at the urban-rural fringe of Torreón and Gómez Palacio, the two other major cities of La Comarca Lagunera. The region serves as a useful case study of land use patterns in regions characterized as satellite manufacturing platforms. Such regions are in many ways disposable, not only to the global economy, but in an aesthetic sense. Global money flows and consumer culture combine with local actors' efforts to capitalize on globalization in the creation of such regions. The never-ending search for low-wage regions of rudimentary manufacturing is a hallmark of late capitalism. By examining the kinds of landscapes they exhibit, we can better understand the social, environmental, and aesthetic implications of the drive to establish low-skill, low-wage manufacturing sites. By extension, we can better see how ideology is etched in the landscape, and we can better understand some of the different forms the capitalist landscape can assume in the global periphery.

In the long run, the continued reliance on denim production to save the economy of Ciudad Lerdo is most likely detrimental, given that the original advantage of Northern Mexico in the realm of textile and apparel production has evaporated under the weight of globalization. Likewise, the traditional town design of walking-scale streetscapes, and mixed land uses favorable to the formation of a sense of community in Lerdo will likely continue to give way to a sprawling, decentralized landscape presenting transportation, infrastructure, and other quality of life problems.

REFERENCES

Adams, J. S. 1970. Residential structure of Midwestern cities. *Annals of the Association of American Geographers* 60 (1): 37 – 62.

Amin, A., ed. 1995. *Post Fordism: A Reader.* Oxford, U.K.: Blackwell.

Araya, A. (Ing.) 2003. Assistant Director of Rural Development, Municipality of Lerdo. Telephone interview. Aug 14.

Arreola, J. 1994. *Coahuila: Monografía estatal* (2nd. edition). México, DF: Secretaria de Educación Pública.

Beauregard, R. 1995. Theorizing the global-local connection. In *World Cities in a World System,* eds. P. L. Knox and P. Taylor, 232 – 248. Cambridge: Cambridge University Press.

Brannon, J., and E. Baklanoff. 1987. *Agrarian Reform and Public Enterprise in Mexico: The Political Economy of Yucatan's Henequen Industry.* Tuscaloosa: University of Alabama Press.

Carlsen, L. 1997. The Corn Conundrum. *Business Mexico* 7 (7): 52 – 54.

Campolina Diniz, C., and M. Razavi 1999. Sao José dos Campos and Campinas: State-Anchored Dynamos. In *Second Tier Cities: Rapid Growth Beyond The Metropolis*, ed. A. Markusen, Y-S Lee, and S. DiGiovanni, 97 – 123. Minneapolis and London: University of Minnesota Press.

Campolina Diniz C., and F. B. T. Santos. 1999. Mana: vulnerability in satellite platform. In *Second Tier Cities: Rapid Growth Beyond The Metropolis*, ed. A. Markusen, Y-S Lee, and S. DiGiovanni, 9, 125 – 145. Minneapolis and London: University of Minnesota Press.

Cervantes, L. 2003. Personal Interview. January 7.

Conocer 2000. *Análisis sectorial de las industrias textil y del vestido*. Mexico, D.F.: Conocer (Consejo de normalización y certificación de competencia laboral) and Editorial.

Corona Paéz, S. A. 2002. Historia e identidad en la Comarca.Lagunera, *Acequias*, 20: 2 – 6.

Dear, M., and S. Flusty. 1998. Postmodern urbanism. *Annals of the Association of American Geographers* 88 (1): 50-72.

Edmonds, E. E. 1997. Fiscal decentralization and municipal governance in Mexico: The case of Chihuahua. Paper presented at the 1997 Annual Meeting of the Latin American Studies Association, Guadalajara, April 17 – 19.

El Financiero. 1998. Changes in land tenure promote investment, *El Financiero*. International Weekly Edition. June 14: 10.

El Siglo de Torreón. 2002. *Resumen Económico de la Comarca Lagunera*. Special Edition. January 1.

Esparza, H. 2002a. Los acuíferos, en manos de 15 familias, *Revista de Coahuila* 12 (129): 16 -- 19.

————. 2002b. El TLC: S impactos negativos en la región, *Revista de Coahuila* 13 (135): 14-17.

Estado de Durango. 1999. *Enciclopedia de los Municipios de México. Durango. Lerdo*. Centro Nacional de Desarrollo Municipal, Gobierno del Estado de Durango.

Expansión. 2001. Torreón-Gómez Palacio-Lerdo. De reconversión en reconversión. 38 (828): 78 – 83.

Feagin, J. 1987. The secondary circuit of capital: office construction in Ho- ton, Texas. *International Journal of Urban and Regional Research* 11(2): 172 – 191.

Galindo, L. 2002. Personal interview July 24.

Garloch, L. 1944. Agricultural economy of the Laguna region *Economic Geography* 20 (4): 296 – 304.

Gereffi, G. 1997. Global shifts, regional response: Can North America meet the full-package challenge? *Bobbin* 39 (November): 3, 16.

Gereffi, G., and J. Bair. 1998. U.S. companies eye NAFTA's Prize. *Bobbin* March. http://bobbin.com/.BOBBINGROPU/BOBINMAG/.

Gereffi, G., and M. Martinez 2000. Torreón's Blue Jeans Boom: Exploring La Laguna's Full Package Solution. *Bobbin* (April).
   http://www.bobbin.com/BOBBINGROUP/BOBBINMAG/apr00/
Goldsmith, W. W. 1997. The metropolis and globalization: The dialectics of racial discrimination, deregulation, and urban form. *American Behavioral Scientist* 41 (3): 99 – 310.
Grant, R., and J. Nijman. 2002. Globalization and the corporate geography of cities in the Less-Developed World, *Annals of the Association of American Geographers* 92 (2): 320 – 340.
Hart, J. M. 1986. Agrarian Reform. In *Twentieth-Century Mexico,* ed. W. Dirk Raat and W. H. Beezley, 6-16. Lincoln, NE and London: University of Nebraska Press.
Harvey, D. 1978. The urban process under capitalism. *International Journal of Urban and Regional Research* 2 (1): 101 – 131.
———. 1985. *The Urbanisation of Capital.* Oxford: Blackwell.
Herbert, D., and C. Thomas. 1997. *Cities in Space; City as Place.* London: David Fulton.
INEGI. 2001. *Cuaderno Estadístico Municipal. Edición 2001, Lerdo, Durango.* Aguascalientes: INEGI (Instituto Nacional de Estadística Geografía e Informática).
———. 1993. *Cuaderno Estadístico Municipal. Edición 1993, Lerdo, Durango.* Aguascalientes: INEGI.
Joseph, G. M. 1982. *Revolution from Without: Yucatan, Mexico, and the United States, 1880-1924.* Cambridge: Cambridge University Press.
Joseph, G., and A. Wells. 1982. Corporate control of a monocrop economy: International Harvester and Yucatan's Henequen industry during the porfiriato. *Latin American Research Review* 17 (1): 69 – 99.
Krauze, E. 1995. *General Misionero. Lázaro Cárdenas.* México, D.F.: Fondo de Cultura Económica.
Leitner, H. 1990. Cities in pursuit of economic growth: The local state as entrepreneur. *Political Geography Quarterly* 1 (2): 146 – 170.
Ley, D. 1987. Style of the times: liberal and neo-conservative landscapes in inner Vancouver. *Journal of Historical Geography* 13 (1): 40 – 56.
Litchfield, G. 2000. Survey Mexico: If not for NAFTA, when? *The Economist* M7-M9. October 28.
Maquila Directory. 2002. Mexico's Maquila Online Directory.
   http://www.maquiladirectory.com/maquila/maquiladirectory256.pdf.
Marcos, A. J. 2002. Personal interview. July 29.
Markusen, A. 1999a. Four structures for second tier cities. In *Second Tier Cities: Rapid Growth Beyond the Metropolis*, ed. A. Markusen, Y.-S. Lee, and S. DiGiovanna, 21 – 41. Minneapolis and London: University of Minnesota Press.

————. 1999b. Studying regions by studying firms. In *Second Tier Cities: Rapid Growth Beyond the Metropolis*, ed. A. Markusen, Y.-S. Lee, and S. DiGiovanna, 43 – 63. Minneapolis and London: University of Minnesota Press.

Markusen, A., and S. DiGiovanna. 1999. Comprehending fast-growing regions. In *Second Tier Cities: Rapid Growth Beyond the Metropolis*, ed. A. Markusen, Y.-S. Lee and S. DiGiovanna, 3 – 19. Minneapolis and London: University of Minnesota Press.

Martin, R. 1994. Stateless monies, global financial integration and national economic autonomy: The end of geography? In *Money, Power and Space*, ed. S. Corbridge, R. Martin, and N. Thrift, 253 – 278. Oxford: Blackwell.

Méndez, J. L. 1998. Descentralización y Administración del desarrollo urbano local. En *Reunón sobre ciudades Mexicanas ante el nuevo milen*, ed. SEDESOL (Secretaría de Desarrollo Social), 127 – 137. Mesa Temática 8, México, DF: SEDESOL El Colegio de México.

Moreno, J. 2002. Land and loss: corn farmers in Mexico say NAFTA is driving them out of business. *Houston Chronicle*. October 20.

Municipio de Lerdo. 2003. Unpublished data. Departamento de Catastro Municipal (Municipal Cadastral Department).

————. 2002. Directorio de Empresas en Lerdo, Dgo. (Directory of Manufacturing Plants in Lerdo, Durango). Unpublished data.

Nijman, J. 2000. The paradigmatic city. *Annals of the Association of American Geographers* 90(1): 135 – 145.

Porfirio Hernández, A.1975. *¿La explotación colectiva en la Comarca Langunera es un fracaso?* México, D.F.: B. Costa-Amic Editor.

Public Citizen. 2001. *Down on the Farm: NAFTA's Seven-Years War on Farmers and Ranchers in the US., Canada and Mexico*. Washington, DC: Public Citizen's Global Trade Watch. (June).

Ramos, E. T. 2003. Personal interview. January 11.

Rea Becerra, R. T. 2002. La economía regional atrapada por los procesos de globalización. *Acequias* 20 (Summer): 7 – 11.

Reforma. 2002. El campo, a punto del colapso. *Reforma*. 13 October. (By Claudia Salazar, Ivonne Melgar, and Leonardo Valero).

Rentería, A. 2002. Personal interview July 24.

Rodríguez, V. E. 1997. *Decentralization in Mexico: From Reforma Municipal to Solidaridad to Nuevo Federalismo*. Boulder, CO: Westview Press.

Rowland, A. M. 1999. Planeación y gesión de pequñas ciudades: diferencias de grado o diferencias cualitativas? *Ciudades* 42 (April-June): 34 – 38.

Santos Valdes, J. 1973. *Matamoros. Ciudad Lagunera*. Mexico City: Editora y Distribuidora Nacional de Publicaciones, S. de R.L.

Scott, A., and M. Storper. 1986. *Production, Work, Territory*. London: Allen and Unwin.

Siglo de Durango. 2002. Pavimentarán 17 mil metros en Cd. Lerdo. May 5. http://www.elsiglodurango.com.mx/comunidad.nID/9155.

Siglo de Torreón. 2002. *Resumen Económico de la Comarca Lagunera, 2001.* Special Edition. January 1.

Spener, D., and R. Capps. 2001. North American free trade and changes in the nativity of the garment industry workforce in the United States. *International Journal of Urban and Regional Research* 25 (2): 301 – 326.

Thomson, M. 1977. *Great Cities and their Traffic.* Harmondsworth, U.K: Penguin.

Tomas, F. 2000. Ciudades medias, descentralización y globalización en América Latina. *Anuario de Espacios Urbanos* 7: 23-30.

Twin Plant News. 2001. Durango, *Twin Plant News* (November): 40.

Van Dooren, R., and O. Verkoren 2002 Transformación rural de La Laguna. *Couvades* 54 (April-June): 46 – 54.

Villegas, M. 2003. Personal interview. January 9.

Ward, P. 1999. *Colonies and Public Policy in Texas and Mexico: Urbanization by Stealth.* Austin: University of Texas Press.

Warf, B. 1988. Regional transformation, everyday life, and Pacific Northwest lumber production. *Annals of the Association of American Geographers* 78 (2): 326 – 346.

Yoder, M. 1993. The Latin American plantation economy and the World-economy: The case of the Yucatecan henequen industry, *Review* 16 (3): 319 – 337.

———. 2000. Northeast Mexico in the global economy: The contemporary urban geographies of three mid-sized cities. In *Working Paper College of Arts and Humanities,* ed. J. Thompson. Texas A&M International University, Aldo Tatangelo Annual Lecture, College of Arts and Humanities.

———. 2001. Social housing in northeastern Mexico: aesthetics, the ideology of subsidy, and the personalization of living space, *Urbana* VI (1) (Fall).

8

The Urban Corona Effect and Retail Change in Small Cities: The Case of Central Iowa

Thomas L. Bell and Margaret M. Gripshover
University of Tennessee, Knoxville

INTRODUCTION

The retail landscape of the United States has undergone tremendous change in the past few decades. Most geographic studies of retail change have focused on the rapid diffusion of particular retail chains (Graff 1998; Graff and Ashton 1994; Laulajainen 1987; Laulajainen 1988) or the emergence of new retail forms such as the power center and/or big box retailers such as Home Depot or Circuit City (Hartshorn 1992). Except for allusions to the rural and small town origins of the Wal-Mart chain, few of these studies have looked at retailing changes in small cities.

The relatively few studies that have focused on small cities began their search for explanations of retail change with an examination of relative location: the proximity of small cities to larger central places (Hodge 1965; Borchert and Adams 1963; Hart and Salisbury 1965; Bell 1973). The classic research of Borchert and Adams on retailing within small cities of the upper Middle West and Great Plains states has been updated in recent years by Anding, et al (1990) and Casey (1999).

As the focus of retail studies in geography shifted to "big-box" retailers like Wal-Mart and their impact on retail structure in cities, geographers and economists parted company in their approaches. In general, geographers have focused on phenomena such as the reverse hierarchical diffusion of Wal-Mart that disrupted the standard model of business location expansion theretofore (Graff 1998; Graff and Ashton 1994; Laulajainen 1987; Laulajainen 1988) while economists have focused on the revenue impact on the city following the arrival of Wal-Mart, without much attention to relative location of cities within which these developments occur (see, for example, Stone and Artz 1999a).

This chapter adds to the geographic literature on retailing by examining the changing retail landscape in small towns/cities in America. It builds on Bell's (1973) study to examine the changes that have occurred in retailing in central Iowa from 1973 to 2003. In particular, it examines several factors affecting the changing retail landscape in small cities in central Iowa including the importance of political status, relative location to Des Moines, proximity to interchanges of the Interstate highway system, and declining agricultural activities in the region. Several hypotheses relating to these factors are investigated. The impact of Des Moines, the state capital and largest city in Iowa, on the retail activities in the small towns is particularly emphasized. It is argued that there is a causal relationship between Des Moines's position as a central place and retail viability of small towns and cities in central Iowa. We hypothesize that the closer the small city or town is to Des Moines, the less viable is the small city's retail sector. We also posit that the relationship between Des Moines and the smaller central places around it can be likened to the behavior of the sun's corona (outer atmosphere) within our solar system. As alternating periods of low and high sunspot activity cause streamers to break out through the sun's corona to negatively affect atmospheric features of planets such as Earth, so does the high retail concentration in Des Moines negatively impact retail fortunes of small cities in central Iowa. We assert that this phenomenon, which could be aptly referred to as the "urban corona effect", could hold the key to explaining much of what has occurred in the retail landscape in central Iowa.

The chapter is organized into four sections. In the next section, we review perspectives on retail change in small cities, within the context of central place ordering principles. Next, we present empirical evidence to show the changes that have occurred in retailing in central Iowa from 1973 to 2003. We next investigate the factors that have caused this and, finally, we draw out implications for small cities elsewhere and for future research.

PERSPECTIVES ON CHANGING RETAIL LANDSCAPE IN SMALL CITIES

When one looks for an explanation of retail decline in small cities these days, there is often a big yellow smiley face involved. Much ado have been made in the literature, both academic and popular, about the chilling effect that Wal-Mart and other big-box retailers have had upon smaller, often locally owned, businesses (Beaumont 1997a; Beaumont 1997b; Humstone and Muller 1997; Marx and Salant 1996; Shils 1997; Stone 1995). In the popular literature there is a seemingly endless variety of articles that focus on Wal-Mart and its impacts on the local retail landscape. Our consumer society seems to have a love-hate relationship with the world's largest retailer. The average price that consumers pay for a market basket of basic goods from Wal-Mart is, no doubt, cheaper than that same market basket of goods obtained from the smaller, often independent merchants that the retailing giant may have driven out of business. One trade off is that often fewer and lower paying jobs are available in the retail and service sectors after the construction of a Wal-Mart store than was the case before the Wal-Mart located in the town (see, for example, Hiltzik 2004; Levine 2003; McKay 2004; Useem 2003; Wood 2003).[1]

The normal pattern for retail store expansion has been to capture large markets first and, if successful, filter down the urban hierarchy to smaller towns and more rural environments. However, Wal-Mart has reversed this standard business location model having its origins (in 1962) in rural Arkansas and growing subsequently by dominating such rural and small town environments before moving into the larger suburban and now, even central city, locations. Wal-Mart, in essence, turned the standard business location expansion model on its head (Graff 1998; Graff and Ashton 1994; Laulajainen 1987; Laulajainen 1988). Wal-Mart has made the transition from small to large markets with tremendous success although they are currently facing serious problems expanding further into certain markets such as California and Germany overseas.

Economists, on the other hand, have more often tried to quantify the loss of jobs and the retail leakage caused by Wal-Mart as it enters previously uncharted territory. Using Iowa as his testing ground, economist Kenneth Stone and his associate Georgeanne Artz have, by their own admission, written more about small town retail and service changes caused by the incursion of Wal-Mart than any other scholars (Stone and Artz 1999a; Stone and Artz 1999b; Stone and Artz 1999c). Their research is extremely relevant as background for the present research. They have been, however, more concerned about county-level structural adjustment in the retailing and service sectors than they have been about the adjustment of individual places. When they have considered towns *per se*, they have not paid heed to the location of those towns relative to each other or to larger central places such as the local county seat or Des Moines.

Geographic studies of retailing generally draw their inspiration, if not their concepts and testable hypotheses, to the two versions of central place theory posited first by Christaller (1966), and later by Lösch (1954). Central place theory attempted to explain theoretically the size and distribution of settlements, both large and small, within an economic landscape. Christaller's version of the theory might be said to be descriptive as it was based on his empirical observation of the size and spacing of settlements within his study area in

Germany. On the other hand, Loch's version of the theory was normative; a discussion of what the pattern of settlements should look like if consumer welfare were maximized and excess entrepreneurial profits were kept to a minimum.[2]

One of the lynchpin concepts in central place theory is the location of a settlement relative to competing centers of equal or larger size. The hexagonal arrangement of settlements deduced from the postulates of classical central place theory is one consequence of spatial competition among central places over a flat, homogeneous (i.e., isotropic) plain (Rushton 1971).

One would not expect such a regular arrangement of places in real world economic landscapes, but Hodge (1965) noted the effects of spatial competition among central places in southern Saskatchewan. Specifically, he defined a "zone of functional attrition" that extended up to twenty-five miles away from the larger towns and cities in southern Saskatchewan. Within this zone, smaller villages and hamlets may have been increasing in population, but they were losing their central place viability for shopping goods. Bell (1973) noted the same phenomenon in central Iowa. Other studies including Borchert and Adams (1963), Hart and Salisbury (1965), Hart et al. (1968), Anding et al. (1990), and Casey (1999) have all demonstrated the depressing effect on retail viability that nearby larger central places have on their smaller counterparts.

Now, in this present era of big-box retailing, has the central place viability of small cities and towns located within a reasonable commuting range of a much larger central place been hurt? If so, what are the main factors that have caused this decreased retail viability and what lessons can we learn from the spatial competition among small cities?

METHODOLOGY

We chose an eight county study area in central Iowa to investigate these questions. The counties that are wholly or partially within the defined study area include Boone, Story, Dallas, Polk, Jasper, Madison, Warren, and Marion (Figure 8.1). Within the study area are 49 central places including Des Moines itself that were purveyors of at least some retail and/or service activities in 2003. Table 8.1 presents a list of those places, their counties of location, and their 2000 population (Bureau of the Census 2002). Some of these places are too small to be called cities, by US definition. However, for the sake of simplicity, we will refer to these places as either small towns or cities. The table also includes two variables that require a bit of explanation. The first is an ordinal measure of the degree of retail viability of each central place. That measure can vary between the value of –2 and +2 for the 48 extant central places. An 'X' appears in that column for the 14 small towns that were viable central places in 1973 but which were nonviable in 2003. A value of +2 would indicate that the town was performing better than average for a place of its size in the state of Iowa over two

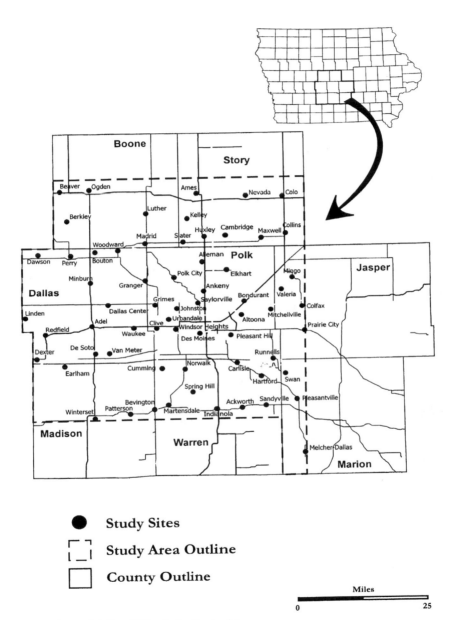

Figure 8.1 Retail Trade in Central Iowa

Table 8.1 Measures Related to Retail Viability in Central Iowa Towns

Place	County	Retail Viability	% Increase Long Commute '90-'00	Population 2000
Ackworth	Warren	X	500	85
Adel	Dallas	-2	55	3,435
Altoona	Polk	-2	97	10,849
Ankeny	Polk	-2	66	27,117
Berkley	Boone	X	100	24
Bevington	Madison	X	600	58
Bondurant	Polk	-2	43	1,846
Bouton	Dallas	2	200	136
Cambridge	Story	-2	8	819
Carlisle	Warren	-2	-34	3,497
Clive	Polk	1	183	12,855
Colfax	Jasper	1	6	2,223
Collins	Story	-2	29	499
Colo	Story	-2	9	868
Cumming	Warren	2	0	162
Dallas Center	Dallas	-2	32	1,595
Dawson	Dallas	-2	150	155
Desoto	Dallas	X	28	1,009
Dexter	Dallas	X	300	689
Earlham	Madison	2	51	1,298
Elkhart	Polk	2	58	362
Granger	Dallas	2	21	583
Grimes	Polk	-2	91	5,098
Hartford	Warren	-2	56	759
Huxley	Story	-2	16	2,316
Indianola	Warren	-2	3	12,998
Johnston	Polk	-2	175	8,649
Kelley	Story	X	300	300
Linden	Dallas	X	200	226
Luther	Boone	X	-57	158
Madrid	Boone	-2	60	2,418
Martensdale	Warren	2	0	467
Maxwell	Story	-2	67	807

Table 8.1 Continued

Place	County	Retail Viability	% Increase Long Commute '90-'00	Population 2000
Melcher-Dallas	Marion	-2	72	1,298
Minburn	Dallas	2	300	391
Mingo	Jasper	-2	50	269
Mitchellville	Polk	-2	18	2,037
Norwalk	Warren	-2	39	6,884
Patterson	Madison	X	-50	126
Perry	Dallas	-2	140	7,633
Pleasant Hill	Polk	-2	78	5,070
Pleasantville	Marion	-2	-19	1,537
Polk City	Polk	-2	33	2,344
Prairie City	Jasper	2	175	1,365
Redfield	Dallas	-2	375	833
Runnells	Polk	2	14	352
Sandyville	Warren	X	0	61
Sheldahl	Boone	X	38	336
Slater	Story	2	19	1,306
Spring Hill	Warren	X	150	92
Swan	Marion	X	-400	121
Urbandale	Polk	-2	2	29,072
Valeria	Jasper	X	-55	62
Van Meter	Dallas	2	-24	866
Waukee	Dallas	-2	273	5,126
West Des Moines	Polk	-2	168	46,403
Windsor Heights	Polk	1	214	4,891
Winterset	Madison	2	24	4,768
Woodward	Dallas	-2	64	1,200

measured time periods (1996 and 2000). In a similar manner a score of -2 would be assigned to a town that performed worse than expected for a town of its size both time periods. The fourth column of Table 8.1 is derived from census data on commuting patterns and indicates the increase (decrease) in the percentage of persons taking more than 29 minutes to commute to work. The reason for the inclusion of the retail viability and commuting variables will become clear as the chapter progresses.

Our selection of the study area was based on two main factors. First, we wanted to know what changes have occurred in the area's retail since Bell's (1973) study. So we chose the same area that he had studied. Second, the eight-county area is dominated by Polk County, the largest urban county in Iowa. The county contains the state capital of Des Moines, which is the highest order (i.e., largest and most important) central place in Iowa. The Des Moines metropolitan area is expanding mainly in a western and southern direction. The largest regional malls and employment centers are located on the western and southern sides of the city. Thus, if there was anywhere in Iowa that the pattern of the retail and service hemorrhaging from the smaller contiguous counties in the study area would conform to both classical central place principles and the conceptual basis of spatial interaction models, it would be in this area. For example, one would expect that the retail viability of small towns and suburbs to the west and south of Des Moines would be imperiled by retail expansion of the city. One might also assume that the smaller towns to the east and north should be able to remain more viable from a retailing perspective as their trade area hinterlands are allowed to expand to a greater degree in the path of least resistance (Zipf 1949). Similarly, if the retailing and service sector of Des Moines is differentially expanding to the south and west, we would expect a greater zone of functional attrition, to use Hodge's (1965) term, in the southerly and westerly directions (i.e. a directional bias). Finally, we would also expect counties contiguous to Polk County to the north and east to demonstrate less retail leakage to Polk County, and thus presumably to Des Moines, than do their southerly and westerly counterparts.

We used three measures to investigate the extent of retail change in the study area. The first measure was county retail sales surplus or leakage. The second was the number of central places that existed in 1973 compared to that of 2003. The third measure was retail sales expectations. Expected retail sales both at the county (i.e., regional) level and within the individual central places in the study area were calculated using a measure developed by Iowa State economists Kenneth Stone and Georgeanne Artz (Stone and Artz 1999d). This method is used to estimate expected retail and service sales according to the following formula:

Expected (Potential) Sales = Town Population x Average Pull Factor x Average per Capita Expenditure x Index of Income.

The average per capita expenditure is obtained from the annual Iowa Retail Sales and Use Tax Report compiled by the Iowa Department of Revenue and Finance from state sales tax returns. The income index data come from *Survey of Buying Power*, published by *Sales and Marketing Management* Magazine updated annually from census baseline data. Market Pull Factors are a type of location quotient based on the average expenditure by Iowans for various goods and services. A value of 1.07 in a town would, for example, indicate that it was seven percent above the state average for the purchase of goods or services in that particular product category. Generally speaking, pull factors are a positive function of population size.

Suppose we wanted to calculate the potential sales for eating and drinking establishments in a town with a population of 3,500 in a county with an 87% index of income. The average pull factor for this merchandise group in this size town is 1.11, and average annual per capita expenditure for Iowans in this category is about $741. Therefore:

Expected Sales = 3,500 x 1.11 x $741 x 0.87 = $2,504, 543

Our quantitative analysis of sales expectations supported some aspects of classical central place theory and spatial interaction models, but not entirely so. In order to gain more insights in what was actually happening on the ground, we undertook a field investigation of the cities in the study area conducted over two "field" seasons—2002 and 2003.[3] In the following sections we will first present the evidence of the changing retail landscape in the study area, and investigate the extent to which the changes conform and not conform to these general expectations.

RETAIL CHANGE IN CENTRAL IOWA

The county retail sales showed that only Polk County, the county in which Des Moines is located had a sales surplus (45%). All the remaining seven counties posted leakages ranging from as low as -1.4% for Story to as high as 62.5% for Warren County. In general, counties to the south and west of Polk County showed the greatest degree of sales leakage (presumably to Polk County and Des Moines) in keeping with expectations derived from classical spatial interaction and hinterland studies (see for example Reilly 1931, McKenzie 1933, Green 1955). With respect to the number of central places, in the 1960s there were 59 towns in the eight-county study area that could be considered central places (i.e., having one or more central retail and/or service functions). By 2003, that number had dwindled to 45 in the same study area.

In a departure from the scale at which Stone and Artz normally calculate retail sales expectations, we applied their formula at the scale of the individual central places in the region for two time periods for which data were available— 1996 and 2000.[4] There were few changes in that four-year period so only the 2000 map of retail sales expectations (i.e., retail viability) is shown (Figure 8.2).

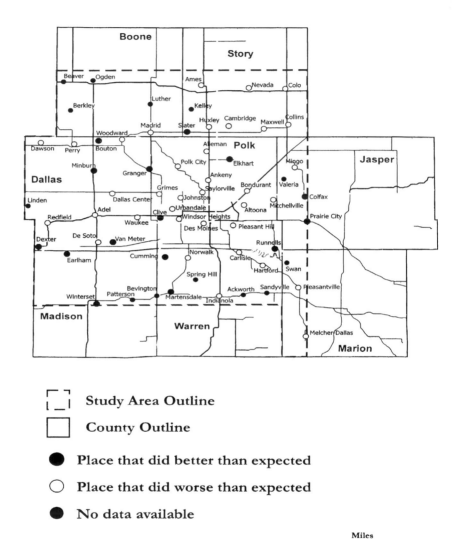

Study Area Outline

County Outline

● Place that did better than expected

○ Place that did worse than expected

● No data available

Miles

0   25

Figure 8.2 Total Retail Sales for 2000

Of the 14 small cities that met or exceeded their expected sales in 2000 (from among the total of 45 small cities in the study area), only one, Clive, a relatively affluent suburb of Des Moines in Polk County, exceeded retail expectations for a city of its size in 2000, but not in 1996. There were no places that exceeded their sales expectations in 1996 that did not also exceed them in 2000. We might conclude, therefore, that the pattern of retail viability displayed in Figure 8.2 has become relatively stable since the mid 1990s.

In slow-growing Boone County, only five small places in the southern half of the County closest to rapidly growing Dallas County and Polk County were included and all were faring poorly as retail centers. In rapidly growing Dallas County, Lösch's (1954) concept of the "tyranny of space" seemed *a propos*. In Lösch's normative version of central place theory, he tried to eliminate situations that bothered him about real economic landscapes, namely that entrepreneurs located in isolated towns facing little or no competition, were able to gouge their customers. That is, because of the tyranny of space, such disadvantaged customers were charged higher prices for the goods they purchased than customers buying their goods from comparable retail outlets in cities facing more competitive pressures. Four small central places that were the most isolated from larger centers in Dallas County (Bouton, Granger, Minburn and Van Meter) displayed better-than-expected retail sales in both 1996 and 2000. Only the western townships of Jasper County were included in the study area and the two largest and most accessible places (i.e., Colfax and Prairie City) exceeded their expected retail sales in 2000 lending credence to the importance of relative location to retail viability. In Madison County, two retail centers exceeded expected retail sales. Winterset, the county seat and a tourist destination did well, as did Earlham, a much smaller place located near an Interstate highway interchange. In Polk County, there were, in 2002, five Wal-Marts, three in Des Moines proper including one Sam's Club and one Supercenter and two other Supercenters, one each in Ankeny and Altoona. The only town near Des Moines that was holding its own from a retailing standpoint was Clive, with upscale shopping opportunities located in the main path of Des Moines's growth. Elkhart and Runnells, much smaller and more isolated places, were also able to exceed retail expectations. The southernmost townships in Story County contained only one small place (Slater) capable of exceeding retail expectations perhaps because of its relative isolation. Finally, Warren County had three towns (Ackworth, Sandyville, and Spring Hill) that ceased to function as viable central places between the 1970s and 2003. Two other small places (Cumming and Martensdale) were able to exceed retail expectations largely as a result of their accessibility to major highways. In addition, neither place showed an increase in long-distance commuting among its gainfully employed populations.

While our quantitative analysis of sales expectations supported some aspects of central place interaction models, some questions still remained unanswered. For example, the expected directional bias of functional attrition caused by the southerly and westerly expansion of Des Moines was more evident at the county scale of analysis than at the level of the individual town. Also, relative location to the Interstate highway network seemed to be a much greater indicator of retail viability in 2003 than it was thirty years earlier. In order to gain more insights in what was actually happening on the ground, we undertook a field investigation of the cities in the study area conducted over two "field" seasons—2002 and 2003.

Retail District Blowout and "Boutiquization"

We expected to find the individual central places located in counties to the north and east of Des Moines to be more viable than those to the south and west. However, our field observations in, for example, the town of Bondurant, a small central place in Polk County to the north and east of Des Moines, revealed a business district considerably less prosperous than central place principles would have predicted. If Bondurant were located in the Old West, we imagined tumbleweeds rolling down the middle of Main Street!

In stark contrast to Bondurant, the county seat towns of Indianola and Winterset to the south and west of Des Moines were pleasant surprises.[5] Our quantitative analysis revealed that retail sales in Indianola in both 1996 and 2000 were below what would be expected of a town of its size and locational pull, so Indianola may be on the right path to viability, but still has a way to go. Winterset, however, demonstrated greater than expected retail sales in both 1996 and 2000 vis-à-vis comparably sized towns throughout the state. Winterset had the added benefit of being a tourism destination.[6]

Surprising to us was the proliferation of non-franchised coffee houses in an area so far from the coffee culture hearth of Seattle. The threshold for these ubiquitous landscape features appears to be almost as low as for the tanning parlor and the video rental store. Similarly, if there were clothing stores located in the downtown shopping district at all, they were, more often than not, second-hand consignment shops or those specializing in vintage clothing. This lack of retail diversity led us to develop the following rule of thumb to test Main Street retail shopping viability: Can you find an outfit for Saturday night in the shopping district? The answer in many of these towns is, sadly, 'no.' In most cases, you would be hard-pressed to outfit yourself for any occasion—work or play.

What has replaced higher order shopping goods in these places might be called the "boutiquization" of small-town retailing. Vacant stores are common. Even more to the point is the adaptive reuse of retail space into service and office functions. Former hardware stores, grocers, clothing stores, appliance stores and other high order shopping goods have been replaced by antique stores and boutiques specializing in the type of discretionary paraphernalia that one normally associates with tourist towns. Even the ubiquitous feed store has fallen to this trend, a sign of the restructuring of the agricultural economy in central Iowa. These land use changes appear to be the result of the acts of desperate landlords eager to fill vacant retail space with something: anything. These stores seem oriented to tourists rather than supplying the needs of the local resident population.

The decline of the retail core of small cities or towns in the study area is reinforced by a cursory examination of the websites in the study area obtained through the Iowa League of Cities (www.iowaleague.org). We perused the websites of the 13 towns of 3,000 or greater population shown in Table 8.1 for which data on specific retail categories of sales tax receipts could be obtained.[7] Eleven of the 13 had developed their own website. One of those missing was, surprisingly, Winterset, although there was a link to the Madison County Chamber of Commerce's website. Sadly, many of these towns seem to have given up on even mentioning Main Street retailing touting instead: 1) their relative accessibility to Des Moines; 2) their proximity to recreational opportunities; or 3) the amenities of suburban living. Only a few mentioned or included photographs of their downtown area and some of these were historic rather than contemporary.

Whereas county seat towns in the study area seem unable to retain a traditional retail mix, they are proving to be a magnet for personal and professional services. One is more likely to find a dentist or a branch of Edward Jones investments than a retail store specializing in high-order retail goods. The threshold for stock brokerage houses seemed to us surprisingly low. In fact, consumer services of all kinds appear to be displacing or simply replacing retailing from the commercial centers of the county seat towns of central Iowa and presumably elsewhere in the state. Financial services, lawyers' offices and health practitioners seem to dominate this service-based landscape. While these services are undoubtedly welcomed and frequented by local residents, land use theory would suggest that such services should not be able to bid rents high enough for such accessible land under normal circumstances (Alonso 1964). We think that their presence is evidence of a diminution of the land value gradient to the point where more extensive land uses such as services can finally afford the rents that would have precluded their central location a few decades previously. The land value gradient of small cities or towns forced such services to the periphery of the downtown three decades ago, but now these services are in-filling the vacuum left by departing retail stores.

FACTORS AFFECTING RETAIL CHANGE IN CENTRAL IOWA

In addition to the factors related to classic central place theory that we examined in a previous section, we discuss here four others that we posit as important based on our field investigation. These factors include: 1) the importance of political status; 2) location relative to the primary and Interstate highway system; 3) the decline of agriculture and concomitant necessity of long-distance commuting, and 4) the" urban corona effect" of Des Moines on the study area.

The Importance of Political Status and Relative Location

In the previous section we argued that Winterset and, to a lesser extent, Indianola, have a legitimate claim to the tourist dollar. Both are county seat towns, and county seats throughout the study area appeared as if they were also trying to attract tourist populations. Designation as a county seat is important to the viability of towns in the Middle West. Their remarkably uniform spacing may be, as Berry (1967) has pointed out, the equilibrium outcome of an historical process of spatial competition. County seat status confers to the town so designated an initial advantage that is difficult for nearby competitors to overcome. Even if the competitor is initially comparable in size and central place offerings, the initial advantage afforded the county seat is often amplified in a positive feedback mechanism (Myrdal 1957). The political status of the county seat creates a built-in economic advantage. Ever since the horse-and-buggy era, residents of the county had to conduct their official business affairs in the county seat. While they were in the county seat they would often shop for higher order shopping goods and services not generally available in other central places thus further exacerbating the initial advantage the county seat enjoyed over its non-county seat competitors. Furthermore, if the competitor was located too close to the county seat, in time that town could even cease to exist as a viable central place because of this circular and cumulative causation (i.e., positive feedback) process. In our field study we found only one non-county seat town that was more viable than its respective county seat and that was Perry (2000 population 7,633), northwest of Des Moines. We will now examine the factors that account for this special case.

The Special Case of Perry, Iowa

Perry was nearly twice the size and seemingly more prosperous than Adel, the county seat of Dallas County. Overall, however, Perry is still a declining central place that was much more vital thirty years ago than it is today. If only purely economic factors were at work, because of its relative location, Perry should be negatively impacted by the westerly direction of Des Moines's growth. Perry's retail sector has, however, been bolstered by two factors that would be difficult to incorporate into an economically driven location model: 1) the serendipitous and unexpected infusion of investment capital by a former resident; and 2) a large influx of Latinos into the town because of a nearby meat processing plant and the subsequent changes to the retail and commercial sector in response to this in-migration. Each will be considered in turn.

Perry was a railroad town and, like many other such towns at the beginning of the twentieth century, it contained a railroad hotel. Built in 1913, the Hotel Pattee was an architectural gem of the Arts and Crafts design period. By the

1960s, the Hotel was dilapidated and had been converted into low-income apartments. In the 1980s a former resident of Perry, Roberta Green Ahmanson and her husband Howard, decided to buy the hotel and to renovate it. The purchase price for the multistoried hotel that takes up almost a full city block was $38,000. Over the next several years, Ms. Ahmanson and her husband poured in over $12 million dollars to have it restored to the way that it looked in 1913. [8]

It is unclear whether the Hotel will ever be able to recoup the initial investment that these wealthy patrons of the town have made, but it is doubtful that they really care. It is an example of spectacular philanthropy that would be seemingly impossible to predict with a deterministic model. Most recently, Ms. Ahmanson was able to convince television personality Pat Sajak, with whom she serves on a charity board, to help dedicate "Hometown Perry, Iowa", a new museum project that "tells the story of small Midwestern towns and the immigrants who settled them" (Associated Press 2004).[9]

The influx of a large Latino population in the area has changed the look of the downtown area in Perry. The town is now more than 25% Hispanic (Bureau of the Census 2002). There is even a Spanish language chapter of Alcoholics Anonymous now available in the downtown area! The influx of this population has kept the downtown area of Perry viable, but not without a lot of changes in the nature of the retail space. There are now *tiendas* and *mercados* where there were previously businesses reflecting the majority native white population.

The Importance of Proximity to the Interstate System

To investigate the importance of relative location and to the Interstate System, we examined closely the pattern of those cities and towns that did or did not meet total retail sales expectations in 2000 (Figure 8.2). As can be seen from the map of these data, location relative to Des Moines and to the Interstate and US Highway system seems to play an important role in retail viability. Proximity to Des Moines had a deleterious effect on expected retail sales regardless of accessibility. Some of Des Moines's contiguous incorporated suburbs (e.g., Johnston, Urbandale) displayed less than expected retail sales even though they were located on Interstate or primary highways with high traffic volumes. And those places that are quite close to Des Moines such as Grimes or Waukee failed, for the most part, to meet their retail sales forecast.

Once we go beyond that immediate attrition zone surrounding Des Moines though, central place viability seems to be based more on relative access to the Interstate and major highway system than to distance per se. Bell (1973) found that Perry, Winterset, and Indianola were able to carve out a "tyranny of space" thirty years ago (Lösch 1954). To a certain extent their relative distance from Des Moines and the county seat status of the latter two places still preserves the viability of their surrounding local retail hinterland. However, if Lösch's tyranny of space is still a valid concept in the early 21st century, we would expect that central places off the beaten path would be doing relatively better than their counterparts that were more accessibly located with respect to Des Moines. Such is not generally the case within the study area. In fact, the reverse is often true. Central places that are not located on a major highway are generally doing poorly and those located on well-traveled routes are usually doing better than expected. Polk City (population 1,900) is, for example, about the same distance from Des Moines and is much larger than Van Meter (population 800). However, Polk City is located on less traveled highways and Van Meter is located just off of Interstate 80 near an interchange. Van Meter exceeded retail sales expectations in both 1996 and 2000, while Polk City sold a less than expected amount of retail goods during the same two time periods.

The Importance of Changes in the Farm Economy on Small Town Retail Viability

A major factor fueling the changes in small town Iowa retailing is the general decline in farming and the farm population in our study area. Expansion of non-agricultural land uses in central Iowa seems to have had a detrimental effect on local retailing of some of the smaller towns in the region, especially towns such as Adel in the path of the continual sprawled suburban development of the metropolitan region of Des Moines.

With the demise of specialized agriculture comes more off-farm employment, longer commuting distances, and more multiple-purpose trip shopping to larger, more complete central places within the urban hierarchy. Such trip-chaining activity of consumers is exacerbated by the fact that many jobs are no longer linked to the local economy. As commuting distances have become greater, the dependence on nearby central places for the provision of goods and services has lessened.

Many of the smaller, less accessible, central places are experiencing the greatest increases in the percentage of their residents who take between 25 and 29 minutes to commute one-way to their places of employment (Table 8.1). In some smaller towns (e.g., Dexter, Kelley Redfield) the percentage of workers having to spend this much time commuting tripled between 1990 and 2000 (Bureau of the Census 2002). The poor retail viability of less accessible places may be related to an increasing zone of consumer indifference created by these long commutes. The increased distance required to commute to work carries over to the journey-to-shop. The greater distances involved with shopping at central places with a more complete array of consumer goods and services may be perceived as inconsequential relative to the distance required to shop at closer but less complete central place alternatives (Rushton 1969).

The Urban Corona Effect and the Changing Retail Landscape

If principles derived from classical central place theory are unable to address all of the changes in the retail landscape of the study area, is there a model or concept that can? Probably not, but there may be an illustrative analogy between the way small places interact with Des Moines and the manner in which the planets in our solar system interact with the sun. At a much more modest scale of difference, the studies by Hodge (1965) and those of Hart and Salisbury (1965) demonstrated that cities as small as 25,000 can have a deleterious effect on the retail provisioning of surrounding smaller places within a 25 mile radius. What if the city were an order of magnitude larger as is the case of Des Moines relative to surrounding smaller places in the study area? One might expect that both the magnitude and areal extent of the negative impact on retailing would be even greater than the "zone of functional attrition" found in those earlier studies. The relationship between Des Moines and surrounding small retail centers may be like the relationships of the sun to the planets, moons and other satellites in our solar system. Such an analogy is not that far-fetched as it might first appear. The attraction of heavenly bodies, in fact, provides the theoretical basis for a whole family of gravity and spatial interaction models that geographers, planners and regional scientists have found useful in forecasting migration, commodity, and other movements between dyads of cities (Isard 1960).

The analogy that we are suggesting here is based on the properties of the sun's corona, visible to the naked eye during a total eclipse of the sun. Arguments by analogy had their greatest importance in human geography in the 1960s.[10] In a good analog model, there is a one-to-one correspondence between each element of the less-well-known system that the researcher is trying to understand and the better-known system to which it is argued to be analogous. So, what do we know about the solar corona and why might it be an apt analogy for the central place structure of smaller towns surrounding a much larger central place?

The "urban corona effect" as we are calling it here, is drawn from the subfield of astronomy known as solar physics. In solar physics, the corona refers to the extended outer atmosphere of the sun. The corona has several interesting features, among which are streamers, loops and holes. Streamers (sometimes called helmet streamers) correspond to regions in which the magnetic field lines are capped or closed in a loop, thus trapping coronal gases, not allowing their energy level to be dissipated. These streamers can be detected by enhanced X-ray emissions caused by the increase in gas densities in the streamers. Coronal loops are closed magnetic field lines that are found around sunspots and active areas. These field lines link magnetic regions on the solar surface. Coronal holes, on the other hand, are open magnetic fields in the corona that appear dark in color. These holes allow coronal gas to flow outward into space and produce the solar wind, thus dissipating the energy of the coronal gases. The size and shape of the corona is affected by sunspot activity, which is cyclical. During periods of high sunspot activity (i.e., an active sun period), the corona contains many streamers emanating from the sun at all angles. Some of these streamers may break off creating coronal holes out of which solar wind is generated.

If sunspot activity is analogous to changes in retailing structure, then during active periods of change, such as the introduction of "big-box" retailers into a system theretofore composed of smaller, often locally owned retailers might be quite devastating. As noted earlier, in the study area there were five Wal-Marts extant in 2002, all of them located in Polk County. Several studies in the growing literature on the negative impact that such superstores have on small towns, the effect of a superstore's entry into the retail mix can have far-reaching impacts, ironically more often on towns surrounding the place where the big-box retailer actually locates (Beaumont 1997a; Beaumont 1997b; Humstone and Muller 1997; Marx and Salant 1996; Shils 1997; Stone 1995). If we have entered a period of "increased sunspot activity" in which Wal-Mart and big-box retailers are analogous to the sunspots, we would expect helmet streamers to emanate from the sun (i.e., Des Moines) in a variety of directions, not limited to leakage through the coronal holes as happens when there is low sunspot activity. However, these helmet streamers might break up as well as, for example, when the downtown shopping district of a small town that has created and nurtured a symbiotic relationship with a shopping district on the town's outskirts is eventually squeezed by the outlying center that it spawned and is dissipated by the "solar wind" emanating from the new retail complex.

Thirty years ago retailing was in a period of "low sunspot activity". That is retail change was gradual and predictable in response to population growth, decline and redistribution. Before the advent of big-box retailing, the nature of retail competition among central places in a regional setting around Des Moines was also more predictably related to expansion in the paths of least resistance. The continued expansion of Des Moines's development path created a barrier making it more difficult for "surface gases" (i.e., retail and service facilities) to escape. During such quiescent times, solar winds are generated mainly by the "dark spots". The dark spots may perhaps be analogous to the economic shadow that larger nearby competing centers cast over their smaller, most vulnerable counterparts. Tears in the fabric of the surface cause the holes through which the gases could escape. In a central place context, that fabric could be "torn" by either: 1) benign neglect of places that are usually located in the opposite direction of the continued retail expansion; or 2) declining circumstances not directly related to retailing or service provision such as industrial plant closures. Such declining circumstances have a "domino effect" on retailing and service provision as measured by the nature of the multiplier effect (see Berry 1967 for example). The gases escaping through the holes in the sun's corona cause the "solar wind", that may be analogous to the cleansing winds of creative destruction that, according to Joseph Schumpeter (1962), is symptomatic of a dynamic capitalistic system.

The most profound sign of increased "sunspot" activity over the last thirty years in the study area has been the thinning out of the number of central places. Whereas in the 1970s there were 60 places that distributed at least one good or service within the eight-county study area, by 2003 the study region had experienced a loss of 14 formerly viable central places.

Our research indicates that the construction of the Interstate highway system in the central Iowa study area created "closed loops" in the retailing system. These "streamer" highways expedited the flows of goods and people among centers privileged with easy access along the loop. Interestingly, in practically every case of the 14 small central places that met or exceeded their expected retail sales in 2000, the volume of traffic as determined by official traffic counts decreased significantly beyond that small central place in a direction away from the Des Moines "sun". The connection between Des Moines and these favored smaller places reinforces the viability of retail activities located within such "loop endpoint" locations if the loops emanate far enough away from the Des Moines "sun".

Sunspot activity is not always predictable. Sunspots, like retailing activities, are sometimes subject to seemingly random perturbations. One such perturbation in the central Iowa retail milieu was the unexpected investment by a wealthy patron in Perry's Hotel Pattee and, more recently, in a museum that will be focus on the contribution made by immigrant populations to the small towns in the Middle West.

These perturbations are also capable of creating a helmet loop, making our knowledge of the exact nature of these loops less predictable in times of high sunspot activity than it is during times of low activity. Forecasting retailing viability during this present era of "high sunspot activity" (i.e., the dramatic changes taking place in the format and supply chains by which retail goods and services are distributed and sold) is less predictable than it was in a time of "low sunspot activity" (e.g., the 1950s and 1960s).

Without a great deal more astronomical knowledge of the behavior of the sun's corona, it is difficult to extend this analog model (or metaphor) any further, but the possibility of further isomorphism is intriguing.

SUGGESTIONS FOR SMALL TOWN VIABILITY AND RESEARCH

So what can the leadership of a small central Iowa towns learn from the research presented here? First, Wal-Mart and other big-box retailers can be blamed for only part of the decline in small town retail viability. Loss of viability appears attributable as well to a number of structural factors including the changing employment base, the decline of employment in agriculture, suburbanization of metropolitan areas, and urban sprawl that has taken farmland out of production and has led to increased commuting times for the journey-to-work of many rural towns in central Iowa residents. Increased long-distance commuting leads, in turn, to concomitant increases in the length of the discretionary journey-to-shop. Multiple-purpose trip shopping to larger but distant central places is often viewed as a rational consumer response to this increased geographic scale of activity. The leadership of small cities and towns should remain vigilant to the telltale signs of retail decline, turnover and abandonment. When large amounts of formerly viable retail space in the downtown area offering new products and services give way to shops distributing mostly used or consignment items, this is a sign of impending trouble.

In the 1930s, before the advent of rural free delivery, a lynchpin activity that contributed to retail viability was the town post office. Rural residents had to travel to the central place to pick up mail and while they were there they also purchased a market basket of goods and services. When it was no longer necessary to pick up mail in smaller places, other business started dropping out of the retailing system as well (Berry 1967; Bell 1973). Our recent field observation of towns in central Iowa points to the importance of the locally owned bank serving this stabilizing function today. As banking deregulation has driven many local banks out of business, the often-imposing bank edifice has undergone adaptive reuse often serving now as the town's main eating and drinking establishment. The owner of a rather forlorn pharmacy in Dexter, Iowa, a town best known for a shoot-out between police and the notorious Bonnie and Clyde in 1933, confirmed our conjecture by noting that Dexter started its downward retailing spiral with the closure of the local bank.

Large cities are also grappling with the problem of a decline in retailing in their central core areas but, unlike, smaller places, retailing in larger places may remain viable in shopping districts outside the central area. The decline of the small town Main Street or the courthouse square has a proportionally larger impact on the psyche of the town's citizens than on their city counterparts. It is, therefore, important to keep up the appearance and façades of the original retail emporiums not simply for nostalgic value but in anticipation of future changes. Smith (2000) discovered that such business edifice preservation under the aegis of the Main Street program supported by the National Trust for Historic Preservation was most successful in Kentucky small towns that were located away from the economic shadow of their larger neighbors or in amenity areas near major rivers or lakes. A small town with an attractive downtown and a preserved architectural heritage is more likely to lure new non-retail related business and tourism than one that has already suffered from retail blowout of the central area.

Retail and service viability in central Iowa has been approached from a variety of perspectives in this study. The results have been synergistic; each of the approaches has reinforced the other. To argue retail change based solely on conceptual principles derived from classical central place theory as one of the co-authors attempted to do more than thirty years ago (Bell, 1973), would not have predicted, for example, the infusion of external capital into the former railroad town of Perry. Likewise, classical central place theory was based on a consumer behavior postulate of distance minimization. While this postulate accords with Zipf's (1949) notion of the principle of least effort, it is not an accurate description of modern consumer shopping behavior. Rushton's (1969) preference structure delimitation is a much better descriptor of actual consumer behavior because it takes into consideration both distance and town size and would provide a more accurate prediction of shopping behavior in light of the increased commuting distances experienced by small town residents throughout the study region.

The interpretative analysis of retail and service provision completed over two "field seasons" (2002 and 2003) of observation was an excellent way to corroborate the empirical findings that relied solely on secondary source data. Yet, qualitative assessment alone would not have been sufficient to uncover some of the relationships found in the present study. For example, analysis of secondary data made it easier to spot regional-scale trends that are not so easily detectable at the scale of the individual central place.

There will also be a need for a more detailed content analysis of the nature of boosterism inherent in official websites of the larger central places in the study area. It is interesting that the Chamber of Commerce websites of many of the places near to Des Moines have banded together to form a metropolitan consortium. Interestingly, Indianola's Chamber is a part of that consortium but Winterset's is not. Indianola did less well as a retail center than other cities of its size in Iowa whereas the more independent Winterset was better able to carve out its own niche and remain a more viable central place.

Finally, if the analogy between the distribution of goods and services within a central place system and the behavior of the sun's corona is to be further advanced, a great deal more work needs to be done. This task should include the close collaboration between geographers and astrophysicists, an interface that has, heretofore, been uncommon.

ENDNOTES

1. Many websites are devoted to advising towns how to keep Wal-Mart out. The National Trust for Historic Preservation has even taken the unprecedented step of declaring the entire state of Vermont "endangered" because of the potential invasion of Super Wal-Marts (i.e. the hybrid of a general merchandise store and a grocery store) into the state where none now exist.

2. A more thorough discussion of the nuances of central place theory may be found in most standard economic or urban geography textbooks such as Wheeler, et al., (1998) or Hartshorn (1992).

3. We wish to acknowledge the Professional Development Award program of the University of Tennessee for providing financial support to conduct the field research portion of this project.

4. We are indebted to Mr. Kevin Sadrak for helping with the quantitative analysis and mapping for this project as part of an Undergraduate Research Experience at the University of Tennessee.

5. Indianola was home to an excellent gourmet restaurant on the courthouse square and there were few vacancies or retail abandonment in the downtown core. Educational and cultural opportunities including Simpson College, a small liberal arts school, and the National Hot Air Balloon Museum, give Indianola the potential for a livelier atmosphere. To what extent tourists actually flock to such a destination is, however, unknown.

6. In fact, the town has two tourist-related factors: 1) it is the birthplace of Marion Morrison—better known as the actor John Wayne; and 2) it is the county seat of Madison County, home to several wooden covered bridges that have now been immortalized in fiction in The Bridges of Madison County. There is even a covered bridge that is preserved in the town's city park!

7. Because of disclosure problems with these sensitive data, tax receipts for specific, though still broadly defined, categories of retail and service activity are only available for towns of 3,000 or greater in the state.

8. The hotel is quite unique. The lobby and public areas are all done in the understated elegance of the Arts and Crafts (or mission) period. The booths in the attached restaurant are festooned with hand-tooled leather railroad-themed dioramas and the walls contain huge murals that pay homage to train travel through the ages. In fact, David's Milwaukee Road Restaurant has been featured on the Food Network's The Best Of series. One may not expect to find a world-class restaurant in such a small place, but it is certainly a delightful surprise. Not surprisingly, in the hotel there is a Gustav Stickley Room with period pieces by the person who is synonymous with the Arts and Crafts movement. But, every room in the Hotel Pattee is themed. No two are alike and the decorative treatments run from the tasteful to the whimsical.

9. Sajak quipped that Perry is "what Mayberry would look like if Aunt Bee had money" (Associated Press 2004).

10. Berry and his students, drawing on the language of von Bertelanffy's General Systems Theory, theorized cities as sets of nested hierarchical systems interrelated to each other at a variety of scales. The title of one of Berry's (1964) article "Cities as Systems within Systems of Cities" summarizes well the thinking of the time. Berry's student, Michael Woldenberg (1968) went further drawing analogies between the ratio of the number of cities at various hierarchical levels and the bifurcation ratio found in Horton's stream laws and the vessels and capillaries of bovine livers among others.

REFERENCES CITED

Alonso, W. 1964. *Location and Land Use.* Cambridge, MA: Harvard University Press.

Anding, T. L., J. S. Adams, W. Casey, S. de Montille, and M. Goldfein. 1990. *Trade Centers of the Upper Midwest: Changes from 1960 to 1989.* Publication No. CURA 90-12. Minneapolis: Center for Urban and Regional Affairs, University of Minnesota.

Associated Press. 2004. Sajak helps dedicate Iowa town's museum. *Netscape News* (on-line), September 26.

Beaumont, C. 1997a. *How Superstore Sprawl Can Harm Communities and What Citizens Can Do About It.* Washington, DC: National Trust for Historic Preservation.

————. 1997b. *Better Models for Superstores: Alternatives to Big-Box Sprawl* (Washington, DC: National Trust for Historic Preservation.

Bell, T. L. 1973. *Central place Theory as a Mixture of the Ordering Principles of Christaller and Lösch: Some Empirical Tests and Applications.* Unpublished PhD. Dissertation. Iowa City, IA: University of Iowa, Department of Geography.

Berry, B. J. L. 1964. Cities as systems within systems of cities. *Papers and Proceedings of the Regional Science Association.*

————. 1967. *The Geography of Market Centers and Retail Distribution.* Englewood Cliffs, NJ: Prentice-Hall.

Borchert, J. R., and R. B. Adams, 1963. Trade centers and trade areas of the Upper Midwest. Upper Midwest Economic Study. *Urban Report No. 3.* Minneapolis: University of Minnesota, Center for Urban and Regional Affairs.

Bureau of the Census. 2002. 2000 Census of Population and Housing Washington, DC: Department of Commerce.

Casey, W. 1999. Trade Centers of the Upper Midwest: 1999 Update Minneapolis: University of Minnesota. Center for Urban and Regional Affairs.

Christaller, W. 1966. *Central Places in Southern Germany.* Tr. C.W. Baskin, Englewood Cliffs, NJ: Prentice-Hall.

Graff, T. O. 1988. The location of Wal-Mart and K-Mart supercenters: contrasting corporate strategies. *Professional Geographer* 50 (1): 46 – 56.

Graff, T. O., and D. Ashton. 1994. Spatial diffusion of Wal-Mart: contagious and reverse hierarchical elements. *Professional Geographer* 46:19 – 29.

Green, H. L. 1955. Hinterland boundaries of New York City and Boston in New England. *Economic Geography* 31: 249.

Hart, J. F. and N. E. Salisbury 1965. Population change in Middle Western villages: a statistical approach. *Annals of the Association of American Geographers* 55 (l): 140 – 60.

Hart J. F., N. E. Salisbury, and E. G. Smith, Jr. 1968. The dying village and some notions about urban growth. Economic Geography 44 (4): 343 – 49.

Hartshorn, T. 1992. *Interpreting the City: An Urban Geo*graphy. New York: John Wiley and Sons.

Hiltzik, M. 2004. Wal-Mart's costs can't always be measured. *Los Angeles Times* (on-line). February 2.

Hodge, G. 1965. The prediction of trade center viability in the Great Plains. *Papers and Proceedings of the Regional Science Association* 15: 365 – 81.

Humstone, E., and T. Muller. 1997. *What Happens to Downtown When Super stores Located on the Outskirts of Town*: A Report on Three Iowa Communities with a Statistical Analysis of Seven Counties. Washington, DC: National Trust for Historic Preservation.

Isard, W. 1960. *Methods of Regional Analysis*. Cambridge, MA: MIT Press.

Laulajainen, R. 1987. *Spatial Strategies in Retailing* Dordrecht, Netherlands: D. Reidel.

———. 1988. Chain store expansion in national space. *Geografiska Annaler* 70B: 293 – 299.

Levine, D. 2003. Wal-Mart's big city blues. The Nation (on-line), November 24

Lösch, A. 1954. *The Economics of Location*. Wolgom and Stopher Tr. New Haven: Yale University Press.

Marx, J., and P. Salant. 1996. *Rural Communities in the Path of Development: Stories of Growth, Conflict, and Cooperation*. Washington, DC: The Aspen Institute Rural Economic Policy Program.

McKay, F. J. 2004. Wal-Mart nation: the race to the bottom. *The Seattle Times* (on-line) February 18.

McKenzie, R. D. 1933. *The Metropolitan Community* New York: McGraw-Hill.

Myrdal, G. 1957. *Rich Lands and Poor*. New York: Harper Brothers.

Reilly, W. J. 1931. The Law of Retail Gravitation. New York: Knickerbocker Press.

Rushton, G. 1969. Analysis of spatial behavior by revealed space preferences. *Annals of the Association of American Geographers* 59: 391 – 400.

———. 1971. Postulates of central-place theory and the properties of central-place systems. *Geographical Analysis* 3:.140 – 156.

Schumpeter, J. A. 1962. *Capitalism, Socialism and Democracy* 5th. ed. New York: Perennial. (First published in 1942).

Shils, E. B. 1997. *The Shils Report: Measuring the Economic and Sociological Impact of the Mega-Retail Discount Chains on Small Enterprise in Urban, Suburban and Rural Communities*. The Wharton School: Philadelphia: University of Pennsylvania.

Smith, C. 2000. *Kentucky Main Street Programs 1980-1997*. Unpublished PhD Dissertation. Knoxville: University of Tennessee. Department of Geography.

Stone, K. E. 1995. *Competing with the Discount Mass Merchandisers*. Ames, IA: Department of Economics, Iowa State University.

Stone, K. E., and G. M. Artz. 1999a. Iowa Retail Market Share of Various Size Towns Ames: IA: ISU Extension Retail Trade Analysis Program.

———. 1999b. *Threshold Levels for Selected Retail & Service Business in Iowa 1998-1999*. Ames, IA: Iowa State University. University Extension.

———. 1999c. *Determining the Market for Your Goods & Services*.. Ames, IA: Iowa State University. University Extension.

———. 1999d. *Iowa County Retail Surplus or Leakage* Ames, IA: Iowa State University. University Extension.

Waller, R. J. 1992. *The Bridges of Madison County*. New York: Warner Books.

Woldenberg, M. 1968. *Hierarchical systems: cities, rivers, Alpine glaciers, bovine livers and trees.* Harvard Papers in Theoretical Geography No. 19. Cambridge, MA: Harvard Graduate School of Design.

Useem, J. 2003. One nation under Wal-Mart. *Fortune* (on-line), February 25.

Wheeler, J.O., G. I. Thrall, and T. M. Fik. 1998. *Economic Geography.* 3rd Edition. New York: John Wiley and Sons.

Wood, D. B. 2003. Wal-Mart rollout—or rollback? *Christian Science Monitor* (on-line). December 24.

Zipf, G. K. 1949. *The Principle of Least Effort*. Reading, MA: Addison-Wesley.

9

Location Dynamics of Economic Activities in America's Small Cities: The Experience of Five Wisconsin Cities

Benjamin Ofori-Amoah
University of Wisconsin-Stevens Point

INTRODUCTION

Location dynamics of economic activities in urban areas have attracted numerous studies in urban geography and related disciplines for over five decades (e. g. Mayer and Kohn 1959; Sternlieb 1963; Cassidy 1972; Hamer 1973; Adams 1976; Vise 1976; Quante 1976; Muller 1981; Semple and Phipps 1982; Daniels 1982; Erickson 1980, 1982; Scott 1982, 1983a, 1983b; Gad 1985; Erickson and Straussfogel 1986; Holloway and Wheeler 1991; Frieden and Sagalyn 1990; Lloyd 1991; Simmons 1991; O hUallachain and Reid 1991, 1992; Hartshorn 1992; Williams 1992; Waddel and Shukla 1993; Gong and Wheeler 2002). These studies have established that since World War II, economic activities in US urban areas have generally shifted from their traditional downtown or city center locations to suburban or outlying locations. These studies have also provided insights regarding the effects of such shift and the programs and policies that have been implemented in many urban areas, to stem the complete outflow of activities and eventual collapse of city centers.

However, almost all of these studies have focused on large cities. The result is that there is very little information as to whether or not the trends that have been identified in large cities also exist in small cities. In the same vein, planning and economic development professionals in small cities, who have to deal with problems resulting from the changing geography of their communities, have to rely on models and policies that may be more suited to large cities than to small cities. In the meantime, the relatively little geographic research on small cities shows that location patterns and trends in small cities and the forces that influence them can be distinctively different (see for example, Zelinsky 1977; Lamb 1985; Mattingly 1991).

The central thesis of this chapter is that the geography of small cities is changing, and even though small and large cities are part of the same national urban system, there may be some significant differences between them due to their differences in size and the factors that have historically shaped their development. It is therefore important to focus specifically on small cities so as to better understand them. This chapter investigates the location dynamics of economic activities in America's small cities, from 1950 to 2004, using five Wisconsin cities as case studies. Specifically, the chapter investigates five main questions. 1) Have there been any location changes of economic activities in small cities? 2) If so, what has been the direction of the changes? 3) What are the causes and effects of the changes? 4) To what extent are the direction, causes and effects of the changes similar or different from the established trends in large cities? 5) What are the implications for research and policy?

METHODOLOGY

Five Wisconsin cities, namely Appleton (69,000) Fond du Lac (40,000), Green Bay (101,596), Oshkosh (60,000), and Wausau (38,700) were selected for study. The cities were chosen for their suitability to the objectives of the study and for their proximity to Stevens Point, which is the residence of the author. The fieldwork for the study began in 1996 with subsequent updates in 2000, 2001, and 2004. Initially, I compiled evidence of location changes since 1950 in all the five cities from publications on local histories, back numbers of local newspapers, city directories, and profiles of local businesses. Next, I conducted interviews with city and county planning officials, community and economic development officials, city managers and administrators, shopping center managers, business owners and leaders of community business associations, such as Chambers of Commerce and Economic Development Corporations. A random sample of individual business owners located at city centers and outskirts were also interviewed. In all 20 city officials, including city managers, and city and county planners, 10 shopping center managers, and 150 business owners were interviewed. These interviews focused on evidence, causes, and effects of changes in location and their implications for the future. Preliminary results of this study were first reported in Ofori-Amoah (1997), on which much of this work is based.

The rest of the chapter is divided into six sections. The first section outlines the stylized facts of location dynamics of economic activities in urban areas that have been established by previous studies. The second section provides an overview of the location and growth of the five cities that were studied. The third section documents the location dynamics of economic activities in the cities, from 1950 to 2004. The fourth and fifth sections discuss the causes and effects of the changes, respectively. The sixth section examines the similarities and differences, if any, between existing knowledge and the experience of the five cities and outlines further research and policy implications.

PERSPECTIVES ON LOCATION DYNAMICS OF ECONOMIC ACTIVITIES IN URBAN AREAS

Research on location dynamics of economic activities in US urban areas shows that until the turn of the 20th century, economic activities in US cities were predominantly located in the central business district (CBD) or downtown areas. The centrality of the CBD and the limitation imposed by transportation and communication technology required activities to locate in downtowns. However, before the turn of the 20th century activities began to move away from downtown (Steed 1976; Erickson 1986; Berry and Horton 1970; Hamer 1973; Berry and Karsda 1977).

Manufacturing activities were the first to leave. Centrifugal forces in and around the CBD such as congestion, lack of space, and rising land values versus centripetal forces of the outskirts such cheap land, low taxes and improved access by the railroad gave outlying locations an advantage over the CBD (Muller 1981; Berry and Horton 1970; Berry and Karsda 1977). However, it was not until the 1960s that the CBD began to lose its grip as a center of manufacturing activities. According to Muller (1981) three new factors reinforced the location advantages of suburbs. First, the rise of new production technologies in the form of increasing automation and assembly line required expansive industrial sites that were only available in the suburbs. Second, the completion of urban freeways as extensions of the Interstate Highway System increased the accessibility and visibility of outlying areas. The interchanges of the urban freeways and the Interstate systems instantly became prime business locations. Third, the new freeway systems also made possible the achievement of scale economies on intraurban trucking over short and medium distances. These advantages of the outlying areas were further strengthened by the proliferation of industrial parks. By the end of the 1960s, it was clear that the CBD's regime as the manufacturing center of the city was over.

Retailing was the next to leave downtown. This began about the late 1940s and early 1950s (Berry and Horton 1970; Bluestone et al. 1981; Lloyd 1991; Hartshorn 1992). Availability of generous housing loans, increasing demand for single-family housing, increasing ownership of the automobile, and the fear of increasing crime all contributed towards rapid suburban growth after World War

II. With the market now living in the suburbs, retailing followed suit to be in close proximity, and new stores began to appear in the suburbs. The success of this "consequent" retail development strategy, as this early shift was called, led to a "simultaneous" retail development strategy in the suburbs, during the 1960s (Jones and Simmons 1990). In this strategy, new suburban residential developments came with their shopping centers. In the 1970s, the simultaneous development strategy was replaced by a "catalytic" development strategy, where large shopping centers were built as growth poles for undeveloped areas. As a result, these shopping centers were purposefully established on "greenfields" at the intersections of major highways (Jones and Simmons 1990). In the 1980s and 1990s, retail location in cities followed an in-filling strategy, by which store location returned to the central city and old suburbs to fill in vacant areas skipped over in the retail suburbanization phase.

In the case of office functions, the decentralization of office activity accelerated during the 1960s (Gad 1985; Semple and Phipps 1982; Holloway and Wheeler 1991). Once again, the availability of space, labor, ease of communication and the need for visibility all began to erode the advantages that the CBD formerly had over the suburbs, in terms of office location. After some initial success stories of a few manufacturing sales offices in the suburbs, large routine departments of insurance business followed suit. Soon, a host of other service firms followed, as they decentralized their office functions (Muller 1981; OhUallachain and Reid 1991; Hartshorn 1992).

As a result of all of these, US cities became more multinucleated as the CBD lost its grip and reputation as the only center of economic activities in the city. As the CBD began to feel the effects of these changes, downtown revitalization became an essential strategy to stem the eventual demise of the CBD in US cities (Holocomb and Beauregard 1981; Friedan and Sagalyn 1990). Among the many projects of this strategy were the building of downtown malls, hotel and convention centers, offices, and sports arenas. In the remaining sections of this chapter, I examine the extent to which these trends have played out in the five study cities.

LOCATION AND BACKGROUND OF STUDY AREAS

All but one of the five study areas are clustered in the northeast portion of the state of Wisconsin, from the southern tip of Lake Winnebago to the southern tip of Lake Michigan's Green Bay (Figure 9.1). Both Fond du Lac and Oshkosh are located on Lake Winnebago, while Green Bay is located on Lake Michigan. In addition, Oshkosh, Appleton, and Green Bay are all situated on the Fox River, while Wausau, the fifth city is located on the Wisconsin River, in the heart of Central Wisconsin. All five cities serve as administrative seats for their respective counties—Appleton for Outagamie County; Fond du Lac for Fond du

Figure 9.1 Map of Wisconsin Showing the Study Areas

Lac County; Green Bay for Brown County; Oshkosh for Winnebago County; and Wausau for Marathon County.

All five cities were established between 1830 and 1847 (Table 9.1). Wausau was established in 1830. Green Bay followed in 1835, Oshkosh and Fond du Lac in 1836, and Appleton in 1847. With the exception of Appleton, which owes its origins largely to the establishment of Lawrence Institute (now Lawrence University) all of the cities originated as fur trading centers. In 1852, Fond du Lac became the first of the five cities to incorporate as a city. Oshkosh followed in 1853, Green Bay in 1854, Appleton in 1857, and Wausau in 1872 (Table 9.1).

Availability of local raw materials, cheap water transportation by way of the Wisconsin and the Fox Rivers, which was later strengthened by the coming of the railroad, and selection as county administration seat boosted the growth of all five cities. By 1870, all of the cities had gained a collection of forest products

Table 9.1: Establishment, Incorporation, and Growth of Study Areas (1870 – 2000)

City/Vicinity	Year Es-tablished	Year Incor-porated	Population					
			1870	1900	1950	1970	1990	2000
Appleton	1847	1857	4,521	15,085	34,010	56,377	65,695	69,103
Vicinity			3,921	23,324	54,120	85,893	102,616	111,555
Urban area			8,442	38,409	88,130	142,270	186,311	180,658
Green Bay	1835	1854	4,666	18,684	52,735	87,809	96,466	101,596
Vicinity			7,503	9,484	19,550	46,074	66,108	74,321
Urban area			12,169	28,168	72,285	133,883	162,574	175,917
Oshkosh	1836	1853	12,673	8,284	41,084	53,104	55,006	60,240
Vicinity			4,704	5,438	9,400	12,903	13,464	13,273
Urban area			13,944	13,722	50,484	66,007	68,470	75,513
Fond du Lac	1836	1853	12,765	15,110	29,936	35,515	37,755	40,389
Vicinity			1,271	1,280	4,762	7,182	6,602	6,764
Urban area			14,036	16,390	34,698	40,697	44,357	47,153
Wausau	1830	1872	1,349	12,354	30,414	32,806	37,060	38,700
Vicinity			2,403	7,361	17,767	30,207	37,421	41,229
Urban area			3,752	19,715	48,181	63,013	74,481	79,929

Source: Wisconsin Blue Book, various years.

and food processing industries, with Fond du Lac as the second most populous city in Wisconsin, following only Milwaukee. Between 1880 and 1890, depletion of nearby forests caused the center of the lumber industry to move northwards from Fond du Lac to Oshkosh. Oshkosh quickly became the largest of the five cities, and also in Wisconsin's Fox Valley. However, between the two World Wars, Oshkosh grew very slowly compared to the rest of the five cities. Green Bay and Appleton particularly experienced more growth due largely to expansion in the paper and appliance industries, sports, and public entertainment. Thus, between 1930 and 1946, Oshkosh's population increased just by 764 people compared to Green Bay's 15,028, Appleton's 8,625, and Fond du Lac's 3,469. By the end of World War II, Oshkosh had ceded its century-old position as the largest city in the Fox Valley to Green Bay.

Transportation and industrial development in the Post World War II period brought growth to all five cities, but once again it was Green Bay and Appleton that experienced the most growth. For Green Bay, the main factors in this growth included the opening of the Austin Straubel Airport in 1948 and the St. Lawrence Seaway in 1959, the completion of a number of important highways including US 41 and Interstate 43, the consolidation with the town of Preble, and the growth in paper and food processing industries (Ofori-Amoah 1997). By the end of the 1950s, Green Bay had established itself as a major transportation hub as well as a dominant retail center of northeastern Wisconsin and the Upper Peninsula (UP) of Michigan. In addition, it had become an industrial center, specializing in paper and allied products, power shovels and cranes, and food processing. Between 1950 and 1995, Green Bay's population doubled from 45,000 to 96,000. For the other four cities, the main engines of growth were the expansion of the paper industry, in the case of Appleton and Wausau, and the development of steel and metal works in the case of Oshkosh and Fond du Lac. In addition, like Green Bay, Appleton, Fond du Lac and Oshkosh all benefited from improvements to US 41, while Wausau did the same from improvements to US 51.

By 2000, Green Bay had become the largest of the five cities, with an estimated population of 101,596, followed by Appleton (69,000), Oshkosh (60,000), Fond du Lac (40,389), and Wausau (38,700). However, by the size of the urban area, Appleton was the largest, with an estimated population of 180,658, followed by Green Bay (175,917), Wausau, (79,000), Oshkosh (73,513), and Fond du Lac (47,153) (Table 9.1).

LOCATION DYNAMICS OF ECONOMIC ACTIVITIES IN THE FIVE CITIES, 1950 – 2004

At the beginning of the 1950s, the overwhelming majority of economic activities in the five cities were located in their respective downtowns. By 2000, the number of economic activities located in the downtowns had considerably declined (Table 9.2). In what follows, I provide the main highlights of this development, taking each city in turn in alphabetical order.

Table 9.2 Number of Downtown Economic Activities 1950 – 2000

Downtown	1950	1960	1970	1980	1990	2000
Appleton	508	579	445	582	514	244
Fond du Lac	757	586	581	479	572	464
Green Bay	908	887	717	494	375	179
Oshkosh	595	493	472	395	336	283
Wausau	412	318	265	256	172	189

Source: Compiled from City Directories

Appleton

In the 1950s, College Avenue, in downtown Appleton, was the dominant commercial street of Appleton (Figure 9.2). Together with other adjacent streets in the downtown area and the Fox River Valley, College Avenue, boasted 508 businesses. City growth bumped up the number of activities in downtown to 579 by 1960, but the tendency that economic activities would locate outside downtown had already begun to show when in 1954 the Valley Fair Mall, an enclosed mall, opened to the south of the city. The expansion of US 41 into a four-lane highway with an overpass, as well as entrance and exit ramps by the end of the 1950s, laid the foundation for business location along West College Avenue, which was located in the Town of Grand Chute, a township to the north and west of Appleton. In 1969, a strip mall with a Kohl's store opened in the northern outskirts of the city along the Northland Avenue, an arterial road in the Town of Grand Chute. This later became the Northland Mall. The opening of the Outagamie County Airport to the west of Appleton in 1965 provided further impetus for growth along West College Avenue, in the Town of Grand Chute. As economic activities began to locate along the avenue, the Town of Grand Chute constructed frontage roads along it to make it more attractive. Increased traffic along West College Avenue led to its expansion into a four-lane highway. By 1974, when it was completed, the 1.1-mile long strip had become the home of hotels, restaurants, discount shopping centers, auto dealers, gas stations, banks, lumber companies, drug stores and tire distributors, and a very strong competitor to downtown Appleton.

Downtown Appleton attracted some economic activities between 1970 and early 1980s, especially with the opening of the Paper Valley Hotel and Convention Center in 1982. However, these were not enough to stem the tide of

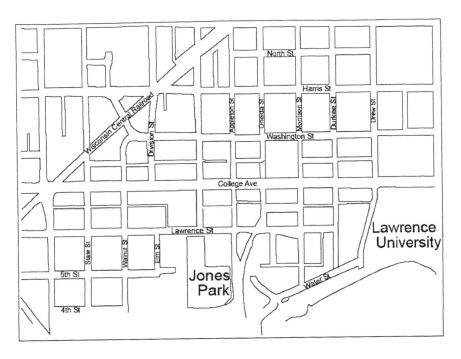

Figure 9.2. Downtown Appleton in the 1990s

flow of retail activities from the downtown. In 1981, J. C. Penny moved out of downtown Appleton and located in the West College Avenue strip. Elsewhere in the city, especially along West Wisconsin Avenue (US 10), also in the Town of Grand Chute, another strip development began to woo economic activities away from downtown Appleton. To make matters worse for downtown Appleton, in 1984 the Fox River Mall opened at the intersection of US 10 and US 41 in the Town of Grand Chute, a few miles north of the West College Avenue strip. The mall opened with Sears, Roebuck and Company as the sole anchor, but it took Sears away from downtown Appleton.

Determined not to lose its retail dominance to the new outskirts mall, Appleton built the Avenue Mall, an upscale downtown mall, to compete with the outskirts mall, in 1987. However, in 1989, H. C. Prange,[1] one of the mall's anchors left for the Fox River Mall, and in 1991, Marshal Fields, the last anchor of the downtown mall, also left for the Fox River mall. After failing to keep most of the anchors of the downtown mall, the owners of the mall went bankrupt, and in 1991, a group of local investors became the new owners of the mall. Convinced that downtown Appleton would no longer become the retail center of the area, the new owners of the downtown mall decided to focus more on office and residential development. Initial efforts boosted the occupancy rate from 17% in 1991 to 85% in 1996, including a medium-sized department store.

However, from the mid-1990s, retail firms, professional services, and light warehousing activities continued to leave downtown Appleton for outskirts locations. The intersection of US 10 and US 41, and West College Avenue, all in the Town of Grand Chute became the center of Appleton's regional market—an agglomeration of department stores, big box retailers, specialty stores, and banks, hotels, and restaurants. Some manufacturing firms also relocated their warehouse facilities at the peripheral areas, in several industrial parks and along the Highway 441 by-pass, even though their production facilities remained in the industrial flats of the Fox River, in downtown Appleton.

In 1999, city officials and business leaders began to refocus downtown Appleton on office functions, professional activities, and the arts and entertainment (Vandenberg 2002). With substantial donations from local businesses, a new performing arts center was opened in 2002 in downtown Appleton. At the same time, College Avenue was reconstructed to make it more pedestrian-friendly. The Avenue Mall was repositioned and renamed City Center Plaza, and in 2004 the Clover Leaf Hotel opened in the downtown as Appleton's first boutique hotel.

Fond du Lac

With over 700 businesses located in it, downtown Fond du Lac, in the 1950s, had no competition in business location in the Fond du Lac area. At the center of this clustering of activities was Main Street, which in 1955 had over 252 retail stores providing all types of modern merchandise. The only exceptions were the manufacturing activities along the Fond du Lac River and the small grocery stores that dotted the neighborhoods (Ofori-Amoah 1997). US 41 was a country road with nothing but farmlands along it. However, activity location in the city had already begun to show a tendency towards the outskirts. As early as 1953, the Schreiner's Restaurant moved out to the US 41. Soon after that the Red Owl Food Store also located along the highway.

The upgrading of US 41 in the late 1950s was followed by construction of two frontage roads, Pioneer Road to the east side and Rolling Meadows Drive to the west side. Immediately, these frontage roads became prime location sites. In 1964, Super Value and a second Red Owl Food store opened on Pioneer Road. The heavy advertisements, coupons, and bargains that accompanied the opening of these new stores brought streams of customers to them and people began to get used to shopping by car. The small neighborhood grocery stores closed down in rapid succession. By the end of the 1960s, a cluster of activities had started growing away from the settled areas and along major transportation arteries.

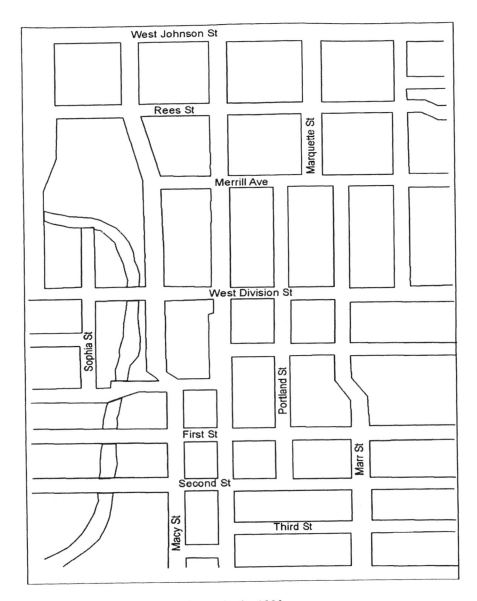

Figure 9.3. Downtown Fond du Lac in the 1990s

The biggest boost to this trend came in 1973, when the Forest Mall opened near the intersection of West Johnson Street and Pioneer Road by US 41. The mall opened with Montgomery Ward, J. C. Penney, and H. C. Prange as anchors.

Prior to that J. C. Penney was located in downtown Fond du Lac, together with other stores such as Sears and Woolworth. In 1975, J. C. Penney closed its downtown store. Sears also moved from downtown to the Forest Mall in 1978 and in 1985, Shopko, a regional discount store, followed suit. The area around the Forest Mall became the location of choice, starting off an intense location activity that would later extend along Pioneer Road and Rolling Meadows Drive. Thus, in 1979, K-Mart opened across from the mall. In 1989, a shopping center with Copps Food Store, a large local grocery chain, opened to the north of the mall, while another commercial strip opened to the east of the mall. In 1991, development spilled over US 41 with a Wal-Mart store opening on Rolling Meadows Drive. In the following year, Target, Toys R Us, Payless Shoes, and Jo-Ann Fabrics all opened near Wal-Mart. A year later, a Cracker Barrel Old Country Store, a Super 8 Motel, and a Red Lobster restaurant opened on Pioneer Road on the opposite side of US 41.

Activity location outside the downtown was not confined to the frontage roads of US 41 alone. Local arterial roads that linked up with the frontage roads also attracted business location. Among these were West Scott Street and South Main, where the Fond du Lac Plaza, a shopping center containing more than 91,000 square feet of retail space, and the Pioneer Plaza, respectively opened in the early 1990s (Ofori-Amoah 1997). This trend continued through 2004, by which time the two frontage roads of US 41 and industrial parks had become the centers of economic activities of the city.

Long-time economic activities in downtown Fond du Lac folded up in the process, but a joint effort between the city and private business brought new activities to downtown.[2] For example, in 1997, a local realty company constructed a new office building in downtown. An insurance company purchased and renovated a former school for office use. In 1998, the Fond du Lac Reporter, the local newspaper, completed a $6 million-pressroom addition to its building in downtown. At the same time, a data processing company located a new call center in downtown. In 1999, the city created the Downtown Fond du Lac Partners (DFP) to rejuvenate the downtown as the social, commercial, and cultural heart of the city. In 2000, the city created a business improvement district and instituted a loan program to help downtown property owners within the district remodel and renovate their property, as a means of maintaining and attracting businesses. In the same year, a new medical office opened and new business started moving into the renovated Woolworth building. The Arts Center was also renovated, while work on the expansion of the Public Library began. By 2004, when the city was awarded a Main Street Program, downtown Fond du Lac had become largely an area of government and professional offices. The total number of businesses there had fallen from 757 in 1950 to 464 in 2000, a drop of 38% (Table 9.2).

Green Bay

In the 1950s, downtown Green Bay, anchored by the Fox River and Main Street, was the center of commerce, retail, and manufacturing in northeastern Wisconsin. Washington and Main streets were the shopping district, while government and professional buildings were located along Walnut Street (Figure 9.4). There were an estimated 908 business activities located in the area in 1950. However, in the 1960s and 1970s, pockets of economic activities, in the form of retail corridors and regional malls, emerged at the interchanges of US 41 and Interstate 43 (I43), and along the major arterial roads in the surrounding communities. Of the retail corridors, the most important was Oneida Street, the business district of the Village of Ashwaubenon and the Oneida Indian Reservation, both of which were to the southwest of Green Bay. Other emerging commercial corridors included Military Avenue and West Mason Street to the west side of Green Bay.

Redevelopment efforts aimed at sustaining the downtown led to the building of the Brown County Library in 1974, the First Wisconsin Building and the Monroe Plaza in 1975, the Port Plaza Mall in 1977, and the IBM Building in 1979 (Maier 1986a, 1986b, 1986c). These projects, especially Port Plaza, boosted the image of downtown as a retail center. Anchored by H. C. Prange and J. C. Penney, the mall was hailed as the savior of downtown Green Bay. For the next two decades, the mall lived up to its reputation. In 1982, it was extended to add a Boston Store franchise as a new anchor. At the same time, a Regency Conference Center was also built adjacent to the mall. In 1988, a second extension brought a food court to the mall. In the early part of the 1990s, the success of the mall even allowed the city to concentrate on a number of downtown revitalization projects, including a Main Street program for West Broadway, a long-neglected part of the downtown west of the Fox River. The program was launched in 1995 and by 2001 it had created a net of 33 new businesses and 427 jobs on West Broadway. By that time, however, things had begun to go sour for Port Plaza Mall. Two regional malls that had opened in the Green Bay area during the 1980s had now gained the upper hand in the competition. The closest of these malls was the Bay Park Square Mall, which opened on Oneida Street between US 41 and WI 172, in the Village of Ashwaubenon. The other was the Fox River Mall, near Appleton, which I have already mentioned. Located at the crossroads of major highways and major city streets, and south of Lambeau Field of the Green Bay Packers Football team, as well as the Packer Hall of Fame, the Bay Park Square Mall quickly became the center of new commercial development in the Green Bay area.

The first signs of trouble for the Port Plaza Mall appeared when several franchise tenants began to seek nonrenewal of their lease, and when in 1999,

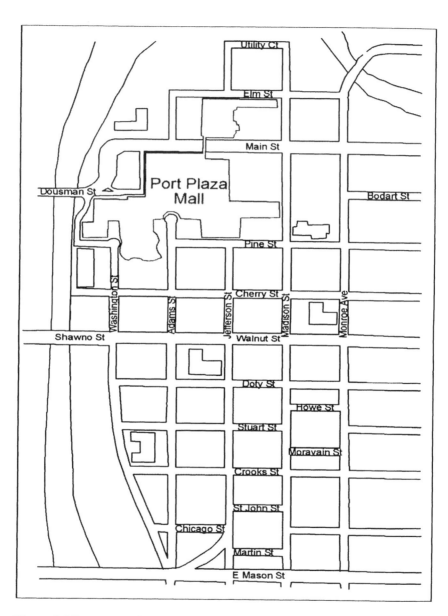

Figure 9.4 Downtown Green Bay in the 1990s

Boston Store, one of the Mall's three anchors, announced that it would close down in 2000, the exit door became wide open (Rentmeester 2004). A mass exodus of mall tenants followed after Boston Store left, beginning with small franchise stores and fast food eateries. Some of the tenants headed for the Bay Park Square Mall, while others headed for the major streets and arterial road corridors. In order to keep the mall from total eclipse, the city purchased it from its owners, and immediately sold it to a group of local investors in 2003. The new owners of the mall changed the mall's name to Washington Commons, renovated it, and added a new food court. However, the food court was closed down at the end of the year. The city also negotiated with the Younkers department store to stay till 2006, but in 2004, Younkers left, leaving J. C. Penney as the only anchor of the almost empty mall.

These developments eroded the dominance of downtown Green Bay as the commercial hub of the city and its region. Between 1970 and 1980, the number of activities recorded to have a downtown location dropped from 717 to 494, a drop of 30%. By 1990, the number was down to 375 and by 2000 it was a mere 179 (Table 9.2). By 2004, downtown Green Bay, had become the home of 8 banks, a hotel and convention facility, a renovated theatre, some specialty stores, restaurants, and some residential apartments, all as a result of some redevelopment project launched in the mid-1990s. However, retail was gone, and although the owners of Washington Commons wanted to convert the former mall to new uses, a city-wide discussion on the future of the former mall, organized by the Green Bay Press-Gazette, the city's newspaper, in 2004 showed there were many ideas, but not an easy task to pick one (Rauen and Rymnan 2004).

Oshkosh

About 595 businesses were located in downtown Oshkosh in 1950, most of them along Main Street (US 45) (Figure 9.5). US 41, which is currently the hub of activities, was in the country, just as it was in Fond du Lac. Location of economic activities along US 41 began in 1962, and by the end of the 1960s, commercial development had leapfrogged the highway, and a mixture of retail, service, and manufacturing activities had replaced most of the farmlands (The Sunday Times 1967). The trigger for this was provided by the upgrading of US 41 into a four-lane highway at the end of the 1950s. After the upgrade, the city built two frontage roads, Koeller Street to the east and Washburn Street to the west of the highway, just as Fond du Lac had also done. With the 28-mile long and 10.5 mile-wide Lake Winnebago to its east side, and hemmed in to the north and south by other cities, Oshkosh could only expand westwards, towards and along US 41.

The opening of Park Plaza Mall in downtown Oshkosh in 1970 brought additional hopes to the downtown. The mall opened with H. C. Prange, Sears, and

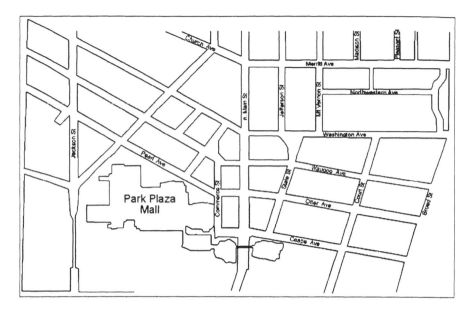

Figure 9.5 Downtown Oshkosh in the 1990s

Kohl's Food Store as anchors. Throughout the 1970s the mall attracted stores and reached an occupancy rate of 96%. Expansion in 1984 and 1991 added more stores including J. C. Penney and a Food Court (Ekvall 1966; Miner 1968).

However, hotels, restaurants, and discount stores continued to pop up along the frontage roads of US 41 (Ofori-Amoah 1997). In 1985, the Koeller Center, a 155,000 square-foot retail space, opened along Koeller Street and by the end of the 1980s, the center had 16 stores and offices. In 1990, the Horizon Factory Outlet Mall, now Prime Outlet Factory Stores, opened with 60 stores on the Washburn Street frontage road. Other stores that located along US 41 around the same time were Wal-Mart and Target. Soon, the attraction along US 41 began taking its toll on downtown business. Five businesses relocated by US 41, while five others closed their Oshkosh operations completely. Eventually, the trend caught up with Park Plaza Mall. In 1986, Kohl's left the mall. General Nutrition followed suit in 1995. In 1996, J. C. Penney relocated by US 41, and by the end of the year, Younkers, the only remaining anchor of Park Plaza, had also closed down. With all its anchors gone Park Plaza Mall became another statistic of a failed downtown mall. Other downtown shopping areas that were experiencing problems, such as Murdock and Jackson Streets and Lake Area Shopping Center began turning into more offices and financial district.

The local family that owned the mall developed a plan to convert 70% of the first floor into office space and 30% into retail space. The retail was targeted at downtown employees and convention participants that would use the nearby Hilton Convention Center. The second level was to be utilized by Hilton to expand for convention activities. A number of businesses had already started moving in to take advantage of the office space conversion.

With a steep decline of property values in downtown Oshkosh, the city decided to seriously look at redevelopment possibilities in 1999. In 2000, a new Downtown Plan of Action was adopted. Among other things, the plan included plaza improvements in the Opera House Square, Main Street improvements, expansion of a Riverside Park area and Convention Center, and developing and making promenade improvements along the river front (Hentz 2003). The Opera House Square improvements were completed in 2002 and the rest of projects are in progress. In 2003, a seven-story 62 luxury apartment complex with first floor commercial space was also completed on the 100 block of Main Street.

In the meantime, a group of local investors purchased the Park Plaza Mall, in 2001, renamed it City Center, and continued with the renovation plans the former owners had developed. By 2004, it was over 65% full. Among the tenants in the center are the University of Wisconsin-Oshkosh, Fox Valley Technical College, 4imprints, and Oshkosh Symphony Orchestra.

Wausau

In Wausau, the story was no different from the four cities already discussed. Most economic activities were located in downtown Wausau, especially along Third Street (Figure 9.6), with manufacturing activities located along the Wisconsin River. Around the mid-1950s, economic activities began to locate north and south of the downtown. These included shopping centers and plazas along North Third Avenue and Grand Avenue. Throughout the 1960s, arterial roads and major intersections of US and state highways became the foci of economic activity location. For example, three new shopping plazas were built at 1st Avenue and Clinton Street, Grand Avenue and Gaywood, and at US 51 and WI 29, respectively. As the 1970s rolled in neighboring communities began attracting business location. Two more shopping plazas, including a K-Mart store, opened on Grand Avenue in the early 1970s. Four new hotels opened at the outskirts of Wausau, one in Wausau, and the remaining three in the Town of Rib Mountain, a township to the southwest of Wausau. From the mid-1970s, many restaurants mushroomed along Grand Avenue, converting it to a restaurant strip. Manufacturing activities also began to relocate outside Wausau as all the surrounding communities developed industrial parks.

In the meantime, economic activities such as department, furniture, and other specialty stores as well as hotels were leaving downtown Wausau. By the late 1970 about 51 buildings in downtown Wausau had vacant or underutilized

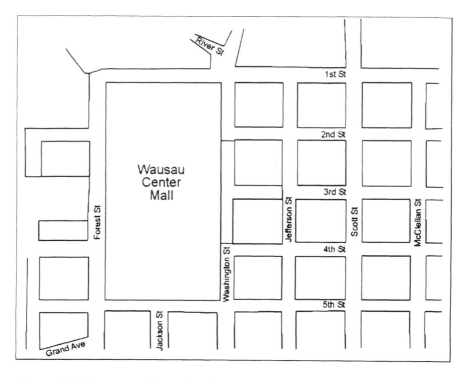

Figure 9.6 Downtown Wausau in the 1990s

commercialized space (Berger 1978; 1979a; 1979b; 1982). However, urban renewal efforts kept downtown Wausau active. In 1975 a 21,000 square-foot retail
space at the corner of Jefferson and Third Street, formerly occupied by the
Woolworth Store, was converted into the Plaza Mall, a mini mall of banks, offices, and restaurants. In 1978, the First American Center, an office complex,
opened on Third Street and Scott Street with the First American National Bank.
A new YMCA addition was constructed on the north end of downtown (Rupinski
1979). Two parking ramps also opened. In August 1983, the Wausau Center
Mall anchored by Sears, Roebuck & Company, H. C. Prange, and J. C. Penney
opened with 30 other stores in downtown Wausau. At the same time, Third
Street was converted to a Pedestrian Mall to integrate the downtown mall with
the rest of downtown. Two months later Washington Square, another renovated
building of a former department store in downtown Wausau, opened with 11
specialty shops and restaurants.

These developments, however, did not deter economic activities from locating outside downtown. From the early 1980s through 2004, the few remaining spots along US 51 as well as in the neighboring communities of Town of Rib Mountain, Village of Rothschild, Town of Weston, and Town of Mosinee, became filled with new activities. A second Shopko store opened along US 51 in 1988, and in 1989 Target opened an outlet in Town of Weston. In 1993, Cedar Creek Outlet Mall opened in the Village of Rothschild and Town of Mosinee area with 33 stores. Soon after that the area around the mall became concentrated with gas stations, hotels, and freestanding chain stores. In 1994, the Mountain View Square (Rib Mountain Mall) opened in the Town of Rib Mountain with Wal-Mart and Sam's Wholesale Club. By 1998, Rogan's Shoes, Fashion Bug, Office Max, TJ Maxx, Best Buy, Kohls, Barnes and Noble, and a host of fast food restaurants had located in the area. Next, the intersection of WI 29 and US 51, in Wausau, became filled with office, hotel, and restaurant development.

With the competition from outlying districts, Wausau city officials began looking for ways to maintain downtown Wausau as a retail and commercial center. This search led to the Wausau Century Project, a simple project conceived in 1992 to build a downtown civic center to create a synergy for nearby property. However, when the project became a $100 million hotel and conference center to be funded mostly by the city, voters defeated the project in two separate referenda in 1998 (Paulsen 2003).

The defeat of the project destabilized efforts to revitalize downtown Wausau, but pieces of the blueprint of the project still remained. At the proposal of a citizen group for an open space in downtown Wausau, the city created an open space from the former building site on the Third Street Pedestrian Mall. In 2000, the city adopted a Central Business District Redevelopment plan and began offering low-interest loans to building owners wishing to renovate their storefronts. Soon private developers jumped into the action and purchased a number of properties on the Pedestrian Mall for renovation. Another group of local investors and philanthropists teamed up to renovate and expand the city's Grand Theatre and Performing Arts Center. In 2002, when Wausau Benefits, a local insurance company, announced that it would build a new office complex, Riverside Place, downtown for 350 of its employees, the city agreed to rebuild an old parking ramp in downtown with a skywalk to a new office building and a retail space on the first floor. In 2003, the Gateway Hotel and Office project, a 62-room hotel, restaurant, and first floor commercial space with skywalk to the parking ramp, began to take shape in downtown Wausau. By 2004, retail was still strong in downtown Wausau, but it was just one of the several retail districts in the area. In addition, downtown Wausau had become home to office, government, arts and entertainment activities.

It is clear from the preceding accounts that in all the five cities there has been a shift in location of economic activities, and that this shift has been from downtown to outskirts, especially for retail and manufacturing. What were the causes of these location changes?

CAUSES OF THE LOCATION CHANGES IN ECONOMIC ACTIVITIES

From interviews with city officials, community business leaders and owners, and newspaper reports, the main factors behind these location changes were identified as limitations of downtown locations, advantages of outskirts locations, downtown revitalization programs, business failures, and the population and settlement geography of Wisconsin. I will examine these factors in detail.

Limitations of Downtown Locations

The downtowns of all five cities had several limitations. First, all of them lacked the physical space for substantial development and expansion. This meant that any such development required the acquisition of built-up property, which was very expensive. This severely limited any new commercial development and expansion of existing business. For example, in 1984 Sears left its 63,000 square foot-store in downtown Appleton for a 107,700 square foot-store in the Fox River Mall (Ofori-Amoah 1997). This was also the main reason for the relocation of all car dealerships, and one of the main reasons for all the outskirts developments.

Second, developers found development requirements and politics in the cities to be too stringent and burdensome compared to those of the outlying townships. As a result, many developers preferred to stay away from downtown projects. Third, all five downtowns had circulation problems. Virtually, all of the commercial development was spread along a single street for a distance of about a half-mile. This meant that shoppers either had to walk long distances from one end of the street to the other end to get what they could not get at their first stop, or they had to move their cars to the place where they wanted to go and risk having nowhere to park. Narrow downtown streets, discontinuity due to either the railroad or drawbridges, and inclement Wisconsin weather made this shopping environment less desirable, in a world of increased automobile ownership and enclosed shopping centers.

Fourth, since it became impossible for shoppers to park right in front of where they wanted to shop, a perception soon developed that downtown had a parking problem. Some of the cities tried to resolve this by building municipal parking ramps, but people did not like them. Finally, city growth and increased traffic also made accessibility to downtown more and more difficult.

In addition to these common factors, city officials in Green Bay and Oshkosh cited, respectively, too many industries and safety issues as contributing factors to the decline in activity location in downtown. For example, the presence of too many industries in downtown Green Bay created an ugly sight and this turned people off from shopping in the downtown area. In Oshkosh, the safety issue related to the Winnebago County Mental Health Institute that occasionally released some of its patients, who would go and hang around the downtown area. This made people uncomfortable to go to downtown Oshkosh.

Ultimately, location dynamics of economic activities are a product of spatial preferences of business owners and developers. For business owners, these preferences are determined by the nature of the business. While destination business does not have to depend on high traffic areas, and are thus comfortable with any location, the high traffic demand of non-destination or convenience business dictates the need for good visibility and immediate access or close proximity to highways. From developers' point of view, the spatial preferences are determined by the availability of a site and expense of development. Given the availability of a site, the expense of development is in turn determined by access and spatial synergy at the site. All these, in turn, depend on the existing geography of the area, type of neighborhood, population size and composition of the area, transportation network, risk level, and availability of investment funds. Potential business locations must be able to deliver on all these. Unfortunately, the downtowns of all five cities in this study fell short in meeting these needs.

Advantages of Outskirts Location

In contrast, the outskirts of all five cities offered all the advantages that the downtowns could not provide. First, land was much more available and cheaper. As a result, it was possible to develop large enclosed malls with large parking facilities at the outskirts. Given the inclement weather of Wisconsin, these enclosed malls were more convenient for customers and for that reason also attracted a lot of customers.

Second, the proximity of outskirts locations to new and improved highway systems and interchanges, such as US 41 in Green Bay, Appleton, Oshkosh and Fond du Lac, Interstate 43 in Green Bay, and US 51/Interstate 39 in Wausau, provided good visibility and easy access. Not only could shoppers from neighboring areas see the advertisement on the billboards by the highways, they could also reach the stores more easily than driving all the way to downtown. These advantages were further strengthened when the cities extended essential services such as sewer, water and frontage roads to the outskirts. An example of this was the development in the Town of Rib Mountain in the Wausau area. Before the early 1990s, the town did not have sewer and water. However, when the well water went bad, the township was left with no alternative but to put in sewer and water systems. This led to a housing boom and several commercial strip developments.

Third, most of the outskirts of the five cities fell under different political jurisdiction of townships and villages. Without the elaborate administrative and planning institutions, staff, and regulations of the cities, these areas had less development requirements, spent less time in scrutinizing and approving development projects, and had less administrative hurdles for developers. With an added advantage of a low tax base, they became very attractive to developers. Indeed, a former City Administrator of Oshkosh singled out the existence of townships in Wisconsin as the leading cause of the demise of downtown Oshkosh as a commercial center.

Downtown Revitalization Projects

Downtown revitalization projects also contributed to the decline in activity location in the downtowns of the five cities. These projects, which often involved the building of downtown malls, performing arts theaters, parking, and other public buildings, required the removal of whole downtown blocks with their existing business occupants. For example, in Appleton, the building of the Paper Valley Hotel and Convention Center and its associated parking ramp in 1982, involved the removal of 16 businesses that were operating in the area. Similarly, the Avenue Mall converted a two-block, three story building complex of about 120,000 square feet of commercial space under one roof (Kellog 1986).

In Fond du Lac, the city's Redevelopment Authority purchased and razed properties in a designated downtown area in 1974. However, as a result of spiraling interest rates and lack of potential tenants for office development, the developers of the project bowed out, leaving the city to figure out what to do with the 48,000 square feet of empty and dusty space (Buchholz 1974; Mentzer 1974; Sandberg 1974a). The city tried to attract a major retailer to the site, but most of the retailers preferred by the city wanted at least 100,000 square feet of commercial space with an extra 5 feet of parking spaces to every 1,000 square feet (Sandberg, 1974b). Apart from this, none of the retailers wanted to move into an island; all of them wanted to be part of a complex so as to have competition next door. This left the city with two options: continue looking for a retailer that was willing to take the site or increase the property size through further land acquisition. It was not until 1978 that an additional space was acquired through the use of a 61-acre tax incremental financing (TIF) district. While the city waited for either of these to happen, uncertainty about the future of downtown Fond du Lac and fear of lowering property values grew, causing some of the businesses that had survived the demolition to leave.

Between 1965 and 1982, Green Bay had two major downtown revitalization projects—the first from 1967 to 1977 and the second from 1978 to 1982. The first one, which culminated in the building of the Port Plaza Mall, removed four downtown blocks along Main Street. This displaced a total of 66 downtown businesses. Of these, 37 (56%) relocated within the city, outside of downtown; 8 (12%) relocated outside the city, while 17 (26%) discontinued business operations (Green Bay Redevelopment Authority 1970). In the second revitalization project, another two-and-a-half blocks of downtown property had to be acquired resulting in the relocation of about 52 businesses and 25 residences (Hutchinson 1981). All together between 1972 and 1982, a total of 118 businesses were displaced from downtown Green Bay. Of these, about 89 (75%) relocated in other parts of the city, 8 (7%) relocated outside the city, 17 (14%) discontinued business operations and 5 discontinued business concerns temporarily. Manufacturing and construction activities in particular were relocated in industrial parks that were at the city outskirts. However, some of the relocation occurred within downtown itself.

In Oshkosh, the revitalization project that resulted in the building of the Park Plaza Mall involved the elimination of railroad traffic, from Main Street and Jackson Street and the clearance of an 18-acre site in downtown Oshkosh (Ekvall 1966). By the time the mall opened in 1970, about 22 buildings with 16 business operations had been removed. For the old established businesses, new facilities were constructed elsewhere in the city, mostly in the industrial parks. In 1980, another revitalization project, which led to the development of the Oshkosh Center, a 182-room Radisson Hotel and a Convention Center, required the acquisition of 19 private parcels in addition to 7 that were already owned by the city, and the removal of about 10 businesses (Combelick 1981; Schulz 1985).

In Wausau, downtown revitalization projects became entangled in a number of citywide contentions. The first was between the supporters of a city mall and those who did not think the city needed a mall. The second was between the supporters of a downtown mall and the supporters of an outskirts mall. The third was between developers and department stores for control over the mall. As these contentions raged on, the future of downtown Wausau became more uncertain causing, Herberger, a major department store, to leave Wausau (Rupinski 1979). This produced a "domino effect" as smaller stores that relied on Herberger began to suffer because of reduced traffic. After voters had supported the mall, the construction of the mall affected about 52 businesses. Of these, 41 (79%) were relocated, while 11 (21%) either went out of business or went out of town. Of the 41 that were relocated, 17 (41%) went outside of downtown (Berger 1978; Oakland 1981a).

Business Failures

Not all the changes in activity location in downtown were due to relocation of existing business or new business start-ups outside of downtown. The failure of both national chains and small family businesses also contributed to the changes. Falling profits of national chains resulting in either bankruptcies or corporate restructuring or both, in turn, led to closing down of stores in small urban areas or relocation to some other place.

With respect to small family businesses, one source of failure was retirement. When former business owners failed to get a family member to take over the business on their retirement, the business merely folded up. In addition, the inability to compete with large chain stores as well as higher rents forced a number of local businesses to fold up.

The Population and Settlement Geography of Wisconsin

Business owners and mangers also cited the population and settlement geography of the state of Wisconsin, and its relationship to market support, as a factor in the relocation of activities from city centers to the outskirts. In particular, the Manager of Forest Mall in Fond du Lac, at the time of this study, observed that Wisconsin has too many cities or communities of around 50,000 people, each of which wants to attract and support major retail stores. This situation is worsened by the fact that in some parts of the state such as the northeast, these cities are too close to each other. For example, Fond du Lac (40,389) is 19 miles south of Oshkosh (60,240), and 39 miles west of Sheboygan (49,676). In turn, Oshkosh is about 10 miles from Neenah-Menasha (37,930), which in turn is about 10 miles from Appleton (69,103). The population sizes of these communities and the communities' close proximity to each other make it difficult for large retailers to stay in them when recruited. For the retailers that choose to remain in these markets, it is absolutely necessary for them to attract potential customers from outside their communities of location. This makes high traffic, high accessibility, and high visibility locations, all of which are outside of downtown, the obvious choice.

EFFECTS OF LOCATION DYNAMICS OF ACTIVITIES ON THE CITIES

By 2004, the location dynamics of economic activities in the five cities since the 1950s had produced two main effects. The first was the transformation of downtown and the second was a change in the morphology of the cities. I examine each of these in turn.

Transformation of Downtown

The changes in economic activity location in the five cities over the past five decades have had several effects on downtown. First, in all five cities, there was a general perception that economic vitality of downtowns had been reduced. This in turn motivated the residents in all five study areas to look for solution to the declining downtowns. In all five cities, there was a strong sense that downtowns needed a new niche—in office functions, government, specialty retail, and arts and entertainment. As several of these projects were planned and implemented, the face of downtown began to change from the center of manufacturing, retail, commerce, office functions, and government to one that is still dominated by government and some professional services, but with manufacturing almost nonexistent and retail considerably reduced to a shadow of its former self.

Effects on City Morphology

In all five cities, as downtown transformed from being the heart of non-farm economic activities, new hubs of economic activities emerged elsewhere in the city. These new hubs consist mainly of industrial or business parks, commercial strips along arterial and frontage roads, and agglomerations at the interchanges of national highways with state and county highways. All five cities have at least two industrial or business parks, within their city limits, while the new centers of commercial activities were both inside and outside the city limits. As a result of these, the cities have become poly-nucleated in terms of location of economic activities, with downtown as one of the several centers of activities. In Oshkosh, a few housing units have popped up behind one of the commercial strips along the US 41 frontage road.

CONCLUSION AND IMPLICATIONS FOR POLICY AND FUTURE RESEARCH

The purpose of this study was to investigate whether geographic trends that have been identified in large US cities have also occurred in small cities in terms of their patterns, causes, and effects. It was hypothesized that even though small and large urban areas are part of the same national urban system, the forces that affect location dynamics of economic activities in them may be different because of the differences in their historical backgrounds and sizes. To investigate this hypothesis, five Wisconsin cities, namely Appleton, Fond du Lac, Green Bay, Oshkosh, and Wausau were selected for study.

The study has shown that in all five cities, a location shift of economic activities has occurred since the 1950s, just as it has occurred in large cities. In general terms, this shift has been from downtown to the outskirts. This has mostly occurred in retailing and manufacturing, while with other service, professional, and government businesses, downtown continues to dominate. The only exception is Wausau, where retail is still strong in downtown.

The causes of this shift were several and they include limitations of downtown location, advantages of outskirts locations, urban revitalization programs, business failures, and population and settlement geography of Wisconsin. While some of these mirror image trends in large cities, others do not. In large cities, the dispersal of manufacturing activities, for example, followed technological innovations in transportation—canals, railroads, and beltways—and finally to industrial parks. In the five small cities, manufacturing activities located along waterways, and then in industrial parks.

In large cities, the location shift in retail evolved in four phases. In the first phase, retail activities moved from city centers to new residential suburbs. In the second phase, new retail centers were developed in conjunction with new suburban development. In the third phase, retail moved out to undeveloped fringes with the view to spurring new residential and commercial development. In the fourth and final phase, retail activities went back to the central city to fill in vacant spots that had been skipped over in the suburbanization process. In the five small cities, the evolution of retail location largely skipped the first two phases. Mostly, they followed the third phase.

In large cities, the causes of location shift of activities from the city centers to the suburbs included such factors as suburbanization of residences, availability of relatively cheap and undeveloped land, the completion of the urban freeways, increasing use of the automobile, and innovations in production technologies that required changes in production organization. In the five small cities, the main reasons included lack of land and developable space in the city center, lack of parking spaces, existence of high access highways at the outskirts, changing consumer behavior, the population and settlement geography of Wisconsin, the need for visibility, and downtown revitalization.

In addition, it is important to note that most downtown revitalization projects in large cities came after most of the businesses had left the downtown and thus was not a major factor in creating the shift in activity location. In the case of the five cities, downtown revitalization projects were undertaken when most of the businesses were still in downtown and thus played a major role in creating the shift.

In large cities, the combined effect of all these factors was the loss of downtown retail dominance to the suburbs. In the absence of retailing, downtowns built concentrations in professional and office functions, government, entertainment and hotel, and convention activities. In the five small cities, the effects of the shift have been similar. Four of the five cities, Appleton, Fond du Lac, Green Bay, and Oshkosh have lost their retail dominance to the outskirts, even though in other service areas, professional and government businesses, downtown is still dominant. In Wausau, the existence of successful downtown malls makes the downtown still dominant in retailing.

In large cities, the decline and deterioration of downtown retail activities, for example, raised a lot of concerns about the future of downtown. This often translated into downtown redevelopment projects, which in turn took the form of downtown malls, designing innovation, and historic preservation building. In the five small cities, people raised similar concerns for city centers as in large cities. Thus, in all five cities residents recognize the importance of a strong downtown, and they have engaged in on-going downtown revitalization plans, though the extent to which they feel about downtown varies from city to city. In all the cities, concerns about whether more money needs to be invested in downtown on a continuous basis are real, even though such concerns may be in the minority.

There is no doubt that downtowns of small cities have faced competition in location of economic activities just as their large city counterparts have. It is inevitable that these trends will continue. Given the similarity of location dynamics of economic activities between large and small cities, it is tempting for small cities to adopt the models large cities have used to deal with the situation. However, by the late 1990s it was clear that such models may not be appropriate for small cities, as four of the cities had either lost or were on the verge of losing their downtown malls.

From this experience, one may surmise that an aggressive downtown policy aimed at reversing the trend of location shift will most likely fail. Instead, small cities need to concentrate on policies that will complement downtown development with what is happening at the outskirts. Such policies need to focus on identifying new niches for downtown. By a process of natural selection, government, professional services, and other office functions have clearly become one such niche. Other niches may include residential development and support for more destination business. For cities that have relatively vital retail downtowns, like Wausau, a key to maintaining this dominance lies in the availability of retail space need for downtown's ability to attract traffic.

This has been a preliminary study. More studies will be needed to examine the real cost of location changes on small cities. In particular, the question of location shift of economic activities between city centers and outskirts will have to be evaluated in terms of employment and revenue gained versus employment and revenue lost. Such studies will be relevant because it will provide a better picture of the actual impact of location trends in economic activities within small cities.

ENDNOTES

1.   H. C. Prange was a regional department store established in 1882 in Sheboygan, Wisconsin. With the emergence of discounters in American retailing, H. C. Prange established Prange Way as its discount store. However, in 1990 it spun off Prange Way and after a series of financial troubles, H. C. Prange itself sold out to Younkers of Des Moines, Iowa, in 1992. At that time H. C. Prange had 22 stores in Wisconsin, Michigan, Minnesota, and Iowa.

2.   I am grateful to Mr. Wayne Rollin, the Community Development Director of the City of Fond du Lac for sharing his annual progress reports from 1996 – 2001 for this section.

REFERENCES

Adams, J. S. ed. 1976. *Contemporary Metropolitan America 4: Twentieth Century Cities.* Association of American Geographers Metropolitan Analysis Project. Cambridge, MA: Ballinger Publishing Company.

Berger, T. 1978. Price tags placed on south, north, downtown malls in Wausau. *The Daily Herald* Wausau-Merrill. March 15.

———. 1979a. Downtown Wausau Shows Signs of Trouble. *The Daily Herald* Wausau-Merrill. January 25.

———. 1979b. Mall controversy two years old. *The Daily Herald* Wausau-Merrill. March 26.

———. 1982. Store closings in city fewer than 5 years ago. *The Daily Herald* Wausau-Merrill. December 6.

Berry, B. J. L., and J. D. Karsda. 1977. *Contemporary Urban Ecology.* New York: Macmillan Publishing Company Inc.

Berry, B. J. L., and Y. S. Cohen. 1973. Decentralization of commerce and industry: The restructuring of Metropolitan America. In *The Urbanization of Suburbs,* ed. L. H. Masohi and J. K. Haddan, 431 – 455. Beverly Hills: Sage Publications.

Berry, B. J. L., and F. E. Horton. 1970. *Geographic Perspectives on Urban Systems.* Englewood Cliffs: Prentice Hall.

Bluestone, B., P. Hanna, S. Kuhn, and L. Moore 1981. *The Retail Revolution: Market Transformation, Investment, and Labor in the Modern Department Store.* Boston: Auburn House.

Buchholz, H. 1974. Demolition work to start Thursday. *Fond du Lac Reporter.* June 5.

Cassidy, R. 1972. Moving to the suburbs: when business flees the city. *The New Republic* 166: 20-23.

City of Green Bay. 1979. Inventory: Economic Systems. *Green Bay Comprehensive Plan. 1979 – 2000,* B1.10-1 - B1.3 – 5. Green Bay: City of Green Bay.

Combelick, J. 1981. Hotel Firms Interested in Downtown Oshkosh. *Oshkosh Daily Northwestern.* January 1.

Daniels, P. W. 1982. An exploratory study of office location behavior in Greater Seattle. *Urban Geography* 3 (1): 58 – 78.

Ekvall, P. A. 1966. $9 million commercial development announced for downtown Oshkosh. *Appleton Post-Crescent.* May 27.

Erickson, R. A. 1980. Environment as 'Push Factor' in the suburbanization of business establishments. *Urban Geography* 1 (2): 167 – 178.

————. 1983. The evolution of the suburban space economy. *Urban Geography* 4 (2): 95-121.

Erickson, R. A., and D. L. Straussfogel. 1986. The spatial patterns of employment change in large American metropolises: 1947 – 1977. *Urban Geography* 7 (5): 385-396.

Fond du Lac. 1995. *Comprehensive Plan. Volume 2: Plans and Policies.* Fond du Lac: City of Fond du Lac.

Frieden, B. J., and L. B. Sagalyn. 1990. *Downtown Inc. How America Rebuilds Cities.* Cambridge, MA: The MIT Press.

Gad, G. 1985. Office Location dynamics in Toronto: suburbanization and central district specialization *Urban Geography* 6 (4): 331 – 351.

Garbo, S. 1983. Highway 41 Location generates businesses. *Oshkosh Daily Northwestern.* February 20.

Gong, H. and J. O. Wheeler. 2002. The location and suburbanization of business and professional services in the Atlanta Metropolitan area. *Growth and Change* 33 (3):341 – 369.

Green Bay Economic Development Department. 1996. Overview City of Green Bay Downtown Redevelopment. Green Bay: City of Green Bay.

Green Bay Redevelopment Authority. 1970. A Report on Gregby 1 Business Relocation. *Green Bay Press-Gazette.* April 4.

Grey, D. 1991. Kline's is pulling out. *Oshkosh Northwestern.* September 5.

Haas, S. 1995. Combating blight in the city. *Oshkosh Northwestern.* Nov. 7.

Hamer, A. M. 1973. *Industrial Exodus From Central City: Public Policy and the Comparative Costs of Location.* Lexington, MA: D. C. Heath and Co.

Hartshorn, T. A. 1992. *Interpreting the City: An Urban Geography* 2nd Edition. New York: John Wiley & Sons Inc.

Hentz, C. 2003. Revitalized. *Marketplace* 14 (9):17.

Herald Staff. 1957. A new shopping center on Grand Avenue. *The Recorder-Herald* October 17.

Holocomb, H. B., and R. A. Beauregard. 1981. *Revitalizing Cities.* Washington, DC: Association of American Geographers.

Holloway, S. R., and J. O. Wheeler. 1991. Corporate headquarters relocation and changes in metropolitan corporate dominance, 1980-1987. *Economic Geography* 67 (1): 54 – 74.

Hutchinson, D. 1981. Phase II Redevelopment begins. *Green Bay News-Chronicle Report.*

Jones, K., and J. Simmons. 1990. *The Retail Environment.* London and New York: Routledge.

Kellog, C. 1986. *College and Oneida.* Appleton: Outagamie County Historical Society, Inc.

Kurschner, D. 1988. West side Shopko plan nearly complete. *The Wausau Daily Herald.* January 13.

Lamb, R. F. 1985. The morphology and vitality of business districts in upstate New York villages. *Professional Geographer* 37 (2): 162 – 172.

Lloyd, W. J. 1991. Changing suburban retail patterns in Metropolitan Los Angeles. *Professional Geographer* 43 (3): 335 – 44.

Mattingly, P. F. 1991. The changing location of physician offices in Bloomington-Normal, Illinois: 1870-1988. *Professional Geographer* 43 (4): 465-474.

Maier, H. 1986a. A decade of development. Press-Gazette Special Report. *Green Bay Press-Gazette* September 6.

————. 1986b. Gregby launched Green Bay's Redevelopment. *Green Bay Press-Gazette* September 7

————. 1986c. Gregby looks at 20 years *Green Bay Press-Gazette* Sept. 7.

Mayer, H. M., and C. F. Kohn, ed. 1959. *Readings in Urban Geography.* Chicago: The University of Chicago Press.

Mentzer, M. 1974. Downtown demolition of buildings underway. *Fond du Lac Reporter.* June 12.

Miner, J. 1968. 18-acre site cleared downtown. *The Paper* June 21.

Muller, P. O. 1981. *Contemporary Suburban America.* Englewood Cliffs, NJ: Prentice-Hall, Inc.

Ndavu, J. M. 1972. A Study of Downtown Redevelopment in the City of Oshkosh. An Unpublished Report.

Oakland, D. 1981a Mall relocation plan is working for business. *The Daily Herald* Wausau-Merrill. May 23.

————. 1981b. Third Street plan unveiled. *The Daily Herald Wausau-Merrill* November 25.

————. 1982. Downtown council picks pedestrian mall. *The Daily Herald Wausau- Merrill* January 22.

————. 1984. Restaurant, grocery top wanted list for Downtown Wausau. *The Wausau Daily Herald* February 25.

Ofori-Amoah, B. 1997. *Geographic Shift in Economic Activities between Downtowns and Outskirts of Small Urban Areas. A Study of Five Wisconsin Cities.* Stevens Point, WI: University of Wisconsin-Stevens Point, Department of Geography and Geology.

O hUallachain, B., and N. Reid. 1991. The location and growth of business and professional services in American metropolitan areas 1976 – 1986. *Annals of the Association of American Geographers* 81 (2): 254 – 70.

————. 1992. The intrametropolitan location of services in the United States. *Urban Geography* 13: 334 – 354.

Paulsen, D. 2003. Rebirth of central city started with mall in 1983. *Wausau Daily Herald* May 8.

Perle, E. D. 1981. Perspectives on the changing ecological structure of suburbia *Urban Geography* 2 (3): 237 – 254.

Quante, W. 1976. *The Exodus of Corporate Headquarters from New York City.* New York: Praeger.

Rauen, K., and Ryman, R. 2004. Downtown: Beyond Perception. *Green Bay Press-Gazette.* October 10 – 14.

Rentmeester, K. 2004. Green Bay officials create a "new" downtown. *Marketplace* 15 (11): 34.

Rupinski, P. 1979. Business and industry grew. *The Daily Herald*, Wausau-Merrill. December 28 – 29.

Sandberg, S. 1974a. Downtown office-retail complex out; major store is sought. *Fond du Lac Reporter.* July 18.

———. 1974b. Jaycees to beautify downtown. *Fond du Lac Reporter.* Aug. 21.

———. 1974c. Entire downtown block slated in 3-Phase urban renewal plan. *Fond du Lac Reporter.* October 17.

———. 1988. 65-acre development announced. *Fond du Lac Reporter* Nov. 16.

Sauer, M. 1995. *The Vision Thing* Brown County Plans and Visions Special Report 2 – 7. Green Bay: Brown County.

Scott, A. J. 1983a. Industrial organization and the logic of intrametropolitan location I: theoretical considerations. *Economic Geography* 59 (3): 233 – 250.

———. 1983b. Industrial organization and the logic of intrametropolitan location II: a case study of the printed circuits industry in Greater Los Angeles region. *Economic Geography* 59 (4): 343 – 367.

———. 1982 Locational patterns and dynamics of industrial activity in the modern metropolis. *Urban Studies* 19: 111 – 142.

Schulz, B. 1985. Ground broken for Oshkosh Center. *Oshkosh Northwestern.* February 17.

Semple, R. K., and A. G. Phipps 1982. The spatial evolution of corporate headquarters within an urban system. *Urban Geography* 3: 258-278.

Simmons, J. 1991. The regional mall in Canada. *Canadian Geographer* 35: 232 – 40.

Steed, G. P. F. 1976. Centrality and locational change: printing, publishing, and clothing in Montreal and Toronto. *Economic Geography* 52 (3): 193 – 205.

Sternlieb, G. 1963. The future of retailing in the downtown core. *Journal of the American Institute of Planners* 24: 162 – 172.

Stevens Point Journal. 1997. Century project draws fire – again December 11.

Stilwell, B. 1992. Motel, restaurant plans on track. *Fond du Lac Reporter.* Jun. 30.

Storm, S. 1995. Leisure time crafts closing doors. *Oshkosh Northwestern.* May 4.

UW-Bureau of Research. 1951. *Oshkosh Economic Survey.* Madison, WI.

Thayer, E. B. 1925. *Early History of Wausau, Marathon County, WI.* Mimeo.

The Sunday Times. 1967. Development along US 41 fast, furious. *The Sunday Times.* September 17.

Vandenberg, E. 2002. Arts and Economics. *Marketplace* 13 (14):38 – 40.

Velden, P. V. 1986. Kohl closes Oshkosh store. *Oshkosh Daily Northwestern.* January 9.

Vernon, R. 1959. *The Changing Economic Function of the Central City.* New York: Committee for Economic Development.

Vise, P. D. 1976. The suburbanization of jobs and minority employment. *Economic Geography* 52 (4): 348 – 362.

Waddell, P., and Shukla, V. 1993. Manufacturing location in polycentric urban areas: a study in the composition and attractiveness of employment subcenters *Urban Geography* 14: 277 – 96.

Wausau Area Urban Planning Committee. 1964. *Comprehensive Planning Studies: Economic Analysis.* Memo Report No. 3. Wausau, WI.

Williams, C. 1992. The contribution of regional shopping centres to local economic development: threat or opportunity? *Area* 24: 283 – 8.

Zelinsky, W. 1977. The Pennsylvania small town: an overdue geographical account. *Geographical Review* 67 (1): 127 – 147.

Part III

Planning and Managing Change in Small Cities

10

Revitalizing Small City Downtowns:
The Case of Brandon, Canada

Doug Ramsey, Derrek Eberts, and John Everitt
Brandon University

INTRODUCTION

Like most cities in North America, Brandon, Manitoba (2001 population 39,716,[1] see Figure 10.1), has undergone significant spatial reorganization over the past half century, principally driven by a reconfiguration of its commercial structure represented significantly, though not wholly, by the emergence and dominance of suburban shopping centers (strip malls, a regional shopping mall, and more recently, big box developments). The adverse impacts of these developments have been felt most strongly in the downtown, consisting of the old central business district and the residential areas immediately surrounding it. Although the literature on downtown decline and revitalization goes back at least four decades (*e.g.* Sternlieb 1963; Vernon 1959), for the most part, this literature has focused on large cities/metropolitan areas, and is therefore not well suited to the case of small cities like Brandon (the collection of papers in Burayidi (2001) is a notable exception). So-called 'Main Street' initiatives have also been the subject of study in North America (*e.g.* Holdsworth 1985; Dane 1997; Francaviglia 1996). This chapter will describe the efforts undertaken to reinvigorate the downtown core of Brandon, in terms of its functions both as a place of business and as a residential neighborhood, from about the late 1960s to the present. The chapter is organized in four sections. First, we will review some

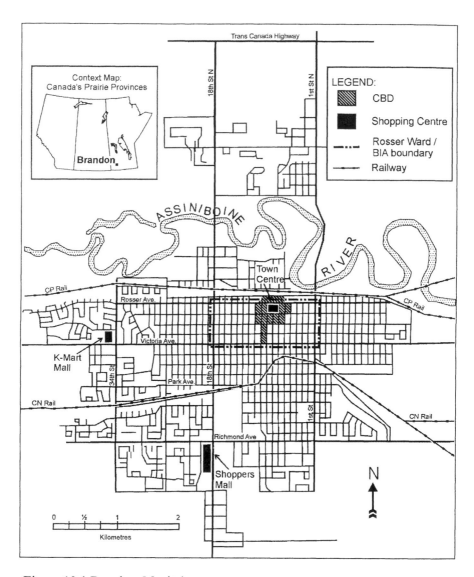

Figure 10.1 Brandon, Manitoba

key contributions on revitalizing the downtowns of small cities. Second, we will outline the evolution and growth of Brandon as a regional service center. Third, we will examine the efforts at revitalizing downtown Brandon with particular reference to the last 20 years. Fourth, we will summarize the lessons learned and their implications for small cities. This we hope will contribute to the small but growing literature on small cities and their downtowns.

PERSPECTIVES ON REVITALIZING SMALL CITY DOWNTOWNS

While small and large cities may often face the same basic problems and challenges, it is also increasingly being recognized that the strategies and solutions for dealing with these problems are quite different between the two types of urban places. The grand projects often envisaged for large cities (see Frieden and Sagalyn 1989) are often impractical and most certainly inappropriate for small city downtowns. This is a direct consequence of the basic truth that small cities and large urban centers are essentially different kinds of places. In a number of ways, small city downtowns are distinct from those of large cities (Robertson 2001):

1. They are smaller, more human scale.
2. They have fewer and/or less severe 'problems' (crime, congestion, etc.).
3. They have lesser 'corporate' presence in physical structure (e.g. office towers) and economic influence.
4. They lack 'signature projects'.
5. They have lesser presence of regional and national chains in the retail structure.
6. They have no specialized 'districts'.
7. They are more closely linked to nearby residential neighborhoods.
8. They have a greater proportion of original (and historic) buildings intact.

In addition, in the Canadian prairies and United States Midwest, the railway had and continues to have a significant impact on the structure of downtown. Further, specifically in the Canadian context, the climate limits the options available in these cities. As a result of these differences and particularities, a number of principles and strategies that would be quite inappropriate for larger cities might effectively encourage the revitalization of small city downtowns.

Several key principles/strategies are argued to be essential to successful downtown revitalization in small cities. Many of these are drawn essentially from the 'Main Street' approach (see National Main Street Center 1988), though there are others that complement this basic approach (Robertson 2001). They include the following:

1. Develop and build on strong public/private partnership.

2. Develop an overall vision/plan for the downtown, addressing functional, physical, social, and economic elements.
3. Be/become multifunctional.
4. Preserve/build on heritage.
5. Link the downtown to the waterfront.
6. Be/become pedestrian-friendly.
7. Establish and follow design guidelines to create an urban streetscape with a unified image.
8. Do not overemphasize parking.

As we shall see, not all of these will be appropriate in the case of Brandon. One example is principle five, as the Assiniboine River is separated from the downtown by the main tracks of the Canadian Pacific Railway running through the city, and the light industrial and warehouse spaces that remain adjacent to the tracks, along the northern boundary of the downtown core (see Figure 10.2). Principle eight is interesting in specifying what *not* to do—most small cities do not have a parking/congestion problem downtown, though the 'big city' strategies will normally make this a primary concern.[2] As we shall see below, downtown parking has been addressed in the past in Brandon, and while it might be perceived as an advantage of the suburban mall, it is in reality probably not a significant challenge facing the city. In this case, those who perceive parking downtown to be a negative issue tend, in fact, to make it an issue.

In a grand way, Kenyon (1989) argues that in the small city, historic preservation and economic development, often considered incongruous, are in fact complementary elements of a shift from Central Business District (CBD) to Central Social District (CSD)—a place within the city that is the center of social life, pulling the community together via festivals, events, and social and cultural amenities that contribute to the city's identity. Robertson (2001) similarly concludes that it is essential that the downtown develop a strong 'sense of place'. This shift in the general function and purpose of the downtown is a strategic way to revitalize the core of the city by becoming distinct from the suburban commercial structure that had threatened it, and at the same time creating opportunities to sustain the often unique commercial activities that linger in the downtown.

In this context, we argue that the revitalization of Brandon's downtown hinges on a variety of individuals and organizations (and their activities), collectively acting in ways more or less consistent with the principles described above. In particular, Brandon has (both deliberately and surreptitiously) followed the basic tenets of the Main Street approach, and focused especially on a) heritage and b) sense of place (broadly) in redeveloping the downtown.

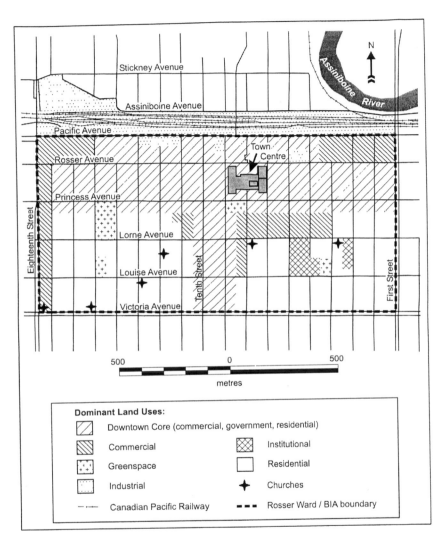

Figure 10.2. Downtown Brandon

EVOLUTION AND GROWTH OF BRANDON

The founding of Brandon was a direct result of the building of the first transcontinental railway in Canada (the Canadian Pacific Railway—the CPR)

(See Everitt and Stadel 1988). Although geographical factors such as the local physical environment, the site's position in relation to other settlements, and perceived economic value, all contributed to its founding, and although favorable conditions for urban growth were present, individual decisions, first by General Rosser and later by administrative officials and residents, were critical in the growth and development of the city. In many ways the decisions of individuals have continued to affect the fate of the city, and the contemporary story of Brandon's downtown revitalization has also hinged on a number of key actors.

Immediately after the selection of Brandon as a town site (with the first passenger train arriving on 11 October 1881), businessmen and speculators rushed to the site, anxious to gain an early foothold. In the following spring there was a permanent population of 1,500 with 120 businesses; and by midsummer it was reported that Brandon was "a full fledged city with complete municipal machinery, nearly 200 businesses, institutions for every class and a permanent population of not less than 3,000" (*Brandon Sun*, quoted in McFadden 1982: 21). Perhaps needless to say these developments were all in what is now considered the 'core' area of Brandon, and this concentration of services within the central city continued for some time.

Although permanent housing was sparse in 1882, a spatial pattern that is still evident today was beginning to emerge. The wealthy were located predominantly on the southwest side of the downtown area. That part of the middle class that did not reside in the downtown boarding houses also lived mainly in the south and west in addition to a small cluster of middle-class houses between Seventh and Tenth Streets. Many of these larger homes have, in recent decades, been converted into apartments, or gentrified. Working-class areas were developing on the east side of downtown, and north of the CPR tracks (Westenberger et al. 1985). As we shall show later, some of these areas are currently subject to redevelopment strategies as part of a provincial program.

Three reasons for this trend-setting pattern can be hypothesized. First, the physical environment of the Assiniboine River floodplain and the existence of the CPR tracks made the north side of the city difficult to reach and undesirable to live in. Second, the prevailing winds from the west and the growth of the railway yards meant that the 'east end' was more noisy and noxious than the south and west sides. Third, once this pattern of development had been established, the higher-class groups moved to the south and west to avoid the people as well as the environment on the other side of the business core.[3]

By 1907 considerable changes had taken place, both in the area covered and in the pattern of development. The downtown area had grown, both in size and significance, and had become better defined as a commercial core. The initial speculative boom had subsided and Brandon residents were now interested in establishing a permanent home, resulting in growth of the residential areas, and a decrease in temporary dwellings close to downtown. Housing had spread southwards to the one hundred-foot wide Victoria Avenue, along which shade trees had been planted and many 'grand' houses constructed (Barker 1977: 28). The working-class zones grew most, so that by 1907 they made up the largest area of any group. Some expansion took place adjacent to the core, in neighborhoods previously occupied by middle and upper-middle-class groups, but most growth was in the south and east ends of the city. This was in part a result of the general broadening of Brandon's economic base, but reflected particularly the construction of the Northern Pacific and Canadian Northern railways to the south, and the expansion of the CPR yards in the east. Ethnically the expansion was significantly Eastern European, mainly by people of Polish and Ukrainian origin.

The Canadian Northern lines also blocked the expansion of upper-middle-class housing to the south, although the earlier elite sector in the west and southwest continued to expand. In fact, the upper class social area consolidated to the west of Tenth Street between 1883 and 1907, although it was surrounded by a middle-class zone which was almost completely cut in half by the expansion of the commercial core south along Tenth Street, even by then the major north-south artery. By 1914 there had been substantial areal expansion but little location change in social areas. The commercial core continued to expand, particularly along the east-west axis of Rosser Avenue and the north-south artery of Tenth Street, a pattern that was reinforced by the short-lived introduction, in 1913, of streetcars that plied these major thoroughfares.

As might be expected, the working-class districts continued to be the largest in the city with pockets of working-class residential development near the core, and with three almost uniformly working-class areas east of First Street, north of the CPR tracks, and in the 'south end' of the city. In all three cases railroad development, and consequently employment, was the critical factor and in all cases the working-class had filled spaces left unused by the other two social groups (middle class and upper-middle class). East of Tenth Street and south of Victoria Avenue the growth of middle-class residential zones was truncated by the active expansion of working-class development. The middle classes abandoned some neighborhoods, and expansion of higher-class housing was deflected into the west end where such social barriers did not exist. These abandoned neighborhoods are the areas now either being used as rental accommodation or undergoing gentrification.

A number of major social and economic forces can be identified that help to explain the development of the city's social areas. First, the upper-middle classes had greater flexibility, freedom of choice, and power in determining residential location than the lower classes; they therefore picked the choice locations. Second, although there are no major relief variations in Brandon, local relief, drainage, and microclimate may have played some role, at least as a reason for the elite avoiding northward expansion onto the floodplain of the Assiniboine River, and eastward expansion into areas affected by air and noise pollution from downtown and the railroad yards. Third, once the upper-middle class had selected its locations, the middle class located close by, a strategy identified elsewhere as a means of minimizing social distance between individuals and the groups they wish to emulate (Timms 1975: 98). As a result, members of the working class had little choice although, as in other cities, a tendency for extremes of the social scale to locate at opposite sides of the city is evident (Duncan and Duncan 1955: 493). In Brandon, a relative lack of mobility and the specific location of economic opportunities reinforced this pattern.

During the late 1950s and early 1960s, many Brandon residents began to trade in their old homes in favor of newer, single-family homes (*Brandon Sun* 1962). This resulted in westward intra-urban movement into new residential development further from the core (such as the Valleyview and Larkhill subdivisions). One consequence was that by the 1960s Brandon was faced with a shortage of low-income housing, as the builders concentrated on middle- and high-income families. This was accompanied by declining housing quality in the older residential sections, which were still being abandoned. Thus, the movement to the outskirts was being accompanied by obsolescence of the housing stock in some of the older residential areas. Also, new shopping areas have sprung up in an outer belt around the city, associated with the decline of the commercial and social dominance of the CBD, a situation that is common throughout North America. Partly to counter this decline, as we shall discuss, a new downtown mall was opened, and in time Brandon began to participate in a province-wide effort to revitalize and spruce up the core area.

REVITALIZING DOWNTOWN BRANDON, 1960 – 2000

The central area of Brandon is characterized by historic buildings, many of which are heritage, as a result of its development processes and lack of land value pressures that in larger cities result in their demolition.[4] It is also characterized by an extensive, although not always economically healthy, commercial area (CBD). In the 1960s, the upper floor spaces generally were poorly used or vacant and were often in a stage of blight as documented in the *City of Brandon –Urban Renewal Study* (Underwood, McLellan and Associates 1967). The upper floors were used predominantly for inexpensive, often substandard, residential suites; manufacturing; wholesaling and storage (often in a condition of blight); inexpensive hotel rooms; offices; and financial services and government functions in more modern or upgraded structures. The inefficiency of upper floor space use was closely related to the age of buildings in the commercial core, many structures dating back to the pre-World War II or even the pre-world War I period, and a failure to maintain the building fabric properly. It is also related to building codes that restrict the possibilities of opening up these floors in specific zones to residential uses. Contemporary attempts at revitalization were hamstrung by this problem that can only be overcome by considerable ingenuity and/or great expense.[5] In addition to the structural deterioration and blight, and the functional obsolescence of buildings, there was also the inability or unwillingness to adapt the buildings to modern requirements and safety regulations. From about the late 1960s, Brandon's CBD became the subject of revitalization studies, reports, and actions, which for purposes of discussion, can be classified as follows: (1) the reports of the downtown studies of 1960s – 1980s (2) The Downtown Mall Project (3) the Downtown Brandon Business Improvement Association and (4) The Neighbourhood Renewal Corporation.

The Reports of the Downtown Studies, 1960s – 1980s

Between the late 1960s and the early 1980s five main reports were issued, all of them identifying what was wrong with downtown Brandon and what needed to be done. The first of these was the *Urban Renewal Report* of 1967 prepared by Underwood, McLellan and Associates. It optimistically characterized downtown Brandon as the

> social and economic hub of the City..., the shopping centre [and] the focus of business and civic life, not just for the inhabitants of Brandon itself, but for a large surrounding agricultural area, the most vital piece of real estate for many hundreds of square miles (Underwood, McLellan and Associates 1967: 69).

The same study recognized, however, that "decay and the need for renewal affect the whole of the city fabric but it is in the Central Business District that the problem is most serious and most difficult to solve," and that "the revitalization of the downtown area is the most important single problem facing the citizens of Brandon" (p. 69). For many people the city center had become old, outgrown, out-of-date, and functionally archaic, and was "showing signs of decay and obsolescence, which reduce its effectiveness and threaten to stifle its future growth and very existence" (p. 69). This problem of the "ugly conditions" (Hodge and Qadeer 1983: 157) of downtown was unquestionably a contributing factor in the emergence of two suburban malls in Brandon during the early 1970s—which then further accelerated the decline of the core area.[6]

In terms of transportation and transport-related land use and problems, the Underwood study noted the prevailing tendency in most downtown areas of

North American cities, at least until the 1970s, to "ease the flow of traffic at the expense of the convenience of the pedestrian" (p. 70), a tendency which could also be observed in Brandon. Yet it was recognized that the major function of the city center should be that of a market place and meeting place, functions that could be stimulated by creating an environment for people on foot. This study concluded that "the provision for both long and short term parking spaces [in downtown Brandon] was inadequate, poorly distributed and an inefficient use of land" (p. 78).

In 1970, the *Brandon Area Transportation Study* (City of Brandon 1970), examining the traffic and parking system, evaluated for the first time the possible effect of closing part of Rosser Avenue from vehicular traffic to create a downtown pedestrian mall, a move that never materialized. An initial concept proposed converting Rosser Avenue between Sixth and Tenth Streets into an enclosed mall with the roof structure becoming a major parking deck made accessible by a series of ramps from the south (City of Brandon 1971). However, this project did not get much beyond the stage of architectural design, and preliminary legal and financial considerations.

In 1971, shortly before the two regional shopping centers (the Brandon Shoppers Mall and the K-Mart Mall) were built outside the downtown, another report, *Brandon Downtown Preliminary Report*, prepared by the Municipal Planning Branch of the Province of Manitoba, stressed the importance of the downtown as a

> major public capital investment in utilities and services, the site of major private investment, a major source of public revenue through both business and property taxation, [and] perhaps the most visible feature of the City [contributing] immeasurably to Brandon's image as a regional service centre and as a potential urban-industrial centre" (Province of Manitoba 1971: 6).

The report optimistically stated that "decentralization of commercial facilities has not yet reached a point where the Brandon downtown has been irreversibly damaged" although it was already recognized that "the parking facilities, improved vehicular circulation, and the climate-controlled mall of the shopping centre development may weigh heavily against the Downtown merchant" (Province of Manitoba 1971: 1). The report went on to brand the CBD as an

> overzoned low-density [area], the retail core of which is threatened by functional obsolescence, inadequate vehicular circulation and parking, increasing competition from decentralized sources, and from the general lack of vitality and dynamics" (p 1-2).

It was also recognized that the initiative for redevelopment must come from both civic administration (through zoning and other measures) and from the private sector (mainly through a financial commitment), the first key principle of successful small city downtown revitalization summarized earlier in this chapter.

In 1975, another city-commissioned report concluded that there was an inefficient use of land in downtown Brandon with a considerable amount of surface parking, vacant land, and vacant building floor space (Damas and Smith 1975). It was pointed out that this was not only visually unappealing but that it also meant a loss of tax revenues. In addition, the appearance of disrepair and neglect, the lack of major attraction, and social problems that appeared to be concentrated in the central area all constituted a constraint for redevelopment and revitalization. Furthermore, the impact of suburban shopping centers on Brandon's downtown had "been felt but [that the situation] is not yet critical" (p. 5). It was also considered that the addition of another suburban shopping center would have a "seriously damaging effect" on the downtown and that "in spite of the defects indicated it is still a central area of considerable viability and potential" (p. 2).

In 1977, the *City of Brandon Development Plan* summarized a number of problems, consequences, and proposals for the CBD. These had been previously prepared, circulated, and discussed as the 1976 *Background Studies* for the plan (Province of Manitoba 1976). The following problems were identified:
1. Excessive amount of vacant but unsuitable commercial floor space in the CBD
2. Lack of compactness and cohesion
3. Lack of suitable major anchors to act as true magnets
4. The obsolescence evident in many of the older, multi-storey buildings which lack one special basic technology to make them more useful and useable, namely an elevator system
5. The zoning by-law which encourages industrial uses in the CBD whilst permitting CBD uses in outlying commercial districts
6. Value and assessment on these older buildings necessarily reflect their obsolescent condition. (Province of Manitoba 1977: 3 – 9)

These problems, the plan stated, had resulted in the following negative consequences for the CBD and the Brandon community as a whole:
1. Loss of public capital investment in the CBD's utilities and services as they are not used to their full capacity and life expectancy
2. Incurment of the costs of additional public capital investments for services and utilities in outlying commercial districts
3. Loss of private capital investments because of declining CBD building and land values
4. Loss of public revenue through reduction of taxes for CBD businesses and property

5. Deterioration of the City's image as a regional service center and potential urban-industrial center
6. Lowering the CBD's attractiveness as a shopping center and as a potential location for investment development
7. Potential loss of jobs, if because of the general unattractiveness, the decline of the central area is accompanied by the inability of the City to draw new commercial development and manufacturing operations to other areas of the City. (Province of Manitoba, 1977: pp. 3-9, 3 – 10)

In its proposals for the CBD, the 1977 *City of Brandon Development Plan* recommended the following policies for the core:

1. It should be restricted in size, with clear demarcation of its limits, and it should be upgraded while maintaining its multi-functional role.
2. It should be preserved as the main pedestrian-oriented retail shopping area, and there should be a ban on the construction of new community or regional shopping centers outside the CBD.
3. It should be zoned as a Central Commercial Restricted Area permitting only intensive core-type uses which should be prohibited outside the CBD.
4. A physical beautification program should be started aimed at creating a pleasant pedestrian-oriented image.
5. Historically important buildings should be protected.
6. A second major magnet (apart from the proposed downtown mall) should be created in the western part of the core.
7. A 'round-the-clock' population should be encouraged within the CBD by the provision of high density residential accommodation with a wide range of facilities and amenities.
8. Government facilities and amenities should be encouraged to locate within the core.
9. Adequate and suitable landscaped parking space should be provided. Parking space should be integrated into new facilities and on-street parking should be reduced gradually by the provision of parking structures at the periphery of the core.
10. Efforts should be made to eradicate the problem of vacant and decrepit floor space and underutilized land.
11. A small portion of the business and assessment taxes should be designate for the purpose of implementing a number of downtown development projects.
12. A downtown development committee, a consultative civic group, should be formed. (Province of Manitoba 1977: 3 – 10, 3 – 11, 3 – 12).

Although many of these recommendations were not implemented during this time period, it is interesting to note that several of these ideas have persisted, and some are currently being implemented, for instance housing and building regeneration (by the Neighbourhood Renewal Corporation [NRC]); heritage preservation (by the City of Brandon through its Municipal Heritage Advisory Committee [MHAC] the Brandon Area Planning District [BAPD]); and Urban Building and Design Standards (through the City of Brandon and a number of other stakeholders including the NRC, the MHAC, and the BAPD). More specifically, from the 1980s, downtown businessmen finally became more committed to revitalization of Brandon's core area. At least four formal initiatives have been undertaken to ensure the preservation of the core of Brandon: the establishment of heritage preservation designations, the development of the downtown mall in 1980 (and regeneration efforts thereafter), the establishment of a business improvement association (having a spatial designation), and a provincial program intended to support initiatives aimed at urban core development in Manitoba (Everitt and Ramsey 2002). The rest of this section will address the last three, as they are most directly aimed at the economic health and vitality of downtown Brandon.

The Downtown Mall

As Kalman (1985: 32) notes, the suburban "shopping mall is the biggest threat to the survival of Main Street", accounting for most of the growth in the urban retail sector since the 1960s (Jones 1991). To counter this trend in Brandon and to energize what had been described by city officials as Brandon's 'lifeless downtown', a city-sponsored construction of a downtown mall ('The Brandon Gallery', subsequently renamed 'The Town Centre') was pursued (see Figure 10.2). This represented the first major attempt to address the problems of downtown Brandon that had been identified in the many previous reports. The mall was completed in 1980. In the early years, the Gallery boasted a 90% occupancy rate. In addition, it appears to have slowed decay and prevented the terminal decline of downtown Brandon. It at least focused attention on the problem, provided much needed breathing space to this area of the city, and enabled downtown to survive until better strategies could be identified and implemented. For example, in 1987, based on a consultant's report with the purpose "to design a plan for the rebirth of the core area" (*Brandon Sun* 25 March 1987), city council committed $350,000 per year over a five-year period for downtown development. This commitment had to be matched by a promise by the local businessmen to form a Business Improvement Area.

However, the mall has had a checkered history. First, it opened amidst controversy. It was opposed by some who felt that the city should have focused more on its other resources, such as heritage architecture and streetscapes. Located on two bulldozed blocks of land assembled by the City of Brandon in the heart of the CBD (Horne 2001), this conventionally designed mall turned its back on the rest of downtown and as Stillinger (1986: 41) notes, The Gallery was left "sitting as [a] giant fortress of retailing in the hostile environment of downtown Brandon." As a result, it represented a use of traditional economic development techniques to solve a problem that was not traditional. Second, it appears that the high occupancy rate that was achieved in the early years was detrimental to the downtown core as vacancy rates outside the mall in the CBD went up. Some retailers, for instance, moved from other CBD locations to new premises within the mall, leaving newly vacant spaces outside the mall. Third, the mall's initial economic success was hampered by a general economic recession in the early 1980s and by the $6.5 million expansion of the Brandon Shoppers' Mall in November 1981 that increased its size by approximately one-third. As the expansion of the suburban mall was not a new regional shopping center, it did not violate the 'letter' of the ban enshrined in the 1977 *City of Brandon Development Plan*. However, it certainly worked against its 'spirit'. At the same time, it touched off considerable controversy. Former Alderman Dyck went as far as to say: "I looked upon the expansion on the same basis as if we had developed a new mall out there. By allowing it, we certainly didn't give the support to the downtown that we were supposedly dedicated to" (*Brandon Sun* 7 July, 1982). Subsequent major losses including two anchors, the Hudson's Bay Company and Eaton's, two of Canada's major department store chains, clearly show that malls such as the Gallery, designed to go head-to-head with their suburban counterparts, were unlikely to succeed in this mission. Through the 1990s, the downtown mall became largely vacant. As a result of this combination of forces, the Gallery has changed hands four times during its history, these ownerships including realty groups in Ontario.

Most recently a group of local investors has taken over. The new operation is being redefined as a service (rather than retail) oriented mall, and has been renamed The Town Centre. This new role is a confirmation of the views of many that central Brandon will never be a competing shopping center to the suburban Shoppers Mall. Retail operations in The Town Centre include specialized niche retailers, and the clientele is predominantly the elderly, partly because there are several seniors housing complexes nearby, and partly because others periodically bus in their residents. The city's primary public transit transfer point is also located proximal to the main entrance to The Town Centre. At the same time, it is hoped that specialized retailing will attract customers from around the city as well as throughout the region. That is, the mall hopes to become a 'destination' for services and niche retailing.

The current incipient success of The Town Centre in its new role has been boosted considerably by the location of the local Regional Health Authority (RHA) within the mall. Not coincidentally, the Director of the RHA was once a Brandon City Manager and a booster of downtown. He recognized that many of the RHA's clientele lived downtown, that the Gallery (as it then was) needed boosting, and that the RHA could help to 'kill two birds with one stone.' Negotiations for its lease were long and drawn out, but the end result gave an important base-rent to the new mall owners. In contrast to the traditional rent structure of malls, where the anchor(s) are given cheap rent so that the smaller businesses benefiting from their drawing power will be willing to pay a premium to be there, in the case of the Town Centre, the RHA is the main bill-payer, allowing the mall to offer inexpensive rent to the principally locally owned, specialized retailers who remain. In a key partnership the city loaned the RHA money for building renovations, to be paid back over the fifteen-year lifetime of the RHA's lease. The 130 staff of the Health Authority represents a boost to traffic downtown, as well as the sales of other mall businesses such as the Food Court.

Another booster for the Town Centre is the Regional Library and Art Gallery that moved into the space abandoned by Eaton's in 1999 (Horne 2000). While amounting to a taxpayer subsidy to the mall owners, this transfer is also likely to have positive spin-offs for this area, at least by increasing traffic in the heart of downtown. This latest initiative was promoted heavily by the mayor at the time, who was anything but a social activist, but did realize the importance to the overall health of the city's economy and society of a vibrant CBD that is attractive to as many citizens of Brandon as possible. The previous library/arts building, located a few blocks away, has now (2004) been recycled into a call center reportedly employing as many as 500 people (*Brandon Sun* 15 Jan. 2005).

An added bonus to the future of downtown Brandon is that the current owners of the downtown mall profess to be less concerned with making money from the mall (although losing money is not an option), and more with improving the center of the city in which they live and work. Thus, community spirit is counteracting the profit motive—at least in the short run. The mall recently received a much-needed facelift, and is likely to continue to be improved over the next few years. Both internal and external beautification initiatives were completed in October 2001 with the grand opening of the new art gallery and regional library taking place in December 2001. By 2003, the Town Centre boasted an occupancy rate of approximately 90%, certainly boosted by the public cultural institutions, the RHA, plus other non-traditional service functions (*e.g.* a fitness center).

The Main Street Program and the Brandon Downtown Business Improvement Association (BIA)

The second initiative involved an attempt to revive the Central Business District of the city through the formation of the Downtown Brandon Business

Improvement Association. For its founding manager, the origins of this initiative could be seen in the Heritage Canada Main Street Program, and the Winnipeg Core Area Initiative.[7] The Main Street Canada Program, instituted in 1980, provided free assistance with storefront designs and helped find sources of funding for renovations. According to a former chairman of the Downtown Development Committee,

> the Program does not supply the money for improvements or promotions but it does get the three levels of government as well as the businessmen involved in looking for ways of reversing the trend away from downtown (*Brandon Sun* 20 June 1985).

In 1985, the Downtown Brandon Association voted unanimously to take advantage of the Heritage Canada Main Street Program. Thus, the city council agreed to "allocate $200,000 to begin the process of improving the image and aesthetics of downtown streets" (*Main Street Brandon* 1986: 1). Furthermore, under the terms of the Heritage Canada Main Street Program, a full-time coordinator was hired.

Although these programs were designed to serve smaller towns and a larger city, respectively, than Brandon, their success did make concerned Brandonites realize what they (and other middle-sized urban places such as Thompson in Northern Manitoba) might be missing out on, and that they would have to be agents of their own change. As a consequence, a few energetic local businessmen invested some seed capital, and the success of their initiative led the City of Brandon and the Downtown Brandon Association (DBA) to successfully sponsor a Main Street Program in 1985.[8] Initially designed for a three-year period, this program was later extended. Its success, plus the credibility of the members of the DBA, and the willingness of the downtown businessmen to invest their own time and money, undoubtedly convinced the City of Brandon to put together a revitalization plan for the downtown area. This included an infusion of city cash, and a compulsory levy upon the businesses in the downtown zone, with these funds being used for marketing and capital redevelopment projects. One key to the success of this plan was the setting up of an organization to stimulate and coordinate changes in the central core of the city, particularly with respect to economic development. Another key was the hiring of an energetic and concerned manager to run this organization.

In the spring of 1987, the consulting firm of Hilderman, Wilty and Associates was hired "to design a plan for the rebirth of the core area" (*Brandon Sun* 25 March 1987). The new chairman of the city's Downtown Development Board, Jeff Harwood, optimistically proclaimed "the whole process of redevelopment and revitalization of the downtown has begun" (*Brandon Sun* 25 March 1987).

City council also committed $350,000 a year for five years to downtown development providing that businessmen in the area agreed to form a Business Improvement Area. This would commit the businesses in the downtown area to paying a special levy for the upgrading and revitalization of the downtown. In January, 1988 the Business Improvement Association was established by downtown merchants and still continues as a significant actor in the redevelopment of Brandon's core[9] with the mission of encouraging the growth and sustainability of downtown Brandon, while at the same time ensuring that the uniqueness of its character and community is promoted, enhanced, and preserved (Horne 2001) (see Figure 10.2). The BIA, along with the Main Street Program, has dramatically improved the infrastructure and physical appearance of downtown, with 'period' lighting, seats, theme-based paving and improved storefronts, and thereby set the stage for further changes within the core area. Over $3 million has already been spent on the beautification of the area, and as a result, the core of the downtown is considerably more 'pedestrian friendly' than it was prior to the BIA's intervention. The founding manager of the BIA has suggested, however, that it was the setting up of a series of public-private partnerships to guide and fund the physical transformations of the city structure that has been the major achievement of the BIA over the past decade.

Representing approximately 500 shops and services, the BIA levy provides the organization with an annual budget of approximately $170,000, a meager amount with which to pay a salary to a full-time manager and minimal support staff, and run programs aimed at achieving the goals of marketing and beautifying the downtown. This highlights the importance of the organization's role to act as a liaison to other agencies that can contribute to the overall project of downtown improvement. One example is Wheat Belt Community Futures, which provides loans and grants to small businesses.

Although some of the downtown merchants were initially skeptical of these attempts, and progress was an uphill battle, most now seem to support it, both in terms of concept and financially (through the levy), and its momentum has increased. A number of achievements can now be tied directly to the efforts of the BIA. First, there has been substantial investment in the appearance of the core of the downtown area, as identified above. Second, the BIA has created special events in an effort to bring people back downtown, including re-establishing the Santa Claus Parade and sponsoring a fall street fair, 'The Pickle Fest' (Horne 2001). Following the withdrawal of Bick's as a sponsor, the Pickle Fest has been discontinued, but in 2002 it was replaced by 'Street Beat', a similar fair designed to provide an attraction (now classic automobiles) to bring pedestrians to the area. The popularity of this festival is indicated by its expansion from a one-day event in its first year, attracting an estimated 7,000 people, to a two-day event subsequently. In addition, beginning in 2003, the main event was supplemented by a series of smaller scale 'BIA Cruise Nights'. Third, the BIA has actively promoted the downtown with marketing campaigns in print and other media, as well as by creating a theme/motto with which to brand a variety of paraphernalia 'giveaways'. In addition to specific initiatives, the BIA is generally active in promoting pedestrianization, the creation of welcoming green space, preservation of the heritage in the built environment— in general creating an 'atmosphere'/'experience'.

Those who are less happy with the changes being implemented by the BIA are often those who are currently excluded (by location) from the areas that have already received a facelift, or those who feel they receive little benefit from the improvement plan. While formally a part of the downtown, they are located at the periphery, beyond the reach of the main activities of the BIA. As a result, there has been a minor revolt, with some individuals contesting the obligation to provide the tax levy to the BIA. For others, while the levy is not opposed, active participation in the BIA's activities is not pursued. As a result, the BIA gets essential input from a minority of businesses, but also coordinates with other groups/agencies which have an interest in the downtown— for example, the City of Brandon and the Neighbourhood Renewal Corporation (described below). Nevertheless, overall the BIA has successfully heightened community pride, and has probably changed many peoples' attitudes with respect to downtown Brandon - although this area still has a long way to go before it is perceived as a prime shopping and social 'place' by many citizens of Brandon.

The Neighbourhood Renewal Corporation (NRC)

Most recently some of the actors involved in the BIA have played a role in facilitating the setting-up of a Neighbourhood Renewal Corporation (NRC) in Brandon, as part of the Provincial "Neighbourhoods Alive!" program that also encompasses Winnipeg and Thompson. It is likely that the extension of this provincial initiative outside the City of Winnipeg owed a lot to the fact that members of the Provincial Legislative Assembly elected from each of Brandon's two ridings were named Cabinet Ministers. One of these was previously manager of the Main Street program, a city councilor for Rosser Ward, a co-founder of the Rosser Ward Citizens Association, and has remained, as a life-long core-area resident, very concerned with the redevelopment of the city.[10]

Under provincial legislation, a Neighbourhood Renewal Corporation was set up to promote a "Neighbourhoods Alive!" initiative of the newly elected (Fall 1999) New Democratic Party (NDP) provincial government.[11] The creation of this body was originally facilitated by the BIA, and there has been some overlap between the memberships of the two organizations. While the province is the sole funder of the "Neighbourhoods Alive!" initiative at present, its birthing was also very much tied to the Rosser Ward, the boundary of which approximates Brandon's heritage area (as defined by the MHAC), and the BIA's area of responsibility. The Rosser Ward has a socio-economically mixed population, including some areas of gentrified housing populated (mostly) by professionals. In November 1994, the Rosser Ward Citizens Association was formally established as a non-profit organization in order to encourage the city to change its attitude towards the core area, for instance, by down-zoning the area to encourage single-family owner-occupied housing.[12] The NRC boundaries have been adjusted since the NRC was set up, in order to allow project partnerships outside the core with other organizations such as the Habitat for Humanity, and Riverbank Inc. (another 'QUANGO' in Brandon) (Repko and Everitt 1999). There is some overlap between the memberships of the NRC, the MHAC, Riverbank Inc., and the BIA, in terms of citizen members, as well as city and local planning district officials. This helps to facilitate the working partnerships, and enables all of these bodies to operate more efficiently, and thus the synergies between the groups have proven to be of key importance.

The Board of the NRC is made up of local citizens who mostly reside in the core area. It has a number of areas of concern including the physical rehabilitation and beautification of parts of the heritage core of Brandon, as well as the promotion of neighborhoods as communities. It has also been concerned with the construction and implementation of a heritage bylaw as a means of achieving its ends. In this context there are interactions between this organization and the MHAC. Since its first year of existence, housing has been improved in some areas, conversions of old commercial spaces into 'affordable' dwellings have taken place, and recreational facilities have been improved in local parks and schools. For instance, the NRC has operated a 'Front and Paint' program since 2002, providing funding to assist with the improvement and/or renovation of residential buildings, aimed particularly at lower income households whose homes might otherwise remain in a generally poor condition. Challenges in the future include improving the visual standards of the non-commercial parts of the downtown area, as well as stimulating neighborhood interactions and a positive sense of place. Most recently, a three-storey modular housing development project was completed on Pacific Avenue, one block north of Rosser Avenue, adjacent to the CP Railway. Developments such as these, which bring people back to the CBD to live, are seen by the NRC as key to the future of Brandon's downtown core. After some original hesitation, the City of Brandon has formally announced a willingness to partner with the NRC on housing development within the NRC boundaries.

SUMMARY AND CONCLUSIONS

Like many cities, big and small, across North America, Brandon has seen a period of decline and decay, both physically and economically, in its downtown core over the past couple of decades. This has been a consequence, in large part, of the decentralization of commercial activities due to the growth and success of the 'suburban' Shoppers Mall, with many social and cultural amenities following the flight out of the core. Having recognized this problem, the city and various key actors within the community have followed a number of strategies to reverse this trend, and revitalize the downtown. A few key conclusions emerge.

First, as the discussion above attests, the efforts that appear to have been most fruitful in reviving downtown Brandon have been those which involve 'public-private' partnerships. Many parties have an interest in the vitality of downtown, but few are willing or capable of acting individually to effect real change. The BIA emerged only with the support, and then legal inducement, of City Council, who supplemented the initiative with cash to 'get the ball rolling.' The NRC, which operates much like a citizens' activist group, has resulted in remarkable improvements in some of the residential building stock of the downtown area, but only with the support of Provincial money.

Second, the role of the downtown has changed, and success has really only followed when this evolution has been embraced. The early failure of the downtown mall was a direct result of the strategy at the time to try to compete 'head-to-head' with the Shoppers Mall. Once it was realized that this was unlikely ever to succeed, and after several ownership changes, the Town Centre has emerged with a new role to play in the city. The mall is now home to regional services, and a smaller selection of mostly very specialized retailers. This has even been accompanied by a new 'model' of mall economics: the biggest tenants (spatially) now 'pay the bills' so that the smaller retailers can be attracted with cheaper rents. While the downtown mall, conventionally conceived, may now be seen as an inappropriate revitalization strategy, the case of Brandon illustrates that it can be put to effective use with some innovative thinking about the role it plays within the city and region.

Third, although not emphasized specifically in this chapter, the major efforts described above have incorporated several additional key strategies, as identified at the beginning of the chapter. All the efforts have included at least some attention to making the downtown more 'pedestrian friendly', whether it is the controlled climate of the mall, the improved streetscapes resulting from BIA investment, or the general improvement in the downtown urban fabric as a result of the NRC's efforts to upgrade many of the buildings. Related to the latter two points, downtown Brandon has generally aimed at preserving the heritage of the downtown, either through designating heritage buildings, or attempting to implement design guidelines to complement existing heritage structures (through the BIA and NRC, for example). In sum, while not all the strategies for small city downtown revitalization have been appropriate to Brandon, several have been pursued with some degree of success, resulting in promise for the downtown whose future looked bleak without these timely interventions.

Not every action to revive the downtown has been effective or appropriate—there have certainly been a few 'false starts' and missed opportunities—but on the whole, we suggest that Brandon is certainly 'doing the right things'. Only time will tell if they will pay off, but as Robertson (2001) argues, what is needed most in redeveloping the downtown is patience. Most recently, with the renewed interest in the downtown mall, programs offered by the Neighbourhood Renewal Corporation, the efforts of heritage preservation and business organizations together bode well for the future of downtown Brandon. As a final note, it is important to recognize the key role played by selected individuals that were often engaged in more than one of the four initiatives.

ENDNOTES

1. The City had a population of 39,716 in 2001, while the Census Agglomeration contained 41,037. In other words, the surrounding area outside the formal City limits is only very sparsely settled, reflecting the context of Brandon being a service center within a predominantly agricultural region.

2. Abundant, free parking is one of the *main* advantages of the suburban mall, argued to be responsible for the decline of downtowns.

3. There was still a cluster of higher status homes to the east of 10th Street, and it has been suggested that these may have been owned by Catholics who wished to live close to the Roman Catholic Church nearby at 327 4th Street. This hypothesis has yet to be tested. (Tom Mitchell, personal communication.)

4. For more detail on this early growth see Christoph Stadel and John Everitt (1988) "Downtown Brandon".

5. An area of apartment units has been built in old upper-floor warehouse space along the 100 block of 10th Street, but this is the exception rather than the rule.

6. One of these malls, (the K-Mart Mall) at the western edge of the geographic city when it was built, has never developed significantly, but the other, (the Shoppers Mall) at the southern edge of town has grown to be a (if not the) major retailing centre for the city (see Figure 10.1).

7. The BIA has had several managers over its relatively short history. Some only held the position temporarily, while others have been a major influence on the association. One of the latter was a valuable informant for our research.

8. The somewhat grandiosely named Downtown Brandon Association actually only included a small number of influential businessmen, who operated and supported redevelopment in the core area.

9. The BIA was based upon similar organizations elsewhere in North America, and particularly in Ontario, British Columbia, and Winnipeg. The boundaries were set, and have remained, as First to Eighteenth Streets, and Pacific Avenue to Victoria Avenue, corresponding to the City's Rosser Ward.

10. In the most recent cabinet shuffle (Fall 2003) the Brandon West MLA stepped down from the cabinet, but the Brandon East MLA is still a cabinet minister.

11. The Neighbourhood Renewal Corporation's boundaries include the entire area of Rosser Ward, plus additional residential areas both north and south of this zone. This corresponds more or less with the older, pre-WWII housing stock of the city.

12. The central historic core of Brandon is largely contained within the Rosser Ward of city council. The members of, and advisors to, the Rosser Ward Citizens Association have often been heavily involved and perhaps instrumental in many of the changes discussed in this paper. Interestingly many have lived and several still live on a few blocks of Sixteenth Street. Depending upon the definitions used, members of this 'Sixteenth Street Mafia' are to be found as members of nearly all of the groups discussed in this paper. An official Rosser Ward representative sits on the NRC and the MHAC. Members of 'The Mafia' were involved with setting up the BIA and the NRC.

REFERENCES

Barker, G. F. 1977. *Brandon: A City 1881-1961*. Altona: Friesen and Sons.

Brandon Sun. 1982. July 7.

Brandon Sun. 1985. June 20.

Brandon Sun .1987. March 25.

Brandon Sun. 2005. Jan 15.

Burayidi, M. A., ed. 2001. *Downtowns: Revitalizing the Centers of Small Urban Communities*. New York: Routledge.

City of Brandon. 1970. *Brandon Area Transportation Study*. Brandon: City of Brandon.

City of Brandon. 1971. *Rosser Avenue Mall Project (RAMP)*. Brandon: City of Brandon, Industrial Commission.

Damas and Smith. 1975. *Brandon Downtown Redevelopment Program*. Brandon: City of Brandon.

Dane, S. 1997. *Main Street Success Stories*. Washington D.C.: National Main Street Center.

Duncan, D., and B. Duncan. 1955. Residential distribution and occupational stratification. *American Journal of Sociology* 60: 493 – 503.

Everitt, J. and D. Ramsey. 2002. Reviving Brandon in the early twenty-first century (Canadian Urban Landscapes Series No.23). *The Canadian Geographer* 46 (3): 266 – 274.

Everitt, J., and C. Stadel. 1988. Spatial growth of Brandon. In. *Brandon: Geographical Perspectives on the Wheat City,* ed. J. Welsted, J. Everitt, and C. Stadel. 61 – 88. Regina: Great Plains Research Centre, University of Regina.

Francaviglia, R. 1996. *Main Street Revisited.* Iowa City: University of Iowa Press.

Frieden, B., and L. Sagalyn. 1989. *Downtown, Inc.* Cambridge, MIT Press.

Hodge, G. D., and M. A. Qadeer. 1983. *Towns and Villages in Canada: The Importance of Being Unimportant.* Toronto: Butterworths.

Holdsworth, D., ed. 1985. *Reviving Main Street.* Toronto: University of Toronto Press.

Horne, R. 2000. Is there life after Eaton's? Paper presented at the Annual Meeting of the Canadian Association of Geographers, Brock University, St. Catharines, June.

Horne, R. 2001. A multifaceted approach to downtown revitalization in Brandon, Canada. In *Downtowns: Revitalizing the Centers of Small Urban Communities,* ed. M.A. Burayidi, 89 – 103. New York: Routledge.

Jones, K., 1991. The urban retail landscape. In *Canadian Cities in Transition,* ed. T. Bunting and P. Filion, 379-400. Toronto: Oxford University Press.

Kalman, H. 1985. Crisis on Main Street. In *Reviving Main Street,* ed. D. Holdsworth, 31-54. Toronto: University of Toronto Press.

Kenyon, J. B. 1989. From central business district to central social district: The revitalization of a small Georgia city. *Small Town.* March-April: 4 – 17.

Main Street Brandon 1986 1 (1): 1.

McFadden, E.M. 1982. Instant city: the birth of Brandon, 1882. *The Beaver* Summer: 14-21.

Mitchell, T. 1993. Personal Communication.

National Main Street Center. 1988. *Revitalizing Downtown 1976 – 1986.* Washington, D.C.: National Main Street Center.

Province of Manitoba. 1971. *Brandon Downtown Preliminary Report.* Brandon: Province of Manitoba, Municipal Planning Branch.

Province of Manitoba. 1976. *Background Studies: Brandon Development Plan.* Brandon: Province of Manitoba, Municipal Planning Branch.

Province of Manitoba. 1977. *City of Brandon Development Plan.* Brandon: Province of Manitoba, Municipal Planning Branch.

Repko, G. L., and J. Everitt. 1999. Down by the riverside: recent developments along the Assiniboine Corridor in Brandon. *Prairie Perspectives* 2: 199 – 213.

Robertson, K. 2001. Downtown development principles for small cities. In *Downtowns: Revitalizing the Centers of Small Urban Communities,* ed. M. Burayidi, 9 – 22. New York: Routledge.

Stadel, C., and J. Everitt. 1988. Downtown Brandon. In. *Brandon: Geographical Perspectives on the Wheat City*, ed. J. Welsted, J. Everitt, and C. Sta del, 123 – 150. Regina: Great Plains Research Centre, University of Regina.

Sternlieb, G. 1963. The future of retailing in the downtown core. *Journal of the American Institute of Planners* 29 (2): 102 – 112.

Stillinger, E. A. 1986. *Downtown Revitalization Strategy: Brandon, Manitoba*. Unpublished M.A. Thesis. Winnipeg: University of Manitoba.

Timms, D. W. G., 1975. *The Urban Mosaic*. Cambridge: Cambridge University Press.

Underwood, McLellan and Associates. 1967. *City of Brandon – Urban Renewal Study*. Winnipeg: Underwood, McLellan and Associates.

Vernon, R. 1959. *The Changing Economic Function of the Central City*. New York: Committee for Economic Development.

Westenberger, M., J. C. Everitt, and C. Stadel, 1985. The development of Brandon's social areas 1881-1914. *The Albertan Geographer* 21: 79 – 95.

11

Downtown Retailing and Revitalization of Small Cities: Lessons from Chillicothe and Mount Vernon, Ohio

Andreas Otto
Dresden University of Technology

INTRODUCTION

Over the last several decades downtown commercial districts in small cities across the United States have seen changes in terms of their overall importance, types of economic activities, and physical appearance of buildings. These changes are due, in part, to the general, social, and economic decline, and, in part, to increasing competition from outskirt locations and their ability to attract not only new but also existing business, a trend which used to be a problem only in large cities. To counteract this trend, small cities have followed the path of their big sisters and engaged in substantial downtown revitalization projects with mixed results. Thus, while a few communities have been able to implement comprehensive strategies that changed their downtown retail tremendously, most places have seen slight changes based on a "mosaic" of various activities by different players, such as local governments, merchants associations, and property owners. These results have informed two notions about the downtown—a pessimistic view of unstoppable decay of the downtown and an optimistic view of downtown revival through such "simple ingredients," as streetscape projects, façade improvements, a couple of antique stores, regional marketing and more parking. This chapter is of the view that none of these notions can be tenable in the face of relative little research on the subject with respect to small cities. To contribute to this research, this chapter examines the state of downtown retail in small cities, using Chillicothe and Mount Vernon, two small cities in Ohio as case studies. In particular, the chapter examines the nature and characteristics of retail activities currently located in the downtowns of the two small cities, the factors that have shaped and continue to shape the activities, and the lessons that can be learned from the experiences of the two cities.

The chapter is divided into four sections. In the first section, I review the general perspectives on downtown revitalization and retail development and outline a framework for analyzing some of the unanswered issues. In the next section, I provide an overview of retail activities in the downtowns of the two cities, including a brief historical background of the two cities, description of the downtowns, and the nature and characteristics of the retail activities. In the third section, I discuss the factors that impact retail activities in the two cities, with special emphasis on the effects of revitalization activities. In the fourth and concluding section I outline the lessons learned and their implications for downtown revitalization and retail development.

PERSPECTIVES ON DOWNTOWN REVITALIZATION AND RETAIL DEVELOPMENT

Downtown problems appear to be well known. As a result of the tremendous suburbanization of both residences and economic activities, the decline and decay of downtown commercial districts became a characteristic of urban development in post-World War II America. Not only have central business districts of large cities suffered from these developments, but also traditional downtowns of small cities. Basic commercial functions have long moved from city centers to city fringes and suburbs. While traditional downtown commercial districts still combine a mix of public and private uses, they are locations of secondary or lower importance when compared to other commercial areas in the city.

Revitalization efforts began as soon as the decline of downtown was recognized. Depending on the prevailing spirit of the age, different ideas formed the character of revitalization strategies and measures (cf. e.g. Teaford 1990). Though to a lesser extent, the clearance of old downtown quarters was applied to small cities in the 1960s and 70s, too. Buildings, which were then seen as just being out-of-date, were often reshaped into a mall-like look or demolished to create room for more parking. Due to growing historic preservation efforts since the 1970s a re-orientation towards maintaining historic structures came slowly into being. Additionally, new buildings had to be increasingly designed in a way to match adjacent historic structures. The 1980s and 1990s followed with more comprehensive and integrated strategies trying to combine physical and capital improvements, e.g. streetscape programs, and economic revitalization, e.g. tools for business redevelopment.

While many cities have achieved a certain success in revitalizing their downtowns, the main objective of permanently stabilizing downtown's economic base or even strengthening its overall socio-economic importance has often not been accomplished. Therefore, research still has to ask many questions about the future of small city downtowns and the development of downtown retail. Whatever the details might be, it seems necessary to say goodbye to the long played "song" of unstoppable downtown decay. The last decades have seen not only decline but also qualitative changes to downtown retail and other types of uses.

Although comprehensive literature and data analysis on small city downtowns is somewhat scarce (e.g. Ryan et al. 1999), several studies suggest potentially far reaching changes of future downtown functions and downtown retail which are mirrored by terms such as "historic downtown retail district" (Moe and Wilkie 1997:172), "central social district" (Kenyon 1989:4), "tourism business district" (Getz 1993: 583) or "downtown as theme park" (Paradis 2000: 65; Sies and Silver 1996: 405). Some authors suggest that the future of downtown might be based on social, cultural and specialized commercial functions rather than conventional commercial functions (cf. Banovetz et al. 2000; Robertson 2001).

Admittedly, any prospects for downtowns to become prime commercial locations for mass market may be quite unrealistic. However, downtowns might have a chance to redefine themselves through niche markets, for the simple reason that downtowns still have certain qualities that keep attracting support from city dwellers. In addition, general conditions on local, regional, national, and international levels seem to support a reorientation of what downtown's future retail function can be. For example,

- Specialized retail and individualized shopping environments have obtained a strong meaning. Downtowns are *the* places of historic, cultural, architectural and symbolic importance. No other part of the American urban landscape shows more individuality. Generally, a strong differentiation of retail and service demands has become an important element of today's individualized society. Downtowns can be predestined locations of commercial specialization as well as destinations of a growing historic tourism. They are considered as having a *sense of place* (Brown 1993; Klebba et al. 2001). Increasing historic preservation efforts and their consequent implementation are closely related to the idea of maintaining downtown's (historic) uniqueness.

- Traditional downtowns are still perceived as important parts of the local community. They are landmarks and figureheads of their respective cities and their symbolic importance might exceed their actual economic importance by far. Since downtowns are places of representation (Turner 2002) it is likely that downtown redevelopment gets a strong community support. Walzer and Kline (2001:251) see this as "commitment to main street USA."

- Associations, be they for-profit or not-for-profit, as well as private initiatives have become crucial factors not only for community life but for the concrete economic development of cities (Hula et al. 1997; Wilson 1991). This might lead to development options allowing more individual features. An example for countrywide initiatives is the Main Street Center of the National Trust for Historic Preservation. Its 4-point-approach of downtown revitalization is applied in more than 1,700 officially dedicated Main Street Cities (NMSC 2004).

However, further research is needed to come to more general and transferable conclusions on the future of downtown retail. In small cities, this need is further accentuated by the following:

- Only some analyses (e.g. Robertson 1999) consider several impact factors of downtown commercial development, their possible association with each other, and cumulative effects.
- Interactions and dependencies between downtowns and other commercial locations are seldom observed in a comprehensive way (e.g. by McClure 2001; Ofori-Amoah 2000).
- Chances and risks of downtown commercial redevelopment as a whole or strengths and weaknesses of specific revitalization measures are scarcely analyzed and evaluated.
- Conclusions from the development of large city downtowns, on which research is focused, cannot cover the specific situation found in smaller cities.

While part of this problem might be due to lack of comparable quantitative data on the sub-city or downtown level (cf. e.g. Walzer and Kline 2001; Burayidi 2001), this chapter is of the view of that good qualitative research undertaken in a more comprehensive way will go a long way in filling some of the existing knowledge gap. Signs of changes of the overall nature of downtown retail, and in particular of increasing importance of specialty retailing, needs to be observed in order to come to conclusions with regard to the role and effects of downtown revitalization. This requires an analysis of the current situation of downtown retail, an assessment of impact factors of downtown retail development, especially on the local level, and an appraisal of mainly local activities of the public and private sectors to enhance retail change.

In the rest of this chapter, I describe and analyze the current state and development trends of retail in downtown commercial districts of Chillicothe and Mount Vernon, Ohio. These two small cities were chosen because of their non-metropolitan location, comparable urban forms, household income and retail sales, and similar governmental functions as county seats. Interviews were conducted with local leaders and business owners in the year 2000. Downtown retail and services and other features of the built environment were analyzed and mapped. In addition, general conditions and tendencies of downtown development were appraised by literature studies and, as far as available, by data evaluations (Otto 2001). Both cities were revisited in 2003 for a follow-up. It is recognized that case study research cannot be representative for the "entirety" of downtown commercial districts. Nevertheless, it is the hope here that the findings from the two case studies will generate ideas for further research.

RETAIL ACTIVITIES IN DOWNTOWN CHILICOTHE AND MOUNT VERNON

In order to provide an appropriate context, I will give a brief background of the two cities and the growth of retail since the 1950s.

Background of the Two Cities

The city of Chillicothe, with population of 21,800 (US Census 2000), is situated about 45 miles south of the state's capital Columbus (Figure 11.1). The city was settled soon after the area became part of the Northwest Territory in 1787, and it was the first capital of Ohio after it became a state in 1803. The opening of the Ohio and Erie Canal in 1831 and the first railroad access in 1852 contributed to the growth of the city, even though it had lost its capital status in 1816. Industrialization in the second part of the 19th century focused on the already existing paper production. Later the production of trucks was introduced as another industrial base. After World War II, the city developed considerable new commercial and industrial areas. Today, Chillicothe is the seat of Ross County, a county of 73,300 people, which is bordered to the north by the Columbus Metropolitan Area. The county has grown slightly, averaging about 6% between 1990 and 2000, compared to the state average of 5%. At $37,117, the median household income of the county is below the average of the state of Ohio ($40,956) (US Census 2000). More than 75% of the workforce in Ross County is based on service industries, with almost one in four jobs in retail (US BEA 2001). About 75% of all the retail trade is accounted for by Chillicothe (US Census 1999).

Mount Vernon, with population of 14,400 (US Census 2000), is located approximately 45 miles northeast of Columbus. Mount Vernon is the main economic and social center of Knox County. The city was laid out in 1805 and became a center of the farming area around it. Railroad access led to a slight industrialization in the second half of the 19th century. Until recently, the city's development has been influenced by the production of agricultural machinery, engines, and turbines. In the 20th century, mineral excavation and glass industry were added to Mount Vernon's economic base. After World War II, commercial areas were developed to the east and south of the city. Like Chillicothe, Mount

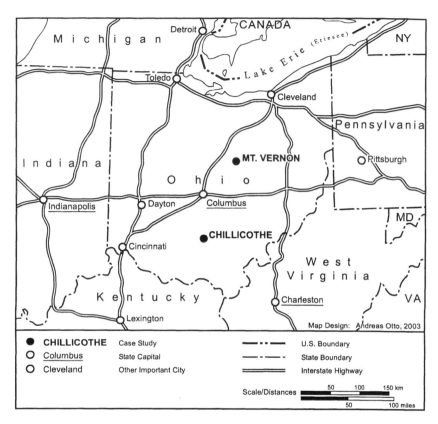

Figure 11.1 Locations of Study Areas

Vernon is also the seat of Knox County, a county with a total population of 54,500, and it accounts for about 75% of the retail sales of the county (US Census 1999). As in the case of Ross County, Knox County is bordered to the south and west by Licking and Delaware Counties, which are both parts of the Columbus Metropolitan Area. Knox County grew considerably in population, about 15% over the decade from 1990 to 2000. Although Knox County's median household income of $38,877 was slightly higher than that of Ross County, it was still below the average income of the state of Ohio (US Census 2000). More than 65% of Knox County's workforce is in service industries, with one in six jobs based in retail (US BEA 2001). Nevertheless, manufacturing plants remain the "heartbeat" of Chillicothe and Mount Vernon, and although both cities are centers of the surrounding agriculture areas, they are mainly seen as "blue collar" cities.

Downtown Chillicothe and Mount Vernon

Chillicothe's downtown district is situated in the historic center of the community and comprises most of its oldest buildings. It covers about six blocks or 70 acres, which are surrounded by residential areas, some commercial uses, and a park (Figure 11.2). It has fairly wide streets compared to other small cities. The area contains a remarkable collection of historic buildings; most of which were built in the second half of the 19th century, but some date back to the early 1800s. The area was listed in the National Register of Historic Places in 1979, and as a result most of the buildings are in fairly good conditions. Some parts on the edge of downtown experienced demolitions of historic buildings and are now characterized by vacant lots or parking areas. At the time of the study, there were 194 buildings in the area, out of which 25% were in good repair, 57% in fair and 18% in poor repair (Table 11.1). Of the 194 buildings, 174 housed 222 businesses. Most of these businesses (82%) used only first floors of the building. In all, 24 or 14% of all commercially used buildings had first floor vacancies.

Like Chillicothe, Mount Vernon's downtown district is also situated in the historic heart of the city around Public Square. With a total area of about 45 acres, Mount Vernon's downtown is much smaller than Chillicothe's and street width are accordingly smaller. The core of the downtown covers an area of about five blocks mainly to the south and west of Public Square (Figure 11.3). Most of the 107 buildings in the downtown were built in the late 19th and early 20th century. While Main Street and Public Square are physically intact areas other parts of downtown experienced major demolitions. At the time of the study about 35% of the buildings were in good repair, 55% in fair repair and 10% in poor repair (Table 11.2). Out of the 107 buildings, 98 buildings were occupied by a total of 141 businesses while 6 buildings had vacant premises on first floors. This translates to 6% of all commercially used buildings. Like Chillicothe, 85% of all businesses use only first floors.

Nature and Characteristics of Retail Activities

Retail activities in both downtowns began to decline from the late 1950s and early 1960s. In the case of Chillicothe, this started with the development of Bridge Street shopping area to the northern fringes of the city and Central Mall and Western Avenue to the western side. Throughout the 1960s Bridge Street especially grew to become the largest commercial location in the county as well as all the surrounding counties in southern Ohio, while Central Mall also grew rapidly into a neighborhood center. Today, Bridge Street offers big box retail and several department stores, while Central Mall is the main seat of county administration. Both locations are only about a mile away from downtown Chillicothe.

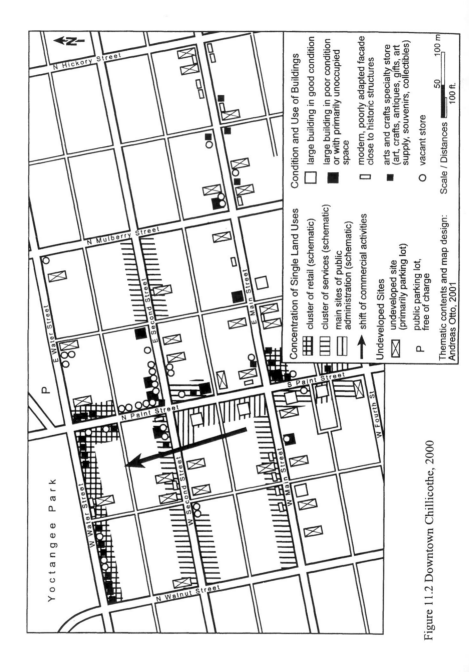

Figure 11.2 Downtown Chillicothe, 2000

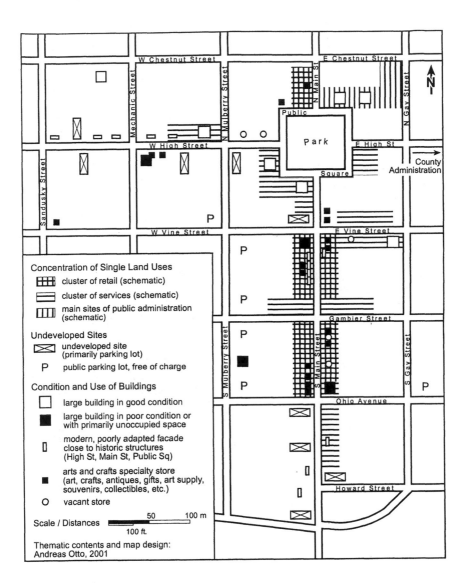

Figure11.3 Downtown Mount Vernon, Ohio, 2000

Table 11.1 Physical Conditions of Downtown Chillicothe and Downtown Mount Vernon*

	Chillicothe	Mount Vernon
Number of buildings	194	107
Percentage of buildings in good repair	25%	35%
Percentage of buildings in fair repair	57%	55%
Percentage of buildings in poor repair	18%	10%
Number of businesses	222	141
Percentage of buildings with actual or potential commercial use	90%	92%
Vacancies in first floors (commercially used buildings)	14%	6%

   * Survey in 2000

In Mount Vernon, the downtown was the only important retail location of the city until the early 1960s. Since 1961, strip developments have continued along Coshocton Road and Harcourt Road. However, unlike Chillicothe, downtown Mount Vernon did not lose its importance immediately after these strip developments. Indeed, as late as the 1990s one could find several department stores in the downtown, and it was only in 2000 that the last downtown department store closed down. Today, however, Coshocton Road is the major retail location in Knox County, offering most of the every-day and long-term needs of the population. It also houses the city hospital and offices, while Harcourt Road, to the west of the city, currently is a strip of car dealers and furniture stores.

Both downtowns have lost their positions as primary centers of retail trade. Nevertheless, retail remains a factor in downtown development. Both cities show a small proportion of convenience retail such as groceries or drugstores, a relatively moderate proportion of comparison retail such as clothing or home appliance stores, and a considerable proportion of specialized retail with arts and crafts, gift and antiques stores.

In 2000, downtown Chillicothe had 71 retail stores. Of these about 40% could be classified as specialty retail (gifts, crafts, art, souvenirs, antiques, art supply, collectible items), 45% were comparison retail (clothing, shoes, furniture, textiles, appliances, sport, electronics, computer, stationary articles, jewelry, etc.), and 15% of stores were convenience retail (groceries, body care, journals, florists, etc.) (Table 11.2). Most of the specialty retail stores had been introduced to downtown during the past 10 to 15 years.

In downtown Mount Vernon, there were 54 retail stores in 2000. Of these, 33% were specialty retail stores, 57% were comparison retail, while 10% were convenience retail. Although this was less than the total number of stores in

Table 11.2 Retail Characteristics in Downtown Chillicothe and Downtown Mount Vernon*

	Chillicothe	Mount Vernon
Number of retail stores	71	54
Ratio of retail stores to buildings	0.37:1	0.51:1
Percentage convenience retail	15%	10%
Percentage comparison retail	45%	57%
Percentage specialty retail	40%	33%
Number of store vacancies	35	6

* Survey in 2000

Chillicothe, Mount Vernon's downtown had a higher density of retail stores in relation to the number of buildings (Table 11.2). Mount Vernon also had a better ratio of retail businesses to other services (1:1.7) than Chillicothe (1:2).

Clearly, retail activities in both downtowns are mere remnants of the heydays of the "old downtown" and retail stores that were once seen as "typical" for downtown continue to disappear. Elderly merchants who are getting close to retiring age run many of these stores. In Mount Vernon, for example, one clothing store and one shoe store closed between 2000 and 2003. Interestingly, most of the retail stores in both downtowns do not feel strong competition from stores in larger commercial locations, because of their unique nature and the differences of the respective merchandise they offer.

Themes and events are common elements of marketing strategies used in most downtowns. In the past decade, major events have been held in downtown Mount Vernon and Chillicothe often based on historic themes or other local features. Downtown retail itself does not yet show a considerable theme or event orientation and many store owners rather complain about negative effects of events due to street closings. Nevertheless, indirect benefits might exist already and business associations and many merchants see a growing theme and event orientation as important or even as the cornerstone of future development. Some merchants have taken advantage of this trend by introducing "heritage oriented retail".

Chillicothe and Mount Vernon are not prime destinations, but they both have potentials for day visits especially for the historic and nature-interested tourist. Both downtowns offer some remarkable specialized retail, which tends to be more tourism oriented than traditional comparison or convenience retail. Most specialty stores in the two downtowns claimed that more than 50% of their customer base was from outside their respective counties of location.

Retail activities in the two downtowns also showed some clustering in their locations. In Chillicothe, the major retail location in the downtown has shifted from the center to its northern edge, along North Paint and West Water Streets (Figure 11.2). A cluster of craft and gift stores, more than 60% of the total number, was concentrated here. In Mount Vernon, about 60% of downtown retail, including 80% of specialty retail, 75% of home appliance stores as well as 65% of jewelries, photo and optics stores, were concentrated on a small two-block strip along South Main Street (Figure 11.3). A small but growing trend of retail stores in the two downtowns did not depend on location for survival. These stores made up to 95% of their sales through deliveries or shipping. Among these were office supplies, floral shops, party equipment, and catering activities.

Like most commercial locations, both downtown Mount Vernon and Chillicothe have seen fluctuations in the number of businesses located in them. To a certain extent this turnover can be seen as a "normal element." However, in the past decades both downtowns have certainly suffered from these fluctuations more than other locations in the area. Both downtowns comprised retail stores, which operated under barely economic conditions. Due to the fact that the owners of these stores had other income sources, these stores did not directly depend on making profit. Instead, they were run as if they were hobbies, and they could be seen as an important means of self-realization for the owner. Most of these stores were newly opened specialty stores.

Apart from a few exceptions, downtown retail in the two cities was locally owned. However, the nature of locally owned retail stores had changed from family businesses in which many family members were involved over generations to individual businesses run by just one or few family members for only a certain period of time.

FACTORS AFFECTING DOWNTOWN RETAIL ACTIVITIES

While macroeconomic factors clearly affect the overall state of small city downtowns, the study assumed that mainly local differences and factors would have a strong impact on the current status as well as the future of retail in the two downtowns. A survey of 40 retail storeowners or managers revealed that most of them were satisfied with their locations. Reasons for the downtown location of their businesses were rooted clearly in market factors (cost and revenue) as well as in personal reasons. Broadly, these factors could be classified as "pull" and "push" factors. The pull factors attract or keep retail downtown, while the push factors drive retail away from the downtown. Table 11.3 summarizes various push and pull factors of downtown retail development as analyzed in Chillicothe and Mount Vernon.

Table 11.3 Push and Pull Factors of Downtown Retail Development

Impact Factor		Nature of Factor
Cost Factors	Rental costs and running costs	Pull
	Real estate and land prices	Pull
	Costs of renovation	Push
	Location related requirements	Pull
	Parking and access	Push
	Availability of premises for start-ups	Pull
Revenue Factors	Sales and profit expectations	Push
	Number of potential clients	Push
	Business aggregation advantages	Push/Pull
Individual Factors	Individual preferences	Pull/Push

Cost Factors

Costs are crucial to the location of every economic activity, including retailing. Thus, although about 50% of the interviewed businesses had at least once thought about moving to another location, the concerns to give up the advantages of lower costs at their downtown location persuaded them to stay. According to the survey rental costs of downtown locations were only half or a third of rental costs of similar premises in shopping centers on the fringes. Furthermore, about 50% of storeowners also owned their premises. For start up businesses, the availability of empty premises in the downtowns of the two cities was an additional cost advantage. At the same time, expensive renovations of downtown premises as well as perceived lack of parking in downtown areas make downtown locations costly for certain types of retail business.

Revenue Factors

The specific "composition" of existing types of uses and functions is important to downtown retail development. The proximity to particular businesses might determine the level of competition and the benefits of agglomeration. Potentials for locating within downtown seem to exist especially for new specialty retail stores. These stores do not often have considerable flexible capital at their disposal, but need a certain clustering among similar stores to draw the critical amount of clients. Evidence for that can be found in the concentration of specialty stores in small areas of the two downtowns.

In both places the historic building stock and the "special atmosphere" of downtown were seen as crucially important for consumer decisions to shop downtown. Both downtowns were also seen as major "public spaces" of the communities. Several downtown festivals and events made them major destinations for residents and visitors. Among other events are the Gus Macker 3 on 3 Basketball Tournament, the Feast of the Flowering Moon and the Christmas Open House in Chillicothe, and a series of summer concerts, the Dan Emmett Music and Arts Festival as well as the Christmas Parade in Mount Vernon. All these generate traffic for downtown retail and services.

In the past decades, downtown retail has been affected by the situation and development of other competing locations. Prime locations such as new shopping centers at the cities' fringes have often determined such important parameters as supply, price, and quality of goods. This has had a clear impact on the situation and development of downtown retail, which is now seen as of secondary importance. Other locations such as Bridge Street or Coshocton Road also appeared to be considered as more attractive because of better supply of goods, better opportunities of combining shopping trips (coupling), lower prices, a better image, and better access conditions. However, as a result of the major retail shift already mentioned, there is barely competition between today's downtown retail and other commercial locations.

At the same time, many traditional storeowners in both downtowns complained about a lack of retail diversity, inconsistent store hours, and the lack of joint efforts in relation to marketing and promotion, as sources of negative impacts on revenue generation of downtown retail stores. In effect, the downtowns of both Chillicothe and Mount Vernon have some strengths and weaknesses that affect retail activities. As seen by the business community, the strengths included:

- Historic buildings and atmosphere
- Attractions and potentials for tourism, events, and festivals
- Location of local government and administration
- Diversified and "interesting" retail supplies
- Good service and high quality retail

Among the weaknesses were:

- Poor parking situation
- Poor building conditions, obsolete infrastructure, and vacancies
- Missing implementation of building codes and regulations
- "New mix" of retail, focus on specialty retail, and lack of diversity
- Different and short store hours
- Problems of marketing

Individual preferences

Pure economic reasons are not the only factors that guide the development of commercial areas. More than other locations, downtowns seem to be characterized and influenced by manifold individual preferences and decisions of business and property owners. About a fourth of the interviewees said that they "wanted to do something to revitalize downtown" or that they have a "deep loyalty" to downtown. The meaning of "self-realization" should not be underestimated when it comes to development of downtown; merchants often want to supply certain goods at a certain location and within an individually designed store. More than half of the interviewees said that they could act and decide more individually and independently than at non-downtown locations. Downtown offers a platform for realizing individual dreams. Aside from demographic and economic factors such as age, education, and income, individual preferences and the perception of a location were crucial elements of consumer decisions, too.

All these mean that downtown Chillicothe and Mount Vernon have become destinations for:

- Businesses which have low flexible capital and therefore cannot afford to relocate (e.g. start-up antique store)
- Businesses which assume that they cannot afford higher costs even in case of higher sales expectations (e.g. gift shop operated as a hobby with low profit expectations)
- Businesses which do not need to be at a certain location due to deliveries or shipping (e.g. florist with marginal walk-in retail)
- Businesses which find agglomeration advantages downtown (e.g. art gallery)
- Businesses which are "bound" to downtown due to owning the premises
- Businesses, which have individual preferences to stay downtown.

The Role of Downtown Revitalization Activities

Market side factors are not the only forces that affect downtown retail. The actions of local governments, downtown associations, chambers of commerce and visitors bureaus, all do affect downtown retail activities. For example, direct local governments actions (e.g. capital improvements, financial, technical and personal assistance) or indirect actions (e.g. regulations, concepts, know how) can have tremendous impact on the fortunes of downtown retail. Similarly, many associations influence downtown's commercial fabric through the marketing of available premises, recruiting of new stores, acquisition of real estate premises, and clustering of certain trades and stores. Chillicothe and Mount

Vernon have both experienced manifolds of these efforts that commonly go under the rubric of downtown revitalization.

Chillicothe

Due to its historic importance, downtown Chillicothe has long been in the spotlight of downtown redevelopment efforts. Instrumental in these efforts have been City of Chillicothe and several downtown as well as business organizations. The city's efforts have included capital improvements, technical assistance, adjustments of legal and administrative settings, cooperation within public-private partnerships, and application of grants from the state of Ohio's competitive Comprehensive Downtown Revitalization Program. During the 1960s revitalization activities in Chillicothe focused on the development of a pedestrian mall. However, this lasted only for a few years. In 1972, a group of downtown business and property owners formed the Downtown Associates (DA) to further economic development and revitalization, through improving marketing activities and lobbying for downtown interests. During the 1980s, revitalization efforts centered of streetscape projects. To support this and other efforts, the downtown was designated as community reinvestment area in 1986 and tax abatements of up to 100% were made available for commercial investments. In 1989, the First Capital District (FCD) a non-profit organization consisting of representatives from business and property owners, the city, the Chamber of Commerce, and Ross County, was formed to coordinate the manifold activities of downtown redevelopment, by pursuing the objectives of the Ohio Main Street Program. A Downtown Plan was formulated in 1990 and updated in 1998. Recent revitalization activities include (cf. City of Chillicothe 1998, 2000):

Streetscape project: The project was carried out in 1989/1990 at the cost of $2.9 million, and was paid for by the city and property owners in a 1:1 ratio.

Building rehabilitation: The city was able to successfully apply for four state grants (Comprehensive Downtown Revitalization Program; formerly: Downtown Revitalization Competitive Program). The grants, along with matching funds, were partially spent to allow building rehabilitations. More than 60 buildings had been renovated in only three years (1994 through 1997). Collaboration between the city and local banks resulted in the Downtown Loan Guarantee Program, which provided businesses with low interest loans for building renovations. Furthermore, private building renovations are supported with the help of a financing tool by the city's economic development office.

Events: Downtown events draw more than 250,000 visitors annually and downtown has seen growing attention as a venue for existing or new events. For

Ohio's bicentennial celebrations in 2003 downtown saw several beautification measures such as murals on former "dead walls".

Mount Vernon

Downtown revitalization efforts in Mount Vernon have also been a joint venture between the city and the business community. Although the city of Mount Vernon sees revitalization as a task for private actors, it has however strongly supported downtown redevelopment through technical as well as personal assistance, support for grant acquisitions, and matching of state funds. Other active partners include the Heritage Center Association (HCA), the Mount Vernon Knox County Chamber of Commerce, the Knox County Convention and Visitors Bureau, and the Mount Vernon Parking Company. The latter association is made up of 30% of downtown retailers, which spend $20,000 annually to maintain downtown parking lots.

First activities of downtown revitalization were carried out in the 1970s when the decline of downtown retail became obvious. In the following years, a streetscape project was planned and realized with a 90% contribution of property owners and businesses. Renovations of private buildings were barely coordinated at this time and many façades were reshaped in an interesting but historically incoherent way. A turning point of downtown redevelopment was the year 1990, when Heritage Center Association was founded to succeed the purely merchant organization that had promoted revitalization activities. The new association was charged with the economic and social redevelopment of downtown with a strong focus of the promotion of downtown retail, while following the goals of the state of Ohio's Main Street Program. In 1993, a part-time downtown manager position was created for mediating between different interests. In 1994, HCA's initiative led to the resolution of an Economic Development Plan for downtown Mount Vernon. With the help of state grants, Mount Vernon was also able to identify resources for heritage tourism. The resulting concept gave downtown Mount Vernon a key position in Knox County's tourism initiatives. More recent revitalization activities include:

Building rehabilitation: With the help of four successful Comprehensive Downtown Revitalization Program grants a number of public and private buildings were renovated. Over 60 buildings had been renovated between 1994 and 2000.

Streetscape project: State grants were also used to help spurring streetscape improvements. Sidewalks were partially improved in 2000; major improvements of streets, sidewalks and street furniture followed in 2003.

<u>Events</u>: As mentioned above, downtown is the venue of a number of annual events. The weekly farmers market, which has been held since 2000 underlines downtown's function as a "public space" for the community.

<u>Cultural facility</u>: Encouraging heritage tourism through the utilization of attractions is one of the objectives of downtown development. The Woodward Opera House of 1851, the oldest authentic 19th century theater building in the US, has been targeted as one such attraction (WDC/KPAC 2000). Due to its location in the heart of downtown and its historic importance, the theater's privately funded $8-9 million revitalization project has become the most significant not-for-profit project in the area.

Downtown revitalization activities in the two cities thus depict three inter-related trends. The first trend is the specialization of retail and services as part of niche marketing. The second is the event and entertainment orientation of commercial and non-commercial types of uses, and the third is the historic designing of buildings, streetscapes and public spaces (Figure 11.4). With respect to retail,

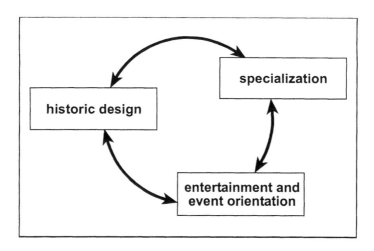

Figure 11.4 Three linked Trends of Downtown Development

these trends in turn show a growing importance of specialized retail, a growing orientation of downtown retail towards specific clienteles such as tourists or higher income, and an increasing association of specialized retail with events and tourism. An important question is to what extent have these trends been successful?

Chillicothe's focus on the physical rehabilitation of its downtown has brought some remarkable success. However, the economic restructuring of downtown has not been a focus of revitalization yet. Vacancy rates in the central parts of downtown are still high. There is no institution that concentrates its work on economic revitalization. FCD and the city mainly work on physical improvements, while the DA (the merchants association) focused on promotional activities. However, after 2003, the DA discontinued its activities due to personal controversies and lack of volunteerism. This is a clear sign for the current lack of interest, a situation that is detrimental to the realization of economic revitalization of the downtown. The future success of downtown redevelopment efforts therefore will strongly depend on the bundling up of available resources that would allow concerted actions.

In Mount Vernon, the close cooperation between HCA, the downtown manager, the visitors' bureau and other players has helped the downtown achieve success in the rehabilitation of buildings and streetscape improvements. With the plans for the renovation of the Woodward Opera House and its surrounding area, a new vision for the economic revitalization and restructuring of downtown has been formulated. An improved marketing of downtown retail as well as the recruiting of new stores and the expansion of existing stores are goals of the downtown business community. However, these goals have not been achieved yet, due in part to lack of stable sources of financing and different interests of downtown organizations.

In both cities the activities of downtown associations, local governments and other semi-public and public institutions have had indirect and to a lesser extent direct influence on the shaping of downtown retail. These effects have been in the areas of planning and regulations, streetscape improvements, incentives for building rehabilitations as well as in terms of marketing and—in a few cases—the recruiting of certain businesses to downtown. Extensive and more direct measures (e.g. acquisition of land and buildings, paying the rents of start-up businesses, saving businesses as common effort) have not yet occurred in the two cities.

In both cities the downtown business communities' expectations of city government's commitment to downtown revitalization as well as the work of downtown associations are very high. Surprisingly, however, not all the members of the downtown merchant groups see themselves as directly responsible for the success of downtown revitalization. The lack of interest and volunteerism as well as inconsistent actions of the downtown business community and other players have been detrimental to the goals of downtown redevelopment plans in both cities. Activating local stakeholders and resources succeeded prior to comprehensive revitalization projects (e.g. the streetscape projects or grant applications), but concerted actions have partly crumbled after the implementation of projects, the planning process or failure of a grant application.

Finally, downtown revitalization activities in both cities have to deal with funding uncertainty. In recent years, state grants have been the main sources of funds. However, these aids are limited and the application procedures are often time and resource consuming. At the same time, further assessments of business and property owners seem rather unlikely. The repayments for streetscape improvements have just ended or are still ongoing. Other stable financial resources have to be found to guarantee the continuation of downtown redevelopment.

As a result of all these, although downtown merchants in both cities welcomed the recent revitalization efforts, they listed a number of areas that needed improvement. These areas included planning and regulations, physical improvements, the enhancement of retail trade, marketing and promotion, and organization and cooperation (Table 11.4).

Table 11.4: Necessary Improvements in Downtown as seen by the Business Community*

Category	Necessary Improvements
Planning and Regulations	Elaboration of downtown business plans and concepts
	Improved consideration of downtown issues in planning processes
	Change/improved implementation of codes and Regulations
Physical Improvements	Continued building rehabilitation and infrastructure improvements
	Extension of public parking
	Implementation of urgent maintenance measures
	Improved access during downtown events and festivals
	Creating more opportunities for downtown housing
Retail Supply Side	Improved consideration of individual demands of clients
	Reducing the conversion of retail into office space
	Increasing benefits of events for downtown retail
	Introducing consistent store hours
Promotion and Marketing	Recruiting new retail stores
	Focusing downtown marketing on specific clienteles
	Improved marketing of attractions and events
	Learning from examples of shopping center marketing

Table 11.4 continued

Category	Necessary Improvements
Organization, Cooperation, and Financing	Hiring a full-time downtown manager
	Improved communication, coordination and cooperation
	Securing financing of projects and technical assistance
	Clarifying of responsibilities and addressing problems specifically
	Restructuring of downtown associations

Notes: Order of objectives and measures follows the total number of answers within categories. Answers were not pre-defined.
* Survey in 2000

CONCLUSION

This study set out to contribute to the relatively little research on downtown retail activities in small cities, using the cities of Chillicothe and Mount Vernon, Ohio as case studies. It examined the nature and characteristics of these activities and the factors that affect them and the implications for future retail development. The study has shown that first, retail activities in the downtowns of the two small cities have transitioned from the traditional comparative retail type towards more and more specialized retail type. Second, there is a growing orientation of downtown retail and services towards few specific clientele such as tourists or higher income residents. Most of these activities also tend to be small, locally owned, and are subject to sales fluctuations. In addition, some of them tend to be hobby-like in nature, while a few tend not to be location-dependent.

The factors that have influenced retail activities in the two downtowns are several and they include cost and revenue factors, individual preferences, and downtown revitalization activities. In particular, the local business communities in both cities have very high expectations of the local government and downtown associations to use revitalization to improve downtown retail. However, downtown revitalization activities have not really made the economic restructuring of the downtown as a focus. Instead, direct emphasis has been on "historic designs," and event and entertainment orientations of commercial and non-commercial types of uses. There is still a considerable gap between successful physical improvements and satisfactory economic revitalization.

The concentration on specialty retail can secure downtown's function as a commercial location. It might also attract more activities and contribute positively towards other services as well as cultural facilities. Moreover, property values and tax revenue might both go up. However, conflicts can arise when downtown concentrates on a small niche that might hinder adjustments to the overall market or is susceptible to local changes.

It seems necessary to achieve a certain balance between downtown's orientation towards local residents and out of town visitors in order to maintain its function as being of importance for an entire community. Niche marketing can guide new clientele into downtown, but it might involve a certain danger of ignoring local needs. This is because niche marketing favors certain interests, e.g. specialized retail, and allows these groups to benefit from economic advantages. Other groups, who might already suffer from weak economic conditions, could stay further behind. This becomes particularly detrimental when certain groups start feeling excluded or are not able to address their needs anymore.

Due to economic and structural changes downtown might experience an upgrading of its image and become perceived as being "different" from other locations. An improved image of downtown can even increase the recognition of an entire city. However, if more small cities follow the same ideas and create similar niches for their downtowns, consumers might feel oversaturated. The situation might become counterproductive to the original goal of achieving uniqueness.

Renovations back to old looks as well as historically contributing new structures are important conditions to maintain downtown's individual character. While this was controversially discussed a couple of years ago, it now seems to be a consensus of downtown redevelopment efforts. The success of a specialized niche might even depend on certain historic characteristics. However, preservation efforts should not prevent necessary investments or lead to the creation of a "downtown museum" which is physically and economically uncoupled from the rest of the city.

The redevelopment process is often initiated and supported by strategies and activities of the public sector and the not-for-profit sector. However, rising financial and organizational problems are detrimental to downtown's revitalization that is dependent on concerted action. Whatever specific direction redevelopment is heading for in the future, the commitment of local governments and stakeholders is needed more than ever to support downtown's survival as a retail location and an important place in the heart of small communities.

Downtown commercial districts in small cities show strong tendencies of specialization even if there is no concerted action of retail change in place. This might allow them to develop a niche that will differentiate them from other commercial locations in the future. At the moment, downtowns have barely achieved true and stable market niches. More studies and comprehensive analysis as to how small cities can achieve this will be needed.

REFERENCES

Banovetz, J., D. Dolan, and J. Swain. 2000. Overview of local economic development. In *Main Street Renewal. A Handbook for Citizens and Public Officials*, ed. R. Kemp Jefferson, 16-31. London, U.K.: McFarland & Company.

Brown, S. 1993. Retail location theory: evolution and evaluation. *The International Review of Retail, Distribution and Consumer Research* 3 (2): 182 – 229.

Burayidi, M. A. 2001. An assessment of downtown revitalization in five small Wisconsin communities. In *Downtowns, Revitalizing the Centers of Small Urban Communities*, ed. M. A. Burayidi, 47 – 64. New York, NY, London, U.K.: Routledge.

City of Chillicothe. 1998. *Downtown Development Plan, Revised 1998*. Chillicothe, OH.

City of Chillicothe. 2000. *Economic Development Department City of Chillicothe Annual Report for 1999*. Chillicothe, OH.

Getz, D. 1993. Planning for tourism business districts. *Annals of Tourism Research* 20 (3): 583 – 600.

Hula, R., C. Jackson and M. Orr. 1997. Urban politics, governing nonprofits, and community revitalization. *Urban Affairs Review* 32 (4): 459 – 489.

Kenyon, J. B. 1989. From central business district to central social district: the revitalization of the small Georgia city. *Small Town* 20 (2): 4 – 17.

Klebba, J. M., M. Garrett, A. Radle, and B. Downes. 2001. Downtown redevelopment in selected Oregon coastal communities: some lessons from practice. In *Downtowns, Revitalizing the Centers of Small Urban Communities*, ed. M. A. Burayidi, 65 – 88. New York, NY, and London, U.K.: Routledge.

McClure, K. 2001. Managing the growth of retail space: retail market dynamics in Lawrence, Kansas. In *Downtowns, Revitalizing the Centers of Small Urban Communities*, ed. M. A. Burayidi, 223 – 248. New York, NY, London, U.K: Routledge.

Moe, R. and C. Wilkie. 1997. *Changing Places. Rebuilding Community in the Age of Sprawl*. New York, NY: Henry Holt and Company.

NMSC (National Main Street Center). 2004. http://www.mainstreet.org..

Ofori-Amoah, B. 2000. Geographic shift in economic activities between downtowns and outskirts of small urban areas: a study of five Wisconsin cities. Pittsburgh, PA. April 4.8.

Otto, A. 2001. Strukturwandel und Standortgestaltung in klein- und mittelstädti schen Stadtzentren in Ohio, USA. *Thesis at Dresden University of Technology*. Dresden, Germany.

Paradis, T. 2000. Conceptualizing small towns as urban places: the process of downtown development in Galena, Illinois. *Urban Geography* 21 (1): 61 – 82.

Robertson, K. 1999. Can small-city downtowns remain viable? A national study of development issues and strategies. *Journal of the American Planning Association* 65 (3): 270 – 283.

Robertson, K. 2001. Downtown development principles for small cities. *Downtowns, Revitalizing the Centers of Small Urban Communities,* ed M. A. Burayidi, 9 – 22. New York, NY, London, U.K.: Routledge.

Ryan, B., J. Braatz and A. Brault. 1998. *Retail Mix in Wisconsin's Small Downtowns: An Analysis of Cities and Villages with Populations of 2,500 – 15,000.* Madison, WI: Center for Community Economic Development, University of Wisconsin - Extension. Staff Paper Number 98.3.

Sies, M. C. and C. Silver. 1996. *Planning the Twentieth-Century American City.* Baltimore, MD: Johns Hopkins University Press.

Teaford, J. C. 1990. *The Rough Road to Renaissance—Urban Revitalization in America, 1940 – 1985.* Baltimore, MD: Johns Hopkins University Press.

Turner, R. S. 2002. The politics of design and development in the postmodern downtown. *Journal of Urban Affairs* 24 (5): 533 – 548.

US BEA (U.S. Department of Commerce, Bureau of Economic Analysis). 2001. http://www.bea.doc.gov/bea.

US Census (U.S. Department of Commerce, Bureau of the Census). 1999. *1997 Economic Census. Retail Trade—Geographic Area Series, Ohio.* Washington, DC.

U.S. Census (U.S. Department of Commerce, Bureau of the Census). 2000. *United States Census 2000.* http://www.census.gov

Walzer, N. and S. Kline. 2001. An evaluation of approaches to downtown economic revitalization. In *Downtowns, Revitalizing the Centers of Small Urban Communities,* ed. M. A. Burayidi. 249 – 274. New York, NY and London, U.K.: Routledge.

WDC/KPAC (Woodward Development Corporation, Knox Performing Arts Coalition). 2000. *The Restoration Proposal for the Woodward Opera House – America's Oldest Authentic 19th Century Theater.* Mount Vernon, OH.

Wilson, M. 1991. The role of community based organizations in contemporary urban America. In *Contemporary Urban America. Problems, Issues, and Alternatives,* ed. M. Lang, 335 – 354. Lanham, MD: University Press of America.

12

Managing Downtown Revitalization Projects in Small Cities: Lessons from Kentucky's Main Street Program

Christa Smith
Clemson University

INTRODUCTION

For the past several decades, geographers have attempted to identify the latest patterns and processes occurring in America's rapidly changing cities. Of particular interest to geographers are the effects of downtown decentralization in America and the numerous strategies employed by municipalities to halt decline in central business districts throughout the nation. A vast amount of research has been conducted on the outcomes of urban revitalization efforts and urban economic development schemes across America (Bryce, 1967; Holcomb, and Beauregard 1981; Frieden, & Sagalyn 1989; Gratz, & Mintz 1998; Filion, Hoerning, Bunting, & Sands 2004). The majority of these studies however, focus almost exclusively on the physical and economic renewal of large urban places.

To date, little research has been done on decentralization and decay in small towns and cities, particularly in urban areas with populations of less than 100,000. A number of case studies on small and medium-sized cities have been published, but these reports have been largely empirical assessments and have failed to provide a theoretical framework to explain the causes and effects of decentralization. Burayidi (2001) voiced his concern on the paucity of information on these small "free standing" urban areas, and claimed a more systematic analysis of small town America must be offered if planners and politicians are to respond effectively to decline in these important urban places.

Small and medium-sized cities, like their larger counterparts, have tried many different lines of attack to decrease decentralization and encourage revitalization in their communities. This study examines the effects of one such strategy, the National Trust's Main Street program, on small communities in Kentucky. To accurately assess the impact of the Main Street program on these small urban places, a systematic examination was undertaken of every Kentucky Main Street community. The study focused specifically on the factors contributing to the active or inactive status of Main Street towns and cities in this state. Data were gathered on 37 Main Street communities from 1979 – 2000. A logistic regression analysis revealed three variables—downtown business vacancy rates, whether or not the town was within the sphere of influence of a metropolitan area, and the composition of Main Street board leadership—were the most important predictors of on-going Main Street activity (i.e., success of the programs). Two Kentucky Main Street communities were further analyzed to ascertain how location and board composition contributed to the success or failure of Main Street programs in Kentucky.

The chapter falls into four sections. The first section provides an overview of downtown decline, the Main Street program, and economic viability of places. The second section describes the methodology of the study highlighting the logistic regression model that was used to analyze the data. The third section presents the case study. The concluding section outlines the lessons from the case study and their implications for small cities. Throughout, the terms town, city, and community will be used interchangeably.

DOWNTOWN DECLINE AND THE MAIN STREET PROGRAM

During the past fifty years, a number of approaches have been employed to combat decentralization and decay in America's downtowns. Programs designed to solve urban ills ranged from the New Deal slum clearance schemes, which focused on rebuilding low income rental housing, to the post-World War II urban renewal plans, which involved razing older buildings in the commercial core to make room for new high-rises, hotels, and convention centers (Clark 1985). The ultimate goal of these early revitalization strategies was the creation of a modern urban landscape, all designed to halt commercial and residential flight to the suburbs.

During the 1970s and 1980s, dissatisfaction with previous urban regeneration programs caused a backlash against urban renewal schemes that involved the alteration or destruction of the historic built environment. Urban designers instead adopted the more current historic preservation strategies, which advocated the protection, preservation, and rehabilitation of historic structures in the downtown district.

One of the most popular preservation strategies presently used across America is the Main Street program. This program, created by the National

Trust for Historic Preservation, seeks to reverse economic decline in small and medium-sized towns and cities by stimulating economic development within the context of historic preservation. The program centers on a "Four Point Approach," which includes design improvements, promotion of downtown businesses, organization, and economic restructuring. To disseminate information about the Main Street approach, in 1980 the National Trust created the National Main Street Center (NMSC). The National Main Street program has grown considerably since its inception. Over 1,650 communities across the United States can claim to be, or have been, Main Street towns. As indicated by the Main Street website, these communities can boast of a total of 88,700 building rehabilitations, and combined public and private reinvestments of $16.1 billion dollars since 1980 (http://www.mainst.org/about/numbers.htm).

The NMSC maintains that by using the Four Point Approach, revitalization can take place in any town, regardless of size or location. While many of these Main Street communities have experienced various degrees of economic revitalization, it must be noted that a number of these towns, while aesthetically pleasing, are no more than empty shells devoid of commercial, social or cultural development. The key question is why do some Main Street communities, given that they have identical downtown development strategies, fail in their attempts at economic revitalization while others succeed? Are there common factors that could assist future Main Street municipalities in developing more successful programs?

Within geography the theoretical framework that appears to provide some partial answers to these questions is Christaller's central place theory (Christaller 1933). The theory argues that cities exist for economic reasons, and that is to provide goods and services to their complimentary region or hinterland. Under the assumptions of an isotropic plain, characterized further by (1) an even population distribution, (2) a steady state-economy, (3) rational economic persons (4) perfect competition, the theory's central question is what will be the number and sizes of cities if they existed mainly as service functions and how will they be distributed? The theory defines a central place as any settlement that offers a good or service. It classifies goods and services on the basis of the threshold of the good (or minimum demand required to support the good or service) and the range of the good or service (or how far people are willing to travel to purchase the good or service). Low order goods have small thresholds and short ranges while high-order goods have large thresholds and long ranges. The theory argues that central places exist in a hierarchical order on the basis of the goods and services they offer. Low order central places offer low order goods and high order central places offer both high order goods and low order goods. Christaller believed that consumers would almost always shop for a good or service at the nearest place providing that good. It is implicit from this then that the decline of downtowns is a reflection of the loss of centrality within their complimentary region. In this case it could also be argued that downtown revitalization seems to imply an attempt to restore the centrality of the downtown as a central place.

However, in a groundbreaking research, Rushton (1969) compared the consistency of actual travel patterns of rural farm and nonfarm populations in the state of Iowa to the classical version of central place theory as developed by Christaller. Rushton argued that both distance and town size (a surrogate of the number and variety of central place offerings) matter when consumers are deciding where to purchase goods and services. Rushton provided empirical evidence from Iowa that showed consumers were willing to travel farther to a larger place than a smaller one, because among many other possible reasons, multipurpose shopping was more feasible in a larger central place that offered a wider variety of goods and services. This was contrary to Christaller's belief that consumer's would be indifferent to town size, but not to distance. It is clear that the relative location of a small city to a larger city might hold some key to predicting the success or failure of a downtown revitalization program. The question again is could there be any other factors? The investigation of this is the focus of the next section.

METHODOLOGY

Kentucky was chosen for this study because, according to Roger Stapleton, the director of the Kentucky Main Street program, it was the first in the nation to implement a statewide Main Street program (Stapleton 1999). The state's preservation office, The Kentucky Heritage Council (KHC), initiated the Kentucky Main Street program in 1979, and until 1998, it was the state's first and only comprehensive downtown revitalization program.

From 1979 to 2000 a total of 54 cities were admitted to the Kentucky Main Street program. This admission allowed each city to receive state funding for six years, after which they were considered "graduate" communities. Of the 54 Main Street towns during this study period, 26 were classified as graduate cities, 11 categorized as inactive, and the remainders were in various stages of the six-year funding cycle. Communities categorized as inactive are those that either chose to voluntarily discontinue the program, or were dropped from the Main Street roster by the KHC. This study analyzed the 26 graduate and the 11 inactive Main Street towns (Figure 12.1).

Data for this study were collected from the KHC Main Street office; federal, state, and county censuses; the state of Kentucky's Economic Development Office, and local newspapers. A survey was also conducted with Main Street managers. The data were analyzed using a logistic regression (LR). An LR model is a multivariate statistical technique that predicts the probability values of a binary dependent or response variable from a set of independent or explanatory variables. Multiple regression analysis and discriminant analysis are two related

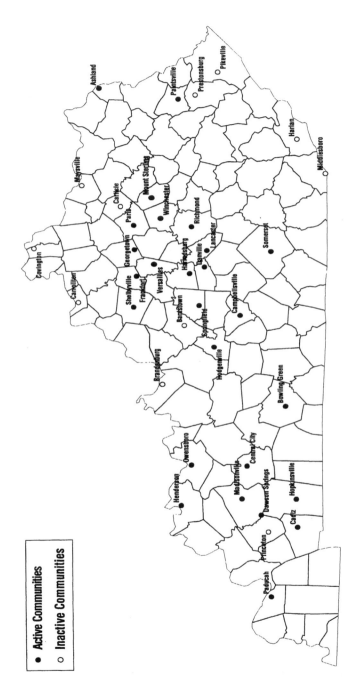

Figure 12.1 Kentucky's Main Street Communities

techniques that could have been used. However, these "techniques pose difficulties when the dependent variables can have only two values—an event occurring or not occurring" (SPSS 1998, 17).

The logistic regression prediction equation is written as:

$$\text{Probability of event occurring} = \frac{1}{1 + e^{-\beta}}$$

Where $\beta = b_0 + b_1X_1 + b_2X_2 + \ldots + b_nX_n$

After mathematically deriving the best estimators of these parameters (β) using a maximum likelihood method, these estimates are then tested to determine if they are significantly different from 0. The Wald test for example, tests the hypothesis that a particular Beta = 0. An explanatory variable with a LR coefficient (β) significantly different from 0 is a good predictor of the occurrence of the event (SPSS 1998). Other associated statistical results such as partial correlations, likelihood functions, and odds ratios, can be used to interpret the relationship between explanatory variables and the response variables (SPSS 1998). The covariates (i.e., the independent variables of the logistic regression analysis model) are listed in Table 12.1 below. A forward stepwise procedure was used

Table 12.1 Logistic Regression Variables and Code Names

Variable Name	Code Name
Location of Main Street towns	Region
Metropolitan status	Metro
Number of store vacancies	Vacancy
Jobs that were netted during the period	Netjobs
Availability of a loan pool	Loan pool
Total business investment	Businves
Total dollars invested in rehabilitation	Rehabinv
The board composition	Boardcom
Total dollar amount of rehabilitation credits	Rehabcre
The number of technical assistance requests	Techasst
The total dollar amount of public improvements	Pub impro

for automated logistic regression model building. In this method, the variable with the smallest significant level for the score statistic (less than 0.05), is entered into the model at each step. Table 12.2 displays the variables not in the equation.

Table 12.2 Variables not in the Equation at Step 0

Variable	Score	df*	Significance
Metro(1)	11.191	1	.001
Region	4.835	2	.089
Region(1)	4.677	1	.031
Region(2)	.466	1	.495
Vacancy	7.722	1	.005
NetJobs	1.329	1	.249
LoanPool(1)	5.580	1	.018
Businves	.735	1	.391
Rehabinv	1.124	1	.289
Boardcom	10.865	2	.004
Boardcom(1)	.895	1	.344
Boardcom(2)	10.638	1	.001
Rehabcre	.856	1	.355
Techass	6.513	1	.011
Pubimpro	.883	1	.347

*df = degrees of freedom

For each variable not in the model, the score statistic and its significance level, if the variable were entered next into the model, is shown. The variables of metro (1), vacancy, and boardcom and boardcom (2) had the smallest observed significance levels less than 0.05, the default value for entry, so they were entered into the model. The metro and board composition variables were indicator, or dummy variables. The metro variable was a two-category variable that was coded as 0 and 1. The code of 0 represented non-metro communities, and a 1 for a metro Main Street town. The board composition indicator variable had three categories, and was coded as follows: a code 1 was given to program board of directors that were grassroots-controlled and 0 otherwise. A code of 2 was assigned to boards controlled by political leaders, and a 0 otherwise. The value of majority business boards was represented by codes of 0 for both of these variables.

FACTORS AFFECTING MAIN STREET PROGRAM PERFORMANCE IN KENTUCKY

The results from the LR in this study revealed which variables were more likely to contribute to the continuance of Main Street programs in Kentucky. Table 12.3 contains the estimated coefficients (under the column head β) and related statistics from the logistic regression model that predicts Kentucky Main Street activity using the variables metro, vacancy, and board composition. Since a large standard error (S.E.) was found with boardcom (1), the variable of

Table 12.3 Variables in the Equation

Variable	β	S.E.	Wald	df	Sig.	Exp(β)
Metro(1)	-3.984	1.892	4.433	1	.035	.019
Vacancy	.481	.251	3.669	1	.055	1.617
Boardcom			4.392	2	.111	
Boardcom(1)	6.724	58.853	.013	1	.909	831.883
Boardcom(2)	-4.285	2.048	4.376	1	.036	.014
CONSTANT	.470	1.619	.084	1	.772	1.599

board composition was re-categorized. A value of 1 was assigned to politically controlled boards and a 0 for all others. Table 12.4 shows the variables in the equation and the changing statistics after the variable of board composition was re-categorized.

Table 12.4 Variables in the Equation after Re-categorization of Board Composition

Variable	β	S.E.	Wald	df	Sig.	Exp(β)
Metro(1)	-4.229	1.888	5.019	1	.025	.015
Vacancy	.473	.251	3.550	1	.060	1.605
Boardcom	-4.410	2.074	4.522	1	.033	.012
CONSTANT	.818	1.522	.289	1	.591	2.266

The logistic regression equation for the probability of Kentucky Main Street programs being active is written as:

$$\text{Prob (being active)} = 0.818 - 4.22 \text{ (metro1)} + 0.47(\text{vacancy}) - 4.41 \text{ (boardcom)}$$

After deriving the best estimators of these parameters (β's), the estimates were then tested to determine if they were significantly different from 0. The Wald statistics from this table test the hypothesis that the logistic regression coefficients for metro1 (–4.229), vacancy (.473) and boardcom (–4.410) were significantly different from zero. The hypotheses were evaluated using the p-value (Significance Level) for each test, generally comparing them to an alpha = .05. The Wald tests showed that all three coefficients were significantly different from 0, and therefore had an effect on the outcome.

The outcome of the logistic regression can best be explained by examining the odds ratio, which is labeled Exp (β). Direction of the change in odds is determined by the sign of the explanatory variable's Beta (β). If Beta is positive, then the odds of an event occurring increases by a factor of Exp (β). If Beta is negative, the odds decrease by a factor of Exp (β). The coefficient of Metro1 is negative and the Exp (β) is .015. This means the odds of having an active Main Street decrease by .015 going from metropolitan to nonmetropolitan. So according to the logistic model, nonmetropolitan Kentucky Main Street towns are more likely to have inactive programs. It was determined that nonmetropolitan towns were more likely to be designated 'inactive" because they were economically healthier than metropolitan communities and therefore were less likely to faithfully follow the Main Street Four Point Approach. Major deviations from the Main Street Approach would garner an "inactive" (failure) status from the KHC.

The next coefficient, vacancy, is positive and the Exp (β) is 1.605. Thus, the odds of a Main Street town being active increase by 1.605 with every 1unit change in vacancy. In other words as vacancy goes up the likelihood that the Main Street community is active increases. This indicates that downtown commercial real estate in these active communities was experiencing high turnover due to the "boutiquization" (Bell 1999) of small town America. Many of these specialized retail and service establishments had difficulty making a profit, and often closed their stores after a short period of time. This led to an increase in vacancy rates.

Finally, the coefficient of board composition is negative and the Exp (β) is .012. This indicates that the odds of a Main Street town being active decrease .012 when boards are comprised of political leaders. It is more likely, therefore, that the boards of active Main Street programs are either majority grassroots or business controlled. While the odds ratio is small for this coefficient, it is retained in the logistic regression predictive equation because it substantially improves the classification rate. Without it in the equation, only 86% of the communities were correctly classified; with board composition in the prediction equation, 95% were correctly classified.

A survey of Main Street managers revealed that majority of respondents strongly believed that board composition has an influence on the program's active status. The respondents further stated, however, that board composition, while important, rarely appeared to be the primary cause of a Main Street program's demise. This finding is contrary to the results of the logistic regression analysis, which identified board composition as one of the predictor variables for an active Main Street.

DETAILED CASE STUDIES

Two Kentucky Main Street programs were chosen to highlight the findings from the logistic regression analysis. Because metropolitan location was the most significant predictor variable for whether a Kentucky Main Street program would be active or not active, two communities, one each from a metropolitan and a nonmetropolitan area were chosen for a detailed study. The nonmetropolitan community chosen was Pikeville, located in southeastern Kentucky, while the metropolitan community was Harrodsburg, which is in the Bluegrass Basin of central Kentucky.

Nonmetropolitan Main Street Communities

In this study, all but one of the inactive Main Street programs was located in a nonmetropolitan area. Covington is the exception; the largest of the inactive communities, it is located in northern Kentucky and is part of the Cincinnati-Covington MSA. Places with inactive programs ranged in size from 1,639 to 43,264 (Table 12.5). Brandenburg, Carlisle, Harlan, Carrollton, Bardstown, Princeton, Middlesboro and Covington were all given inactive status by the KHC. Maysville, Pikeville, and Prestonsburg were assigned an inactive status on the basis of the author's research.

Table 12.5 Kentucky's Inactive Main Street Programs

Community	Population	Community	Population
Carlisle	1,639	Pikeville	6,323
Brandenburg	1,836	Bardstown	6,801
Harlan	2,785	Princeton	6,940
Prestonsburg	3,558	Maysville	7,169
Carrollton	3,711	Middlesboro	11,328
Covington	43,711		

Field observation in several of these towns immediately indicated that an "inactive" designation might not necessarily mean that these communities had "failed" at downtown revitalization. From all appearances, the majority of these communities looked as viable as their active counterparts. Most had lower program-end vacancy rates (one of the main criterion the NMSC uses to gage success) than the active communities. KHC clarified that these inactive communities were *failures at following the Main Street Four Point Approach*, but not necessarily unsuccessful at downtown revitalization. It was pointed out

> Main Street is not the only approach to downtown and community revitalization that you (a community) may follow; however to continue to use the name and receive the benefits of Main Street services, you must meet our requirements (Stapleton 1999).

Why were so many of the inactive programs located in nonmetropolitan areas? Why did these particular communities not follow the Four Point Approach? There were inactive communities in metropolitan areas as well, but the active metropolitan programs outnumbered the inactive metropolitan communities 2:1. This was consistent with the logistic regression analysis, which revealed active programs were more likely to be located in metropolitan areas than in nonmetropolitan places.

To understand why these nonmetropolitan communities failed to follow the Main Street approach, we first have to look at the conditions of their downtowns at the beginning of the program period. As previously mentioned, Main Street was designed to halt downtown decline. The target communities were those that had high vacancy rates and substantial loss of retail leakage out of the central business district. In theory, only towns that were in serious economic distress were to be chosen as Main Street programs. In the Main Street application, every town competing for designation must supply a variety of information detailing the current conditions of the central business district. This was required so Main Street officials could assess the need for a Main Street Program in a specific community. Some of the questions in the application were highly subjective, and much could be gleaned from the answers concerning the true economic status of an applicant town. After reviewing these applications, it was discovered that a high number of the communities with inactive programs in nonmetropolitan Kentucky were not suffering from serious economic decline at the time they were chosen as a Main Street community. It is believed that such towns were less likely to follow the Main Street Four Point Approach because they did not really need the program for downtown revitalization. Many of these towns, by virtue of their central place locations and functions as county seats, had ample economic activity to keep them viable communities. In essence, they could afford to ignore the Main Street office when the KHC requested the agreed upon deliverables. These cities wanted the Main Street designation, and the money and prestige which followed, but did not want to go through the onerous reporting processes required to retain the title of "Main Street City".

The Case of Pikeville, Kentucky

Pikeville, Kentucky (Figure 12.2) is located in the southeastern portion of the state, in the center of one of the most productive coalfields in Appalachia. The application was prepared by the president of the Pikeville-Pike County Industrial Development and Economic Authority (P-PC/IDEA), which was a newly formed industrial development and economic organization funded through a public/private partnership between the city, county and private sector. Even though Pikeville completed the six years required to become a graduate Main Street town, it was assigned an inactive status by the author due to the absence of progress reports and board meeting during the last two years of the program, which, according to the KHC, was a requirement to retain an "active" status.

Overall, the Pikeville Main Street application revealed a strong, diverse downtown district, with little economic decline. The only real downtown weak-

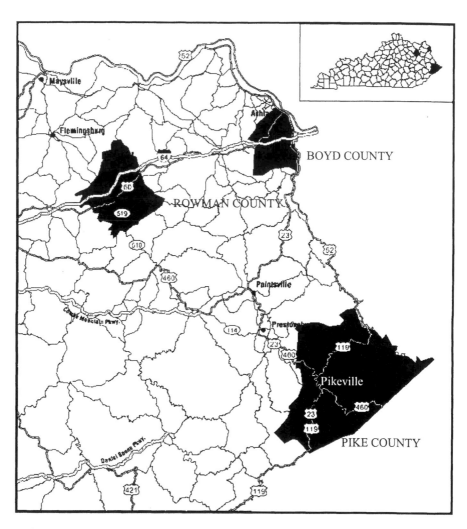

Figure 12.2 Pikeville, Kentucky

ness stressed in the application was "the lethargic attitude on the part of some property owners to attractively maintain their buildings" (Kentucky State Historic Preservation Office 1989). Given that one of the primary foci of the Main Street program is the historic preservation and rehabilitation of existing buildings, this was deemed a serious weakness. On the whole however, Pikeville in the 1980s witnessed a huge investment of both public and private dollars in the CBD. The ground floor vacancy rate for this time period was 9%, compared to the average of 11% (Kentucky State Data Center 1995). With the exception of strip development on the US Route 23 bypass, which could potentially impact the downtown by diverting some of the retail trade from the business district, Pikeville appeared to have a solid economic future. So why was this community even chosen to be a Main Street town?

In 1989, Pikeville was officially designated a Main Street community. During the first year, the program adhered faithfully to the concepts of the Main Street program. The city submitted a budget, hired a Main Street manager, formed a board of directors, and implemented a low interest loan-pool. It conducted training workshops for board members and volunteers on how to implement the Main Street Four Point Approach. So impressed was the KHC with the first year efforts of Pikeville Main Street that they awarded the community an extra $5,000 for a "job well done" (Kentucky State Historic Preservation Office 1989).

Over the next three years, the Pikeville Main Street program continued to more or less adhere to the Main Street principles. Thirty-five new businesses located in the downtown district. Fifteen façade improvements were completed (although most of these improvements consisted of a new coat of paint or a new sign) and four major building rehabilitations were undertaken. Main Street downtown promotions, though sporadic, were organized. At the end of the fourth year, the program began to exhibit problems with implementing the Four Point Approach. One of the biggest obstacles to the continuance of the program was the inability to keep a Main Street manager. In less than four years, Pikeville had hired three different full-time managers. Other signs that the program was veering off course were the absence of any board or committee meetings and the lack of progress reports to the KHC. Even more serious was the fact that the Main Street program manager was being paid by the P-PC/IDEA. This was significant because the Pikeville Main Street program had to be a stand-alone, non-profit organization to legally obtain state and federal funding. Four years into the program, Pikeville Main Street had never applied for non-profit status, which they were supposed to have done at the beginning of the funding period. By the fifth year, the Main Street manager was not getting her agreed upon salary, and she repeatedly threatened to sue the city for back pay. The city maintained that it was not responsible for her pay, and that the Main Street manager was supposed to raise the funds for his or her own salary. The KHC was very unhappy with the whole situation because each year they provided state funding specifically for the Main Street manager's salary, and did not understand why the Pikeville Main Street manager was not being paid.

Despite these problems, the KHC continued funding the city until the end of the six-year program cycle, upon which it became a graduate community. In 1994, state and national Main Street representatives performed a program exit evaluation on Pikeville's Main Street program. According to the evaluation, when locals were asked about the overall impact of the program, they were unable to name a "single thing that Main Street could accomplish to have a successful program." When pressed to elaborate on what they felt the program could do to improve the CBD, a common reply was "to clean up the trash from the downtown area" (Kentucky State Historic Preservation Office 1994).

Location as a Predictor of Main Street Activity in Pikeville

The majority of nonmetropolitan Main Street communities, such as Pikeville, had location advantage over their metropolitan counterparts because they served as the central places for the exchange of goods and services in their respective areas. Pikeville fits into central place theoretical framework in a number of ways. First the settlement pattern in Pike County is consistent with Christaller's hierarchy of cities. As the largest central place in Pike County, Pikeville is surrounded by three towns of slightly smaller population and 30 considerably smaller hamlets and villages. Additionally, the city of Pikeville offers a high number of medium to high-order goods and services, which are typically only found in central places atop the hierarchy of cities. A review of the type and number of businesses in Pikeville at both the beginning and end of the Main Street program illustrates this point. Pikeville had over 100 functions in the downtown district alone, with well over one-half identified as medium or high-order goods and services. For example, there were 33 law offices in Pikeville, with 100 attorneys practicing in the downtown district. It was the Big Sandy Valley region's primary financial and health center. Pikeville's solid retail mix also dominated the region. In 1987, the total retail sales in the Big Sandy Valley were $371,438,000, of which 67% were from the city of Pikeville alone (P-PC/IDEA 1989).

Pikeville's central place status is further strengthened by the complexity of the topography of eastern Kentucky and transportation network in the area. Pikeville has the good fortune of being situated in an area that permitted the construction of a major transportation artery into the complex topography of eastern Kentucky. As a result, the high volume of through traffic in the area supports more functions in the Pikeville CBD than might have otherwise been possible. Without the threat of a considerable economic downturn in the downtown district, the "movers and shakers" of Pikeville saw little tangible need for the Main Street program. As such, the program ran adrift and the Main Street Four Point Approach was abandoned. Thus, Pikeville's central place status contributed to the inactive designation of the Pikeville Main Street program.

Board Composition as a Predictor of Main Street Activity in Pikeville

While Pikeville's function as a central place in the region is believed to be the primary reason its Main Street program became inactive, another variable must be considered when analyzing the events that contributed to the inactive designation of the program. That variable is Main Street board composition (leadership). In her study of inactive towns in Iowa, Baxter (1996) listed leadership as the primary reason programs closed in that state. Indeed, in her summary of the top 15 reasons why an Iowa Main Street town closed, five dealt with leadership issues. The logistic regression analysis supports her findings that leadership (in the form of board composition) was a predictor of whether or not Main Street programs would be active or inactive.

The drive behind the Pikeville Main Street program was the P-PC/IDEA, a county-wide entity whose main goal was to diversify the economy of both Pikeville and Pike County. The P-PC/IDEA had nearly universal support from both the county and city political leadership. This is verified by the monetary contributions to the Main Street program ($15,000 annually) from both political divisions, plus the strong participation of local political leaders on the program's board of directors.

Pikeville's Main Street board composition included the Pike County judge executive, the county clerk, the mayor of Pikeville, the city attorney, the president and chairman of P-PC/IDEA, two bankers, two accountants and two merchants. One banker and one accountant were also members of the city council. Committees were comprised of representatives of local industry, professionals, (particularly lawyers and accountants), and employees of the Chamber of Commerce.

It is interesting to note that there were only a few local citizens, merchants or downtown property owners on the board or committees. There were no historic preservationists on either the board or any of the committees. The primary players in the downtown district (merchants and property owners) had little or no interest in the Main Street Four Point Approach because Pikeville's CBD was economically sound during this period, and they saw little need for the program. These groups especially viewed the preservation component of the program, which involved the historic rehabilitation of their properties, as an unnecessary expense.

For the politicians involved however, the implementation of the Main Street program meant recognition, power and possible re-election for implementing a program that was perceived by voters to benefit the community. The chairman and president of the P-PC/IDEA were fulfilling their paid obligations to recruit industry (and jobs) to the area via the Main Street approach, though most of the recruitment was geared toward Pike County, and not the city of Pikeville itself. The Pikeville Main Street managers were reduced to little more than paid figureheads in this organization. The board had so much power that one manager replied in the Program Managers survey "...they (the board) tell me what to do and I do it" (Kentucky State Historic Preservation Office 1998).

In the end, the program became inactive not only because of its location, but because the board leadership, which was comprised mainly of politicians and industry leaders, saw the Main Street program primarily as a public relations tool. They were able to use Main Street money and public exposure to advance their real cause, which was to bring industrial jobs to the wider region. Since Pikeville itself was not in economic distress, the board had little incentive to faithfully follow the Four Point Approach.

The failure of Pikeville's Main Street program is consistent with the LR's outcome, which predicted Main Street communities were more likely to be classified as inactive when the board composition was comprised primarily of local political leaders, and not downtown merchants, property owners, or grassroots organizations.

Metropolitan Main Street Communities

Of the 26 active Main Street programs studied, 18 were located in metropolitan areas. These communities ranged in size from a high of 53,549 in Owensboro to a low of 2,148 in Cadiz (Table 12.6). While these communities varied in the level of the economic "success", they all fulfilled their obligations to the KHC. Many of these towns in fact, truly embraced the Four Point Approach, almost to the point where they were dogmatic in its implementation. This dogmatic approach was probably a reflection on the poor conditions of their downtown areas, and the communities' earnestness to improve the situation via the Main Street program. Field observation revealed that some of the active towns were quite viable, particularly the larger urban areas or those located in nonmetropolitan communities. The programs located within the economic and cultural shadows of the larger MSA central cities however, were the ones that experienced the greatest overall economic decline in their downtown areas.

Table 12.6 Kentucky's Active Main Street Programs

Community	Population	Community	Population
Ashland	23,622	Madisonville	16,200
Bowling Green	40,641	Mt. Sterling	5,262
Cadiz	2,148	Paducah	27,256
Campbellsville	9,577	Paintsville	4,354
Central City	4,979	Paris	8,730
Danville	16,621	Richmond	21,115
Dawson Springs	3,129	Shelbyville	6,238
Frankfort	25,968	Somerset	10,733
Georgetown	11,414	Springfield	2,878
Harrodsburg	8,790	Lancaster	3,421
Henderson	25,954	Versailles	7,269
Hodgenville	2,756	Winchester	15,799
Hopkinsville	29,809	Owensboro	53,549

The Case of Harrodsburg, Kentucky

Harrodsburg, founded in 1774, is the oldest town in Kentucky. The seat of Mercer County, Harrodsburg is situated in the Bluegrass Region of central Kentucky (Figure 12.3). With a population of 7,335, it is the largest urban place in Mercer County. On March 25, 1987, the town of Harrodsburg submitted an application to the KHC requesting to become a Main Street community. The application was prepared as a joint effort of downtown merchants, the tourism commission, and the Harrodsburg - Mercer County Landmarks Association. The Harrodsburg application emphasized the city's "charm and quality of life," and highlighted the fact that the downtown had a plethora of late 19th and early 20th century features. So picturesque was the downtown that it is listed on National Register's list of Historic Places. The application stressed the widespread community support for the program. Numerous merchants, property owners, preservationists, and local citizens expressed their desire for such a program, and many had indicated their willingness to volunteer their time and expertise to this revitalization effort.

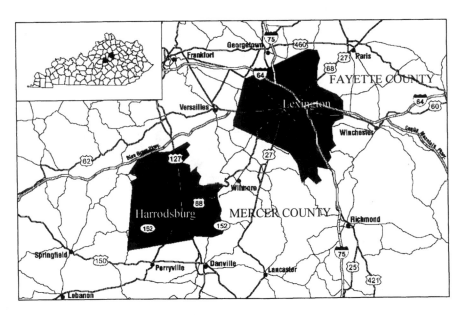

Figure 12.3. Harrodsburg, Kentucky

Despite these strengths, throughout the 1980s retail sales declined in the Harrodsburg CBD. The application reported a 5% decrease in revenues from sales tax from 1980-1987 (Kentucky State Historic Preservation Office 1987).

Further, the application stated that ground floor vacancy rate in Harrodsburg for this same period was 18%, compared to the state urban vacancy rate of 11% (Kentucky State Data Center 1995). The application complained that many downtown property owners lacked the understanding or information needed to ensure historically sensitive renovations to existing buildings, and that in the end, insensitive preservation efforts would inevitably erode the town's historic charm. Additionally, the streetscape of the downtown district was in disrepair; sidewalks needed to be replaced, trees needed to be planted, and street furniture was lacking.

Harrodsburg was awarded Main Street status in 1987, and went by the name of Harrodsburg First. From the beginning, Harrodsburg First embraced the Four Point Approach, and was very active in implementing each facet of the program. Like the Pikeville Main Street program, in the first year Harrodsburg First hired a manager, formed a board of directors, organized committees, conducted training, and submitted a budget to the KHC.

By the KHC and NMSC definitions, Harrodsburg First was a major success story. Throughout the funding period, the program remained committed to the Four Point Approach. During this time, the town witnessed 41 façade improvements, 9 signage projects, 29 building rehabilitations, 28 new businesses, 5 business expansions, and 3 major public improvement projects for a total reinvestment in Harrodsburg of $2,800,500.

Location as a Predictor of Harrodsburg Main Street Activity

A survey of the number and types of businesses in Harrodsburg at the end of the six-year program period revealed a shift in the kind of goods and services offered in the downtown. There emerged a clustering of functions that catered to the tourism industry, such as restaurants, inns and hotels, craft shops and antique stores. This would indicate that local merchants had adopted a strategy of niche marketing. During the same period, the number of medium and high-order goods and services declined. This probably occurred because merchants providing medium and high-order products were not able to compete with the larger urban area, and thus abandoned their operations in the Harrodsburg CBD.

This is consistent with Rushton's (1969) improved consumer behavioral postulate approach to central place theory, because while Harrodsburg is the largest central place in Mercer County, from an economic standpoint it has the misfortune of being located in the economic shadow of a larger metropolis: Lexington, Kentucky. With a population of 250,000 Lexington, located approximately 30 miles northeast of Harrodsburg, is the largest urban place in central Kentucky, as well as the second largest city in the state. Several other Main Street communities, such as Paris to the northeast, Winchester to the east, and Georgetown to the north, have all suffered a similar economic decline in their downtown districts because of their proximity to Lexington and the economic shadow that it imposes.

Board Composition as a Predictor of Harrodsburg Main Street Activity

The program exit evaluation performed by the KHC was full of praise for Harrodsburg First. It was particularly full of accolades for the board and the Main Street manager. As with Pikeville Main Street, the program-end activity in downtown Harrodsburg can be explained, in part, by its board composition. The primary difference between Pikeville and Harrodsburg was in the composition of the board of directors. The Harrodsburg First board was comprised of a wide variety of community representatives, including interested citizens, merchants, property owners, and preservationists. There were no county or city politicians and no industry leaders on the board, and only two politicians were on any of the Main Street committees. Harrodsburg First's board of directors was very active throughout the life of the program (unlike the Pikeville board) and they shared leadership with the Main Street managers. More importantly, the board and the managers had the same goals.

Paramount to these leaders was the aesthetic improvement of downtown Harrodsburg. At the beginning of the program, a number of buildings were in need of façade improvement or rehabilitation. The sidewalks and streets were in a poor state of repair. Additionally, the leaders felt they needed to provide a mechanism to increase both the community's and visitors' appreciation for the historic buildings in the downtown. The organizations and individuals that had a non-vested interest in the economic development of the downtown became involved as volunteers. This cooperation among so many diverse groups was unusual in many Main Street communities, and is a good indicator at how successful the leaders were at mobilizing collective action in Harrodsburg. They were successful because they had created a consensus that the image of their downtown would be one that could serve the needs of Harrodsburg residents, businesses, and tourists alike.

Harrodsburg First emerged as a powerful entity in the community, and was quickly recognized as the "mouthpiece" of downtown. The community ridiculed any dissenters, particularly the local politicians. For instance, a controversy arose over Harrodsburg First's proposal to help property owners replace their sidewalks in the downtown. This angered some politicians who felt that taxpayer dollars (both the city of Harrodsburg and Mercer County contributed to the Main Street's budget) was being used for private gain. One protestor was quoted as saying "pretty sidewalks aren't going to do a damn thing for Harrodsburg...tell me one business or person who will benefit from this project, other than the person who puts in the sidewalks" (The Harrodsburg Herald 1992). Another claimed,

It's foolish to make downtown Harrodsburg look as it did in the 1920s…right now Danville (a neighboring Main Street community) is preparing for the year 2020; that is progressive. Harrodsburg First, on the other hand, wants us to go backward, it wants Harrodsburg to look like it is 100 years behind every other city in the country (Danville Advocate Messenger February 23, 1992:2).

These criticisms met with scathing comment in the local newspaper, in both the editorial section (Figure 12.4) and in public meetings. A similar incident occurred when a local commissioner accused Harrodsburg First of trying to bribe him with a can of peanuts. This commissioner was upset that the Main Street program, and not the city, would oversee the design and construction of new park in the downtown district. He claimed that the city should be in charge because it was city property, and the municipality was "footing the bill." He stated that after he voiced his displeasure at a Harrodsburg First meeting, he soon received a can of peanuts from the organization. "It can't buy my vote" he was quoted as saying (The Harrodsburg Herald 1992). Obviously, this incident was met with much mockery from the community (Figure 12.5).

Figure 12.4 Harrodsburg Herald Editorial Cartoon

...and the winner in the category of "best ridiculous bickering by elected officials" goes to...

Figure 12.5 Harrodsburg Herald Editorial Cartoon

Despite this impressive reinvestment back into the community, and Harrodsburg First's staunch commitment to the Four Point Approach, at the end of the program period, the city of Harrodsburg was no better off economically than at the beginning of the program. Ironically, Harrodsburg First's *success as an active* Main Street program can be attributed to the town's continuing economic distress. In particular, because the viability of Harrodsburg's CBD was threatened, various interest groups (concerned citizens, downtown property owners, merchants, and preservationists) acted collectively throughout the six-year program period to raise awareness and seek ways to increase business activities in the downtown.

Although tourism businesses continue to grow, they did not turn into the major economic opportunity for Harrodsburg as forecasted. The abundance of antique shops and malls in the downtown district is viewed by some as "one step above moth-balling a building" (Stapleton 1999). This approach to downtown revitalization, while deemed a success by KHC standards, did little in the end to increase the economic strength of Harrodsburg's downtown.

CONCLUSION

The KHC has long maintained that the Main Street program has helped halt economic decline in many communities across Kentucky, but seldom addressed the question of why some of these towns did not succeed in their efforts at revitalization using this approach. The purpose of this study was to determine what factors contributed to the active or inactive status of a Kentucky Main Street city. The study first concluded that the KHC definition of success was based on a community's adherence to the Main Street Four Point Approach. The municipalities that followed the Main Street guidelines were awarded an "active" status; those that did not implement the approach were declared "inactive." Any town that was designated inactive during the six-year funding period would not be able to obtain future monetary or technical assistance from the KHC, and would no longer be listed as a "Main Street" city.

The study revealed that Main Street programs located in metropolitan areas were more likely to be active. These communities, particularly those that were located in the shadows of a larger metropolis, typically embraced all four points of the Main Street approach as a means to halt economic decline in their business districts. These communities had the most to lose because local consumers were more likely to abandon these small downtowns in favor of shopping for goods and services in the larger central place. Because the very existence of these communities as viable commercial entities was threatened, interest groups often acted collectively to raise awareness of historic districts and to increase business activities in the CBD. Main Street board members and volunteer groups therefore, were often comprised of a cross-section of individuals from the community, and included property owners, merchants, concerned citizens and preservationists. Niche marketing typically emerged in these active towns as a means of enticing consumers to the CBD. Often this "boutiquization" of small town America led to increased vacancy rates because many of these retail establishments (such as craft shops and antique stores) had a difficult time making a profit and staying in business.

On the other hand, nonmetropolitan Main Street towns were more likely to be declared inactive. Many of these downtowns, by virtue of their isolated locations and their dominance of the surrounding rural hinterlands, were viable, if not thriving, communities. Vacancy rates in the CBD were low because these towns were not in competition with other urban places, and had an abundance of retail and service establishments to keep the street front spaces filled. Implementation and leadership of the Main Street program in these locations were typically county and city politicians, who had the most to gain from such an endeavor. Merchants and property owners were seldom involved in the Main Street process because their economic health was not threatened. Because these downtowns were viable, many citizens of these communities viewed the Main Street program as unnecessary. Apathy concerning the Four Point Approach often set in, and the principles of the program were abandoned. In turn, this led to an inactive designation by the KHC.

To date, geographers and urban planners have not conducted a regional or nation-wide analysis of the effectiveness of the most popular preservation strategy, the National Main Street program. It is believed the conclusions presented in this study can contribute to the greater understanding of the processes involved in downtown revitalization efforts in small and medium-sized downtowns. Future research at the regional or national level needs to be undertaken to further validate the findings in this study. Finally, data obtained in this study could also be used to develop a structural forecasting model to predict success or failure of Main Street communities nationwide.

REFERENCES

Baxter, K. 1996. *Assessment of the Inactive Main Street Programs in Iowa.* Des Moines, Iowa: Department of Economic Development.

Bell, T. 1999. Personal interview. Jan. 10.

Bryce, H. 1967. *Revitalizing Cities.* Lexington, Mass: D. C. Heath Company.

Burayidi, M. ed. 2001. *Downtowns: Revitalizing the Centers of Small Urban Communities.* New York, NY: Routledge.

Clark, D. 1985. *Post-Industrial America.* London: Methuen, Inc.

Christaller, W. 1933. *Central Places in Southern Germany.* Trans. C.W. Baskin. 1966. Englewood Cliffs: Prentice-Hall.

Danville Advocate Messenger, 1992. February 23: 2.

Filion, P., H. Hoernig, T. Bunting and G. Sands. 2004. The successful few: healthy downtowns of small metropolitan regions. *Journal of the American Planning Association,* 70: 328 – 344.

Frieden, B., and L. Sagalyn. 1989. *Downtown Inc.: How America Rebuilds its Cities.* Cambridge, MA: MIT Press.

Gratz, R.B., and N. Mintz. 1998. *Cities Back from the Edge: New Life for Downtown.* New York, NY: John Wiley & Sons.

Holcomb, H.B. and R.A. Beauregard. 1981. *Revitalizing Cities.* Washington, D.C: Association of American Geographers.

Kentucky Heritage Council. 1997-2000. Main Street Files. Frankfort, KY: Kentucky Heritage Council, State Historic Preservation Office.

————. *Main Street Kentucky*. 1988. Frankfort, KY: Kentucky Heritage Council, State Historic Preservation Office.

Kentucky State Data Center. 1995. *Economic Summaries*. Louisville, KY: Urban Studies Institute, University of Louisville.

Kentucky State Historic Preservation Office. 1987. Harrodsburg Main Street Files. Frankfort, KY: State Historic Preservation Office.

————. 1989. Pikeville Main Street Files. Frankfort, KY: State Historic Preservation Office.

————. 1994. Pikeville Main Street Files. Frankfort, KY: State Historic Preservation Office.

————. 1998. Pikeville Main Street Files. Frankfort, KY: State Historic Preservation Office.

National Trust for Historic Preservation. n.d.. *Main Street: Miracle on Main Street*. Washington, D.C.: National Trust for Historic Preservation.

————. Programs and Grants. 2001. www.nationaltrust.org.

Rushton, G. 1969. Analysis of Spatial Behavior by Revealed Space Preference. *Annals of the Association of American Geographers* (59): 391-400.

SPSS Inc. 1998. *SPSS Advanced Statistics User's Guide*. Chicago, IL: SPSS Inc.

Stapleton, R. 1999. Personal interview. September 18.

The Harrodsburg Herald 1992. Editorial Cartoon. February 27: 2.

13

Public Transportation in Small Cities: The Case of Marysville and Yuba City, California

Thomas Irion
Santa Clara Valley Transportation Authority

INTRODUCTION

Transportation is vital to the existence of urban life. Activities are scattered about the city, requiring people to move between residences, retail outlets, places of employment, and other specialized locales (Hanson 1995). Thus, in survey after survey, citizens of urban America cite transportation as one of the primary concerns affecting their daily lives. In urban areas, the vast majority of transportation is conducted by private conveyances. The remainder is conducted by a variety of public modes of transportation: ferries, commuter trains, buses, and light rail vehicles, among others. As cities have grown, transportation infrastructure has become more congested, commute times have lengthened, air pollution from transportation sources has increased, and "road rage" has entered the American lexicon, all of which are symptoms of the urban transportation problem.

However, problems of urban transportation are usually seen as pertaining to only large metropolitan areas. Consequently, urban transportation studies tend to focus on large metropolitan areas, while small cities receive less attention. This chapter is of the view that transportation problems in urban America are not limited to large metropolitan areas alone, but to small urban areas as well. After a brief synopsis of the development of urban transportation in the United States, this chapter will turn its attention to public transportation in small cities, using the case of Marysville and Yuba City, California as an example of the development and atrophy of public transit in small urban areas. The chapter will conclude with an assessment of the problems facing small city public transportation.

PUBLIC TRANSPORTATION IN THE UNITED STATES

Transportation within cities has passed through a number of stages, each being connected with the size of cities. In the United States, these stages have usually been classified as the walking-horsecar, the cablecar, the electric streetcar, and the automobile eras (Muller 1986; Taaffe et al 1996).

The Walking – Horsecar Era (1800 – 1890)

Until cities reached a radius of about two miles, transportation was entirely by foot. By the early 1830's, several cities had reached sufficient size that walking was no longer an adequate means of intra-urban travel. In 1831, horse-drawn omnibuses appeared in both Philadelphia and New York, followed by Boston in 1835 (Vance 1986). These early conveyances served a middle class clientele, the fare exceeding the ability of the ordinary worker to pay (Vance 1986). In 1832, the New York and Harlem Railroad established the first US horsecar line to connect downtown New York with the railroad's uptown terminal. New York City at that time was located entirely on long and narrow Manhattan Island. The island's length made foot travel difficult. A second horsecar line was established between New Orleans and Carrollton, four and one-half miles, later the same year (Vance 1986). These two lines established the technological standard for horse drawn street railways for the life of the industry. In the 1850s, Boston, Philadelphia, Pittsburgh, Cincinnati, and Chicago all established horsecar lines (Vance 1986). The horsecar permitted expansion of cities to about three miles radius, expanding the available area for housing. At the same time, the cost was reduced to a level that put transportation from home to work within the reach of the typical worker. Steam railroad suburbs also developed outside major cities along with horsecar suburbs. The horsecar lines had frequent service, frequent stops, and were cheap to expand. The horsecar was, however, limited by its speed; beyond its reach, some form of mechanical assistance was needed (Vance 1986).

The Cablecar Era (1870 – 1890)

The steam railroad commuter train proved the desirability of applying steam power to suburban transportation. The technology demanded a separate right of way. In cities, this meant elevated or underground lines (Vance 1986). The first New York City elevated line was cable powered, opening on July 1, 1868. Extension of the line in 1871 rendered cable propulsion impractical. The line used small steam locomotives until electrification in 1902. New York City, Chicago, Boston, and Philadelphia built elevated railways, as did Sioux City, Iowa, the only small city to attempt such a venture.

The widespread application of mechanical power to street railways awaited the development of the cable railway. The cablecar appeared in San Francisco in 1873. The cable car increased street railway speeds by 50%, while cutting costs by half (Vance 1986). The cablecar allowed the motive power to be at a distance from the car. The smoke and noise of its steam power plant could be concealed, or at least reduced to tolerable levels (Vance 1986). In hilly terrain, descending cars assisted ascending cars while maintaining a constant speed. There were, however, a number of safety problems with the technology, and construction was quite expensive. Although the cablecar increased average speeds to five to six miles per hour, the cable railway was not the long-sought solution to the horsecar problem (Hilton 1982). With few exceptions, the cablecar was confined to large cities (Vance 1986). It increased the serviceable radius to about four miles.

The Electric Streetcar Era (1890 – 1930)

As early as 1835, the first experiments were undertaken that would lead to electrically propelled transportation. Until 1879, all such projects used battery power. The use of electricity on street railways awaited the development of a practical dynamo. In the 1880's, the pace of experimentation quickened. By 1888, there were eleven electric streetcar systems in operation in the United States with a total of less than 100 cars and 60 miles of track. The main difficulty with each was the transmission of torque from the traction motor to the wheels. Chain drives and rigidly mounted gears suffered high failure rates due to the variations in track surface and alignment.

In 1888, the problem of torque transmission was solved by Frank J. Sprague. Sprague had contracted to build two electric street railways, the first being the Richmond Union Passenger Railway, a 12 - mile system with 40 cars that operated on grades up to eight percent. He devised a system for support of the traction motors that kept the distance between them and the axles constant, the innovation that was needed for the electric railway to succeed. The Richmond system is acknowledged as the first successful electric streetcar system. A few months after the system opened, Sprague demonstrated the simultaneous starting of over one-half the Richmond fleet for Henry M. Whitney, president of the West End Street Railway in Boston. The West End line was a large horsecar system that was considering conversion to cable power. Their management was concerned that an electric system could not sustain simultaneous starting of many cars in dense traffic. Sprague's demonstration allayed their fears. The conversion of the West End lines to electricity was the first in a large city. Within two years, there were 200 electric street railways in operation or under construction. Half of these were furnished with Sprague equipment and fully 90% used Sprague patents. The rapidity of electric railway adoption was startling. By 1902, there were 21,862 miles of electric railway track in the United States. The industry peaked at 41,447 miles of track in 1917 (Middleton 1967). The electric railway was relatively inexpensive and easy to install, and was quite reliable (Vance 1986). The electric streetcar became the major instrument of the geographical expansion of cities (Vance 1990). The streetcar operated at speeds three to five times greater than the horsecar, permitting cities to expand proportionally. It also permitted workers to live at some distance from their places of employment. The improved transportation encouraged factory satellites to locate around the metropolitan core (Vance 1986).

Eventually, electric traction was applied to subway and elevated lines, interurban railways, and main line "steam" railroads. Within cities, streetcar systems flourished into the late 1910's. These years coincided with the years of rising government regulation of transportation. Most street railways operated under some sort of limit on fares, usually five cents per ride without regard to distance. The inflation of costs that occurred during and after the First World War was not matched by a rise in fares. By the early 1920s, this situation reduced many street railway companies to a hand-to-mouth existence that allowed little for new equipment purchases or line extensions. By the 1930s, streetcar abandonment had begun in earnest, especially in smaller cities. The last small town streetcar system in the United States, Johnstown, Pennsylvania, Traction Company, ceased to operate in 1960.

The Automobile (1930 – Present)

The automobile developed just a few years after the electric railway. The auto permitted filling-in of urban space between streetcar lines (Vance 1964). The low cost, mass produced car allowed travel anywhere, any time. No form of public transportation could match its convenience. According to Muller (1986) it was the farmers in rural America that first took to the automobile due to their need to reach service centers. In the city, the automobile was first used for weekend recreational outing. However, as American cities suburbanized car ownership became a necessity and a combination of this with other factors gradually affected the public transportation industry. The commuting public demonstrated an aversion to the streetcar's replacement, the motor bus. The transit industry eventually was reduced to carrying the elderly, the young, and the mobility-impaired, while the bulk of commuters started traveling in their own conveyances, the private automobile.

After several decades of automobile-dependent urban development and growth, the transportation problems in urban America seem to have come full circle. The transportation problem that is so often the subject of surveys, news articles, and legislative deliberations today, is largely a problem of congestion. Commuting speeds on inner-city highways at peak hours are often slower than fifteen miles per hour. The available fuel tax revenue is inadequate to maintain and expand the highway system in the most populous states. Bus transit is affected by the same congestion that afflicts the private automobile. In a number of cities, new electric railways, "Light Rail Transit", have been built in an effort to bypass crowded roadways and attract motorists to transit. Local, state, and federal tax revenues now subsidize the transit industry to varying degrees. Without this tax support, the American transit industry would exist in very few places.

Much of the preceding applies to major metropolitan areas. What about small urban areas? The small urban area is often neglected in discussions of urban transit problems. How does public transportation in small cities compare with that of major metropolitan areas? In the following sections, I will consider the case of Marysville and Yuba City, California, to gain some understanding of public transportation in small cities. How has the development and atrophy of the transit system of these cities differed from that of large cities? What are the future prospects for public transit in these and other small communities?

PUBLIC TRANSPORTATION IN MARYSVILLE AND YUBA CITY, CALIFORNIA

In August 1839, John A. Sutter settled at the current site of Sacramento, having acquired a large grant from the Mexican government. Within a few years, the towns of Nicolaus, Marysville, Yuba City, Oroville, and others were established along the rivers of the Sacramento Valley, later serving as points of debarkation for prospectors traveling into the gold-laden foothills of the Sierra Nevada. These towns continued to function and grow long after the gold fever had ended. The Sacramento Valley became an agricultural gold mine that needed marketplaces, transshipping points, foundries, seats of local governance, and a hundred other supporting functions for the agriculture that developed in the valley. In some of these valley towns, populations were large enough to require some form of urban transportation by the late-19th century.

Augustus Le Plongeon, second owner of a portion of John A. Sutter's Mexican land grant, laid out Marysville in 1849-1850. The town, which is within Yuba County, occupied the northeast quadrant of the confluence of the Feather and Yuba Rivers, a site which constrains its growth (Gudde 1998). The other of the so-called Twin Cities—Yuba City—was laid out in 1849 on a site previously occupied by Maidu Indians, and named after the Yuba River, although it lies within Sutter County. Both cities became important service centers for the surrounding agricultural areas. In the 1860s, much of the Sacramento Valley was planted in cereal grains (Vance 1964). Within twenty years, the Valley's agriculture was beginning to shift to orchard crops. In 1882, the first of many canneries was established in the Twin Cities area (McGowan 1961).

Table 13.1: Historical Populations of the Twin Cities

Year	Marysville	Yuba City	Total
1910	5,430	1,160	6,590
1920	5,461	1,708	7,169
1930	5,763	3,605	9,368
1940	6,646	4,968	11,614
1950	7,826	7,861	15,687
1960	9,553	11,507	21,060
1970	9,353	13,986	23,339
1980	9,898	18,736	28,634
1990	12,324	27,437	39,761
2000	12,268	36,758	49,026

Early Public Transportation

Public transportation came to the Twin Cities in the form of a horse-drawn omnibus. E. H. Pacey began operating his omnibus between Third and D streets in Marysville and Yuba City in November 1861. The fare was "one bit" or 12 ½ cents (Marysville Daily Appeal 1861). Pacey operated the service every thirty minutes (Appeal-Democrat 1960). At least one enterprising soul attempted to compete with Pacey without the benefit of a license, and received a citation for the offense. In November 1864, another omnibus was added under the management of Benjamin B. Wolfe (Marysville Daily Appeal 1864). The Marysville newspaper described it as "new and elegant," but offered no other details. The newspapers announced new equipment from time to time as late as 1889.

In 1861, the state legislature in Sacramento considered a bill authorizing a horse railroad to be laid in the streets of Marysville. The proposed route extended from the Feather River steamboat landing to the central business district, a distance of about one mile. If local sentiment can be gauged by the writings of the *Marysville Appeal*, the proposition was none too popular with the Marysville populace. The *Appeal* was eloquent in its sarcasm directed toward the proposal. The paper said the railroad was not a public necessity, and then went on to surmise that it was probably a ruse to give one of the steam railroads access to public streets as rights of way (Marysville Daily Appeal 1861). The paper scoffed at the need for a horse railroad to handle freight from the river to the merchants in town asserting that the drayage firms could handle the business. The paper's editor summed up his feelings, 'We don't want it' (Marysville Daily Appeal 1861). Until 1870, there was no further mention of a horse railroad. Omnibuses continued to serve passengers. Another horse railroad bill was introduced in the legislature in January 1870 (Marysville Daily Appeal 1870). This one proposed to extend across the Feather River from Marysville to Yuba City. Nothing came of the project.

By 1874, jurisdiction over such local matters as street railroad franchises seems to have passed from the state legislature to the local government. The Marysville City Council passed a street railroad ordinance in June 1874, which the mayor promptly vetoed. The mayor's veto message gave sufficient reason to persuade the councilmen to sustain his veto unanimously. The offending language was removed, the ordinance passed, and the mayor signed it (Marysville City Council 1874). As with the previous proposal it was all for naught, there was no track laid nor cars operated.

In May 1888, the Marysville City Council passed an ordinance granting David E. Knight and three associates the right to construct and operate a street railroad on the streets of Marysville (Marysville City Council 1888). Knight had organized the Marysville Coal Gas Company in 1858, and by 1888 was an important local figure. He took delivery of four cars in August 1889. The fare was five cents. This line was the first street railroad in the valley north of Sacramento (Silsbee 1960) Knight's line used mules rather than horses, a common practice due to the mule's superior stamina. The speed of a horse car was about the same as walking, but without the exertion. The typical car carried 25 to 50 people, including standees. Horsecars and the later electric streetcar enabled people to live farther from the business district than would have otherwise been practical (McGowan 1961). The flat five-cent fare leveled the cost of distance which enabled workers to select housing over a wider area (Vance 1990). One indication of the importance of the horse car to the local economy was summed up in an advertisement for cannery workers in August 1905, "Good wages paid to canners at Yuba City Cannery. Car fare paid to and from Marysville. Apply F. B. Crane, Manager" (Marysville Daily Appeal 1905). The horsecar permitted workers to pick from a wider selection of housing while allowing the employer to recruit from a wider area.

The Electric Railroad Era

The horsecar came to Marysville and Yuba City relatively late in the animal powered railroad era and the cities bypassed the cable car altogether. The electric railroad was also slow to come to Marysville and Yuba City. There had been several local proposals for long distance electric railroad lines between 1901 and 1905 (Marysville Daily Appeal 1905). The first, in 1901, was proposed to run between Marysville and Grass Valley in the Sierra Nevada foothills (McGowan 1961). This line, the California Midland, actually built two miles of streetcar track in Marysville in 1906 and paid the Marysville Levee Commission to strengthen one of the Yuba River levees to take the weight of a railroad, then put its construction on hold "temporarily" (Marysville Daily Appeal 1908). The temporary hiatus turned out to be permanent. The California Midland did not operate the track that was built. Col. E. A. Forbes and his associates put forth a proposal in 1905 to build an electric line from Marysville to the Sacramento River near Meridian, a distance of about 15 miles. The goal of reaching the Sacramento River was inspired in part by the availability of freight boats for most of the year on this stream as far north as Meridian.

The project that finally brought the electric streetcar to the Twin Cities was also proposed in 1905 in the town of Chico, 47 railway miles north of Marysville (McGowan 1961). The Northern Electric Railway (N.E.) began construction in Chico with the goal of reaching Vallejo Wharf on the north end of San Francisco Bay, and a steamship connection to San Francisco. The railroad completed its line between Chico and Marysville on December 3, 1906 with the aid of Col. Forbes and Wendell Hammon, developer of the Yuba River gold fields, who purchased the Marysville-Yuba City horsecar line and passed its franchises to the N.E. (McGowan 1961). Once the Northern Electric began operating on a regular basis, local streetcar service between Marysville and Yuba City supplemented its interurban cars on the line to Chico and Sacramento. By 1909, streetcar service operated every fifteen minutes from 6:20 AM until 6:20 PM, then every thirty minutes until 11:20 PM (Marysville Daily Appeal 1909). The cars could carry about forty seated passengers and up to sixty standees for a five-cent fare.

In 1910, there was a major extension of service proposed on the Marysville end of the line. The proposed line would have added about a mile of track to the existing 2.43 miles of route (Marysville Daily Appeal 1910). None of this extended route was ever placed in service. In 1915, the specter of competition arrived in the Twin Cities in the form of jitneys (Marysville Daily Appeal 1915). These were usually private automobiles operated along fixed routes without the benefit of franchise or license that charged a nickel fare. Many of these jitneys operated along street railway routes, often racing to stay ahead of a streetcar so that the jitney operator could collect a full load before the streetcar arrived. In the absence of regulation, there were few jitneys carrying insurance, operating on formal schedules, or maintaining their vehicles adequately. Only a few jitneys operated in Marysville or Yuba City. Still, their effect on the streetcar ridership of the Northern Electric Railway was substantial. The Marysville city council enacted a requirement for substantial bond against injury to patrons, and a license fee in 1915. The *Appeal* reported that it was expected that the two remaining jitneys would cease operation as a result of the new regulation (Marysville Daily Appeal 1915).

In 1924, a new generation of streetcars designed for one-man operation and low power costs was installed. The style of equipment, known as a Birney Car, had been developed in 1915 and was touted as the savior of the street railway industry. Its costs of operation were about half that of other streetcars, but it only had about half the passenger capacity of the cars it replaced. The negative aspects of this equipment were its rough riding quality, and austere interior appointments.

The first *bona fide* proposal for a bus line for the Marysville-Yuba City route came in August 1918 (Sutter County Independent Farmer 1918). The plan came to naught, and passengers traveling between Marysville and Yuba City continued to ride the streetcar. The streetcar operated over two different routes within Yuba City; via Second Street and the Feather River levee, or via the direct line used by the Northern Electric's interurban trains on Bridge Street.

The Northern Electric entered receivership in 1914. Within a few months of its reorganization as the Sacramento Northern Railroad, the company applied to the California Railroad Commission for permission to abandon the Second Street line (California Railroad Commission 1919). Service continued over the main line of the railroad on Bridge Street where the streetcars shared the track with interurban passenger trains and freight trains. The route was 2.20 miles in length between Second & Oak Streets in Marysville and Cooper Avenue & Reeves Street in Yuba City. In 1931, the company operated the service every fifteen minutes from 6:00 AM to 7:15 PM, then every thirty minutes until midnight. In March 1940, the Sacramento Northern reduced the service to every thirty minutes between 6 AM and 7 AM, then every fifteen minutes until 6:15 PM, returning to thirty minutes until 11:55 PM. The service remained at this level until February 15, 1942, when the company discontinued streetcar service (SNRy 1941). The speed of the streetcar averaged 8.8 miles per hour including "recovery time" at the end of the line (SNRy 1941).

The Motor Bus Era

In October 1941, Lassen Trailways approached the Sacramento Northern Railway and the city councils of Marysville and Yuba City seeking to substitute bus service for the railway's streetcar line. Application was made to the California Railroad Commission to execute the plan. Two buses were ordered from Yellow Coach of Detroit, Michigan (California Railroad Commission 1942). The Railroad Commission approved the substitution of buses for the streetcars, setting the fare at five cents, the same as the streetcar fare. In retrospect, it is incredible that the Commission had continued the nickel fare for over thirty years in the Twin Cities. Although the nickel fare broke the streetcar companies, the Commission would continue to embrace it long after it should have been obvious that the buying power of the 1940's nickel was a mere shadow of the buying power of the same coin in 1906, when the streetcar service began.

The new operation, known as Twin Cities Transit, was under the management of Joseph L. Green and Norman H. Robotham, who had previously been an agent of the Sacramento Northern Railway. Twin Cities Transit provided service every twenty minutes from 6:20 AM until 9:00 PM, then every thirty minutes until 11:30 PM. The average speed dropped to 6.6 miles per hour. The route included a loop around much of Yuba City's residential area south of the railroad line and a crossing of the Feather River into Marysville where buses operated alongside the old streetcar tracks as far as C Street. Twin Cities Transit expected its route to be within two blocks of 95% of Yuba City's population (California Railroad Commission 1942). After a month, the company extended the route to include more of Yuba City's residential areas, both north and south of the old streetcar route, and in Marysville, expanded the route to reach nearly a mile north of the old route (Sutter City Independent-Farmer 1942).

Twin Cities Transit struggled with the five cent fare for six months before returning to the Railroad Commission to apply for a fare increase to 10 cents with commute books available for regular riders at reduced per-trip cost (Independent-Farmer 1942). The same application included a request for rights to operate through larger areas of Marysville. The Commission denied the fare increase, but allowed the extensions (Sutter City Independent-Farmer 1942). Route changes were numerous during the Second World War as the company tried to accommodate the increased ridership resulting from gasoline and tire rationing plus the activity at Beale Army Air Force Base, while revenues remained at five cents per ride. By 1944, the company had reduced the Marysville-Yuba City route until it looked to the editor of the *Sutter County Independent-Farmer* as though it was the old streetcar route. The editor also complained about the tendency of the bus company to change routes and stops without notice on the slightest whim (Sutter City Independent-Farmer 1944). The paper recommended restoring the streetcar service as it would save tires and gasoline "as well as giving assurance to patrons that they would not be left waiting on a route changed overnight as streetcar rails can't be moved that easily."

The residents of South Marysville and the town of Olivehurst received bus service starting August 1, 1944. Nine daily trips were operated, three of those on Sundays (Marysville Appeal-Democrat 1944). In February 1946, A. J. Chapin, who operated bus services in the Salinas and Watsonville areas, and in the suburbs of Sacramento, bought Twin Cities Transit (Sutter City Independent-Farmer 1946). The Railroad Commission approved the transaction a week later. A year later, Robotham repossessed the company. In early February 1948, Twin Cities Transit extended its route to northwest Marysville and the Yuba County Hospital, operating four trips daily. Within two weeks, it was clear that the service was greater than the demand. In the first twelve days, the service carried only 22 passengers. The company quickly deleted one trip from the schedule (Sutter City Independent-Herald 1948).

In mid-1952, the Twin Cities Transit operation was sold again, this time to G. R. Summy. Like the 1946 sale to Chapin, this sale was not consummated. Twin Cities Transit, now in the hands of the widow of Mr. Robotham, abruptly discontinued all service on September 30, 1952, leaving its patrons stranded (Marysville Appeal-Democrat 1952). Operations resumed three weeks later on a much-curtailed schedule operated in rush hours only, supplemented by taxi service in the off-hours. Transit service in the Twin Cities had become so unimportant that the next sale of the company was not even reported in the newspapers. The company, now owned by Messrs. Jarvis and Nelson, applied to raise fares due to the need to re-route the bus line over the Tenth Street Bridge since the Fifth Street Bridge had been destroyed in the Christmas Eve, 1955, flood of Yuba City. The fare increased to fifteen cents for adults, ten cents up to 12 years of age (Marysville City Council 1956). In January 1960, Jarvis was again before the Council asking for a twenty cent fare. The council refused to acquiesce to the request, preferring to remain neutral until California Public Utilities Commission held hearings (Marysville City Council 1960). Twin Cities Transit continued to operate until the early 1960s. The exact date of the last bus run is unknown, but the California Public Utilities Commission revoked the company's operating authority on October 27, 1964 (Martin, 4, 2004). In late 1967, another operator attempted to operate a bus service in Yuba City (Herald 1967). The attempt lasted less than 30 days (Herald 1967). With that cessation of service, the era of privately-owned public transit service ended in the Twin Cities. The next step would require a political change of heart at all levels of government.

Public Transit as Public Enterprise in the Twin Cities

After the final attempt to operate bus service in the Twin Cities, public transit consisted entirely of "for-profit" taxicabs until July 1975. On July 1, 1975, the Hub Area Transit Authority (HATA) was formed under a Joint Powers Agreement (JPA) between Yuba and Sutter Counties. The Authority subsidized taxi service for senior citizens and disabled persons until August 1979, when it replaced the subsidized taxi service with a Dial-A-Ride transit service available to the general public. In September 1982, HATA established its first fixed route bus service. A mid-day intercity run was instituted from Marysville to the University of California-Davis Medical Center in Sacramento. At the beginning of 1988, Sutter County withdrew from the JPA which resulted in the termination of this and all other fixed route service. Another Dial-A-Ride service replaced the fixed route service. The Sacramento mid-day service was restored nine months later. In July 1990, the Sacramento service expanded to include commuter trips to downtown Sacramento, serving the large employment center surrounding the State Capitol.

In January 1991, Sutter County re-joined the JPA. Two years later, HATA became Yuba-Sutter Transit and reintroduced fixed route service to the Twin Cities. Yuba-Sutter Transit acquired new 45-passenger buses for the Sacramento commuter service in 1994 and expanded that service to include a Yuba City-Sacramento route. The JPA instituted a subsidy for weekday evening taxi service to provide local transportation during those hours at reasonable cost, and for a vanpool program to Sacramento. New local routes were implemented in Marysville in 1995.

In mid-1998, Yuba-Sutter Transit established routes to Beale Air Force Base and the town of Sutter (eight miles west of Yuba City). It began Saturday service, expanded the Dial-A-Ride territory, and implemented a number of reduced fare plans. These plans included monthly passes, discount ticket books, and a senior and disabled I.D. card to permit those patrons to pay reduced cash fares. This year was the most active in the history of Yuba-Sutter Transit in terms of expansion of service and encouragement of transit use. The weekday evening taxi subsidy ended in July 1999. The following month saw a retrenchment of the rural routes to Sutter and Beale AFB, and the start of general public Dial-A-Ride service on weekday evenings. The increasing commute population of the Twin Cities led to the initiation of a commute service to Lincoln Airport Industrial Park at the same time. Another Yuba City local route began operating in April 2001. In April 2002, the agency received three new buses to expand the Sacramento commuter service (Yuba-Sutter Transit 2003a).

Today's Yuba-Sutter Transit service within the Twin Cities includes five routes. Service is operated every thirty minutes on two routes, and every sixty minutes on the remaining three. All routes offer hourly service on Saturdays. There are three rural routes: Wheatland (one trip each Tuesday), Foothills (two trips each Tuesday, Wednesday, and Thursday), and Live Oak (one trip on Monday, Wednesday, and Friday). The Sacramento and Lincoln Airport commuter runs continue to operate on schedules designed to match the starting and ending times of the commuter's workday (Yuba-Sutter Transit 2003b).

Considering that neither the Sacramento Northern nor Twin Cities Transit were able to operate at a substantial profit for most of their histories, what has changed to permit Yuba-Sutter Transit to operate and expand its service since its inception in 1975? Clearly, it is the availability of federal, state, and local tax funds that make this service possible. A glance at the operating results posted by Yuba-Sutter Transit tells much of the story (Table 13.2). The table below compares Yuba-Sutter Transit's fiscal years 1993 and 2003. This table shows that the cost of operating Yuba-Sutter Transit is not covered by the fares paid by the passengers (Yuba-Sutter Transit 2003c).

The failure to cover operating costs from farebox revenue is nearly universal in US transit operations. Yuba-Sutter Transit has one of the better farebox recovery ratios found in a random sampling conducted in 2004. The Santa Clara Valley Transportation Authority in San Jose, California, is operating at 15% recovery with fixed route and paratransit service. In Medford, Oregon, Rogue Valley Transit District recovers 22% of its costs from fares for fixed route and Dial-a-ride service. In Twin Falls, Idaho, the town's transit service is entirely dial-a-ride, recovering 6% of its costs from fares.

CONCLUSION

As small cities founded during the nineteenth century, Marysville and Yuba City have followed a public transportation path that is typical of cities large enough to warrant street railway service. Initially, service was provided using animal power. Omnibus speeds were below five miles per hour on dirt streets, the horse car increasing slightly. The next step was the electric streetcar, bypassing the cable car technology used in larger cities due to its expense. The streetcar

Table 13.2 Yuba-Sutter Transit Operating Results

Characteristics	1993	2003 est.
Fleet Size	18	37
Service Hours	32,540	69,900
Passenger Trips Total	184,535	664,000
Fixed Route	45,523	501,000
Dial-A-Ride	110,712	67,000
Commuter	3,344	8,000
Rural Routes	2,118	11,000
Rides per Capita	4.64	4.42
Operating Revenues Total	$1,125,313	$2,813,550
Federal, State, and Local tax funds	892,018	2,008,200
Fares and Miscellaneous	233,295	805,330
Fare per Passenger-Average	1.00	0.95
Operating Cost per Passenger	6.10	4.24
Operating Cost per Service Hour	34.58	40.25
Fare Box Recovery Ratio	17.7%	23.0%

raised speeds to as high as fifteen miles per hour, increasing the radius available for urban development. The next major influence on transportation in urban areas was the automobile which further extended the urban radius. The bus permitted its owners to transfer the costs of infrastructure to the taxpayers in the form of fuel taxes supporting roadway construction and maintenance. Small city transit operations are almost exclusively bus systems. The density of population is not sufficient to support high levels of service. In the Yuba-Sutter Transit example, the best frequency of service is thirty minutes. This is compared to service in Los Angeles as frequent as every five minutes. Rail operations are limited to metropolitan areas and a small number of tourist sites. For small communities, the typical public transit choices are bus service supported by taxes, or no service at all.

The future of public transit in small cities will in large part be dependent upon the level of political support for the expenditure of tax funds to operate the service. The majority of federal transit support is for capital expenditures, equipment and facilities. The bulk of these funds go to metropolitan areas. Federal transit funds for operation are limited. The costs of operation are borne by varying levels of state and local funds that supplement farebox revenues. The service can continue only as long as there is the political will to continue to make up the shortfall in passenger revenue with tax funds. Ultimately, that is determined by the voters. One of the transit industry's challenges is to convince the motorist voters that transit is valuable to them even if they do not use the service. That situation exists in metropolitan areas as well as small cities.

REFRENCES

California Railroad Commission 1942. Decision 34970
———. 1942. Decision 34969.
———. 1919. Decision 6870.
Gudde, E. G. 1998. *California Place Names.* Berkeley CA: University of California Press.
Hanson, S. 1995. *The Geography of Urban Transportation.* New York: The Guilford Press.
Hilton, G. W 1982. *The Cable Car in America*, San Diego, Calif: Howell-North Books.
Martin, K. 2004. Telephone Interview.
Marysville 1941. City Line Timetable.
Marysville City 1960. Council Minutes.
———. 1956. Council Minutes.
———. 1874. Council Minutes, June 15.
——— 1888. Council Minutes.
Marysville Daily Appeal. Various Years.
Marysville Appeal-Democrat.
Marysville Democrat Various.
McGowan, J. 1961. *The History of the Sacramento_Valley*, West Palm Beach, Fla: Lewis Historical Publishing Co.
Middleton, W. D. 1967. *Time of the Trolley* Milwaukee, WI: Kalmbach Publishing Co.
Muller, P. O. 1986. Transportation and Urban Form: Stages in the Spatial Evolution of the American Metropolis. In *The Geography of Urban Transportation*, ed. S. Hanson, 24 – 48. New York, NY: Guildford Press.
SNRy 1941. File 302. December 1
Silsbee, N. 1960. Recollections of the Northern Electric Railway, Known Later as the Sacramento Northern Railway, Sacramento, California.
Sutter County Independent-Farmer Various Years
Sutter County Farmer: Various Years
Taaffe, E. J., H. L. Gauthier, and M. E. O'Kelly. 1996. *Geography of Transportation.* Second Edition. Upper Saddle River, NJ: Prentice-Hall.
Vance, J. E. Jr. 1990. *The Continuing City.* Baltimore, MD.: Johns Hopkins University Press.
———. 1986. *Capturing the Horizon. The Historical Geography of Transportation since the Sixteenth Century.* New York, N.Y. Harper and Row.
———. 1964. *Geography and Urban Evolution in the San Francisco Bay Area.* Berkeley, Calif., Institute of Governmental Studies: University of California, 1964.
Yuba-Sutter Transit. 2003a Summary of Key Events. January.

———. 2003b. Rider's Guide. September.
———. 2003c System Fact Sheet. January.

14

Housing and Urban Development Problems in Small Cities: The Case of Ciudad Guzman, Jalisco, Mexico

Luís Felipe Cabrales Barajas[*]
Universidad de Guadalajara

INTRODUCTION

Since the 1940s, Mexico has experienced rapid urbanization. This has largely been due to the industrialization policies developed since the institution of the modern state that resulted from the Mexican Revolution of 1910. Between 1900 and 2000, Mexico's population grew from 13.6 million to 97.5 million, and the country went from being predominantly rural toward predominantly urban. Thus, at the beginning of the 20th century only 10% of Mexicans lived in urban areas. A century later the population is 61% urban and 39% rural. During the 1960 – 1970 period most of this growth occurred in the three largest metropolitan areas of Mexico City, Guadalajara, and Monterrey, with Mexico City in particular growing at an annual rate of 5.3% compared to the national rate of 3.4%. However, during 1990-2000, small and medium sized cities in Mexico experienced a demographic and urban turnaround, and even though the growth rate greatly varied regionally and with respect to the productive base, on the average it was about 3%, compared to 1.84% for the nation as a whole. At the same time the nation's great metropolitan areas saw a reduction in their

[*] Both the author of this chapter and the editor of this book are grateful to Michael S. Yoder, Associate Professor of Geography, Texas A&M International University, for greatly improving the initial translation of this chapter from Spanish to English. – Ed.

growth rates. Thus, the Metropolitan Zone of Mexico City had a rate of 1.6%, Guadalajara 2.1%, and Monterrey 2.3%.

Within the Mexican academic tradition, a small city is defined as one that has population between 15,000 and 99,999, while a mid-sized city has population ranging from 100,000 to one million people. By these definitions, Mexico had 399 small cities in 2000. These accounted for approximately 13,285,000 inhabitants or 13.6% of the national population. Other estimates credit small cities to be containing about 22.26% of the national population, which is equivalent to that of the three national metropolitan areas. There may be several explanations for the nonmetropolitan turnaround in population. In part, it may be due to the economic model of development, impulses by the augmentation of the tertiary sector, and free trade and State deregulation. To a lesser extent, it may be due to the urban-regional policies adopted since the 1980s, as well as the negative effects of the rural crisis and social and labor problems of the big cities. No matter the explanation, one thing is certain and that is the overwhelming increase in urbanization of small and mid-sized cities translates into problems that they are not prepared to deal with considering their limited management capacity and lack of financial resources. If particular attention is not paid to these problems, there is a high risk of reproducing the same severe social and environmental problems of the big cities. This would run counter to the potential advantage of population redistribution brought about by the nonmetropolitan turnaround in population.

This chapter examines problems of housing and urban development in a small city setting using Ciudad Guzman, a small city in Mexico's Jalisco province, as a case study. The chapter argues the inappropriateness of models of urban development derived from Western developed countries to small cities, and especially those in nonwestern developing countries such as Mexico. It claims that analysis of urban development problems of small cities in Mexico must be placed within broader contexts that go beyond population distribution and economic activity, and able to connect multiple social objectives. This should include the city's capacity to attract and generate employment, environmental relations, quality of life, and development in general. The chapter illustrates these trends with the case of housing and urban development in Ciudad Guzman with particular reference to development before and after the 1985 earthquake that the city suffered. The rest of the chapter is divided into three sections. The first section outlines a critique of regional policies and urban development models in Mexico. The second section provides a brief overview of the location and growth of the case study city—Ciudad Guzman. The third section provides an analysis of housing and urban development in Ciudad Guzman, with particular reference to the 1985 earthquake. The final section provides some concluding thoughts on urban development problems in small cities in Mexico.

REGIONAL POLICIES, URBAN DEVELOPMENT MODELS, AND MEXICO'S SMALL CITIES

Mexico is a country of great social contrasts and regional disparities. While some "winner" regions have reached the articulation to the prevailing economic model, some "loser" regions remain marginalized from development especially the ones located in the south of the country. The history of concentration and regional differences have generated territorial models that are not so easily modified in the medium term, while the vision of the hierarchically constructed pyramidal urban systems has the tendency to be replaced by one of a diffuse network (Borja y Castells 1997). Within this perspective the large metropolitan areas have gained their prestige, because they are recognized as innovative and receptive of command functions for activities that have expanded over wide territories, given the decentralization. Thus, even though a growing portion of industrial employment has been captured by small cities and other remote or rural places, industrial activities of various complexities do in fact remain largely concentrated in metropolitan areas.

Interurban articulations derived from the evolution of the economic model, as well as the lessening of planning activities by the government, have provoked, in the last decade, urban deconcentration and a growing political discourse regarding small and mid sized cities. This discourse has mainly sought to reverse the traditional pattern of income distribution and population that has been concentrated in the large metropolitan areas. For example, in 1991 the "100 Cities Program" was implemented to look for a better quality of life in the intermediate cities, with the aim of ending problems of large city growth. However, urban-regional policies have faced several challenges. For example, an estimated 40 -70% of Mexico's population lives in poverty (Damian & Boltvinik 2003). Most of the paupers and marginal paupers live in urban areas. The rapid growth of nonmetropolitan areas has created sudden appearance of new ways of producing urban space, namely land invasion by the poor, which is having tremendous impact on nonmetropolitan areas.

Apart from this, regional policies have faced the challenge of strengthening the economic conditions of cities, while guaranteeing harmonious relationships with the natural environment. This situation prompted Connolly (1989) to question whether decentralization of the population and economic development to peripheral regions of the country was in fact a fallacy. Similarly, Aguilar et al (1996) argued the need for urban regional policy to be an integral part of the national development strategy. In a recent analysis of the evolution of the urban–regional politics Garza (2003) lamented the "abdication of the functions of planning the national territory" and declared the "100 Cities Program" (Programa de 100 ciudades) as having died at the end of the 20th Century.

Given the pursuit of policies that privilege the actions of the free market and dissuade discourse about the State's ability to reorganize space, it would be prudent to focus attention on analyzing an appropriate model of development of cities through a perspective that goes beyond the geographic distribution of the population and economic activity. Such a model should consider a given city's expansion, its capacity to attract and generate employment, its environmental relations, quality of life, and development in general. In particular, it would be necessary to analyze the behavior of the residential market, given its importance in overall urban land use, and given that the provision of dwellings and infrastructure is a major structural element in social development.

The case presented in this chapter is evidence of the dual processes that small cities experience: in addition to the pauperization phenomenon, informal land uses become intermingled with formal ones. The sudden appearance of new ways of producing urban space, namely land invasions by the poor, is a phenomenon that has notably impacted non-metropolitan cities. The city is an accurate image of the social condition of its inhabitants; social segregation and economic articulation occurs as the city expands. Furthermore, the city experiences structural realities that economic data fail to reveal. One of the key explanations is the dominant economic base. While large metropolitan areas sustained a phase of massive expansion (1940 – 1970) in the dual urbanization-industrialization process, small cities have almost always followed the economic urbanization-diversification standard. They cannot be neatly defined as industrial cities because they remain a part of the agriculture and cattle-raising sector. Moreover, the expansion of the tertiary sector has been accentuated. These cities have experienced their growth at a time between the era of the agrarian reform and that dominated by commerce and services, without the mediation of the classical stages of industrial Fordism and Keynesianism. This means that their pattern of accumulation of capital varies when compared to the logics developed by the national metropolitan areas.

In order to understand the expansion pattern and its environmental impact, it is pertinent to consider the probability of discovering some empirical regularity. The more proven theoretical instruments regarding expansive models of cities usually come from the Anglo-Saxon and German schools, especially those giving more importance to the spatial dimension. The ecological approaches from the Chicago School of Urban Sociology mainly those of Ernest Burgess, Homer Hoyt, and Harris and Ullman are classic. However, some explicative aspects hidden under these expansive models of city form constitute enough justification for caution in their application and interpretation.
For example:

- The urban societies that have inspired the said patterns observe a more balanced social pyramid (better income distribution), an aspect that acquires a spatial reflection of the materialization of the city.
- The predominance of a private ownership regime of urban land in those countries contrasts with the diversity of land ownership patterns in Mexico. In the latter case, a considerable part of urbanization is supported by the

public land system. It produces a series of political strategies that "distort" the liberal scheme of urban expansion, thus implying difficulties from the formal point of view as well as the sociological, cultural, and juridical position.

- As a result of the above mentioned, Mexico faces a juridical system that even though is *de jure* has clear *de facto* rules. It is fragile, permissive and therefore complex. The urban irregularity in Mexican cities involves three aspects; one regarding land holding, another trespassing the urban law, and finally those regarding the deficit and anarchy on the service supply issue. Azuela (1989) refers to the fact that Mexico has a legislation system called "juridical order". This is superseded by "political or conventional order" based in custom and personal relations. This explains a high degree of urban permissiveness.

- The diverse schemes of enlargement of the industrialized countries generate consolidated urban spaces. Meanwhile, Mexican and other Latin-American cities show a rapid expansion that includes half finished urbanization works, or urban renewals. This leaves "urbanicity" in those locations where agricultural economies marginally survive.

Thus, in contrast to developed countries cities where land, building, and location, are considered important factors in the real estate market, in Mexico those elements are subject to different logical operations, except in consolidated city center areas. In the urban peripheries, a portion of the land is unsecured property, and therefore, urban renewal is precarious. In the meantime, the building process is open, especially in self-constructed settlements. The location factor is also relative when it comes to the incipient traffic flow and the transportation system. This means a disarticulation exists regarding the consolidated areas of the city.

While in the developed countries' cities an eminent urban culture is observed, Mexican cities reflect multiple and fragmented urban cultures living together with rural codes resulting from country migrations. One characteristic trait of urbanization in the most developed countries is political and economic autonomy of local governments. The negotiations surrounding urban development favor social participation or at least counts for the rationalization of financial resources due to the fact that priorities are perceived in a more direct way. In Mexico, it is evident that this autonomy will be necessary for fiscal reform to provide local governments with more financial resources. Direct participation from the municipalities is around 5%. This ranks the country in a similar position with Paraguay, Uruguay, and Venezuela. On the other hand, countries like Chile, Argentina, Brazil, Costa Rica, and Colombia give more resources to their municipalities: participation fluctuate between 11% and 24%. Evidence that mature democracies promote local authority is the fact that participation is over 30%. In the United States and Canada, for example, participation is as high as 36%, in Norway it is 45%, and in Sweden 59% (Victory 1999). In addition to the problems already mentioned concerning the existing theoretical models, they additionally are anachronistic, even in Canada and the United States. Thus, the North American urban pattern tends now to be more spatially diffused than it used to be, without specific industrial districts. All these imply that urban expansion models and theories must now adapt to issues that were nonexistent some decades ago: structural crisis, interdependence and globalization, the shrinking of the state, federalist claims, augmentation of private capital, environmentalist paradigms, and a series of social demands.

Clearly, local models of housing and urban development will be more appropriate for the purposes of this study. In Mexico, Jaramillo (1982: 177 – 212) identified five types of house production that can be used to study housing and urban development in Ciudad Guzman. Theses are:

Self-construction: Unitary housing built with labor force of final user. The final user has the technical control as well as the economic one of the production. It is about a self-provided system of housing motivated by the use value.

By order: Final user has economic and technical control of production and hires a professional contractor—individual or enterprise—to develop the technical control over the construction. Architectural designs are usually unique and are a good quality.

Private completed housing. Houses are built according to a standardized architectural design. The constructor is usually an individual or enterprise. The free market regulates the behavior of production in this type of housing, normally financed through bank credit.

Official: Housing generally built by a private enterprise through a state contract that reduces the requirements for private capital by means of diverse instruments (subsidies, transfer of public land, etc.). Assignments of housing are also controlled by the State. The archetypical example is INFONAVIT (the National Fund for Worker Housing). Although in recent years, especially since 1992, the State has modified the mechanisms, INFONAVIT now functions as a credit institution. Once granted the worker selects the dwelling in the free market which means that there are no more housing developments built entirely by the State.

Non-Construction: When the process of housing construction (independently of the predictable classification) has not been initiated, then the non-constructed category is used. We will now examine the main forms of housing and urban development that have taken place in Ciudad Guzman.

A major force underlying the recent reconfiguration of the city was the earthquake of September 19 1985, which greatly impacted the city and its immediate vicinity. The seismic phenomenon accelerated the rhythm of urbanization and reoriented the growth pace.

HOUSING AND URBAN DEVELOPMENT IN CIUDAD GUZMAN

Location and Background

Ciudad Guzman, capital of the municipality of Zapotlan el Grande registered a population of 85,118 in 2000. It is located in western Mexico, 125 kilometers from Guadalajara, at a site that presents both great advantages and big problems for human settlement. Among the great advantages is its location in a rich agricultural and forest region that is heavily devoted to corn, pasture, oats, and to a lesser amount tomatoes and chick-peas (Ayuntamiento de Zapotlan 2001). At the municipal level 39% of the population is engaged in agriculture. Livestock raising (cattle, sheep, and hogs) is the most profitable activity, followed by crop cultivation. Forestry follows agriculture as the next most important activity, engaging 34% of the population. In 1993, 2,132 cubic meters of wood were extracted. By 1998 the total volume of wood extracted had reached 79,278 cubic meters (Ayuntamiento de Zapotlan 2001), which denotes not only a booming activity but also the environmental deterioration given the irrational pattern of exploitation. In 1998, 74% of the wood production was pine and 23% was oak.

The economic (industrial, commercial, and services) census of 1995 registered 3,449 economic units, of which 407 (12%) were manufacturing establishments, 1910 (55%) were commercial businesses and 1,132 (33%) were services (INEGI 1995). Of the 9,319 employed in these activities, 1,738 (19%) were in manufacturing, principally in food and beverages, metallic products and wood industry. Commerce employed 4,561 (49%) and services 3,020 (32%). Cuidad Guzman is also an economic node of southern Jalisco, a region that consists of 16 municipalities and constitutes a site that has historically performed functions alternating with the city of Guadalajara, the second largest metropolis in the country, and the city of Manzanillo the country's principal port of the Pacific.

The Zapotlan Valley, where the city is located, has a complex landscape framed by the Sierra del Tigre, El Volcan de Colima, and Laguna de Zapotlan. In particular, the site of the city has severe geological and hydraulic tensions. Physical conditions have influenced even the cultural perspective of the area to the extent that it has been recorded in Mexican literature. Thus, the great writer Juan Jose Arreola offers a fitting metaphor of the place in his work La Feria. He writes:

> I don't mean to scare you, but don't place all the weight of your body over the ground. This town is built on an alluvium valley and its fertile lands are purely

superficial: they hide a colossal geological fault and you're standing over an eggshell (Arreola, 1963: 25).

The valley is a receptacle of volcanic deposits located on a system of geological faults oriented from the northeast to the southwest. These characteristics make the valley hypersensitive to seismic movements tied to the activity developed at the juncture of the North American and Cocos tectonic plates. Like two pieces of a puzzle these two plates join at the Pacific Coast, in a contact zone known as the Trench of Acapulco. Both plates are engaged in a permanent struggle. The Cocos plate, which is oceanic, lies underneath the continental North American plate. Tectonic drift occurs at a rate of 6 to 7 centimeters per year, resulting in frequent seismic activity in that part of Mexico.

The region also stands on a transverse neo-volcanic axis which is one of the most active faults in the world. The Colima Volcano, 3,960 meters high, and one of the most active volcanoes in the world, is located 26 kilometers from Cd. Guzman. Furthermore the city is seated in an enclosed sedimentary basin, where the natural dynamics hardly contributes to the quality of water recycling. For this reason the Zapotlan lagoon that borders Cd. Guzman, is a discharge reservoir that has transformed into great deposit of still water. East of Cd. Guzman is the Tigre Sierra Mountain, which is now the location of the Montaña Oriente (East Mountain) suburban development. Given the steep slopes in this area, about 20%, and due to deforestation and soil erosion, landslides are common in this area, creating challenges to human settlement.

Provision of Housing in Ciudad Guzman

There are no historical documents to prove the date of the colonial origin of the old Zapotlan. Some testimonies indicate that Fray Antonio de Padilla founded it in 1533 (Vizcaino 1991). In the 19th century, the city became the capital of the region, a role that was historically held by the neighboring town of Sayula. At the beginning of the 20th century it had only about 17,596 inhabitants. The accelerated demographic process started in Cd. Guzman during the 1950s and reached its most expansive period in the 1960s (Figure 14. 1 and Table 14.1).

Demographic stagnation during the first half of the 20th century is due in part to the arrival of the railroad. The region has historically functioned as a transit point between the Pacific region and the interior, specifically Guadalajara. According to De la Peña (1977), the introduction of the Guadalajara-Manzanillo rail line, which began operating in 1910, impacted the region negatively. Transportation of goods into the region from elsewhere became cheaper, and these goods increasingly were preferred to those that were locally produced. Furthermore, the rail line served to displace economies of towns it bypassed.

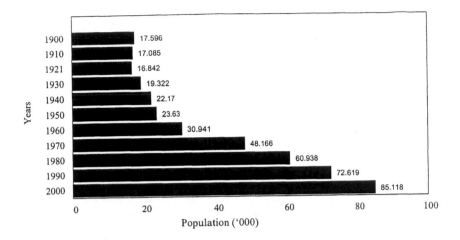

Figure 14.1 Ciudad Guzman Demographic Evolution 1900 – 2000
Source: Author's research and Mexican General Population Census

Table 14.1 Ciudad Guzman: Population Growth Rates 1900 – 2000

Period	% Rate
1900-1910	-0.29
1910-1921	-0.13
1921-1930	1.54
1930-1940	1.38
1940-1950	0.64
1950-1960	2.73
1960-1970	4.53
1970-1980	2.38
1980-1990	1.77
1990-2000	1.60

Source: Mexico General Population Census.

While urban and agricultural usages clearly place pressures on the natural environment, one must also consider the inherent physiographic complexity of the city's site. As already pointed out, the Zapotlan Valley constitutes a natural receptacle of eroded and transported materials, including volcanic ash deposits from the surrounding mountains. These elements underlie the development of fertile lands for agriculture, which contain an average 696 millimeters of volcanic deposition. The suburban zone especially contains agriculturally rich soils, which explains the widespread establishment of collective farm land, or *ejidos*, surrounding the city after the Mexican Revolution. If the drainage difficulties are taken into account, it is quite clear that natural factors alone present strong limitations to the conversion of these lands to urban uses.

In terms of urban development, the city can be divided into three easily recognizable zones (Table 14.2). The first is the historic city center, which corresponds to the urbanized area before 1900. The second is the medium zone, which was built between 1900 and 1967, around the historical center and before the subsequent rapid urban growth. The third is the peripheral city, which emerged after 1967. This zone falls into two sub-areas: the first inner circle formed between 1967 and 1985, and the second circle formed after the 1985 earthquake. For the detailed study, we consider the development up to 1995.

Intense competition for land in Ciudad Guzman was initiated in 1950. Residential construction accelerated in 1967 and lasted until 1995. There were 466 urbanized hectares during the period, consisting of 88 developments, in

Table 14.2 Urban Development Zones of Ciudad Guzman

Urban sector	Period	Area (hec-tares)	Population 1995	Houses 1995	Density per hectare
Center	1533-1900	117	33,456	7,095	56
Medium	1900-1967	485			
Peripheral city					
First circle	1967-1985	159	48,264	4,344	104
Peripheral city					
Second circle	1985-1995	307		6,285	
Total		1,068	81,720	17,724	73

Source: Author's research

which 10,629 houses were built (Table 14.2). This means that 44% of the urban land was produced within the last 28 years, while the remaining 56% was built during the prior four centuries. This recent massive expansion of the urbanized zone is more than simply an extension of the preexistent city, but represents a new cycle of urban life.

The principal type of housing identified in the peripheral zone of Ciudad Guzman in 1995 was self-construction. This type of housing occupied 54% of the incorporated land in the peripheral zone. It also accounted for 48% of the city's housing units that were mostly built during the 1980s (Table 14.3). The occupation index (the number of occupied houses divided by the number of landed property incorporated to the market of the land) of the self-construction settlements was of 52.10 (Table 14.4).

Table 14.3 Land and Housing Production in the Peripheral City Zone of Ciudad Guzman

Typology	Land Production		Housing Production, (Number of houses)	
	Hectares	%	No. of Houses	%
Self construction	253	54.29	5,141	48.3
By order	84	18.03	1,431	13.46
Private completed	8	1.72	533	5.02
Official or assisted	80	17.16	3,517	33.09
Non Construction	41	8.80	6	0.06
Total	466	100	10,628	100

Source: Author's research

Table 14.4 Occupation Index of Housing in Ciudad Guzman

Type of Housing	Occupation Index
Self construction	52.10
By order	64.63
Private completed	100.00
Official or assisted	94.14
Non construction	0.23
Total	60.00

Source Author's research

The "Constituyentes" development is a good example of self-construction in Ciudad Guzman. With a total of 2,507 lots, each measuring some 7 meters deep by 20 meters wide, and covering an area of 69.49 hectares, this development housed an estimated population of 8,720 in 1995. Negotiations for public land expropriation began in 1983. In 1984, a preliminary urbanization judgment was issued. However, in 1985, construction was restricted due to the limitation of the sewage system brought about by the earthquake. This settlement became the target of several collaborative efforts, led by the State Commission of Reconstruction of the southern Jalisco region, to provide popular housing to earthquake survivors. In spite of the presence of State and NGO-assisted housing most of the residential production was by self-construction. Given the large number of lots, there were still 526 vacant lots, which was 21% of the total in 1994. In addition, public infrastructure was far from adequate.

The housing by order absorbed 18% of the land, which was comparable to the 18% taken by the official housing category. However, in terms of housing production, the by order promotion generated only 14% of the houses, while the official housing accounted for 33%. An emblematic development of the housing by order is *Mansiones de Real*, which first appeared in 1969, north of Ciudad Guzman. Of its 184 lots of 200 square meters each, 155 (84%) had been built by 1995. Although there are 20 developments where housing by order dominates, this category is less important now than during the 1970s, when production of housing by order reached its apogee.

The dramatic presence in recent years of official housing is due to the heavy involvement of state assistance or public funds, which resulted from the 1985 earthquake and the reduction in the housing by order category. The earthquake of September 19, 1985 registered 8.1 degrees on the Richter scale, while the one on the following day registered 7.8 degrees. According to Garcia de Alba (1988) out of 9,804 inspected houses that comprised a large share of the total housing, 34% suffered total damage, 26% partial damage, and 40% slight damage. This left 21,000 survivors or 32% of the city's population without adequate shelter. This obviously brought in immense government assistance. In this case, the earthquake served as a catalyst to the production of official or public assisted housing. It brought together the State and the community to confront the social problems unleashed by the seismic devastation. By 1995, government housing accounted for 16% of all housing in Ciudad Guzman.

Private completed housing was marginal because it covered only 2% of the residential land area, even though its occupancy level was 100%. *Pintores* and *Lomas Altas* were the only two zones representing this type of housing. Together they constituted a mere 5% of the city's total number of housing units produced between 1967 and 1995. The non-constructed category covered 9% of the residential land area. This percentage was low compared to cities of similar size, thus reflecting the predominance of the value in use over the value in exchange.

Before the earthquake, the land market in Ciudad Guzman operated predominantly on free market principles. However, the state became a dominant player after the earthquake of 1985. During the period 1985-1995, for every 100 houses constructed, official agencies such as INFONAVIT and FOVISSSTE, produced 46. This is in contrast to what happened in other small cities in Jalisco. For example, official housing as a percentage of overall housing, over several decades, was 16% in Lagos de Moreno, 5% in Tepatitlan de Morelos, and 33% in Ciudad Guzman. A more eloquent indicator is the occupation index, which showed that Ciudad Guzman, with occupation index of 60%, made an effective use of the parcels incorporated to the land market, more than Tepatitlan de Morelos, with an index that scarcely reached 34%, and Lagos de Moreno with 38% (Cabrales 1997: 157). This shows a more rational model of land market was in operation in Cd. Guzman.

Ordinarily, the increasing role of the government in the housing production market is explained by the devastation created by the earthquake. However, the relative formal coherence and public participation in Ciudad Guzman, seemed to have its origins in the irregular occupation of the *ejidal* land. Metaphorically speaking, the disaster was converted into a passport for a massive access to the *ejidal* land. This in turn amplified the well-rooted, long-standing conflict in land tenure. The *ejidal* land occupied for urban purposes reached new heights of 279 hectares by 1995. Of these, 87% were formally incorporated, after 1985. This data supports the argument about the overall tolerance that characterized the post-seismic urbanization. The urgency of the moment eased restrictions on opening the land for settlement, but beyond a certain point, permissible attitudes no longer dominated.

In order to avoid concentration of property, the Federal Government passed an expropriation decree for the ejidal land, which guaranteed tenancy in favor of the occupants. The execution plan was consistent with the desire to check rampant speculation. It specified not only that the size of the lot cannot exceed the average lot size, but title could only be transferred, according to social interest for a reasonable price. Furthermore, only one lot per head of the family could be used as a residence, provided that none of its occupants is a real estate speculator. If a resident possessed a lot whose area was larger than the one assigned for the type lot of the zone, he or she could acquire the excess portion of the land at the normal value, according to the valuation made beforehand. Unoccupied lots within the expropriated area that were not used could be transferred, but only for construction of popular dwellings. The philosophy of the decree was consistent with the social policy as well as with the rational usage of the ground because it opened the historical opportunity of counting with an internal reservation.

CONCLUSION

When analyzing the urban problems of small cities one can easily see the similarities with those of large metropolitan areas. However, small cities in many ways are better suited than large cities to realize the effects of actual planning, because of their manageable size, and because they have better chances to potentially reach high standards of quality of life and territorial regulation. Beyond the logic of the economic model, Mexican cities, be they small, medium size or large, require a clear definition of urban policy that may contribute to the improvement of the quality of the urban environment and enhance the city's competitiveness.

The case of Ciudad Guzman illustrates an urban growth model that reflects unique social and environmental problems, but at the same time represents national urban problems. It is a style of urbanization that generates pockets of vacant land, segregation, and a failure to meet the real life necessities of the population. It is a model associated with inadequate provision of infrastructure and facilities that generates a negative impact on the environment.

As a metaphor, we can affirm that the incorporation of the land to the urbanization advances at a rate of 100 kilometers per hour, while the construction of houses advances at rate of 50 kilometers per hour, and works and services at 25 kilometers an hour. A working mechanism to synchronize these three velocities must be found, if the gap between urban growth and development, and social development can be bridged. This calls for a dynamic participation from the public.

Nevertheless, current urban policy seems not to be conscious of this matter. The *Plan de Desarrollo Urbano* of 1997 (the Urban Development Plan) considered urban reservation zones of 171.34 hectares in the short term, (three years) and 428.55 in the long term (six years) (Ayuntamiento de Zapotlan 1997). This means the incorporation of 600 hectares, which constituted massive vacant land inside the city.

It is important to remember that self-constructed housing accounts for more than half of the urban space, resulting in noteworthy social and environmental dilemmas. Each housing development occupies modest amounts of space, exhibits high variability in the quality, and generally lacks basic services. This ultimately has an impact on the quality of the environment.

The lack of synchronization between agrarian and urban land uses has been a common problem in urban peripheral zones throughout Mexico. Since the Mexican Revolution in 1910, but above all, from the 1930's onwards, a granting of the *ejidal* land intended for agricultural production for the rural poor was initiated. However, the reality of rapid urbanization required the use of those areas, thus generating illegal practices of occupation and simultaneously producing a cheap land offering for the poor people. The conflict between agrarian and urban land requirements, insofar as they overlap, creates a pressure that lies at the roots of the Mexican urbanization model. While the problem traditionally was limited to the periphery of the metropolitan areas, nowadays it can be seen in small cities.

Ciudad Guzman illustrates these kinds of tensions; however, beyond the competition between different land uses, the dilemmas of the environment ultimately prevail there. The city has encountered limitations for its expansion: the active geological faults that cross the city and the presence of unstable hillsides at the *Montaña de Oriente* that create the risk of slides and falls. Towards the west, the flood-prone land and the Laguna de Zapotlan reservoir gather much of the pollution produced by the city. The land granting practices in Mexican cities should no longer include a search for land reserves further from the current urbanized zone of each. The economic difficulties of financing infrastructure, as well as the threat to natural resources (particularly land and water) should encourage the creation of policies of higher urban density, accompanied by an effort to create public spaces of a high quality.

One of the findings as a result of this urban analysis is that if the economic rules of neoliberal capitalism cannot realistically be modified locally, a heavier commitment should be made to implement active urban policies in order to contribute to proactive urban regulation and a higher quality of life. Urban management should consider the fragile nature of the territory as well as the limitations to continue consuming land in an indiscriminate form. For this reason it is pertinent to compare the valley of Ciudad Guzman with an eggshell.

REFERENCES

Aguilar, A. G., B. Graizbord y A. Sánchez Crispín (1996). Las ciudades intermedias y el desarrollo regional en México. México, D.F.: Consejo Nacional para la Cultura y las Artes.

Arreola, J. 1963. La Feria. México, D.F. Joaquín Mortiz.

Ayuntamiento de Zapotlán el Grande, Jalisco 1997. Plan de Desarrollo Urbano, Ciudad Guzmán, Jalisco. Inédito.

Azuela de la Cueva, Antonio 1989. El significado de la planeación urbana en México, en Gustavo Garza–compilador- Una década de planeación urbano-regional en México, 1978 1988, 55 – 77. México, D.F.: El Colegio de   México.

Borja, J., y M. Castells 1997. Local y global. La gestión de las ciudades en la era de la información. Madrid: Taurus.

Cabrales Barajas, L. F. 1997. Mercado de suelo urbano y tipologías de vivienda en Lagos de Moreno, Tepatitlán y Ciudad Guzmán, en *Realidades de la utopía: demografía, trabajo y municipio en el occidente de México*, 115 – 183. D. Lorey y   B. Verduzco, compiladores, ed. J. Pablos México: Universidad de Guadalajara, UCLA Program on México.

————. 2003. Mapa urbano nacional de México, año 2000. Ponencia presentada en el 9º. Encuentro de Geógrafos de América Latina, Mérida, Yucatán (en prensa).

Connolly, P. 1989. Programa Nacional de Desarrollo Urbano y Vivienda, 1984. en Gustavo Garza, Una década de planeación urbano-regional en Mexico, El Colegio de México: 111 – 120.

Damián, A., y J. Boltvinik. 2003. Evolución y características de la pobreza en México, en Comercio Exterior, 53 (6): 519 – 531.

de la Peña, G. 1977. Economía y sociedad en el sur de Jalisco: notas para un enfoque diacrónico. En Controversia, No. 2. Guadalajara: Centro Regional de Investigaciones Socioeconómicas.

García de Alba García, R. 1988. Micro-regionalización sísmica del Valle de Zapotlán, Jalisco. Tesis profesional para obtener el título de licenciado en geografía. Facultad de Geografía, Universidad de Guadalajara.

Garza, G. 2003. La urbanización de México en el siglo XX. México, D.F.: El Colegio de México.

INEGI 1991. XI Censo General de Población y Vivienda. Aguascalientes: Instituto Nacional de Estadística, Geografía e Informática.

INEGI 1995. XIV Censo Industrial, XI Censo Comercial y XI Censo de Servicios. Aguascalientes: Instituto Nacional de Estadística, Geografía e Infortica.

INEGI 2001. XII Censo General de Población y Vivienda. Aguascalientes: Instituto Nacional de Estadística, Geografía e Informática.

Jaramillo, S. 1982. Las formas de producción de espacio construido en Bogotá, en Emilio Pradilla –compilador-, Ensayos sobre el problema de vivienda en América Latina 150 – 212. México: Universidad Autónoma Metropolitana.

Victory, C. 1999. Gobiernos municipales y desarrollo local en Iberoamérica", en Revista Cidob d´Afers Internacionals, No. 47: 15 – 49. Barcelona: Fundación Cidob.

Vizcaíno, J. 1991. La fundación de Zapotlán el Grande. En Estudios Jaliscienses, No. 5: 5 – 10. Guadalajara: El Colegio de Jalisco.

15

Public Policy and Development of Small Cities: The Experience of Israel's Development Towns

Erez Tzfadia
Sapir Academic College

INTRODUCTION

In the years 1949 – 1963, the young Israeli state planned and established twenty-eight small towns, mostly in remote regions of the Negev and Galilee (Figure 15.1; Table 15.1). These towns became known as "development towns" (DTs). The planning and the building process of the DTs paralleled other key political, geographic, and demographic events. These included the expulsion and escape of 750,000 Palestinian refugees during the war of 1948, the abandonment of 320 of Palestinian villages and towns (Morris, 1987), questionable definition of the state borders which were expended during the war, influx of 800,000 Jewish immigrants, mostly from Arab countries in North Africa and the Middle-East (Lissak 1999) (usually identified as *Mizrahim*, which means Easterners or Oriental Jews), the conversion of the young state to a landlord of more than 90% of the land within its sovereign territory, some of which was expropriated from the Palestinian refugees (Kedar 2001), and the establishment of centralist regime with durable planning system, backed up with Zionist ideology (Aravot and Militanu 2000).

Several years after their establishment, the towns became sites of poverty and deprivation according to various indicators. Most of the towns continue to be dependent on the transfer of central government funds for the provision of

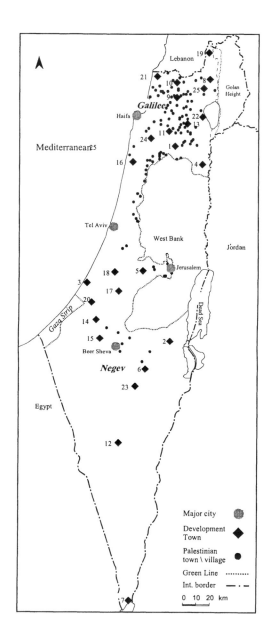

Figure 15.1 Israel's Development Towns
(The numbers represent the towns. See Table 15.1 below for the names)

Table 15.1 Israel's Development Towns by Name and Population, 2002

No. on the Map	Name of Town	Population	No. on the Map	Name of Town	Population
1	Afula	41,748	14	Netivot	23,297
2	Arad	27,748	15	Ofaqim	24,654
3	Ashkelon	112,607	16	Or Aqiva	16,918
4	Bet She'an	17,583	17	Qiryat Gat	52,084
5	Bet Shemesh	54,905	18	Qiryat Mal'akhi	21,628
6	Dimona	37,162	19	Qiryat Shemona	23,708
7	Elat	54,476	20	Sederot	21,812
8	Hazor Hagelilit	9,515	21	Shelomi	5,596
9	Karmi'el	47,573	22	Tiberias	44,886
10	Ma'alot-Tarshiha	21,959	23	Yeroham	9,172
11	Migdal Haemeq	26,477	24	Yoqne'am Illit	17,875
12	Mizpe Ramon	5,526	25	Zefat	29,817
13	Nazerat Illit	51,158			
	Total				799,884

Source: Ministry of Interior, 2003

local services and for the viability of much of the local employment. For these reasons they are commonly viewed as the social and geographic periphery. The great majority of the residents in the DTs are *Mizrahim*. In the 1990s low-status immigrants from the Former Soviet Union and Ethiopia were settled in the DTs as well (Tzfadia 2000). In 1995, the DTs population accounted for 1.09 million residents, constituting 20% of Israel's total population (Yiftachel 2000a). Most of them (800,000) lived in peripheral DTs (Table 15.1).

The inherent challenge of establishing 28 new peripheral towns within less than two decades, the relatively disadvantaged state of their populations, and the towns' ethnic homogeneity, attracted academic attention from almost all fields within the social sciences, as to why the towns had failed. Until the early 1990s two explanations led the academic discourses in relation to the towns and their relative disadvantaged state: the first, which was identified with the modernist-functionalist school of thought, focused on the planning programs and processes. The second, which was identified with the neo-Marxist school of thought, undermined the logic behind the making of the towns. It claimed that the affiliation of nationalism and capital accumulation resulted in the making of the towns. During the 1990s, a third explanation was launched, which related the planting of the DTs with the colonial ambitions of Israel and its Zionist ideology.

Basing on the analysis of these explanations, this chapter argues that the making of towns *beyond the metropolis* and the typical socio-economic problems that such towns have experienced are associated with social-political-spatial structures and power relations within broader spatial scales, such as states. Furthermore, the chapter argues that the location of the towns beyond the metropolis was a means to advance the interests of dominant groups by controlling social relations and spatial processes. To advance this argument, the chapter first outlines the making of the DTs within the context of the theorization of planning and growth of small cities, and presents several indicators on the socio-economic difficulties facing the towns. Next, it critically examines the three explanations given for the difficulties the towns have been facing. Finally, some implications of public policy on the growth and development of small cities will be outlined.

THE ESTABLISHMENT OF ISRAEL'S DEVELOPMENT TOWNS

Shortly after the Second World War mega-acts of new towns planning took place in many countries that had been involved in the war (Taylor 1998). Planning new towns with new scientific techniques was portrayed as having economic and social merits: economically, new towns were a public answer to land and property market failures that had concentrated people and economic activities in big urban centers (Webster 1998). Remote new towns were regarded as centers of economic growth, mainly in peripheral rural regions, which would likely increase the regional basis of taxpayers, to function as regional service centers, and to facilitate the exploitation of remote natural resources. These economic merits and the location in pleasant surroundings were supposed to advance social balance; design friendly communities; increase social involvement and participation in the local social life, hence increasing the grass-roots democracy—contrary to the urban mass-society (Phillips and Yeh 1987; Palen 1997).

Like in most other states, these ideas were well fused into the young Israeli establishment, academia (Ram 1999), and planning institutions, (Elhanani 1998). In particular, it answered the desire for spatial development by employing "modern" and "rational" methods, which probably answered two main problems that bothered the Israeli establishment. One of these problems was spatial population polarization. The "frontier" (or peripheral regions) contained numerous tiny rural settlements with a small amount of Jewish population, and in the geographic center there existed a few big urban centers where the vast majority of Jewish population concentrated (Lipshitz and Massam 1998). The second problem was an influx of a large wave of Jewish immigrants, which had tripled the population within eight years. Most of the immigrants were *Mizrahim* (Lissak 1999).

The "solution" was found in the first national plan, known as the *Sharon Plan* (Sharon 1951). The plan was influenced by several popular "scientific techniques" such as Ebenezer Howard's (1985) Garden City *model* and Walter Christaller's (1966) central place theory. Both Howard and Christaller constructed models that promoted urban dispersal (Yiftachel 2000a). Indeed, one of the major principles of the *Sharon Plan* was dispersing 28 urban centers all over the state's territory, which were envisioned as regional, economic, and service centers for remote agricultural settlements (Krakover 1979), as well as sites of absorption of new immigrants. These communities came to be called development towns. By the 1960s, the DTs had enabled the Israeli state absorb 200,000 Jewish immigrants and offer them places to reside in public housing projects (Lewin-Epstein et al 1997). However, the towns did not attain the prescribed social and economic goals set for them. Several indicators show a gap between the socioeconomic level of the towns and mainstream Israeli society (Table 15.2).

Table 15.2 Selected Socioeconomic Characteristics of Development Towns

Indicator	DTs	Israel
North African and Asian origin (1983)[1]	81%	44%
Mean salaried income (monthly)(2000)[2]	5520 NIS	6494 NIS
Ownership dwelling (percentage of households) (1995)[3]	66%	73%
Percent of work-seekers of aged 15+ (1999)[4]	4.8%	3.3%
Percent of recipients of income-maintenance (1999)[4]	3.7%	1.9%
Percentage of employed persons in manufacturing (1995)[5]	30.1%	19.5%
Percent of students of aged 20-29 (1999)[4]	8.6%	12.2%

1. Central Bureau of Statistics, 1983.
2. Swirski and Konor-Attias, 2001.
3. Central Bureau of Statistics, 1995.
4. Central Bureau of Statistics, 2002.
5. Central Bureau of Statistics, 1998.

EXPLANATIONS OF GROWTH DIFFICULTIES OF DEVELOPMENT TOWNS

What are the reasons behind the growth difficulties of Israel's development towns? Countless articles have dealt with this question. The intention here is to classify the suggested reasons into three main explanations, namely the modernist-functionalist, neo-Marxist, and the colonial explanations. In the rest of this section, I will discuss these three explanations, with special emphasis on the colonial explanation.

Modernist-Functionalist Explanation

Post WWII rational planning was well embedded in the modernist-functionalist approach. This approach regards society as a set of requirements and problems that the institutions of the nation-state are supposed to solve, while concurrently achieving a public identification with the national agenda. In this context, cultural and social assimilation is the major objective of society within the general project of state and nation building. The assimilation is achieved through modernization, industrialization, and economic development (Gordon 1964; Glazer and Moynihan 1975). Modern, rational, and professional urban and regional planning is pictured as a powerful method for advancing development, spatial regulation, and social justice (Faludi 1973).

From the early stage of the establishment of Israel, the modernist-functionalist approach dominated the academia and planning authorities. The dominancy of the approach soon became evident in the discourse on planning the towns, and mainly in the long-term reasoning of the relative backwardness of the DTs. This reasoning generally criticized the implementation of the planning, without criticizing the concept of rational planning. Rational planning regularly enjoyed the status of a beneficial public policy.

Most planners and social scientists in the Israeli academia claimed that the socioeconomic difficulties resulted from the imperfect planning processes of the towns. Among the criticisms of the planning process were the following:

1. There was no coordination between the construction of dwellings, infrastructure, public services, and employment—and this prevented a consistent development of the DTs (Brutzkus 1970; Efrat 1988).
2. Israeli planners were not experienced enough in urban planning (Cohen 1970; Troen 1994a).
3. The spatial models of Howard (1985) and Christaller (1966) had already proven to be as unsuccessful as models in other states by the time of planning the DTs
4. These spatial models were implemented upon a small-sized geographical territory, and as a result, too many towns were established, too small and in very close proximity with each other (Efrat 1988).
5. The spatial models did not match the topographical reality (Aravot and Militanu 2000).
6. Financial shortage of the new state prevented essential investments in transportation infrastructure, which brought isolation to the DTs in the periphery (Troen 1994b; Efrat 1988).

Several other social scientists pointed at the social and economic planning and policy as the main reasons behind the difficulties of the DTs. For this group, there was an inherent contradiction between the desire to integrate immigrants and the desire to disperse them to peripheral regions, as the dispersion itself generated segregation (Cohen 1970). In addition, it charged that the DTs were inhabited by *Mizrahi* immigrants from underdeveloped states, who were mostly poorly educated, unskilled, and had oversized households (Krakover 1979; Soen and Sharoni 1983). Many other Israeli researchers argued that the long-term economic development policy, primarily the decision to set up local labor-intensive and "traditional" industries, was the main barrier blocking the growth of the towns (see: Gradus and Krakover 1977; Gradus and Einy 1984; Razin 1988).

The wide spectrum of criticism on the planning process could not, and did not, try to find a coherent explanation regarding the difficulties of the DTs. No explanation attempted to scrutinize the structures of power relations in the Israeli society, and to unravel from them the reasons behind the establishment of remote and peripheral small towns, or the reasons behind their backwardness and ethnic homogeneity. The first to do so were neo-Marxist social scientists.

Neo-Marxist Explanation

Perhaps, one of the best expressions of neo-Marxists thought about planning is Fainstein and Fainstein (1979) statement.

> Planning is necessary to the ruling class in order to facilitate accumulation and maintain social control in the face of class conflict. The modes by which urban planners assist accumulation include the development of physical infrastructure, land aggregation and development, and maintenance of land values (Fainstein and Fainstein 1979, cited in Taylor 1998: 106).

Not surprisingly, by the time Fainstein and Fainstein (1979) contributed their cutting edge article to planning discourse, the neo-Marxist thought in Israel had started to criticize the making of DTs. The social and economic gap between DTs and mainstream Israeli society, highlighted by the concentration of labor-intensive industry, unstable employment, and dishonest terms of residence, had brought many Marxist and neo-Marxist researchers to re-examine the reasons behind the making of DTs.

Contrary to the modernist-functionalist explanation, the neo-Marxist explanation argued that the State of Israel in the 1950s was not a modern state, and did not have a developed economy or industrial sector. Only the exploitation of the *Mizrahi* proletarians enabled the development of modern economy (Bernstein and Swirsky 1982). Urban and regional planning produced an uneven and stratified geographical space in terms of investments and wealth. One form of stratification was the location of labor-intensive industrial parks together with *Mizrahi* immigrants in the same remote places. Such policy benefited the capitalists, most of whom were Jews of European origin (known as *Ashkenazim*) (Swirski 1989).

The educational system established by Israel in the DTs trained the young *Mizrahi* generation to be "experts" in labor-intensive industrial branches, according to the dominant branches in each town (Swirski 1990; Swirski and

Shoushan 1985). Together with the educational system, the Israeli land and housing regime contributed to the low stratification of the Mizrahim in the DTs, by maintaining low land and dwelling value and keeping a considerable stock of public housing in the DTs, more than in any other type of settlement in Israel. The stock of public housing functioned as a means to settle relatively weakened inhabitants in the DTs (for example poor Russian immigrants in the 1990s), and to prevent the growth of a developed dwelling market in the towns. Consequently, landlords who sought to sell their apartments in order to leave the towns found that the value of their apartments was not sufficient for living elsewhere in Israel (Law-Yone and Kalus 1994; Kalus and Law-Yone 2002; Yona and Saporta 2002).

What is the contribution of geographical remoteness and isolation for effective exploitation of the towns' residents? Harvey (1993, 1996) argues that capitalist industry utilizes the space, the spatial dispersal and the geographical isolation and remoteness as instruments to oppress and exploit minorities. Such oppression is usually executed in labor-intensive industrial branches. For the capitalists, it is easier to exploit marginal groups in small peripheral towns by maintaining high rates of unemployment and low wages, developing a limited range of occupational resources, and employing unorganized labor. These are all possible because of the distance from public consciousness, and the isolation somewhere in the periphery.

The neo-Marxist explanation is essential to understanding the gaps between *Mizrahim* in the DTs and mainstream Israeli society. However, it fails to explain the function and class-position of the Palestinians in the stratified structure of Israeli society, the place of the Israeli-Arab conflict in the class relations of Israel, and the function of DTs in the conflict. Such deficiency is similar to the failure of the modernist-functionalist explanations. Sociologist Uri Ram describes this specific failure as follows:

> The major trends of Israeli sociology have simply managed to focus on Jewish society while conspicuously omitting the other components... the Arabs and the conflict. Alternatively they have addressed the Arab, and separately the conflict, but without linking either to broad societal issues. (Ram 1999:62).

In order to provide this link, a more comprehensive explanation has emerged since the 1990s, which includes the question of the Palestinians in Israel, the Arab-Israeli conflict, and the Zionist settlement process. This new explanation, which emerged from social scientists' new view of Israel as an immigrant-settler society, became labeled as the colonial explanation, and it is to this that I will now examine.

The Colonial Explanation

The colonial explanation of the failure of Israel's DTs is based on the notion that Israel is an immigrant-settler society, and that the Zionist ideology shares common features with other colonialist movements was first published by non-Israeli Palestinian researchers in the late 1960s (Ram 1999). In Israel, this explanation expanded in leftist radical movements shortly after the war of 1967, when the Israeli army occupied the West Bank, Sinai, Golan Heights, and the Gaza Strip, and a Jewish settlement project was planned in those areas (Silberstein 1999). In the 1970s, the Israeli academia launched studies on the social nature of Israel via the colonial perspective. Apparently, Turner's (1962) American frontier theory and its relation to the Israeli case was the earliest expression for the colonial approach within the Israeli academia. It asserted that the most influential factors on the Israeli society were the geo-political circumstances of the Middle East, namely the Israeli-Arab conflict. Furthermore, the seizing of land in Israel/Palestine by Jews since the late 19th century and their prolonged attempt to establish a presence on the land by settlement were essentials in determining the nature of the ethno-national based hegemony and social structure within Israel (Kimmerling, 1983). Accordingly, some Israeli sociologists and historians use the colonial explanation, as complementary one to the neo-Marxist explanation, to analyze social processes within Israel, viewing the society mainly in terms of power relations between different ethno-class groups.

A starting point of this explanation generates from a statement made by Prime Minister David Ben-Gurion in 1949. He said:

> If you look in the map, you will see that in the South there are numerous empty places, and nothing toss such a fear on me as this emptiness. Not only because nature cannot stand emptiness, but because people do not stand it, and the politics does not stand it (Prime Minister David Ben-Gurion, Government of Israel, 1949, translated from Hebrew by the author).

According to the colonial explanation, this statement generates a lot of questions. What is the meaning of "emptiness" and "empty places" in the map? Emptiness of what? Why did emptiness toss fear? What did this emptiness have to do with the public policy of making small cities? To answer these questions the exponents of the colonial explanation argue that one should get into the roots of the Israeli social and political structure, which corresponds the traditional political-historical context of an immigrant-settler society.

The traditional political-historical context of an immigrant-settler society, aims at describing societies that have facilitated European migration and settlement in other continents. The process of immigration and settlement involved exploitation of indigenous land, labor, and natural resources. By these actions, territories in the Americas, Australia, New Zealand, and Africa were expropriated from native groups. Territorial domination was then consolidated by European settlers mainly through spatial expansion, settlement and the development of a "frontier culture." In the long run the settlers shifted their national loyalty through the founding of a national independent project in the settled territories (Stasilius and Yuval-Davis 1995).

Settler-founder groups usually possess a sense of belonging to the settled territory. They tend to facilitate the myth of eternal affinity to the territory (Garaudy 1977), and regard themselves even as the "chosen people" destined to fulfill the duty of settling their "holy land" (Grosby 1999; Templin 1999). Hence, both settler-founder and native groups are identified as "homeland groups," and this identification intensifies the territorial conflict and the struggle to dominate land and natural resources (Yiftachel 2001). Yet, these two groups are still broad, ethnically sub-divided categories, and should not be seen as homogenous groups.

One common type of these immigrant-settler societies is the "pure settlement colony," which has been shown to be most appropriate to the Israeli-Zionist case (Shafir 1989). Pure settlement colony contains a third social category consisting of later immigrants from different cultural backgrounds. Yet, they do indeed share some common characteristics with the founder group. The readiness to absorb these later immigrants relates to the decreasing number of immigrants from Europe. The affinity between these two groups enables the incorporation of the later immigrant group, and together they establish "the nation." However, the founder group creates a system that incorporates the later immigrants unevenly within the economy and politics of the nation. As a result, the later immigrants are stratified in an inferior status compared to the European group, and in a superior one compared to the natives. Such a kind of incorporation produces a heterogeneous society in terms of ethnicity, class, and race, which tends to preserve and reinforce the ethnic and class stratification. Such a system usually determines the economic and political status of the three groups for generations to come (Pearson 2002; Stasilius and Yuval-Davis 1995; Yiftachel 2000a).

In Israel, the "founding group" is identified mainly with *Ashkenazi* Jews who immigrated to Israel from Europe in the period of Ottoman and British Mandatory rule, some of them out of national and Zionist aspirations. It is in this group's image that "Israeliness" was formed, thus institutionalizing its cultural dominance. The indigenous group is the Palestinians. With them and with the Arab world, of which the Palestinians are part, the State of Israel has been involved in a protracted territorial conflict. The term "later immigrants" generally refers to two noticeable groups: *Mizrahim*—Jewish immigrants from Arab countries, and Russians—Jewish immigrant from the Former Soviet Union, who immigrated to Israel during the 1990s (half of them are not Jews (Lustick 1999)). The nation and state-building project in Israel, which was conducted in the shadow of the conflict, ingathered the *Ashkenazim*, the *Mizrahim*, and the Russians, while excluding the Palestinians.

In settler societies, settlement projects and economic development are particularly important in frontier areas (Anderson and O'Dowd 1999; Kellerman 1992; Kennedy 1987; Kimmerling 1983; Shafir 1989). It is called spatial ethnicization, since it promotes only the spatial dissemination of the members of the founding and immigrant group, while restricting the members of the native group (see Pearson 2002). Aside from its economic and demographic importance, the settlement process has other implicit purposes. To begin with, the process inculcates "collective" values that include myths of conquest of the wilderness, redemption of the frontier, and the transformation of the remote reaches of the territory "from desolation to a breathing land." These myths encourage and normalize the settlement process (Kellerman 1996), remove native significance from the settled space, and impose new meaning upon the space as an object of identification for the settler group (Benvenisti 2000). Secondly, the settlement process helps the dominant group to extend its control over the natives and their lands and resources. Thirdly, by transforming the later immigrants into pioneers, they are kept distant from the centers of power and wealth while at the same time being included in the nation-building project, albeit in a position of inferiority, in such a way that their settlement is kept out of the pantheon of national achievement. Thus, unequal power relations within the entity known as a "nation" emerge, even though it is commonly represented as egalitarian, inclusive, and just.

From the colonial explanation a new academic perspective concerning the establishment and long-term policy towards the DTs has emerged. This perspective was first used by Yiftachel (1997, 2000a, 2000b), and later by Tzfadia (2000, 2001, 2002a, 2002b), Yiftachel and Tzfadia (2004), and Tzfadia and Yiftachel (2004). Deconstructing two central axioms within Zionism facilitated these studies on the DTs, namely the "ingathering of the exiles" and "Judaization dispersal." Both are widely considered within Israeli society to be common sense ideals, and have been twisted into favorite policies by all Israeli governments. Hence, their deconstruction is considered as a critical act (Silberstein 2002).

The first axiom, which had been intensively implemented during the 1950s, is the "ingathering of the exiles." It is the Israeli version of the American single melting pot approach (Gorny 2001), but in Israel it was directed only at the Jews (Shuval and Leshem 1998). The "ingathering of the exiles" represents the ambition to lap the cultural space over the national space. That is, the construction of a national homogenous culture. In Israel, this objective was partially obtained by demanding the *Mizrahim,* who emigrated from Arab countries, to get rid of their Arabic culture, and to adopt Israeli identity. The *Mizrahi* primordial culture was too similar to the native Palestinian culture (Shapiro 1997). The call to produce a homogenous national identity was compatible with secular Zionism, which was created by European founder Jews. The Zionist vision mandated the immigrant Jews to rid themselves of the exilic spirit, and to adopt a secular, modern and western national identity. The vast majority of the population in Israel / Palestine, however, was indeed rooted in the Arabic traditional culture (Shohat 1997).

However, *Mizrahim* were also regarded as inherently part of the Israeli-Jewish nation, a pivotal component in the making of an independent national entity, since the vast majority of European Jews were massacred in the Holocaust (Shohat 1997). Therefore, four years after independence, the Israeli parliament legislated two laws that provided free immigration to Israel for all the Jews around the world, with citizenship granted immediately upon arrival. The widespread stereotypes placed upon the *Mizrahim*'s Arabism and the understanding that only by absorbing the *Mizrahim* might the national project succeed, were fundamental in the formation of an inclusion-exclusion policy. The practice of Judaization dispersal was the spatial appearance of this policy, as we shall see later.

However, there is a third component in the Israeli social structure—the Palestinian population that remained in Israel after the war in 1948, and the land property of the Palestinian refugees. Weaving the links between the Palestinian case and the making of DTs, is considered as one of the major contributions of colonial explanation upon the two other approaches (Ram 1999). About 750,000 Palestinians escaped or were expelled in the war of 1948. They left behind 320 abandoned villages and towns and millions of *dunams*[1] of land (Morris 1987). Following the war, their land was fully transferred to State ownership. In addition, Palestinians who remained in Israel and became citizens of Israel lost approximately 40-60% of the land they had possessed prior to 1948 (Kedar 2001). Most of the Palestinians who remained in Israel lived in Israel's peripheral regions (Negev and Galilee, see Figure 15.1). Their presence was considered as a security problem, which demanded a Jewish presence in these regions, mainly on the expropriated lands of Palestinian refugees. Yoseph Weiss, a personage in the Zionist movement and the first director of Israel Lands Administration, wrote (1950: 143-145):

> Some theorists... think that since the State was established, all the land belongs to it... and therefore the land question solved itself and the land was redeemed... The land is indeed State land, but there is one flaw in it... The rights to the land belong to all the State's citizens, including the Arabs... In this situation, we must ensure that most of the land will belong to Jews... and therefore we must continue with land redemption (Quoted and translated by Kedar 2001)

Weiss (1950: 10) expressed the best way to redeem the land as follows:

> The struggle for redemption of the land is as simple as it sounds—redemption from the hands of foreigners [i.e. Arabs]; a struggle to redeem the land from its shackles; a struggle to conquer the land by settling it; and, finally, the most

important thing—a struggle to strike roots in the land (translated by the author).

Where the phobia from *Mizrahi* culture met the simultaneous desires to incorporate the *Mizrahim* into "the nation," to "redeem" the abandoned Palestinian lands, and to increase Jewish presence in peripheral regions in which Palestinians constituted the majority, the axiom of "Judaization Dispersal" became the ultimate solution, at least according to the colonial explanation. The dispersal was realized by the "Sharon Plan," the first national plan (Sharon 1951). It aimed at planting 28 new towns and dozens of agricultural settlements, most of them in the Negev and Galilee, mainly on the ruins of Palestinian towns and villages.

Mizrahim particularly populated these new settlements and DTs at the "frontiers," often against their wishes. Two major practices were utilized to achieve these goals. (a) Public housing was offered in the DTs to *Mizrahim* who lived in tents or tin huts in provisional absorption camps (Kallus and Law-Yone 2002). (b) *Mizrahim* were often transported in the middle of the night directly from the airport or harbor to public housing in the DTs. Yiftachel and Tzfadia (2004) found that most of the *Mizrahim* who resided in the DTs in the late 1990s, and born outside the DTs, arrived there by one of these two practices, most often against their wishes. Nearly 200,000 *Mizrahim* became forced pioneers in the DTs through these practices. The long-term housing and employment policies enabled the relegation of the *Mizrahim* to the DTs for generations to come, as was well described by neo-Marxist scholars.

Yet, these acts do not suggest a conspiracy against the *Mizrahi* immigrants, but a mishmash of a sense of closeness between European Jews, a European arrogance towards the "orient," and a lack of leadership and property among the *Mizrahim*. Nevertheless, the aims of the establishment of the DTs were to control Palestinian land and population, distance the *Mizrahim* from centers of authority and wealth through geographic isolation, and incorporate them into 'the nation' as essential members of the frontier ethos.

For these reasons the establishment of the new towns was successful, according to the colonial explanation. In particular, it relocated a great mass of people more numerous than any other settlement project in Zionist history – more than what the mythical *Kibbutzim* (cooperative villages) managed to do before statehood or even the endeavor to colonize the occupied territories after 1967. Simultaneously, capitalists managed to "earn" low-priced and obedient labor for the Israeli developed industrial sector. However, the success cannot be measured only by demographic, geographic, or economic terms. The *Mizrahi* residents of the towns themselves regarded the building of the DTs in the 1950s as an important act in the nation- and state-building project. To be part of this project meant that the *Mizrahim* believed they were an integral part at the Israeli-Jewish nation, hence held a sense of mastership upon "inferior" groups (indigenous groups). The building of the towns did not propose that the *Mizra-him* were not aware of their inferior status and deprivation within the Israeli-Jewish nation (Yiftachel and Tzfadia 2004). A sense of bitterness has definitely emerged, which can possibly be channeled to political organizations on an ethnic basis. The bitterness and escalation, however, will not touch the essentiality and stability of the Israeli settler society. Hence, it is logical to claim that the making of the towns should be seen as a success in national terms too.

CONCLUSION

This case study of public policy and the growth and development of small cities has shown that the colonial mentality underlining the planning and establishment of Israel's development towns explains more of the difficulties the towns are facing. This explanation may be seen as an analogue for stratified societies in terms of ethnicity, class and space, which are managed by power relations and domination. Accordingly, public policy in general and planning of small towns beyond the metropolis in particular is an instrument for controlling and preserving such a social structure. "Difficulties" of remote small towns have rarely to do with planning lapses, or with the idea that remoteness generates backwardness. Rather, the "problems" of small towns should be associated with social-political-spatial structures that dominant groups create in order to advance their political and economic interests by maintaining hierarchy according to different social categories, such as ethnic belonging. Geography facilitates and preserves this hierarchy by maintaining an unequal distribution of wealth and power, isolation, spatial fragmentation and walling. It suggests that geography and spatial policy should be seen as channels for obtaining social control and not as procreators of social hierarchy by themselves. Yet, this argument cannot be reduced into single dimension of class relation, as neo-Marxists theoreticians suggest. Rather, a critical attempt should be made in order to dissect official policies, planning, ideologies, cultures and legal structures, and ascertain their influence on various structural stratifications, mainly when the geographical focus is *beyond the metropolis*.

ENDNOTES

1. A unit of land measure equal to 1,000 square meters (about 1/4 acre).

REFERENCES

Anderson, L., and J. O'Dowd, 1999. Borders, border regions and territoriality: contradictory meanings, changing significance. *Regional Studies* 33 (7): 593 – 604.

Aravot, I., and S. Militanu, 2000. Israeli new town plans: physical transformations. *Journal of Urban Design* 5 (1): 41 – 64.

Benvenisti, M. 2000. *Sacred Landscape: The Buried History of the Holy Land since 1948.* Berkeley: University of California Press.

Bernstein, D., and S. Swirsky. 1982. The rapid economic development of Israel and the emergence of the ethnic division of labour. *British Journal of Sociology* 33 (1): 64 – 85.

Brutzkus, E. 1970. *Regional Policy in Israel.* Jerusalem: Town and Country Planning Department., Ministry of Interior.

Central Bureau of Statistics. 1983. *Census of Population and Housing 1983.* Jerusalem: State of Israel, Ministry of the Interior.

———. 1995. *Census of Population and Housing 1995.* Jerusalem: State of Israel, Ministry of the Interior.

———. 1998. *Statistical Yearbook 1998.* Jerusalem: State of Israel, Ministry of the Interior

———. 2002. Characterization and ranking of local authorities according to the population's socio -economic level, 1999.
http://wwwcbsgovil/hodaot2002/13_02_48htm#tabsgraphs

Christaller, W. 1966. *Central Places in Southern Germany.* Trans. C. W. Baskin. Englewood Cliffs, N.J.: Prentice-Hall.

Cohen, E. 1970. *The City in Zionist Ideology.* Jerusalem Urban Studies 1. Jerusalem: Hebrew University.

Efrat, E. 1988. *The New Towns of Israel: a Reappraisal.* Munich: Minerva.

Elhanani, A. 1998. *The Struggle for Independence. The Israeli Architecture in the Twentieth Century.* Tel-Aviv, Ministry of Defense (Hebrew).

Fainstein, N.I., and S. S. Fainstein. 1979. New debates in urban planning: the impact of Marxist theory within the United States. *International Journal of Urban and Regional Research* 3 (3).

Faludi, A. 1973. *Planning Theory.* Urban and Regional Planning Series. Vol. 7. Oxford: Pergamon Press.

Garaudy, R.1977. Religious and historical pretexts of Zionism. *Journal of Palestine Studies* 6 (2): 41 – 52.

Glazer, N. and D. P. Moynihan. 1975. Introduction. In *Ethnicity,* ed. N. Glazer and D. P. Moynihan, 1-28. Cambridge: Harvard University Press.

Gordon, M. M. 1964. *Assimilation in American Life.* New York: Oxford University Press.

Gorny, Y. 2001. The 'melting pot' in Zionist thought. *Israel Studies* 6 (3): 54 – 70.

Government of Israel. 1949. *Protocol of Governmental Meeting* 12/309, 03.05.1949.

Gradus, Y., and Y. Einy. 1984. Trends in core-periphery industrialization gaps in Israel. *Geography Research Forum* 2-6: 71 – 83.

Gradus, Y., and S. Krakover. 1977. The effect of Government policy on the spatial structure of manufacturing in Israel. *Journal of Developing Areas* 11 (3): 393 – 409.

Grosby, S. 1999. The chosen people of Ancient Israel and the Occident: Why does nationality exist and survive? *Nations and Nationalism.* 5 (3): 357 – 380.

Harvey, D. 1993. Class relations, social justice and the politics of difference. In *Place and the Politics of Identity,* ed. M. Keith and S. Pile, 41 – 66. London: Routledge.

———. 1996. *Justice, Nature and the Geography of Difference.* Malden, MA: Blackwell.

Howard, E. 1985. *Garden Cities of To-morrow* (New Edition), Sussex: Attic Books. (First published in 1898 as Tomorrow: A peaceful path to real Reform. T.P.verso).

Kallus, R., and L. H. 2002. National home / personal home: public housing and the shaping of space in Israel. *European Planning Studies* 10 (6):765 – 779.

Kedar, A. 2001. The legal transformation of ethnic geography: Israeli law and the Palestinian landholder 1948 – 1967. *NYU Journal of International Law and Politics* 33 (4): 923 – 1000.

Kellerman, A. 1992. *Society and Settlement: Jewish and Land of Israel in the Twentieth Century.* Albany: SUNY Press.

Kellerman, A. 1996. Settlement myth and settlement activity: Interrelationships in the Zionist land of Israel. *Transactions of the Institute of British Geographers* 21 (2): 363 – 378.

Kennedy, D. K. 1987. *Islands of White: Settler Society and Culture in Kenya and Southern Rhodesia, 1890-1939.* Durham: Duke University Press.

Kimmerling, B. 1983. *Zionism and Territory: The Socio-Territorial Dimensions of Zionist Politics.* Berkeley: The University of California Press.

Krakover, S. 1979. The development of three towns in the northern Negev. In *The Land of the* Negev, ed. A. Shemueli and Y. Gradus, 569-611. Ministry of Defense Publishing House. (Hebrew).

Law-Yone, H., and R. Kalus. 1994. *Housing Inequality in Israel.* Tel Aviv: Adva Centre.

Lewin-Epstein, N., Y. Elmelech, and M. Semyonov 1997. Ethnic inequality in home-ownership and the value of housing: The case of immigrants to Israel. *Social Forces* 75 (4): 1439 – 1462.

Lipshitz, G., and B. H. Massam. 1998. Classification of development towns in Israel by using multicriteria decision aid techniques. *Environment and Planning A.* 30 (7): 1279 – 1294.

Lissak, M. 1999. *Mass Immigration in the Fifties: The Failure of the Melting Pot Policy.* Jerusalem: Bialik Institute (Hebrew).

Lustick, S. I. 1999. Israel as a non-Arab state: the political implications of mass immigration of non-Jews. *Middle East Journal* 53 (3): 417 – 433.

Morris, B. 1987. *The Birth of the Palestinian Refugee Problem, 1947 – 1949.* Cambridge: Cambridge University Press.

Palen, J. J. 1997. *The Urban World.* 5th edition. N.Y: McGraw-Hill.

Pearson, D. 2002. Theorizing citizenship in British settler societies. *Ethnic and Racial Studies* 25 (6): 989-1012.

Phillips, D. R. and A. G. O. Yeh. 1987. *New Town in East and South East Asia.* Hong-Kong: Oxford University Press.

Ram, U. 1999. The colonization perspective in Israeli sociology. In *The Israel / Palestine Question,* ed. I. Pappe, 55 – 80. London: Routledge.

Razin, E. 1988. Ownership structure and linkage patterns of industry in Israel's development towns. *Regional Studies* 22 (1): 19 – 31.

Shafir, G. 1989. *Land, Labor and the Origins of the Israeli-Palestinian Conflict: 1882-1914.* Cambridge: Cambridge University Press.

Shapiro, M. J. 1997. Narrating the nation, unwelcoming the stranger: anti-immigration policy in contemporary America. *Alternatives.* 22: 1 – 34.

Sharon, A. 1951. *Physical Planning in Israel.* Jerusalem: Gov. Printing Office (Hebrew).

Shohat, E. 1997. The narrative of the nation and the discourse of modernization: the case of the Mizrahim. *Critique.* Spring, 3 – 19.

Shuval, J. T. and E. Leshem. 1998. The sociology of migration in Israel: A critical view. In *Immigration to Israel: Sociological Perspectives,* ed. E. Leshem and J.T Shuval, 3-50. New Brunswick: Transaction Publishers.

Silberstein, J. L. 1999. *The Postzionism Debates.* London: Routledge.

Silberstein, L. J. 2002. Problematizing power: Israel's postzionist critics. *Palestine-Israel Journal* 9 (3): 97 – 107.

Soen, D., and S. Sehori. 1983. Migration balance and socio-economic image- the case of Israel's new towns. *Planning Outlook* 26 (1):22 – 27.

Stasilius, D., and N. Yuval-Davis, ed. 1995. *Unsettling Settler Societies.* London: Sage Publications.

Swirski, S. 1989. *Israel: The Oriental Majority* London: Zed Books.

———. 1990. *Education in Israel: Schooling for Inequality.* Tel Aviv: Breirot (Hebrew).

Swirski, S., and E. Konor-Attias. 2001. *Israel: A Social Report 2001.* Tel-Aviv: Adva.

Swirski, S., and M. Shoushan 1985. *The Development Towns of Israel: Towards a Brighter Tomorrow.* Haifa: Breirot (Hebrew).

Taylor, N. 1998. *Urban Planning Theory Since 1945.* London, Sage.

Templin, J. A. 1999. The ideology of a chosen people: Afrikaner nationalism and the Ossewa Trek 1938. *Nations and Nationalism* 5 (3): 397 – 417.

Troen, I. 1994a. New departures in Zionist planning: the development town. In: *Returning Home: Immigration and Absorption into Their Homelands of Germans and Jews from the Former Soviet Union*, ed. I. Troen and K. Bade, 441 – 459. Beer-Sheva: Ben-Gurion University of the Negev. Humphrey Institute for Social Ecology.

―――. 1994b. The transformation of Zionist planning policy: from rural settlement to an urban network. *Planning Perspective* 3: 3 – 23.

Turner, F. J. 1962. *The Frontier in American History*. New York: Holt, Rinehart and Winston.

Tzfadia, E. 2000. Immigrant dispersal in settler societies: *Mizrahim* and Russians in Israel under the press of hegemony. *Geography Research Forum*. 20:52 – 69.

―――. 2001. Competition over political resources: the development towns' municipal elections. *Ofakim Be-Geographia* 53: 59 – 70. (Hebrew).

―――. 2002a. Immigrants in Peripheral Towns in the Israeli Settler Society: Mizrahim in Development Towns Face Russian Migration. Unpublished PhD. Thesis. Beer-Sheva: Ben-Gurion University of the Negev (Hebrew).

―――. 2002b. Between nation and place: localism in Israeli development towns fronts Russian immigration. *Studies in the Geography of Israel*. 16: 97 – 122 (Hebrew).

Tzfadia, E. and O. Yiftachel. 2004. Between urban and national: political mobilization among Mizrahim in Israel's 'development towns.' *Cities: The International Journal of Urban Policy and Planning* 21 (1):41 – 55.

Weiss, Y. 1950. *The Struggle Over the Land*. Tel Aviv: Taversky. (Hebrew).

Yiftachel, O. 1997 Nation-building or ethnic fragmentation? Ashkenazim, Mizrahim and Arabs in the Israeli frontier. *Space and Polity*, 1 (2): 149 – 169.

―――. 2000a. Ethnocracy and its discontents: minorities, protest, and the Israeli policy. *Critical Inquiry* 26 (4): 725 – 756.

―――. 2000b. Social control, urban planning and ethno-class relations: Mizrahi Jews in Israel's development towns. *International Journal of Urban and Regional Research* 24 (2): 418 – 438.

―――. 2001. The homeland and nationalism. *Encyclopedia of Nationalism* 1: 359 – 383.

Yiftachel, O., and E. Tzfadia. 2004. Between periphery and 'Third Space': Identity of Mizrahim in Israel's development towns. In *Israelis in Conflict: Hegemonies,,Identities and Challenges*, ed. A. Kemp, D. Newman, U. Ram, and O. Yiftachel. Sussex Academic Press.

Yona, Y., and I. Saporta. 2002. The politics of lands and housing in Israel: a wayward republican discourse. *Social Identities* 8 (1): 91 – 117.

Webster, C. J. 1998. Public choice, Pigouvian and Caosian planning theory. *Urban Studies* 35 (1): 53 – 75.

Conclusion

16

The Future of Urban Geography as if Small Cities Mattered

Benjamin Ofori-Amoah
University of Wisconsin-Stevens Point

INTRODUCTION

This book was born out of the need to fill a gap in urban geographic research, namely the study of small cities. Specifically, the authors believed that in spite of the considerable representation of small cities in the urban system of North America and elsewhere, there has been a relative neglect in the study of these cities within the traditional context as well as in emerging themes in urban geography. To this end, each author examined a topic in urban geography within the context of a small city either for purposes of comparison with large city trends or as a stand-alone study. In this concluding chapter, it is only appropriate to ask the question: "What have we learned about small cities and what are the implications of these lessons for future research on small cities in urban geography?" I answer these questions with respect to each of the three broad categories of study that were used in the book.

THE EVOLUTION AND GROWTH OF SMALL CITIES

The chapters that focused on the evolution and growth of small cities have informed us that the growth paths of small cities and the factors that influence them may not be very different from those of large cities, but there are also a few significant differences. For example, the story of Prince George from a frontier outpost to the regional metropolis of Northern British Columbia, by Halseth, Sedgewick, and Ofori-Amoah, mirrors the general evolution of the large cities that dominate the Canadian urban system. This growth was strongly influenced by relative location, transportation development, government policies, and corporate strategies, factors that have been identified with the evolution and growth of large cities. However, there is a time lag between the periods of transition of Prince George's growth and that of the large cities in Canada, perhaps due to Prince George's western location and the effect of hierarchical and spatial diffusion within the urban system. In addition, the transformation that has resulted is now posing new challenges that are more difficult for Prince George to deal with, compared with its large city counterparts.

If the phases of growth of Prince George replicate the growth experience of large cities, the urbanization of Minnesota's countryside identified by Adams and VanDrasek is new in terms of our conventional understanding of urbanization. Specifically, in conventional understanding, it is population growth that drives urbanization. However, in Minnesota, small cities are urbanizing rapidly not because of population growth but because of transportation development in the countryside, which in turn has led to an extension of commuting fields around small cities. As expected, this transformation is also posing new problems, such as high housing prices, problems which were formerly not associated with small cities.

Demographic changes in small cities in both the US and Mexico, over previous decades, also reflected some similarities and differences with large city trends. In both countries, we learned that the fortunes of small cities close to large urban areas are inextricably tied to those of nearby metropolitan areas. In both countries, small cities grew considerably faster than medium and large cities. In the US, Brennan and Hoene's work show that small cities were less ethnically diverse than large cities, while in Mexico, Gonzalez Sanchez and Gutierrez de MacGregor show that age and gender structure of population differentiated small cities from large cities. In the US, small cities gained population, between 1990 and 2000, while in Mexico small cities have been losing population since 1970. Thus, small cities in the two countries are facing two different kinds of challenges. In the US, the key question is how to cope with rapidly increasing population growth resulting from the expansion of metropolitan areas and continued increases in the gross population of the country. In Mexico, the problem is how to stem the declining population of small cities due to emigration to large urban areas. Clearly, these questions also reflect the relationship between the level of economic development and the urban system.

The implications of these trends for further research are several. In general, more studies focusing on small cities need to be conducted to investigate these findings. In particular, there are several specific questions that need addressing. For example, why do small cities grow the way they do, or why do small cities remain small? What are the forces behind the demographic changes occurring in small cities? Why are some small cities growing while others are not? Why are there more small cities in Mexico today than decades ago, yet small cities account for a lesser proportion of the country's population than before? Why is the opposite occurring in the US?

THE INTERNAL STRUCTURES OF SMALL CITIES

The analysis of the social and spatial structures of small cities has informed us that small cities are miniature replicas of large cities, but with some significantly different features. For example, Fonseca's analysis of Ohio's micropolitan areas informs us that small cities have smaller proportions of non-white population than metropolitan Ohio, except for the proportions of Hispanics, which tend to be the same as those of their large city counterparts. Small cities also lag behind in income, unemployment, poverty, educational attainment, and housing value. In terms of the spatial structure, each small city in Ohio has also evolved a core and a fringe. As in a large city, the fringe is growing faster than the core. Income is higher and population is less diverse at the fringe than in the core areas. In addition, each small city has evolved its own central business districts, specialized districts, older factory districts with adjoining multifamily and run-down housing, a historic district or strip of well-kept and large older homes, college districts, medical districts, and in general, distinct neighborhoods or sections of the city easily categorized by social class. These districts become more recognizable and distinguishable with increasing city size. Like their large counterparts, small cities are facing the same problems of growth on the fringes, and loss of population in the core.

Yoder's study of Ciudad Lerdo, Mexico, reveals clearly that no place can be sheltered from the power of global capital and neoliberal policies that are shaping the large cities of today. Thus, the desire to promote industrialization for export under a free trade environment has pushed agriculture to the backwaters of Ciudad Lerdo, and has transformed its spatial structure of a rural community into an urban one overnight. However, the effects of these processes on this small city have been far more devastating because it lacks the institutional, managerial, and financial resources that allow large cities to cope under similar circumstances. As rich agricultural lands give way to industrial land uses that fail to deliver the jobs and economic growth they promise, traditional town design gives way to a sprawling, decentralized landscape that is not only wasteful, but accentuates such quality of life problems as poor transportation and infrastructure.

Location dynamics of economic activities within small cities provide a third group of examples of how the internal structure of small cities follows the trends in large cities, but once again with different effects. The most important manifestation of this change is the decline of downtown retail and the rise of new shopping or business districts at the outskirts and along major highway corridors and interchanges. In central Iowa, Bell and Gripshover have shown that big box retailers, such as Wal-Mart, are only a part of this problem. The other part is rooted in structural changes that include the loss of visibility, changing employment base, urban sprawl, and the domineering influence or the "urban corona" effect of Des Moines as a highest order central place in the region. Admittedly, large cities are also grappling with this problem, but retailing may still remain viable elsewhere in the city. In small cities such as those in Iowa, that chance does not exist. As a result, the decline of Main Street retailing has a proportionally larger impact on the psyche of the people who live in those cities. This implies that it is important to keep up the appearance and façades of the original retail emporiums not simply for nostalgic value but in anticipation of future changes. In addition, the leadership of small towns should remain vigilant to the signs of retail decline, turnover and abandonment, since such large turnovers may be a sign of impending trouble.

In Wisconsin, Ofori-Amoah shows that the phases, pattern, and direction of location change in retail, manufacturing, and service activities in five small cities have also followed the trends in large cities except for the causes and effects of the change. Thus, location of retail away from downtown did not occur because of "suburbanization" of residences and the completion of urban freeways, but mainly because of the need for greater visibility, accessibility, relative ease of development in "greenfields" rather than "brownfields," and downtown revitalization projects. In reacting to the effects of retail decline in their downtowns, we have also learned that small cities have mostly followed the strategies of large cities some of which have failed miserably. This has created an on-going search for identity and vitality for the downtown.

In addition to the need for more studies to verify these findings, there are also a number of interesting questions. Can the spatial and social structure identified in Micropolitan Ohio be found anywhere else? Can the spatial structure of small cities be modeled? If so, how many of such models could be developed and how will they differ regionally? Is the social structure of small cities distinct from that of large cities? Do the effects of globalization and neoliberal policies on small cities depend on whether the small cities are in a developed or developing country? Does the capital landscape created in the global periphery differ from that created at the global core? Does the "urban corona" effect really exist? If so how does it impact the well being of small cities? Is there a niche for the downtown of a small city? If so, how does one know it, when it is found? Does activity, such as retail, location away from the downtown, necessarily mean a loss of economic vitality of the downtown? Are there better measures of how well downtown is doing beyond just relocation of some activities? What about employment and revenue measures?

PLANNING AND MANAGING CHANGE IN SMALL CITIES

Change is an inevitable part of the life of a small city just as it is of a large city. Some changes are planned while others are unplanned. Whether planned or unplanned, change must be managed, in order to make cities livable. In small cities, the change that seems to attract the most attention of the general public is downtown revitalization. Most of these revitalization projects have been in response to declining economic activities in the downtown area or physical deterioration of the area. Most of them have also followed the strategies that have been used by large cities. The mixed results of these efforts have raised interest in the question as to what strategies and factors account for the differences in results. For example, from Otto's study of two small cities in Ohio, we can deduce that part of the mixed results may lie in the downtown revitalization projects themselves. In particular, in spite of high expectation from local business communities that downtown revitalization will improve downtown retail, revitalization activities have not really made economic restructuring of downtown as a focus. Instead, revitalization activities have emphasized historic designs, event and entertainment functions. The result is that there is still a considerable gap between successful physical improvements and satisfactory economic revitalization, amidst a number of conflicts. For example, conflicts can arise when downtown concentrates on a small niche that might hinder adjustments to the overall market or is susceptible to local changes. In addition, emphasizing niche marketing might also ignore local needs and if several other small cities follow suit, the whole strategy might become counterproductive due to saturation. The implication of all of these is that there is the need for balance in shaping the future of the small city downtown.

However, Ramsey, Eberts, and Everitt's study of revitalization efforts in Brandon, Manitoba, highlights the fact that the most fruitful results from downtown revitalization occur when there is a partnership between public and private sectors. This is because many parties have an interest in the vitality of downtown, but few are willing or capable of acting individually to effect real change. Also, the role of downtown is evolving, and it is only when a particular phase of evolution is embraced that revitalization efforts can succeed. In this regard, a 'head-to-head' competition with an outskirts or a suburban mall will not work. At the same time, the downtown mall with some innovative thinking could be an effective tool for the downtown. All said, the story of Brandon demonstrates while not every downtown intervention works, those that work provide a secure future for downtown.

In Kentucky, Smith's study of the Main Street program adds another dimension to the causes of mixed results of downtown revitalization efforts, and that is the factor of relative location to large cities. Smith's study informs us that Kentucky's Main Street programs in metropolitan areas are more likely to be active and, for that matter, succeed than Main Street programs in nonmetropolitan areas. This is because small cities located in the shadow of large cities see the program as a matter of survival, as a result of competition. Thus, they become more involved and better organized, and the program is able to gain a broad-based support. In contrast, small cities in nonmetropolitan areas have no competition with other urban places, and have an abundance of retail and service establishments to keep the street front spaces filled. Implementation and leadership of the

Main Street program in these locations are typically county and city politicians, who had the most to gain from such an endeavor. Merchants and property owners are seldom involved in the Main Street process because their economic health is not threatened. Because these downtowns are viable, many citizens of these communities viewed the Main Street program as unnecessary.

Downtown revitalization may be the most well-known change event in small cities, but it is by no means the only one. Public transportation, housing and urban development, as well as general economic development are the other change events in small cities. From Irion's work, we have learned that as small cities founded during the nineteenth century, both Marysville and Yuba City followed the public transportation path typical of cities large enough to warrant street railway service. Thus, from the use of horses, public transportation in the two small cities evolved through the horsecar, the electric streetcar, the automobile, and the bus. However, as a result of small population size, low population density, and high ownership of automobiles, the typical public transit choices in small cities are bus service supported by taxes or no service at all. The majority of federal transit support is for capital expenditures, equipment and facilities. The bulk of these funds go to metropolitan areas. Federal transit funds for operation are limited. The costs of operation are borne by varying levels of state and local funds that supplement farebox revenues. The service can continue only as long as there is the political will to continue to make up the shortfall in passenger revenue with tax funds. Ultimately, that is determined by the voters. One of the transit industry's challenges is to convince the motorist voters that transit is valuable to them even if they do not use the service. While this situation exists in metropolitan areas, it seems to become more problematic for small cities.

The story of Ciudad Guzman, presented by Cabrales Barajas, is a revelation that problems of housing and urban development are not unique to large cities alone, but are characteristics of small cities as well, even though they may be on a small scale. In the case of Cuidad Guzman, these problems generate from a negative demonstration effect of a national urban development pattern that creates pockets of vacant land, segregation, inadequate infrastructure, and a failure to meet the real life necessities of the population. These forces have been exacerbated by a lack of synchronization between agrarian and urban land uses and the city's location in an environmentally fragile zone. The result has been a housing development in which the housing units occupy modest amounts of space, exhibit high variability in quality, generally lack basic services, and for that matter have negative environmental impact. Thus, urban development problems that used to be confined only to Mexico's large cities have now descended on its small cities as well.

Oftentimes, when urban communities are facing economic growth and development problems, inept planning structures and practices, among other things, become the culprit as the causes of the problems. Contrary to this general notion, Tzfadia's investigation into the growth and development problems facing some of Israel's development towns emphasizes the role of public policy and geography. From his analysis, we are reminded once more of how public policy and geography can be instruments for controlling and preserving a social structure, by the dominant group of society, even in planning of small cities. Within this context, the so-called "difficulties" of remote small towns have very little to do with planning lapses, or with the idea that remoteness generates backwardness. Rather, the "difficulties" should be associated with social-political-spatial structures that dominant groups create in order to advance their political and economic interests by maintaining hierarchy according to different social categories, such as ethnic belonging.

As in the previous sections, there is the need for more studies to further investigate these findings. Is retailing completely gone out of small city downtowns? If not what factors explain retail success and failure in small city downtowns? If partnership between the public and private sector is crucial for downtown revitalization projects, are such partnerships project dependent? What types of projects attract such partnerships and how does one cultivate such partnerships? If proximity to a large urban area is a predictor for success of a Main Street program because of competition, could competition among small cities in close proximity also be a determining factor for a successful Main Street program? Is a structural forecasting model for predicting success or failure of downtown revitalization as well as Main Street programs possible? Does housing constitute an urban development problem in small cities in the US and Canada? What factors affect economic development of small cities in peripheral regions?

CONCLUSION

The purpose of this chapter was to review the main findings of the chapters in this book and their implications for future research. The review so far has shown that some of the findings confirm what we already know from the experience of large cities, others have challenged those established conventions, while a few have been completely new. For the findings that confirm what we already know there may be no need to belabor the differences between large and small cities, but there will be the need to look at more small cities to be sure that the trends and patterns are in fact the same. However, for those findings that differ from the trend, pattern, or explanation, or challenge existing notions, there is a real need to pay special attention to them. In addition, there is a vast range of topics that urban geographers deal with that were not touched upon in this volume. Thus, in addition to the several questions I have raised above, those other topics should provide further motivation for more urban geographers to study small cities, not only for purposes of comparison, but also as stand-alone studies in their own right.

Index

About the Editor and Contributors

EDITOR

Benjamin Ofori-Amoah is a Professor of Geography and Chair of the Department of Geography and Geology at the University of Wisconsin-Stevens Point. He received his PhD degree in geography from Simon Fraser University, Burnaby, BC, Canada, in 1991. Ben is an economic geographer and a regional planner with teaching and research interests in industrial location, retail location, transportation, urban geography and planning, technological change, geographic information system applications, small cities, and Africa. He has published articles and book chapters in several of these areas, including one co-edited book *Addressing Misconception About Africa's Development*. His most recent publication is Africa, co-authored with Ezekiel Kalipeni and Joseph Oppong in G. L. Gaile and C. J. Willmott's edited volume *Geography in America at the Dawn of the 21st Century*. Ben's current activities include several writing projects, a four-year Rockefeller Foundation grant to build capacity to use geographic information systems in district planning in Uganda, and faculty and institutional development at the Kwame Nkrumah University of Science and Technology, Kumasi, Ghana.

CONTRIBUTORS

John S. Adams is a Professor of Geography, Planning, & Public Affairs, the University of Minnesota-Twin Cities. He obtained his PhD degree in economic geography from University of Minnesota in 1966. He served as the first director of the Humphrey Institute of Public Affairs at the University of Minnesota, and is the past director of the Urban Studies Program, also at the University of Minnesota. He is a past president of the Association of American Geographers. Dr. Adams has served as a visiting professor and consultant for many institutions in the US, Austria, Poland, Japan, China, and Russia. His courses and seminars included Human Geography; Urban Geography; American Cities. He has written, edited, and co-authored numerous articles, books, and reports on the American city, on regional economic development, intra-urban migration, and on housing markets, urban transportation and urban development in the USA and the former USSR. At present he is co-PI for the NSF-sponsored National Historical Geographic Information System (NHGIS) study at the Minnesota Population Center, 2001-06.

Luis Felipe Cabrales Barajas is a professor and researcher at the Department of Geography at the Universidad de Guadalajara. He received an undergraduate degree in geography at la Universidad de Guadalajara. He obtained the doctorate in geography and territorial ordination at la Universidad Compulutense in Madrid, Spain. His research interests include the production of urban space, the functional and social aspects of historic centers of cities, and the relation between tourism and national heritage, as themes tied to local and regional development. He has taught geography in various universities both in Mexico and abroad. He is member of the National System of Investigators (National Council of Science and Technology). He has approximately 50 publications, and is editor of the journal, *Geocalli, Cuadernos de Geografía*.

Thomas Bell is a Professor of Geography at the University of Tennessee, and a former Assistant Dean for Research at the same university. He received his Ph.D. degree in geography from the University of Iowa. He has authored numerous articles and reviews in the professional journals such as the *Annals of the Association of American Geographers*, the *Professional Geographer, Geographical Analysis, Geographical Review*, the *Southeastern Geographer, Urban Geography, Journal of Geography, World Archaeology*, and the *Journal of Archaeological Research*. He is the co-author of an earlier textbook in economic geography *Economic Growth and Disparities: A World View* with S. R. Jumper and B. A. Ralston published by Prentice-Hall, Inc. He has also been involved with preparing textbook materials in introductory human geography such as (*Human Geography: People, Places and Change* Prentice-Hall *World Regional Geography* W. H. Freeman, 2000; and the tenth edition of Harm deBlij and Peter O. Muller, *Geography: Realms, Regions and Concepts*, published by John Wiley and Sons.

Christiana K. Brennan is a research assistant at the National League of Cities in the US. She received her Masters in Public Policy degree from George Washington University in 2002. Her research interests include community development and land use, families and children, municipal finance, and homeland security. She has presented research on "Demographic Change in Small Cities, 1990-2000" at the Association of American Geographers conference and has also published "Homeland Security and America's Cities" and "Local Elected Officials and the Internet."

María Teresa Gutiérrez de MacGregor is a researcher in the Institute of Geography of the University of Mexico. She received her PhD degree in Geography from the Universidad Nacional Autónoma de México in1965. Her research interests lie in Urban Geography and Population Geography. Her recent publications include Impact of Mexican and USA Urban Growth and Natural Resources in the Northern Border of Mexico in *Latin American Studies, Las costas mexicanas y su crecimiento urbano en Investigaciones Geográficas. Boletín del Instituto de Geografía, Propuesta para fijar 10 mil habitantes como límite de una localidad urbana en Investigaciones Geográficas. México. Boletín del Instituto de Geografía.*

Derrek Eberts is an Assistant Professor of Geography at Brandon University, Brandon, Canada. He received his PhD from York University, in North York, Canada. His research interests include economic restructuring, changing patterns of work organization, neo-artisanal production, rural diversification, small city downtowns, tourism, and (Canadian) brewing industry. His most recent publications include The New Artisan and Metropolitan Space, in *Entre la Metropolitisation et le Village Global*, published by University of Quebec Press, Review of E. Schoenberger,s *The Cultural Crisis of the Firm*, in *Tijdschrift voor Economische en Sociale Geografie*, and New Forms of Artisanal Production in Toronto's Computer Animation Industry, in *Geographische Zeitschrift*.

John Everitt is a Professor of and Chair of the Department of Geography at Brandon University, Brandon, Canada where he has worked since 1973. He received his PhD from University of California-Los Angeles. In recent years, John has been involved in studies concerned with regional planning in Manitoba; economic opportunities on Indian Reserves in Western Manitoba; and elderly support services in Manitoba; the changing status of rural life in the Canadian prairies including the fortunes of small cities, and tourism in Manitoba, Belize, Puerto Vallarta, and the British Virgin Islands. John is a past president of the Canadian Association of Geographers. His recent publications include A Spatial Analysis of Crime in Brandon, Manitoba in *Prairie Perspectives: Geographical Essays*, Reviving central Brandon in the early twenty-first century, in *The Canadian Geographer*, and What the People say: a study of quality of life in three towns in Jalisco, Mexico in *Canadian Journal of Urban Research*

James W. Fonseca is Professor of Geography and Dean of the Ohio University –Zanesville, Ohio. He obtained his PhD in Geography from Clark University in 1974. He previously taught at George Mason University, Fairfax, Virginia, where he served also in various administrative positions including Director at Prince William Campus, Associate Dean of Graduate School, Academic Director of Community College Programs. His most recent publications include Changing Patterns of Population Density in the United States, which appeared in

Professional Geographer, and *Atlas of American Society* with Alice C. Andrews, published by the New York University Press.

Jorge González-Sánchez is Research assistant in the Institute of Geography of the University of Mexico. He received his Masters degree in Geography from the Universidad Nacional Autónoma de México in 1996. His research interests lie in Urban Geography and Population Geography. His recent publications include Cambios en la estructura jerárquica del sistema nacional de asentamientos de México. En: Estudios Demográficos y Urbanos 31, and Tipología sociodemográfica 2000. Hoja del Atlas del Diagnóstico Territorial del Estado de Oaxaca. Instituto de Geografía, UNAM-Comité de Planeación Estatal del Estado de Oaxaca (COPLADE). Sección 2 SOCIEDAD. (Incluye tres mapas escala 1: 500,000).

Margaret M. Gripshover is currently an Adjunct Associate Professor and Lecturer in the Department of Geography at the University of Tennessee. She received her doctorate in geography from the University of Tennessee in 1995. Her dissertation examined the origins and diffusion of the Tennessee Walking Horse. She taught for twelve years in the Department of Geography at Marshall University in Huntington, West Virginia. Her research interests focus on the linkages between rural and urban economies, and cultural landscapes, with regional emphases in the American South and Midwest. She and husband Dr. Thomas L. Bell have collaborated on numerous research and publication projects.

Greg Halseth is an Associate Professor in the Geography Program at the University of Northern British Columbia, and Canada Research Chair in Rural and Small Town Studies. He received his PhD from Queens University, Canada. His courses include economic geography, political geography, and social geography of northern communities. His research examines rural and small town community (economic) development and the social geography of community change. He has published many journal articles and book chapters on small cities. His recent publications include *Building Community in an Instant Town: A social geography of Mackenzie and Tumbler Ridge, British Columbia*, published by the University of Northern British Columbia Press, *(Re)Development at the Urban Edges*, a University of Waterloo, Department of Geography Publication Series, and *Cottage Country in Transition: A Social Geography of Change and Contention in the Rural-Recreational Countryside. Montreal*" published by McGill-Queen's University Press.

Christopher Hoene is the Research Manager at the National League of Cities. He received his Ph.D. in political science in 2000, and an M.A. in public policy in 1996 and from Claremont Graduate University in Claremont, California. His work focuses on municipal finance, regional development, children and families, and homeland security. Previously, he was a Policy Analyst with the Center on Budget and Policy Priorities in Washington, DC and a Research Fellow at the Public Policy Institute of California in San Francisco. His most recent publications include: Fiscal Constraints and the Loss of Home Rule, in *American Review of Public Administration*, Homeland Security and America's Cities, in National League of Cities, Overhaul the Public Finance System in Federal Times, and "The Development of Counties as Municipal Service Providers," Urban Affairs Review.

Thomas Irion is a Rail Integration Project Manager for the Santa Clara Valley Transportation Authority (SCVTA) in Santa Clara, California. He holds a Masters degree in Geography from the California State University-Hayward. He began his career in the transportation industry with the Southern Pacific Company in 1962. In 1966 he joined the Sacramento Northern Railway for three years and went back to the Southern Pacific Company as a locomotive engineer. In 1975 he joined the California Public Utilities Commission's Railroad Operations and Safety Section in Los Angeles, and after six years returned to Southern Pacific Company. In 1987, he joined the SCVTA as a supervisor and instructor with its Light Rail Division, and moved into his current position in 2001. He is the author of several professional reports and serves as reviewer of articles for transportation journals.

Andreas Otto is a Research Associate with the Leibniz Institute of Ecological and Regional Development (IOER), one of Germany's leading research institutions in the field of spatial planning, and a lecturer at the Institute of Geography at the University of Technology at Dresden, (TUD) Germany. He holds a Master of Geography (i.e., German Diplom) with a focus in urban and regional development and planning from TUD, Dresden, Germany. Since 2003, Mr. Otto has been one of several participating faculty members involved in a study abroad exchange program between graduate students at TUD and the Ohio State University in Columbus, Ohio. He is currently completing research toward his doctorate degree in Geography in the area of small city downtown revitalization. He was awarded the TUD Lohrmann-Medal by the Department of Forestry, Geo and Water Sciences for academic excellence.

Doug Ramsey is an Associate Professor of Geography and Chair of the Department of Rural Development at Brandon University in Brandon, Manitoba. He received his PhD degree from University of Guelph, Canada. His research Interests include exploring rural tourism opportunities and constraints, farm diversification, evaluating policies which impact rural communities, hog farming issues in Manitoba, rural community well-being, urban core renewal in Brandon, environmental education, and music-based cultural hearths and cultural tourism.

His most recent publications include "Agricultural Restructuring of Ontario Tobacco Production" in *The Great Lakes Geographer*, "Reviving Brandon in the Early Twenty-first Century (Canadian Urban Landscapes Series No.23)" in *The Canadian Geographer* and "Rural Community Well-being: Models and Application to Changes in the Ontario Tobacco-belt" in *Geoforum*.

Christa Smith is an Assistant Professor of Geography at Clemson University. She received her PhD from University of Tennessee. She is a specialist in Appalachia and Urban Geography, and teaches a variety of geography courses in the department, including World Regional Geography, Economic Geography, and Geography of the American South. She also teaches Introduction to Historic Preservation. Her recent publication includes Predicting Success or Failure on Main Street: Urban Revitalization and the Kentucky Main Street Program, 1979-1999, in *Southeastern Geographer*. She is currently working on a book project entitled Affordable Housing for All.

Erez Tzfadia is a lecturer at the Department of Public Policy and Administration at Sapir Academic College in Israel. He received his Ph.D. from the Department of Geography, Ben-Gurion University (Beer-Sheva) in Israel in 2002. Erez Tzfadia was a Lady Davis postdoctoral fellow at the Hebrew University (Jerusalem) in 2003. His research projects and publications focus on spatial policy and distributional injustice, land regime, migration and spatial policy, territory and national ideology, and intensifying ethnic conflicts.

Barbara VanDrasek is a Research Associate at the Department of Geography, University of Minnesota-Twin Cities. She holds a Bachelor of Arts, Master's Degree, and Ph.D. in Geography from the University of Minnesota has been engaged in teaching and research on cities in the United States and the former Soviet Union for the past twenty years. Much of her work on Minnesota and the Twin Cities metropolitan area has involved the study of transportation systems. VanDrasek is the co-author of a book on the Minneapolis-St. Paul metropolitan region, now under revision for a second edition, as well as seven research reports funded by the Minnesota Department of Transportation. She has also authored two monographs for the Center for Urban and Regional Affairs at the University of Minnesota, and several book reviews, research reviews, and journal and encyclopedia articles.

Michael S. Yoder is an Associate Professor of Geography and Coordinator of Urban Studies at Texas A&M International University at Laredo, Texas, USA. Michael obtained his PhD (Geography) degree from Louisiana State University. His current interests are in globalization and the Mexican and world cities, neoliberalism and changing urban geographies of Mexico, suburbanization in the U.S. and Mexico, and geography and new urbanism. His recent publications include A Mexican Border City in the Global Periphery: Piedras Negras and Steel Manufacturing, 1935-2000; and Social Housing in Northeastern Mexico: Aesthetics, the Ideology of Subsidy, and the Personalization of Living Space both of which appeared in the *Urbana journal*.